Shojo Beat

Absolute Boyfriend

-5-

Story & Art by

Yuu Watase

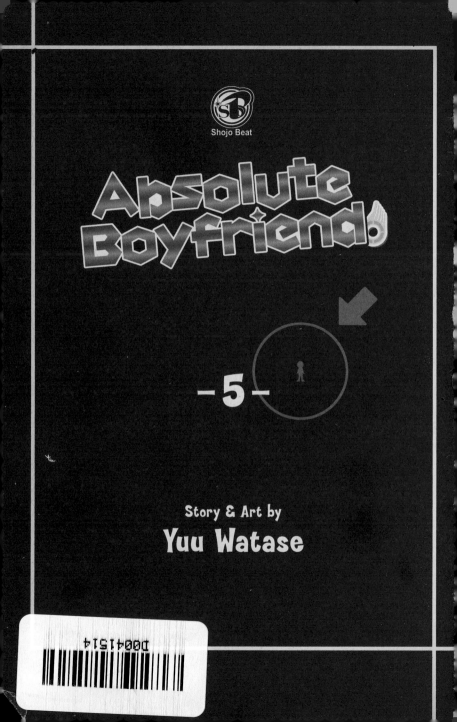

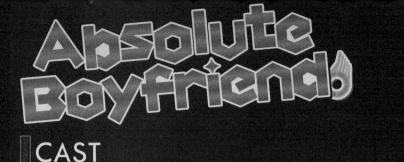

Absolute Boyfriend

CAST

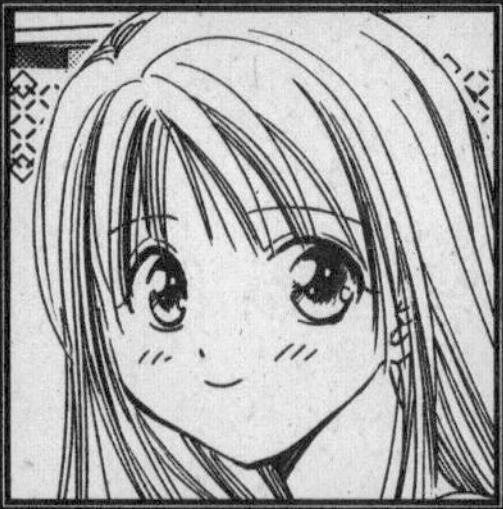

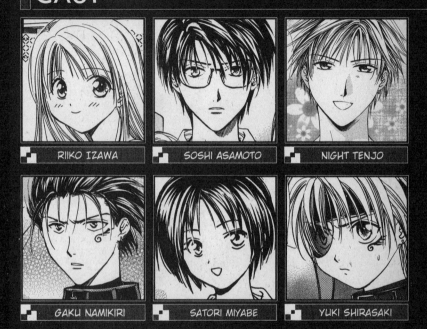

RIIKO IZAWA

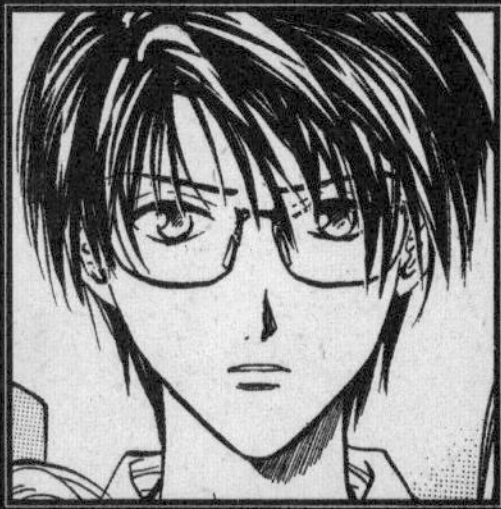

SOSHI ASAMOTO

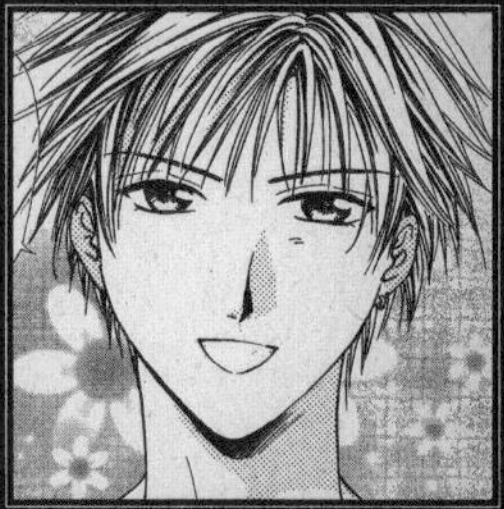

NIGHT TENJO

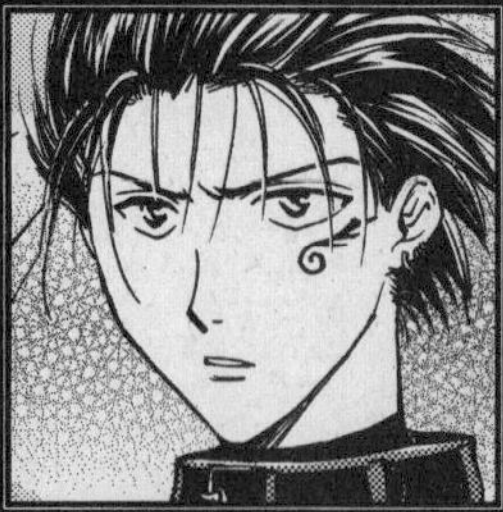

GAKU NAMIKIRI

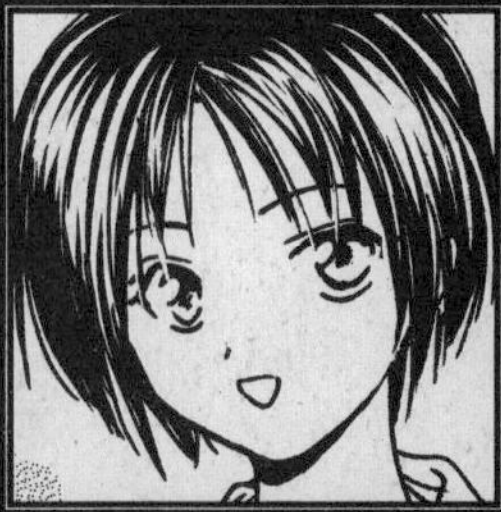

SATORI MIYABE

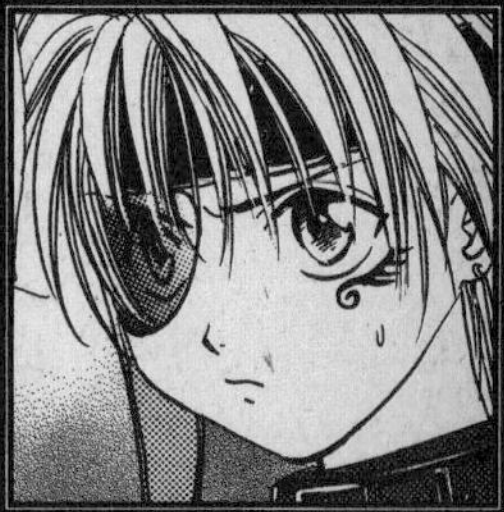

YUKI SHIRASAKI

STORY

DEPRESSED ABOUT BEING REJECTED, RIIKO BOUGHT THE IDEAL BOYFRIEND FIGURE, NIGHT, FROM A STRANGE SALESMAN. ONE KISS MADE HIM HER BOYFRIEND, BUT SOMETHING MORE WAS NEEDED TO MAKE HIS DEVOTION PERMANENT, AND RIIKO WASN'T READY FOR THAT. WHEN NIGHT WAS DAMAGED DURING A FIGHT WITH ANOTHER FIGURE, GAKU TOOK HIM AWAY FOR REPAIRS. BUT NIGHT CAN'T STAND TO BE SEPARATED FROM RIIKO, SO HE RETURNED TO HER IN A TEMPORARY MINIATURE BODY! MEANWHILE, SOSHI DISCOVERS NIGHT'S SECRET AND INFORMS RIIKO THAT HE WILL LIVE WITH HER UNTIL SHE DECIDES WHO WILL BE HER ONE TRUE BOYFRIEND! BUT CAN NIGHT AND SOSHI LIVE TOGETHER WITHOUT BLOODSHED!?

Act 25: The Tiny Boyfriend

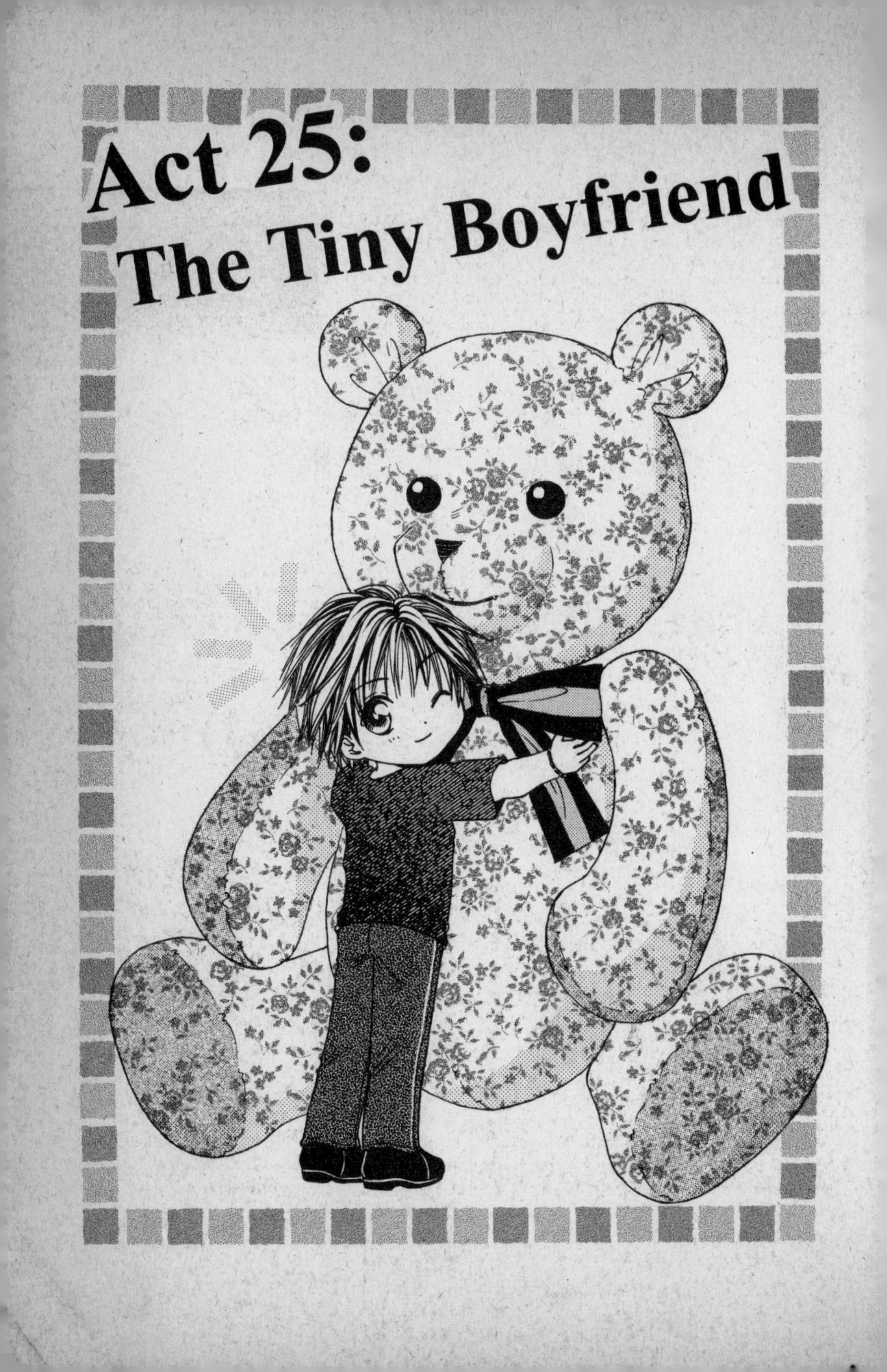

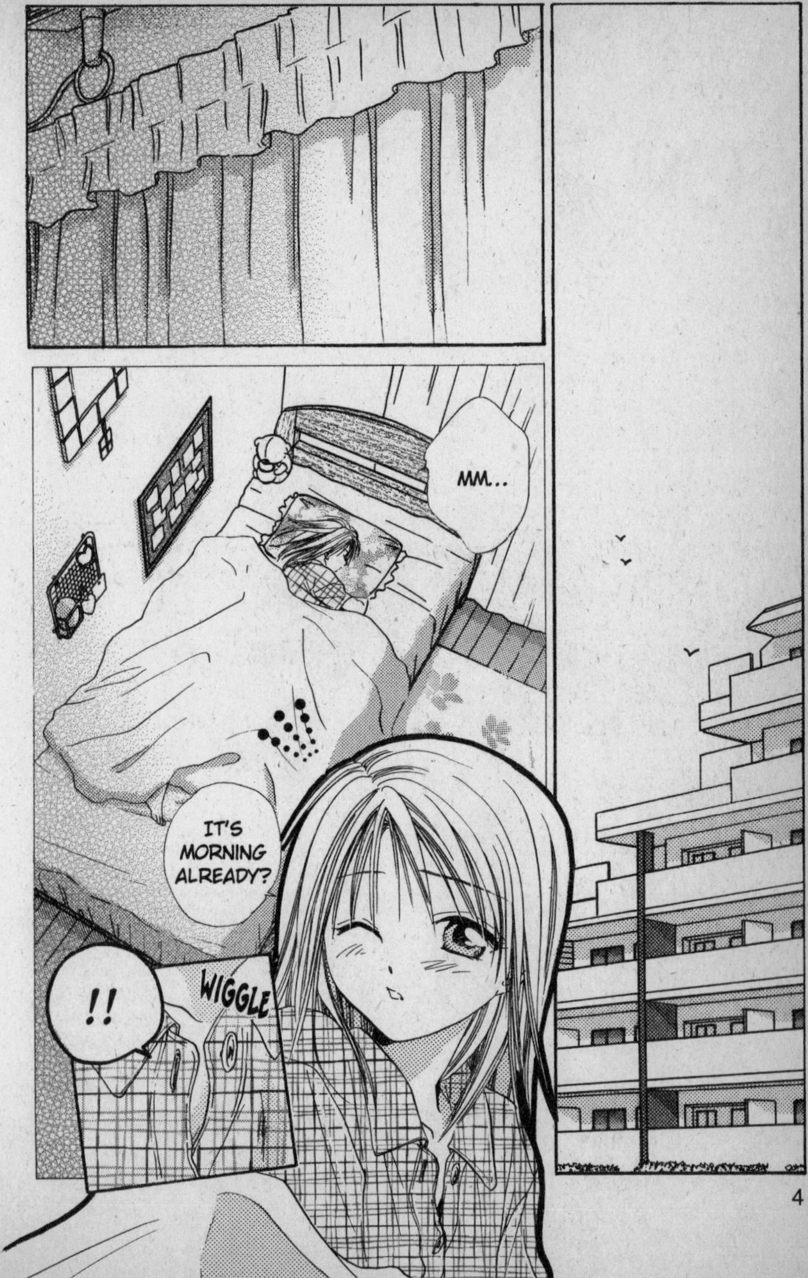
MM..
IT'S MORNING ALREADY?
WIGGLE
!!

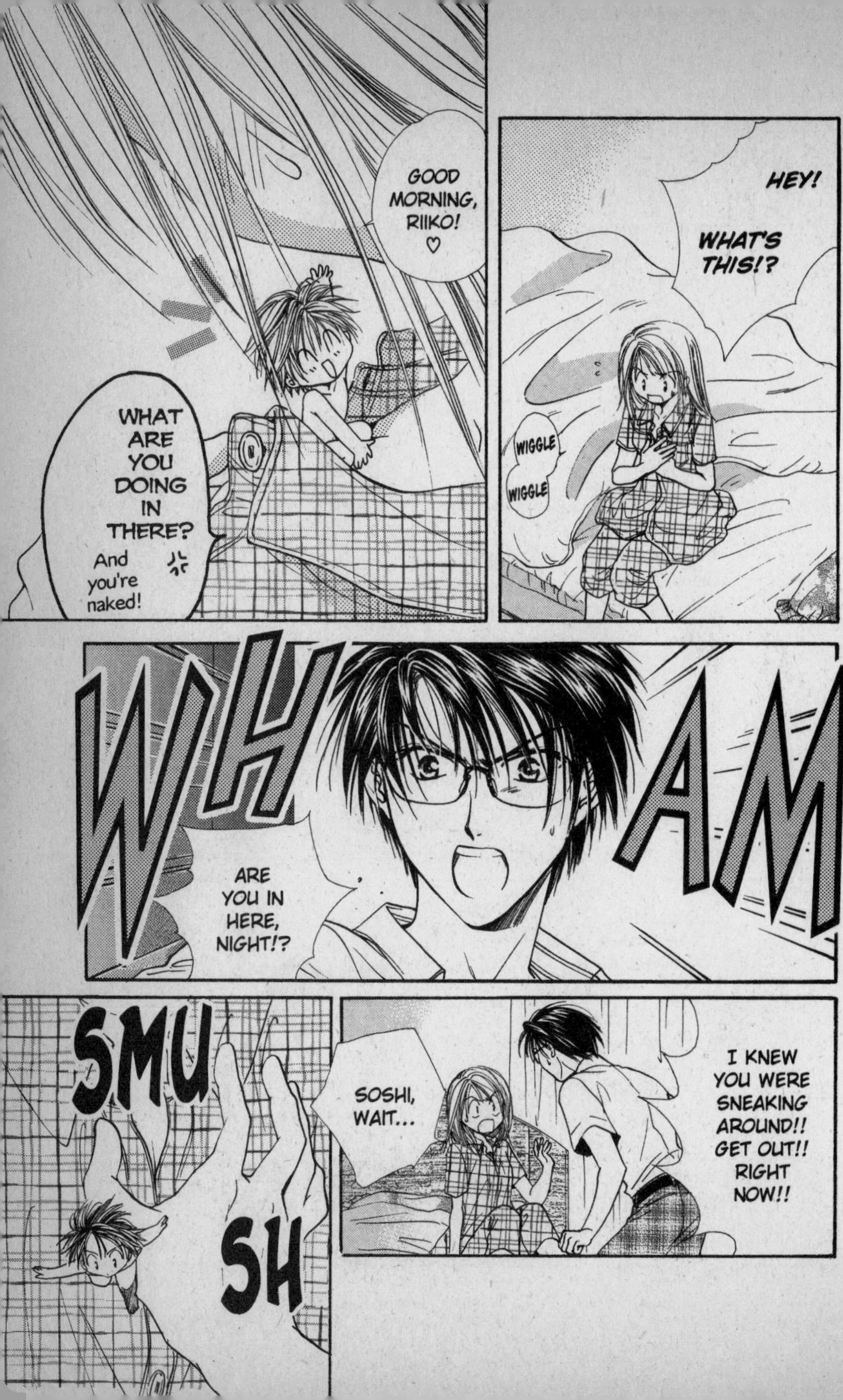
HEY!
WHAT'S THIS!?
WIGGLE
WIGGLE
GOOD MORNING, RIIKO! ♡
WHAT ARE YOU DOING IN THERE?
And you're naked!
WHAM
ARE YOU IN HERE, NIGHT!?
I KNEW YOU WERE SNEAKING AROUND!! GET OUT!! RIGHT NOW!!
SOSHI, WAIT...
SMUSH

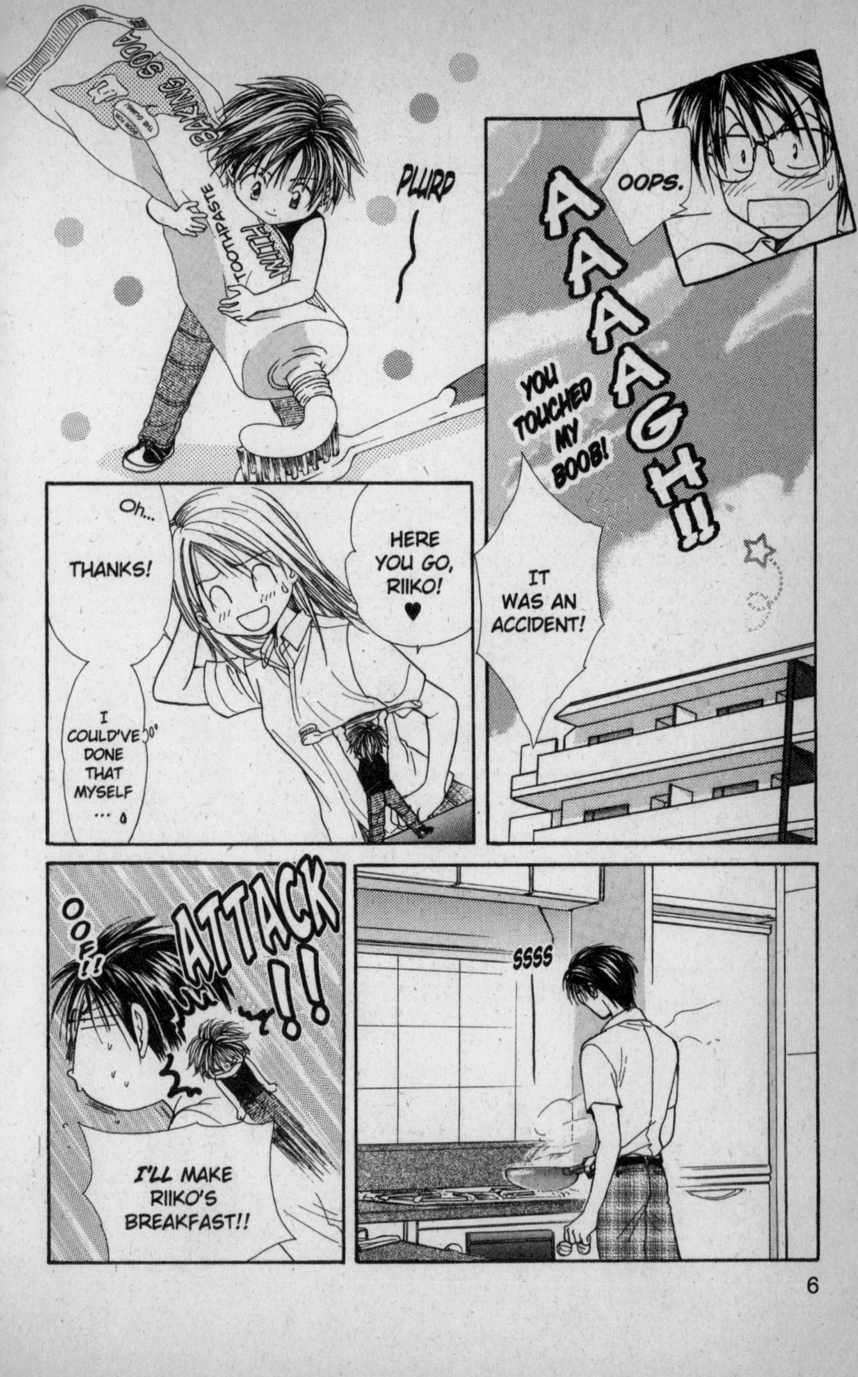
OOPS.
AAAAGH!!
YOU TOUCHED MY BOOB!
IT WAS AN ACCIDENT!
BAKING SODA
WITH TOOTHPASTE
PLURP
HERE YOU GO, RIIKO! ♥
Oh... THANKS!
I COULD'VE DONE THAT MYSELF ...
SSSS
OOF!!
ATTACK!!
I'LL MAKE RIIKO'S BREAKFAST!!

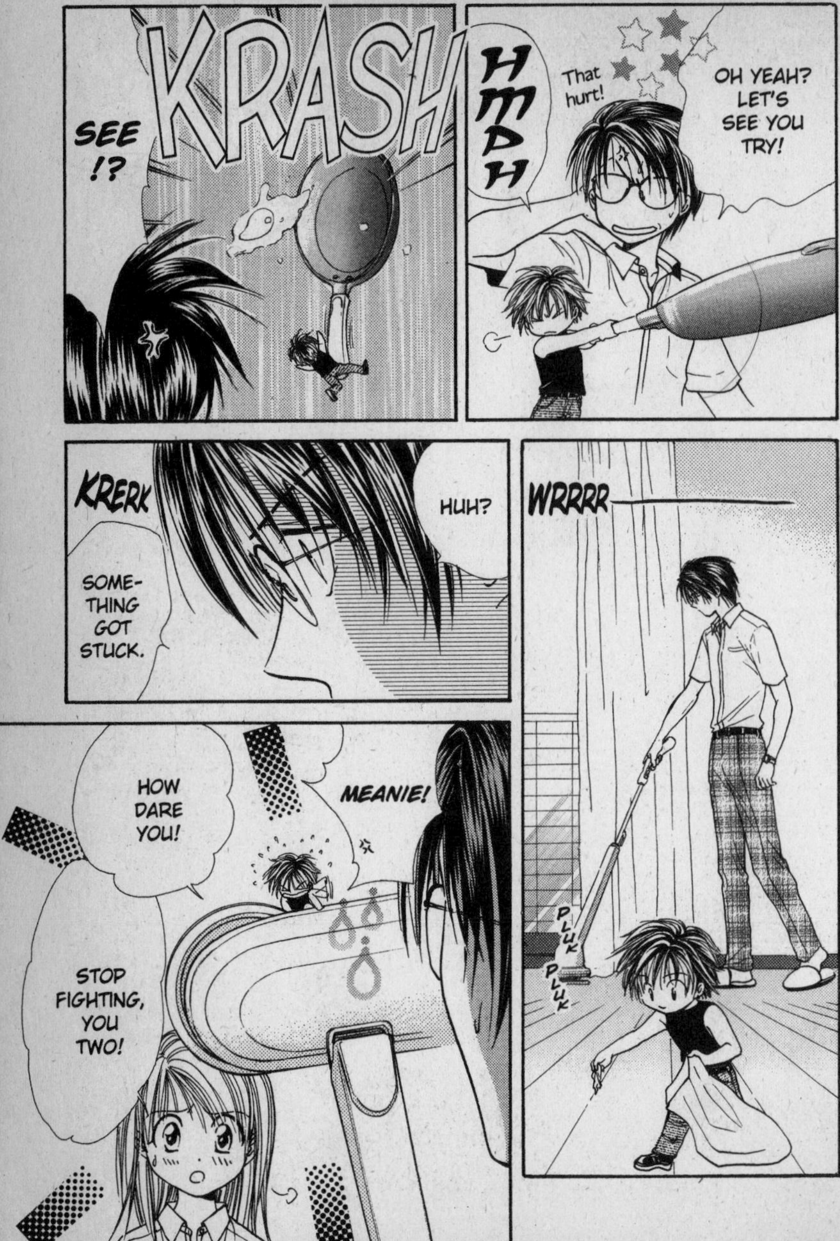
OH YEAH? LET'S SEE YOU TRY!
That hurt!
HMPH
KRASH
SEE!?
WRRRR
PLUK PLUK
HUH?
KRERK
SOME-THING GOT STUCK.
MEANIE!
HOW DARE YOU!
STOP FIGHTING, YOU TWO!

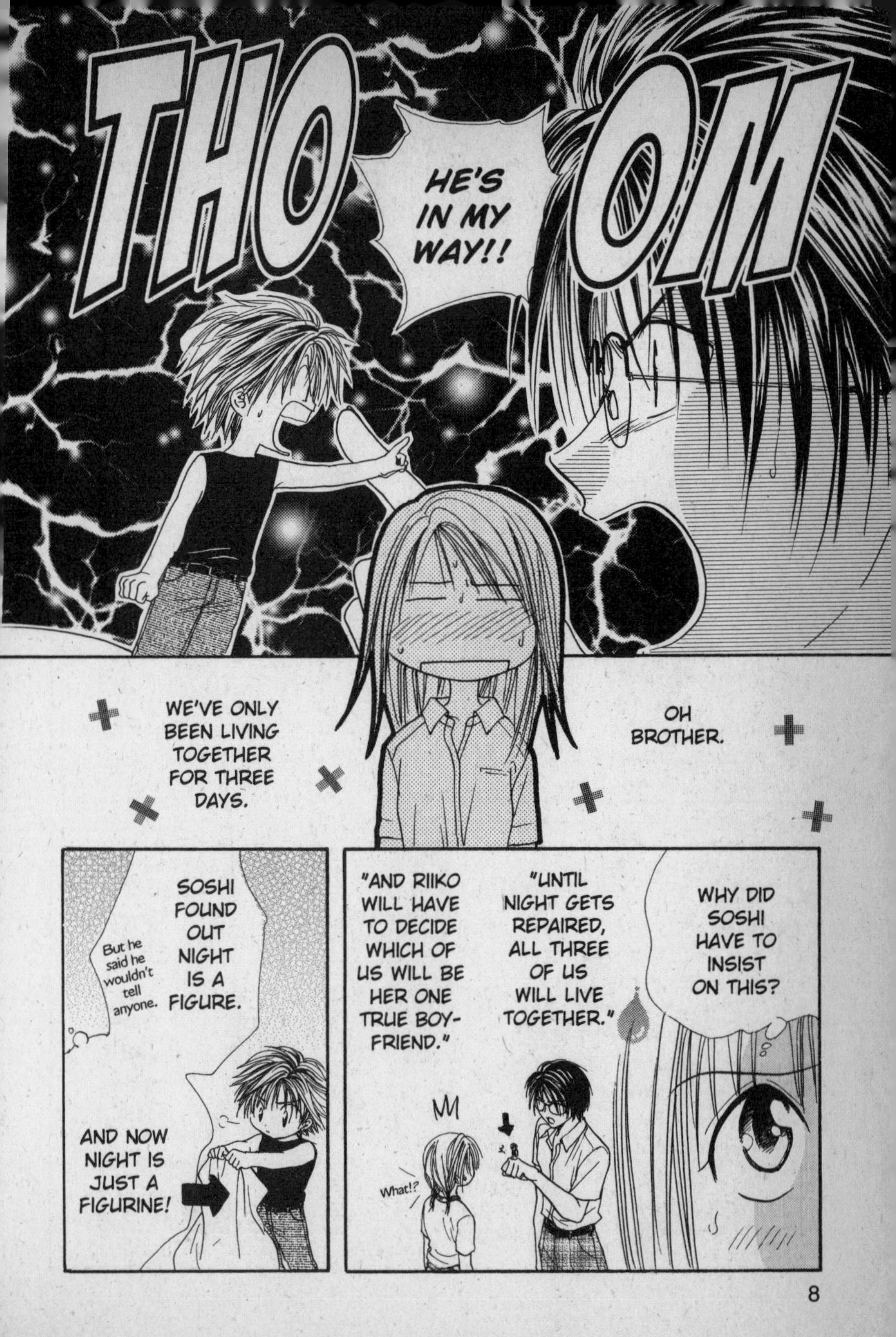
THOOM
HE'S IN MY WAY!!
OH BROTHER.
WE'VE ONLY BEEN LIVING TOGETHER FOR THREE DAYS.
WHY DID SOSHI HAVE TO INSIST ON THIS?
"UNTIL NIGHT GETS REPAIRED, ALL THREE OF US WILL LIVE TOGETHER."
"AND RIIKO WILL HAVE TO DECIDE WHICH OF US WILL BE HER ONE TRUE BOY-FRIEND."
What!?
SOSHI FOUND OUT NIGHT IS A FIGURE.
But he said he wouldn't tell anyone.
AND NOW NIGHT IS JUST A FIGURINE!

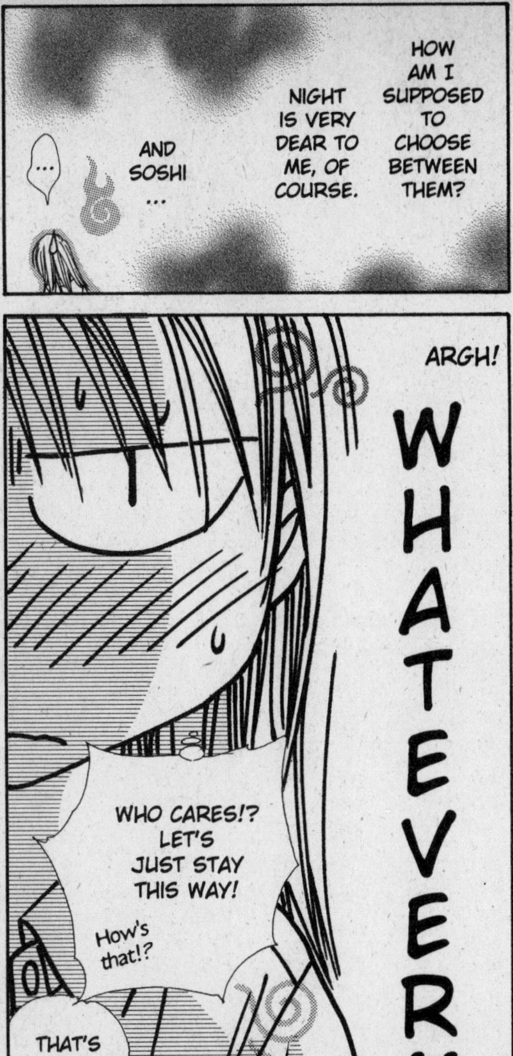
HOW AM I SUPPOSED TO CHOOSE BETWEEN THEM?
NIGHT IS VERY DEAR TO ME, OF COURSE.
AND SOSHI...
...
ARGH!
WHATEVER!!
WHO CARES!? LET'S JUST STAY THIS WAY!
How's that!?
THAT'S WHY I TOLD YOU TO CUT IT OUT!!

Hello, everyone. We're in the fifth volume of *Absolute Boyfriend*, thanks to you. The series has already ended in *Shojo Comics*, but please stay with me to the end.

The drama CD is on sale now, and I'm glad to hear that people like it. I particularly enjoyed "Gaku's Home Shopping Network." (smile) The voice actors really fit the roles--I chose them myself. What do you think?

Fushigi Yugi Perfect World magazine issue 3 comes with a drama CD of its own as a deluxe insert. The voice actors for that one are good too. It's pretty short, so I think it's a comedy written especially for the insert. These audio-drama CDs used to be free mail-in gift offers for all *Shojo Comics* readers. Since it comes with a CD, this issue will be a bit more expensive than usual. Ten years ago, book CDs were all the rage. Now it's just dramas. Everything has a drama CD now.

Anime is more fun. In an audio-drama the characters have to explain what's going on and it sounds kind of weird. Or is that a good thing?

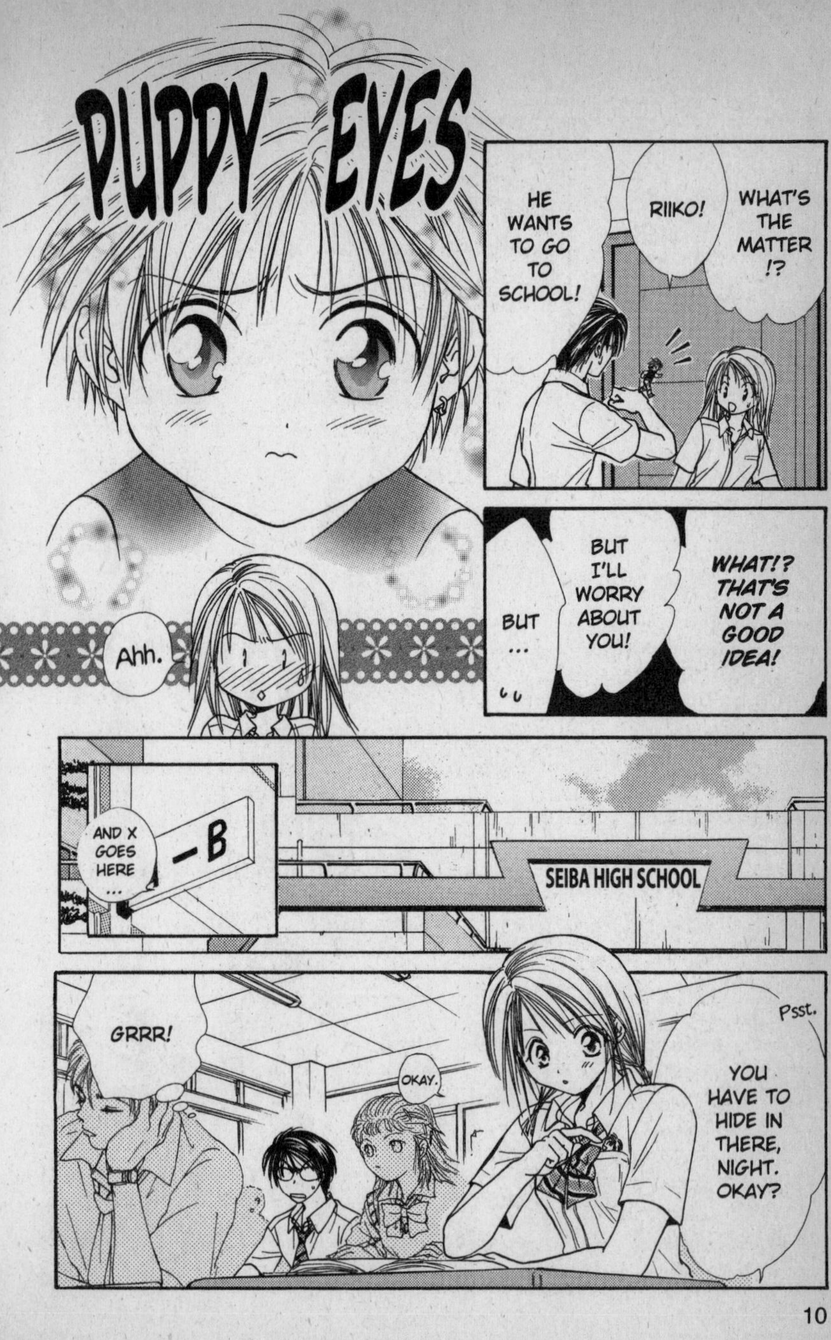
WHAT'S THE MATTER !?
RIIKO!
HE WANTS TO GO TO SCHOOL!
WHAT!? THAT'S NOT A GOOD IDEA!
BUT I'LL WORRY ABOUT YOU!
BUT ...
PUPPY EYES
Ahh.
SEIBA HIGH SCHOOL
-B
AND X GOES HERE ...
Psst.
YOU HAVE TO HIDE IN THERE, NIGHT. OKAY?
OKAY.
GRRR!

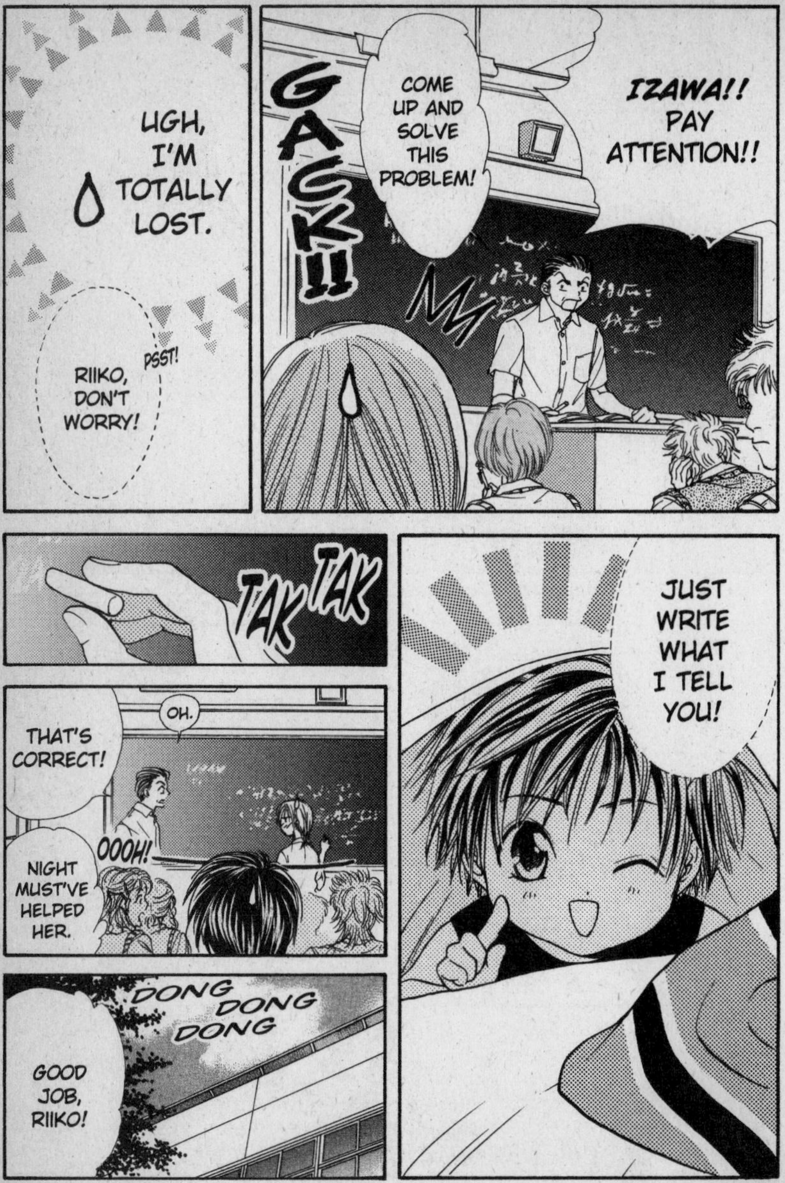
IZAWA!! PAY ATTENTION!!
COME UP AND SOLVE THIS PROBLEM!
GACK!!
UGH, I'M TOTALLY LOST.
PSST!
RIIKO, DON'T WORRY!
JUST WRITE WHAT I TELL YOU!
TAK TAK
OH.
THAT'S CORRECT!
OOOH!
NIGHT MUST'VE HELPED HER.
DONG DONG DONG
GOOD JOB, RIIKO!

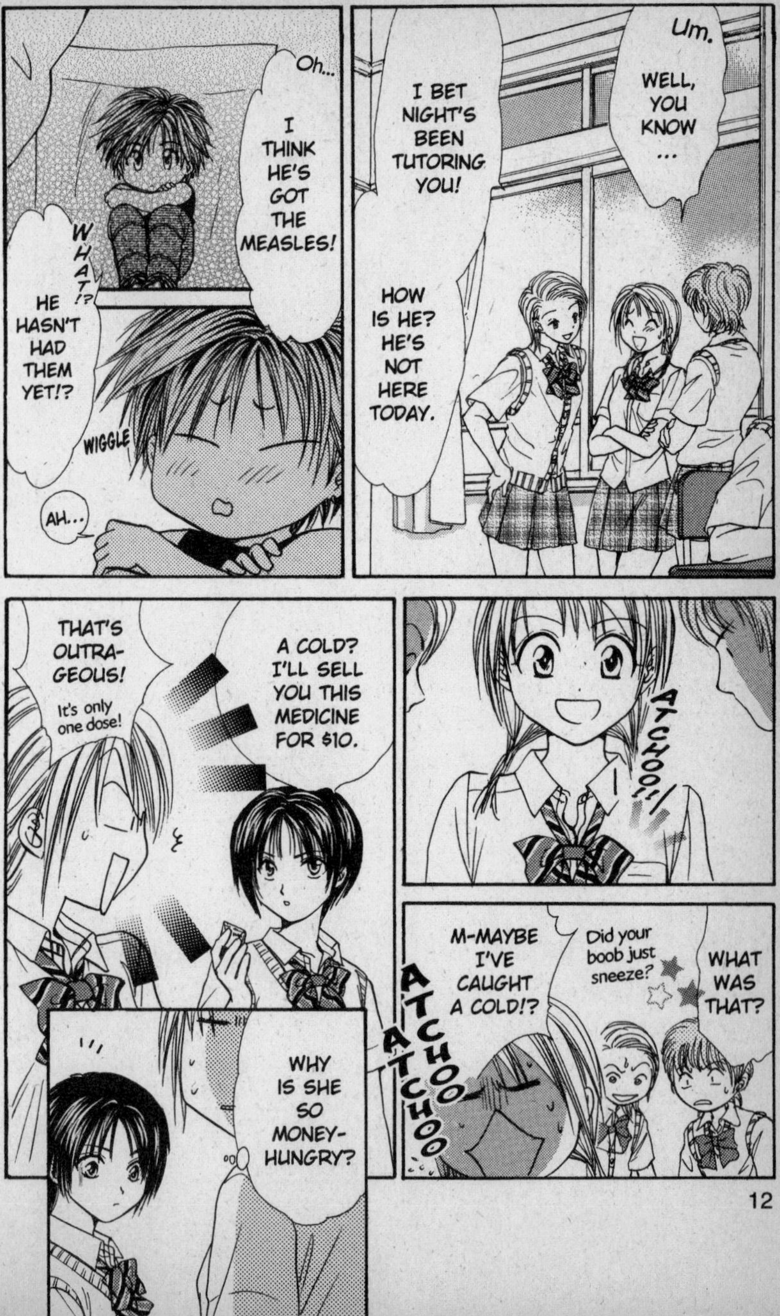
Um.
WELL, YOU KNOW ...
I BET NIGHT'S BEEN TUTORING YOU!
HOW IS HE? HE'S NOT HERE TODAY.
Oh...
I THINK HE'S GOT THE MEASLES!
WHAT!?
HE HASN'T HAD THEM YET!?
WIGGLE
AH...
ATCHOOO!!
WHAT WAS THAT?
Did your boob just sneeze?
M-MAYBE I'VE CAUGHT A COLD!?
ATCHOO ATCHOO
A COLD? I'LL SELL YOU THIS MEDICINE FOR $10.
THAT'S OUTRAGEOUS!
It's only one dose!
WHY IS SHE SO MONEY-HUNGRY?

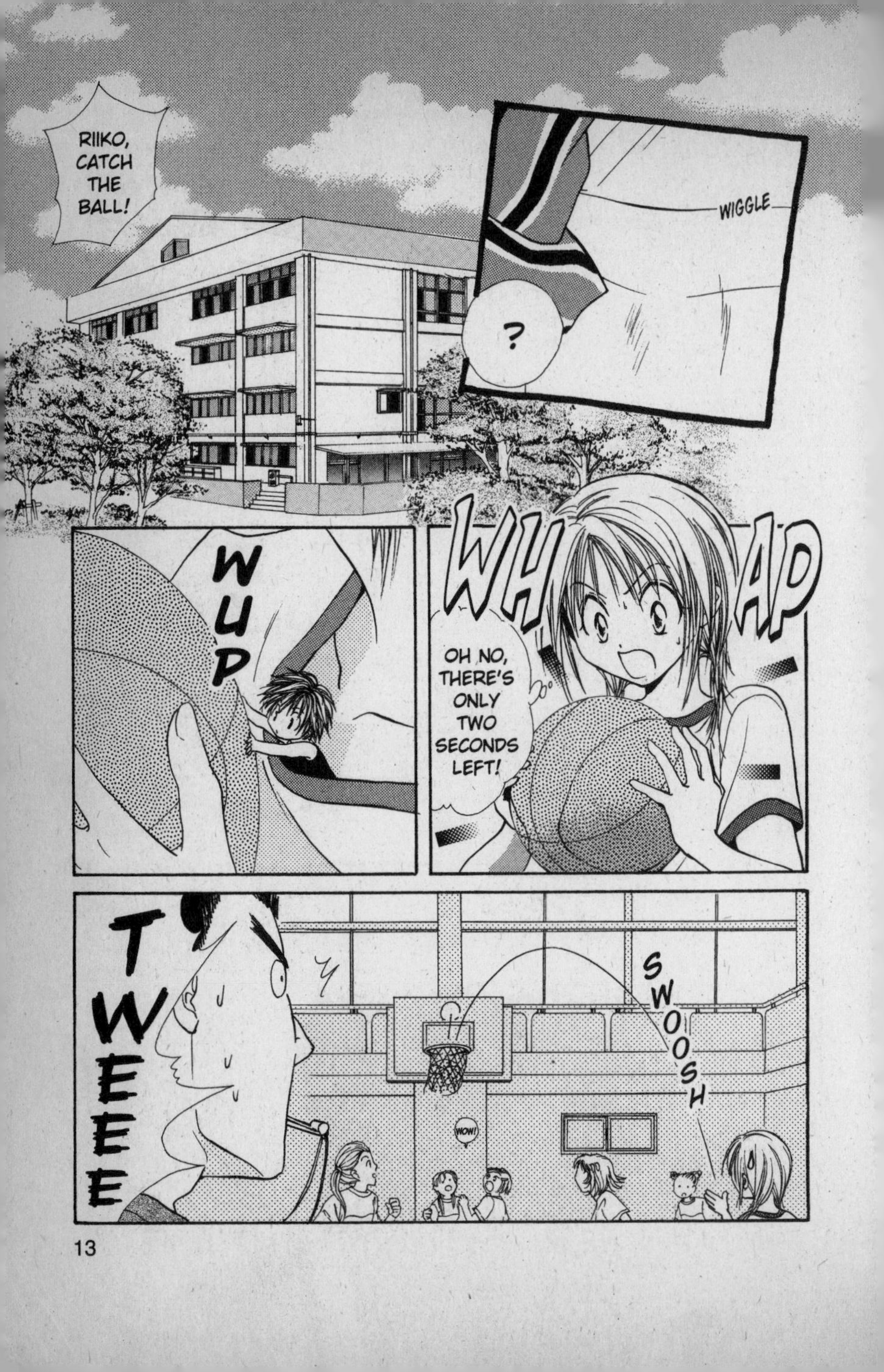
WIGGLE
?
RIIKO, CATCH THE BALL!
WH AP
OH NO, THERE'S ONLY TWO SECONDS LEFT!
WUP
SWOOSH
WOW!
TWEEEE

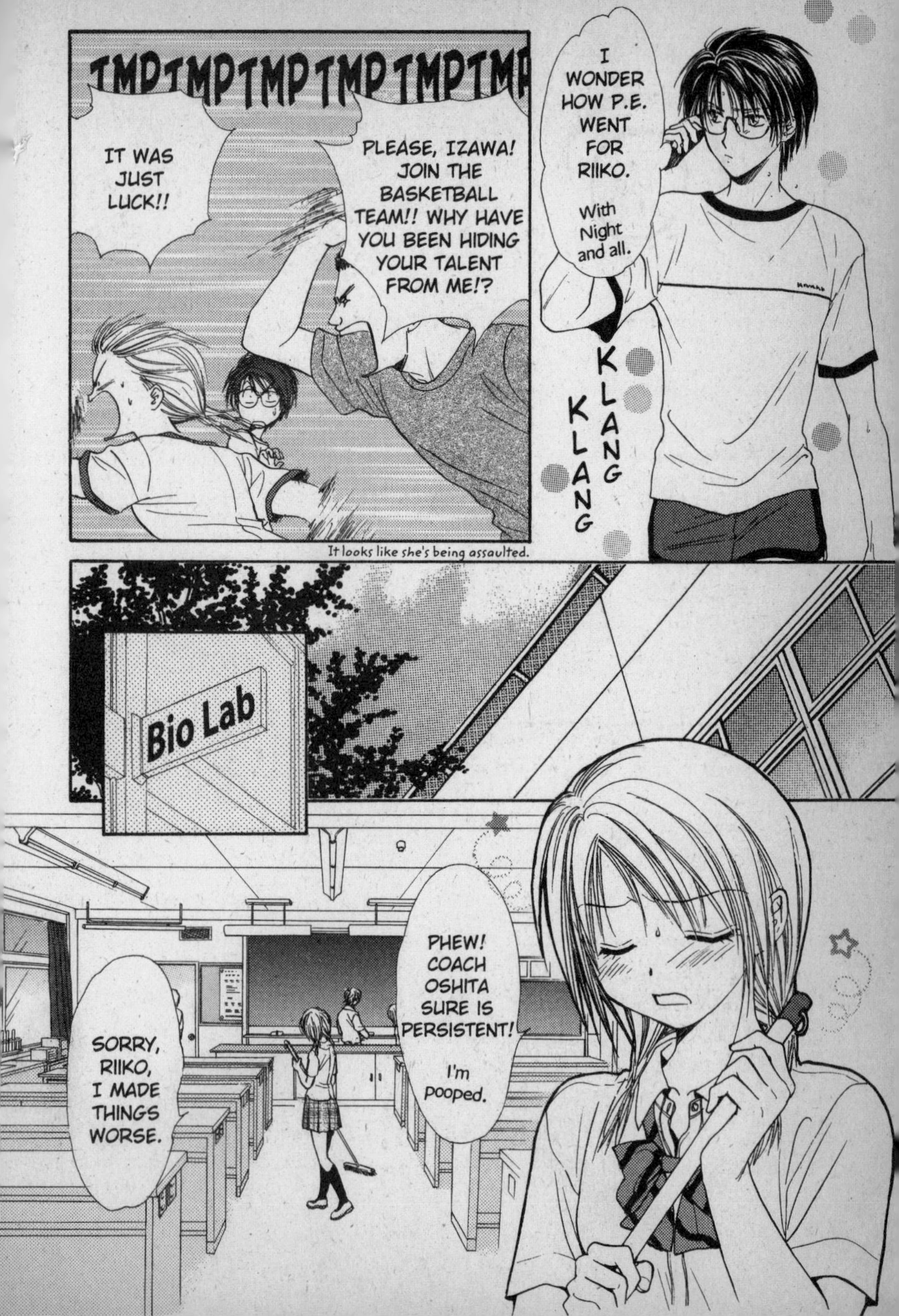
I WONDER HOW P.E. WENT FOR RIIKO.
With Night and all.
KLANG KLANG
TMP TMP TMP TMP TMP TMP
PLEASE, IZAWA! JOIN THE BASKETBALL TEAM!! WHY HAVE YOU BEEN HIDING YOUR TALENT FROM ME!?
IT WAS JUST LUCK!!
It looks like she's being assaulted.
Bio Lab
PHEW! COACH OSHITA SURE IS PERSISTENT!
I'm pooped.
SORRY, RIIKO, I MADE THINGS WORSE.

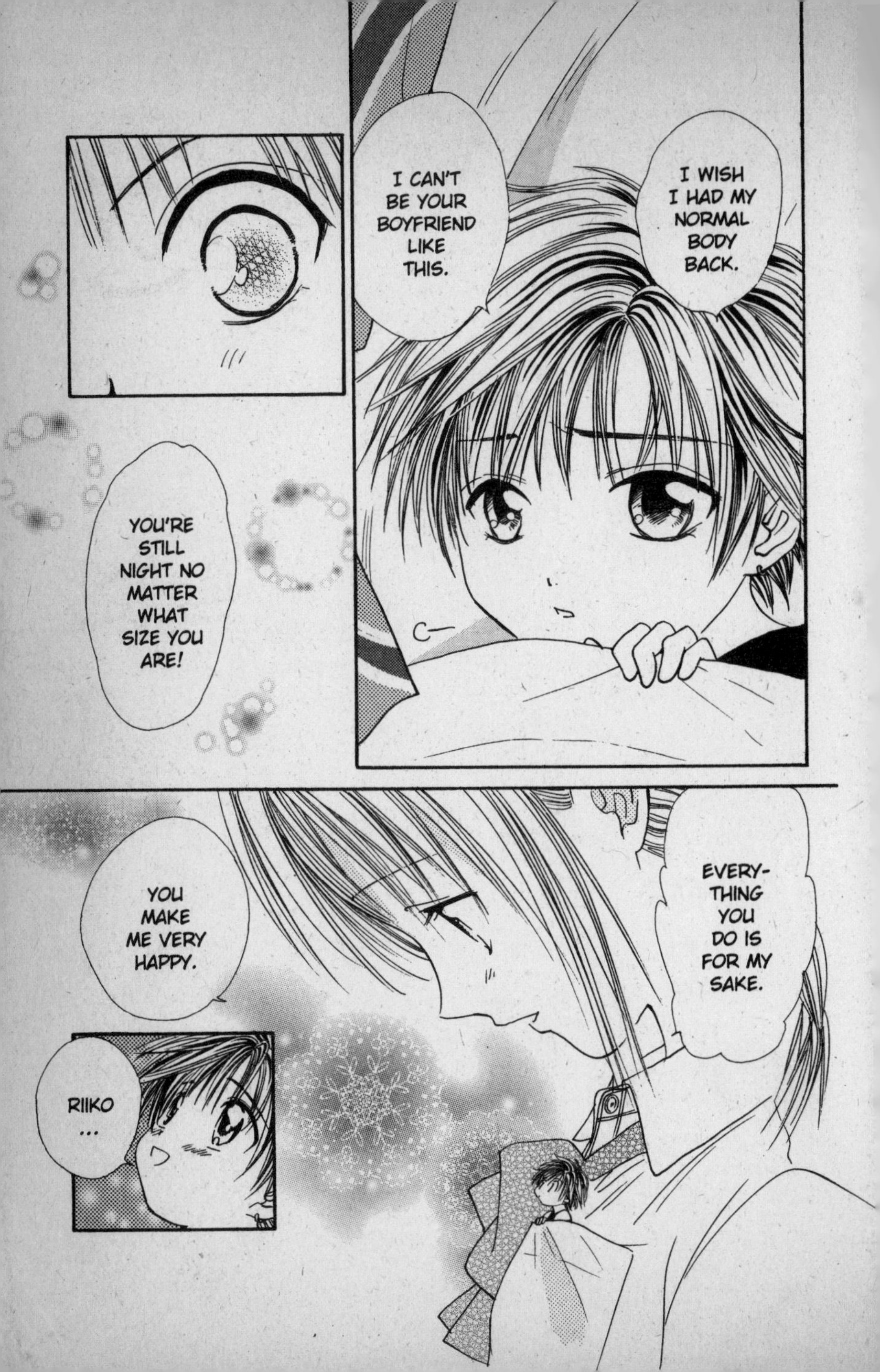
I WISH I HAD MY NORMAL BODY BACK.
I CAN'T BE YOUR BOYFRIEND LIKE THIS.
C—
YOU'RE STILL NIGHT NO MATTER WHAT SIZE YOU ARE!
EVERY-THING YOU DO IS FOR MY SAKE.
YOU MAKE ME VERY HAPPY.
RIIKO ...

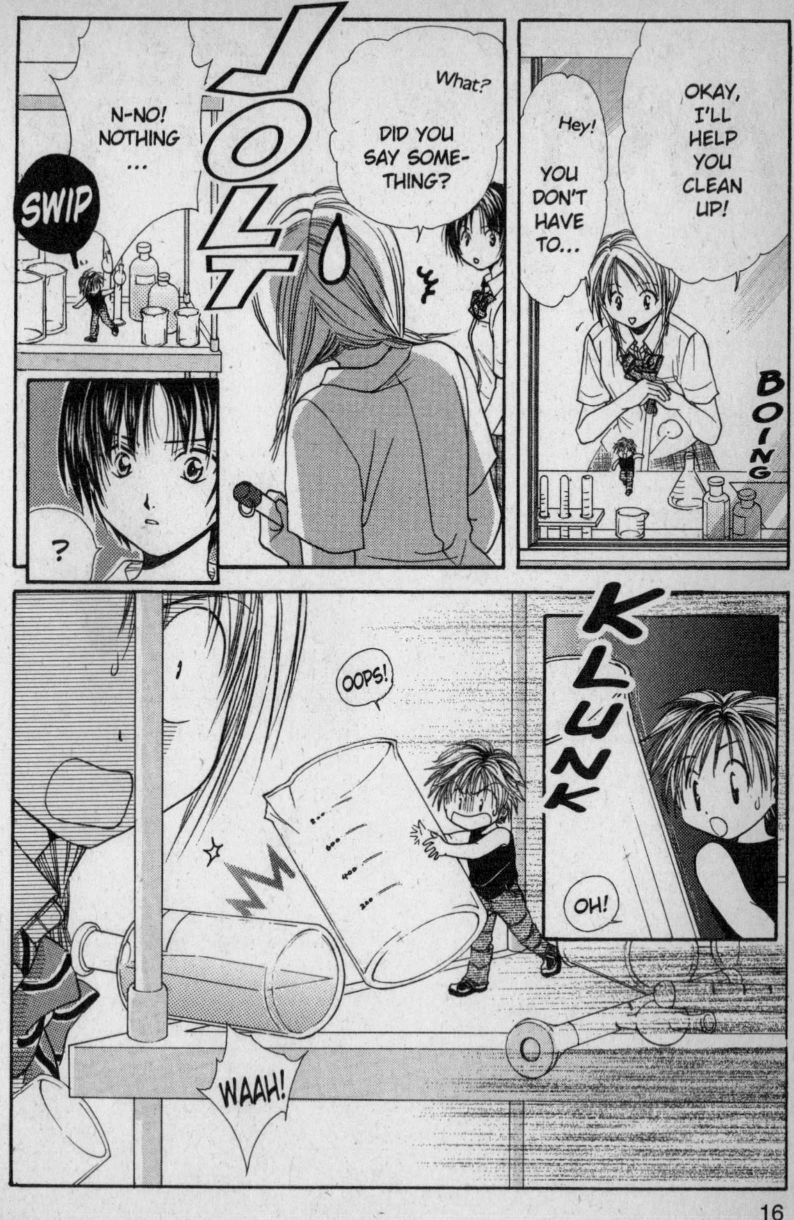

OKAY, I'LL HELP YOU CLEAN UP!
Hey!
YOU DON'T HAVE TO...
BOING
What?
DID YOU SAY SOME-THING?
JOLT
N-NO! NOTHING...
SWIP
?
KLUNK
OH!
OOPS!
WAAH!

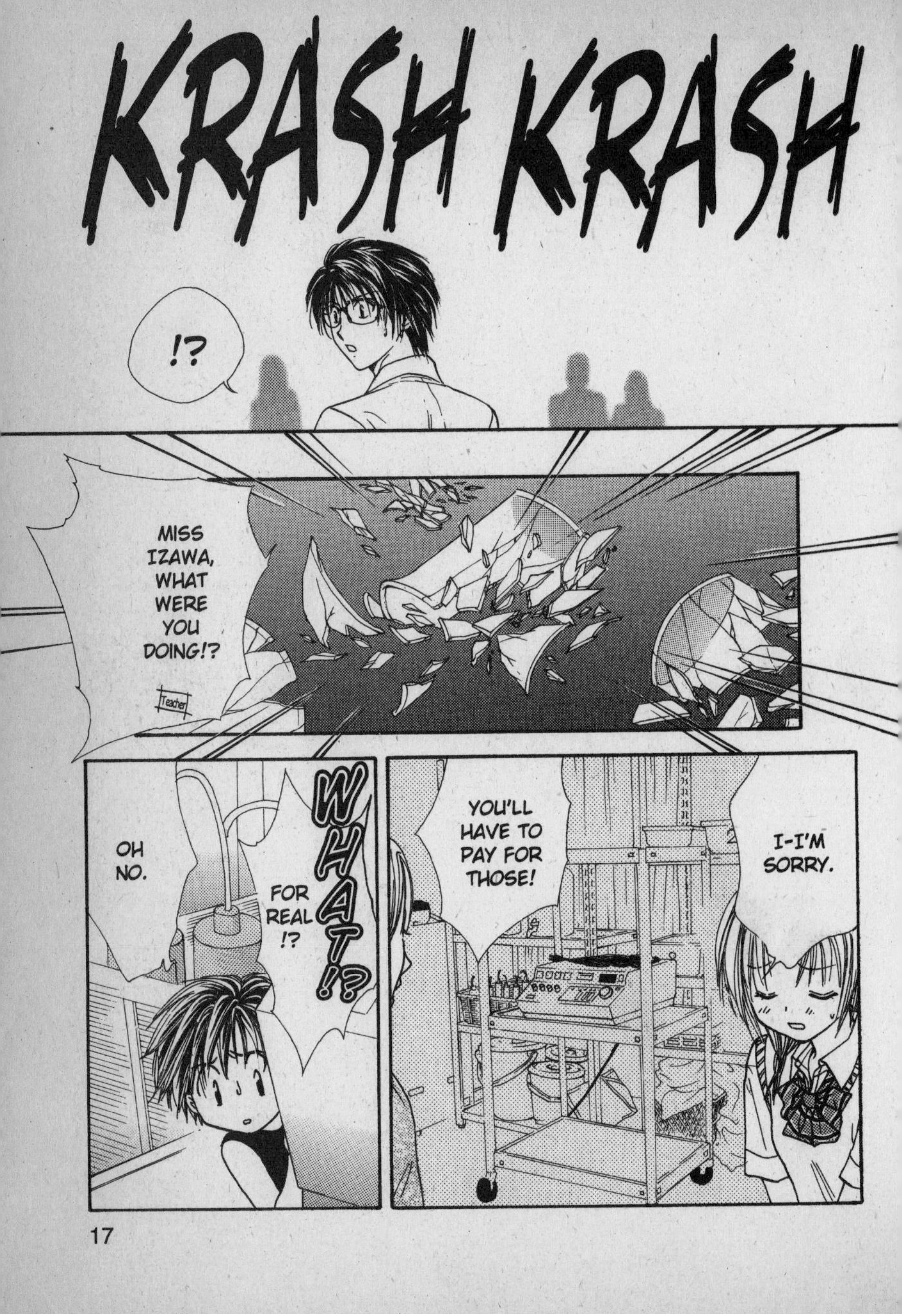
KRASH KRASH
!?
MISS IZAWA, WHAT WERE YOU DOING!?
Teacher
YOU'LL HAVE TO PAY FOR THOSE!
I-I'M SORRY.
WHAT!?
FOR REAL!?
OH NO.

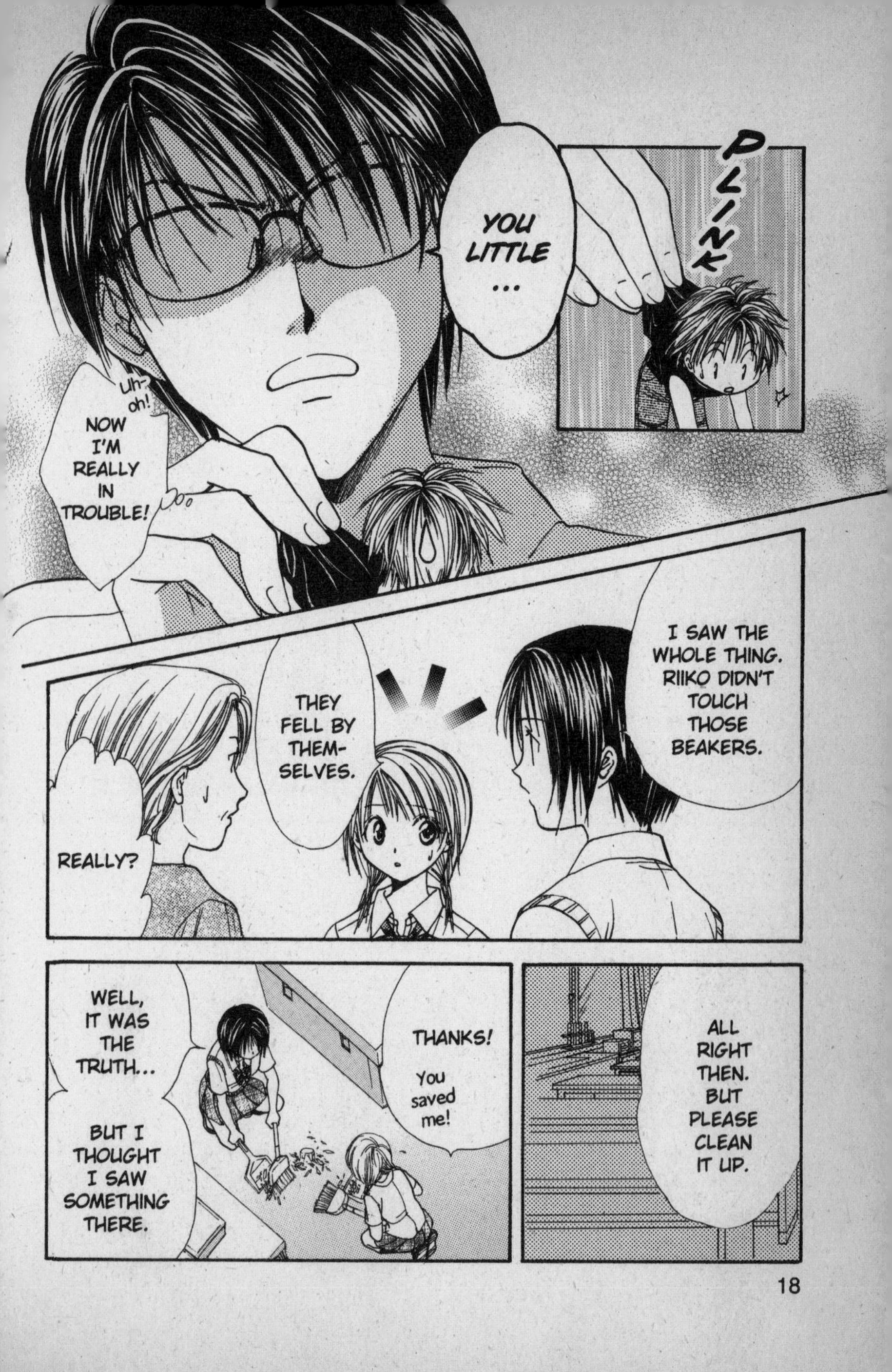
PLINK
YOU LITTLE ...
Uh-oh!
NOW I'M REALLY IN TROUBLE!
I SAW THE WHOLE THING. RIIKO DIDN'T TOUCH THOSE BEAKERS.
THEY FELL BY THEM-SELVES.
REALLY?
ALL RIGHT THEN. BUT PLEASE CLEAN IT UP.
THANKS!
You saved me!
WELL, IT WAS THE TRUTH...
BUT I THOUGHT I SAW SOMETHING THERE.

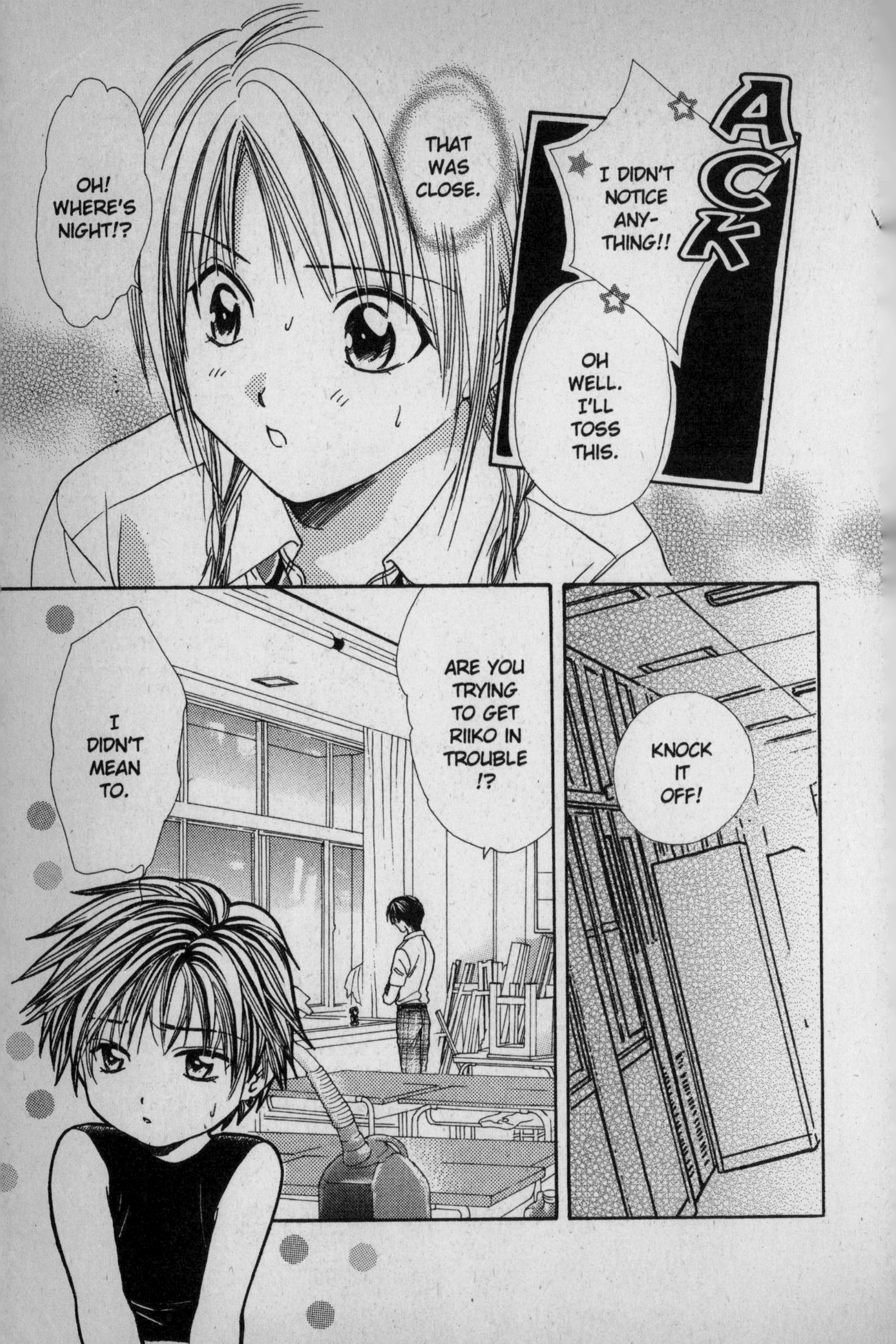
ACK
I DIDN'T NOTICE ANYTHING!!
OH WELL. I'LL TOSS THIS.
THAT WAS CLOSE.
OH! WHERE'S NIGHT!?
KNOCK IT OFF!
ARE YOU TRYING TO GET RIIKO IN TROUBLE!?
I DIDN'T MEAN TO.

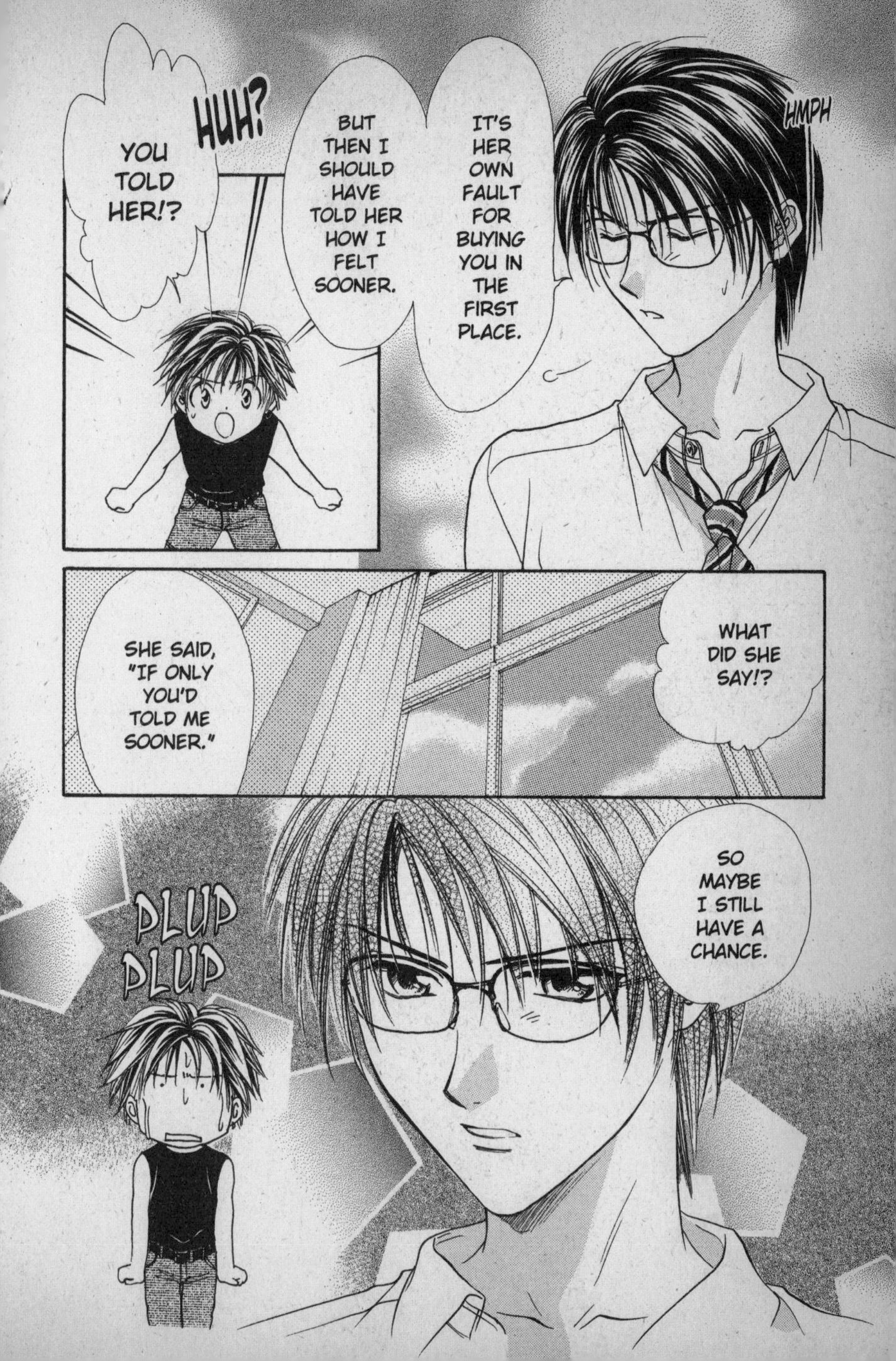
HMPH
IT'S HER OWN FAULT FOR BUYING YOU IN THE FIRST PLACE.
BUT THEN I SHOULD HAVE TOLD HER HOW I FELT SOONER.
HUH?
YOU TOLD HER!?
WHAT DID SHE SAY!?
SHE SAID, "IF ONLY YOU'D TOLD ME SOONER."
SO MAYBE I STILL HAVE A CHANCE.
PLUP PLUP

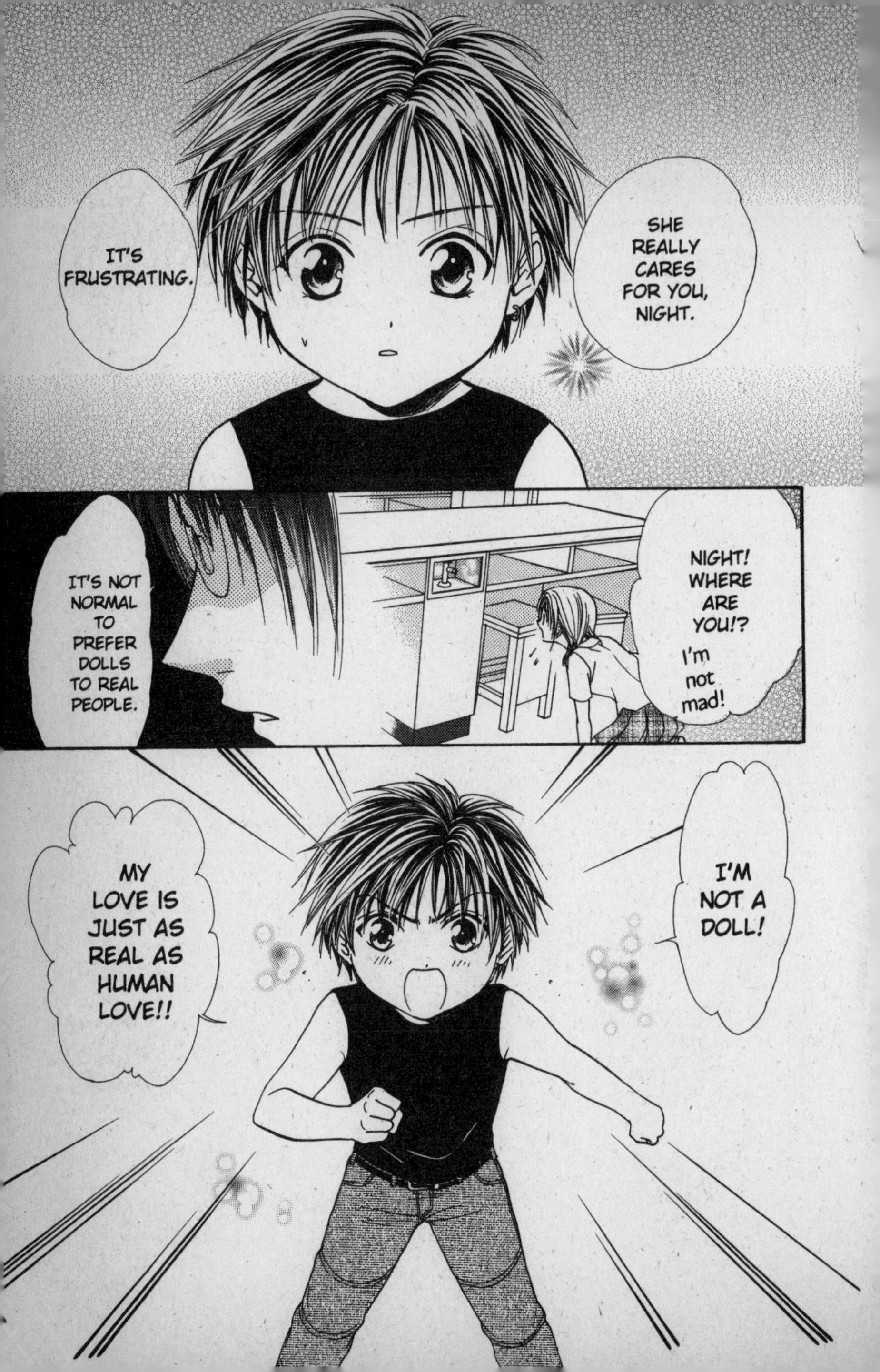
SHE REALLY CARES FOR YOU, NIGHT.
IT'S FRUSTRATING.
NIGHT! WHERE ARE YOU!?
I'm not mad!
IT'S NOT NORMAL TO PREFER DOLLS TO REAL PEOPLE.
I'M NOT A DOLL!
MY LOVE IS JUST AS REAL AS HUMAN LOVE!!

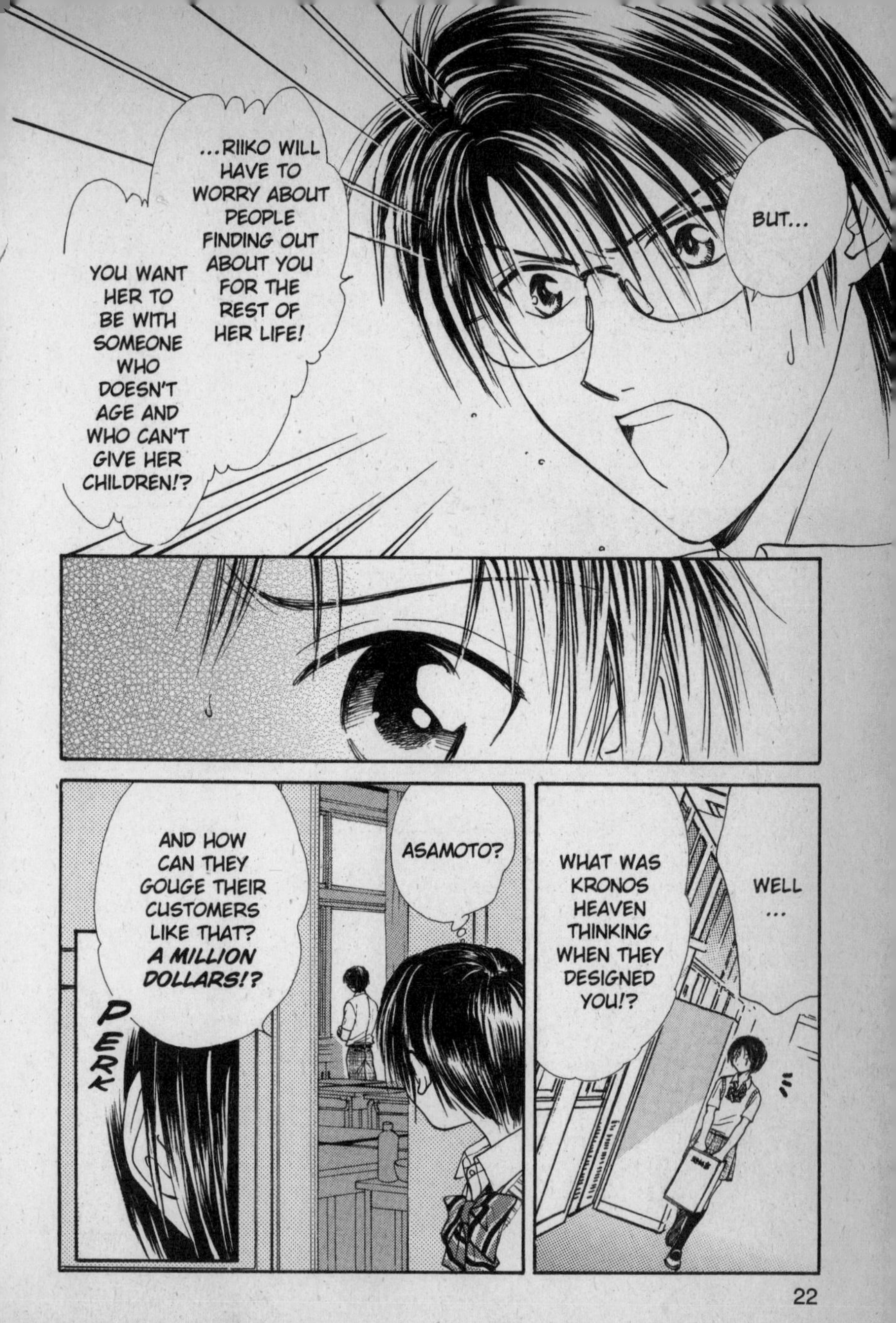
BUT...
YOU WANT HER TO BE WITH SOMEONE WHO DOESN'T AGE AND WHO CAN'T GIVE HER CHILDREN!?
...RIIKO WILL HAVE TO WORRY ABOUT PEOPLE FINDING OUT ABOUT YOU FOR THE REST OF HER LIFE!
WELL ...
WHAT WAS KRONOS HEAVEN THINKING WHEN THEY DESIGNED YOU!?
AND HOW CAN THEY GOUGE THEIR CUSTOMERS LIKE THAT? A MILLION DOLLARS!?
ASAMOTO?
PERK

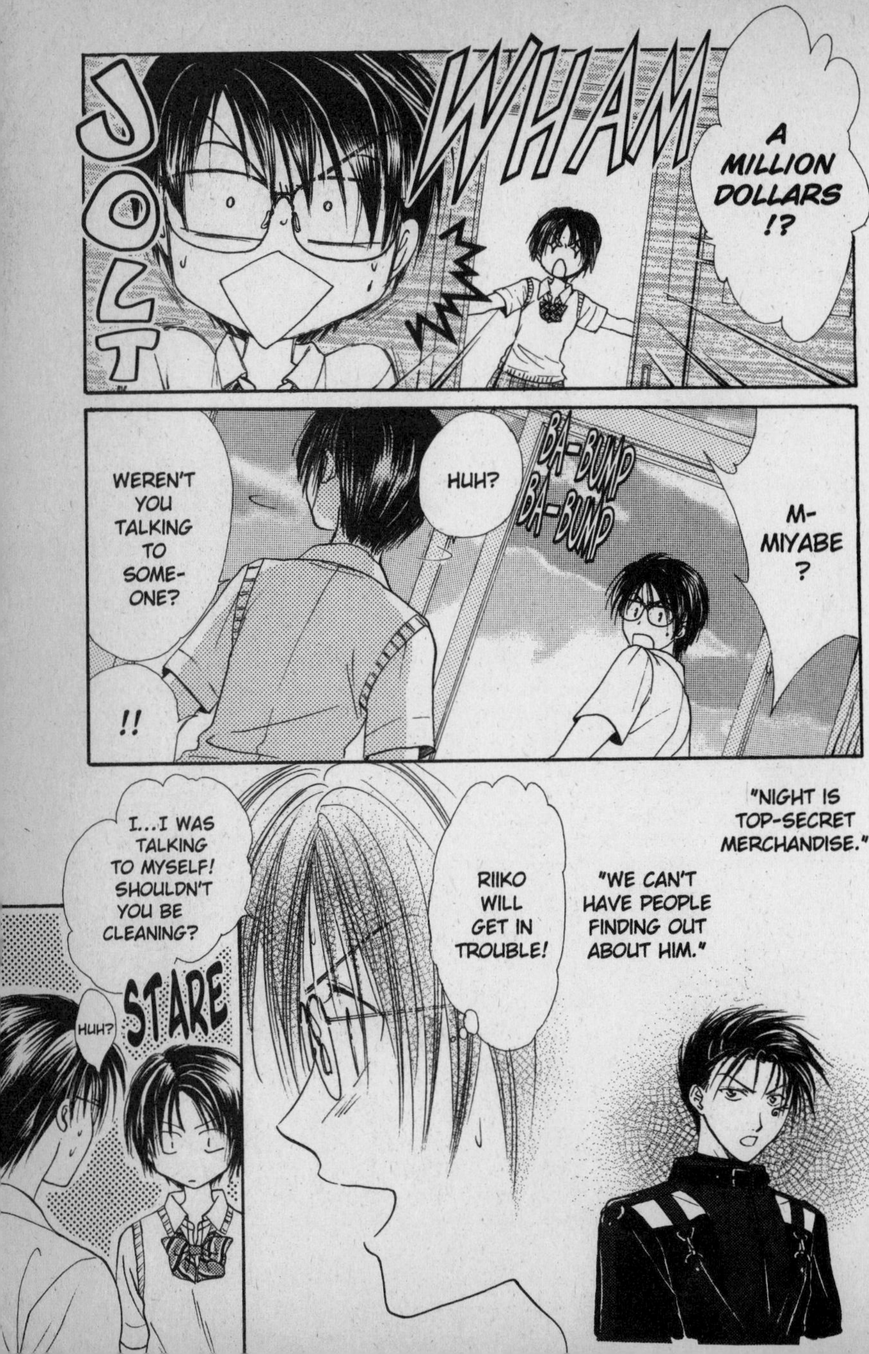
A MILLION DOLLARS !?
WHAM
JOLT
M-MIYABE?
BA-BUMP BA-BUMP
HUH?
WEREN'T YOU TALKING TO SOMEONE?
!!
"NIGHT IS TOP-SECRET MERCHANDISE."
"WE CAN'T HAVE PEOPLE FINDING OUT ABOUT HIM."
RIIKO WILL GET IN TROUBLE!
I...I WAS TALKING TO MYSELF! SHOULDN'T YOU BE CLEANING?
STARE
HUH?

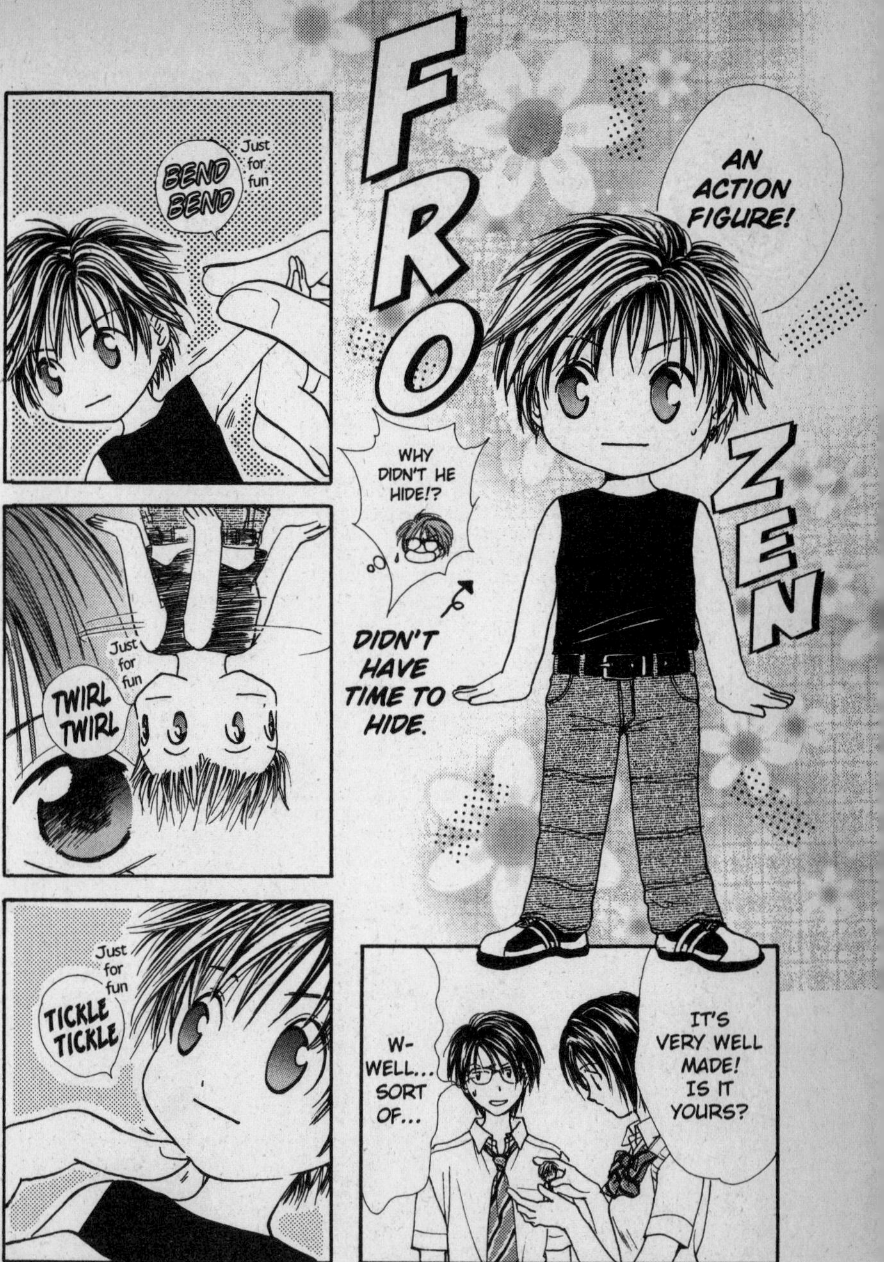
FROZEN
AN ACTION FIGURE!
WHY DIDN'T HE HIDE!?
DIDN'T HAVE TIME TO HIDE.
IT'S VERY WELL MADE! IS IT YOURS?
W-WELL... SORT OF...
Just for fun
BEND BEND
Just for fun
TWIRL TWIRL
Just for fun
TICKLE TICKLE

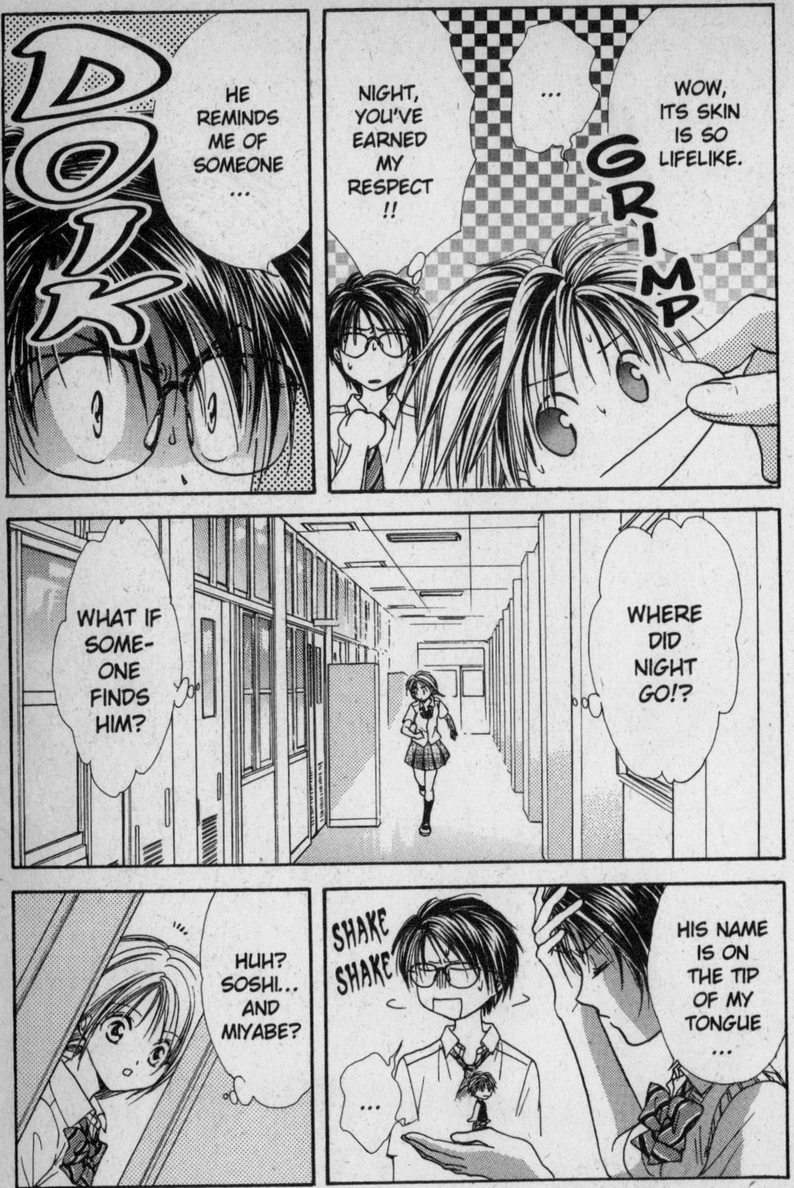
WOW, ITS SKIN IS SO LIFELIKE.
GRIMP
...
NIGHT, YOU'VE EARNED MY RESPECT !!
DOIK
HE REMINDS ME OF SOMEONE ...
WHERE DID NIGHT GO!?
WHAT IF SOME-ONE FINDS HIM?
HIS NAME IS ON THE TIP OF MY TONGUE ...
SHAKE SHAKE
...
HUH? SOSHI... AND MIYABE?

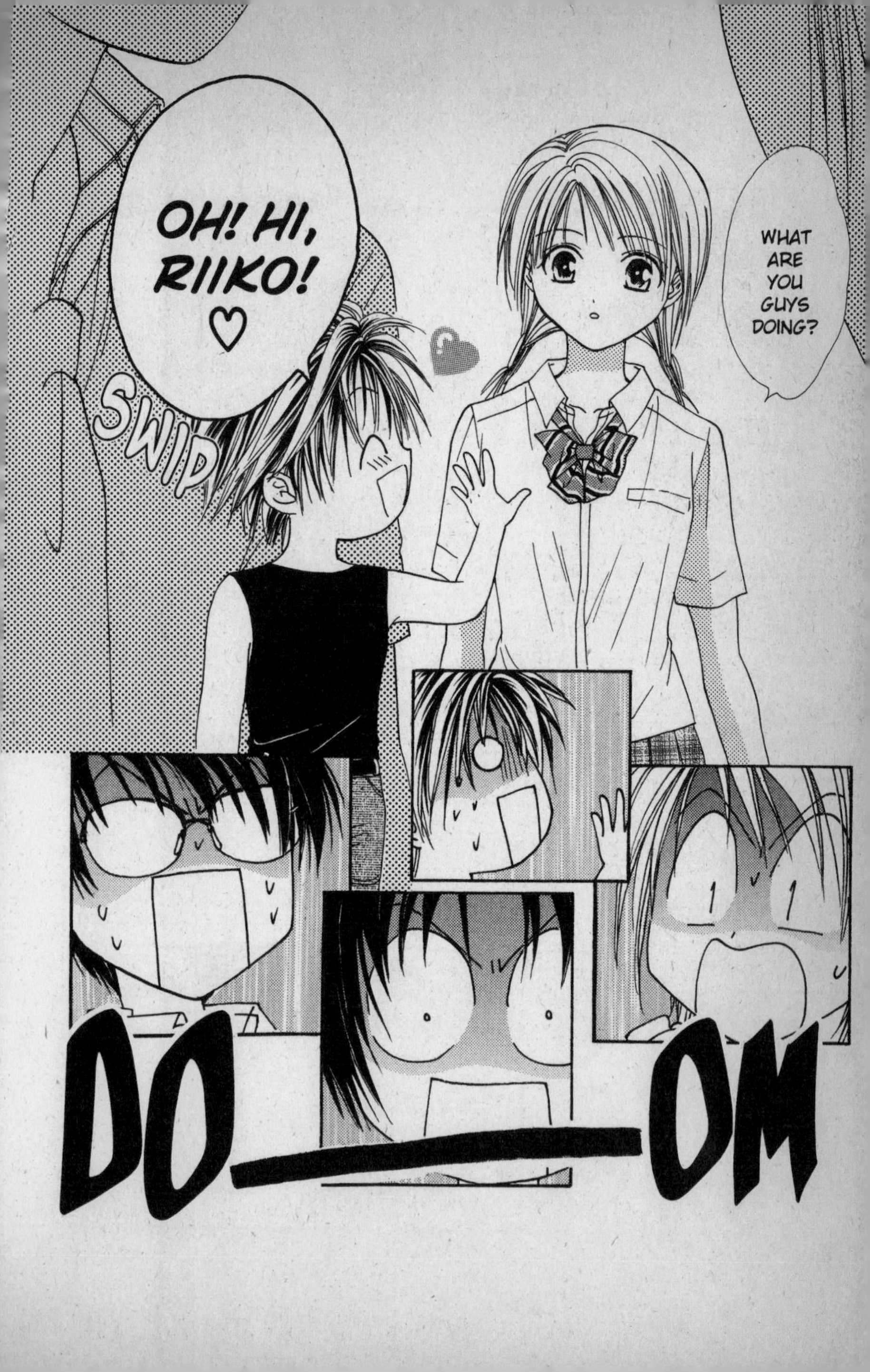
WHAT ARE YOU GUYS DOING?
OH! HI, RIIKO! ♡
SWIP
DO—OM

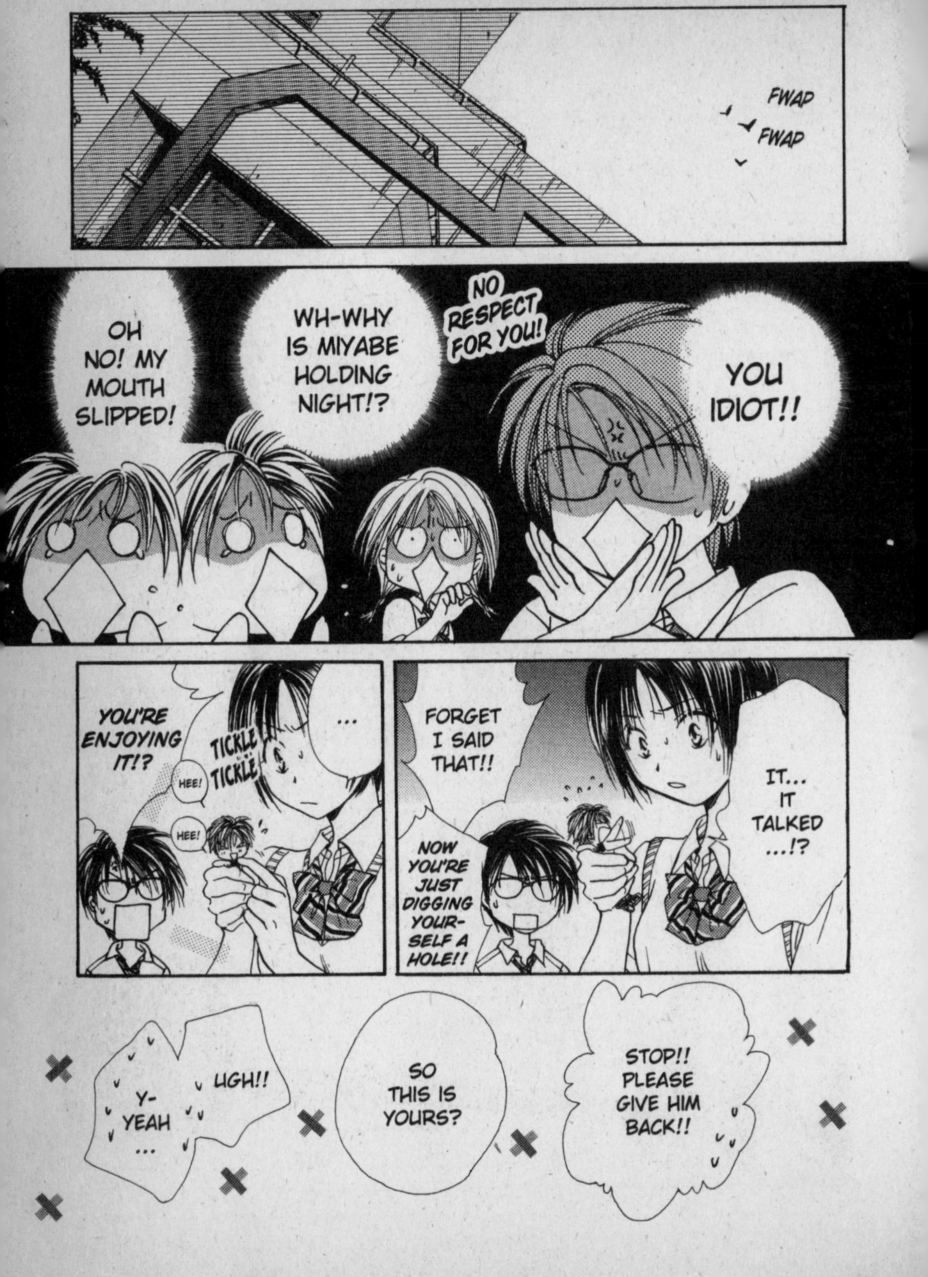
FWAP
FWAP
YOU IDIOT!!
NO RESPECT FOR YOU!
WH-WHY IS MIYABE HOLDING NIGHT!?
OH NO! MY MOUTH SLIPPED!
IT... IT TALKED ...!?
FORGET I SAID THAT!!
NOW YOU'RE JUST DIGGING YOUR-SELF A HOLE!!
...
TICKLE TICKLE
YOU'RE ENJOYING IT!?
HEE!
HEE!
STOP!! PLEASE GIVE HIM BACK!!
SO THIS IS YOURS?
UGH!!
Y-YEAH ...

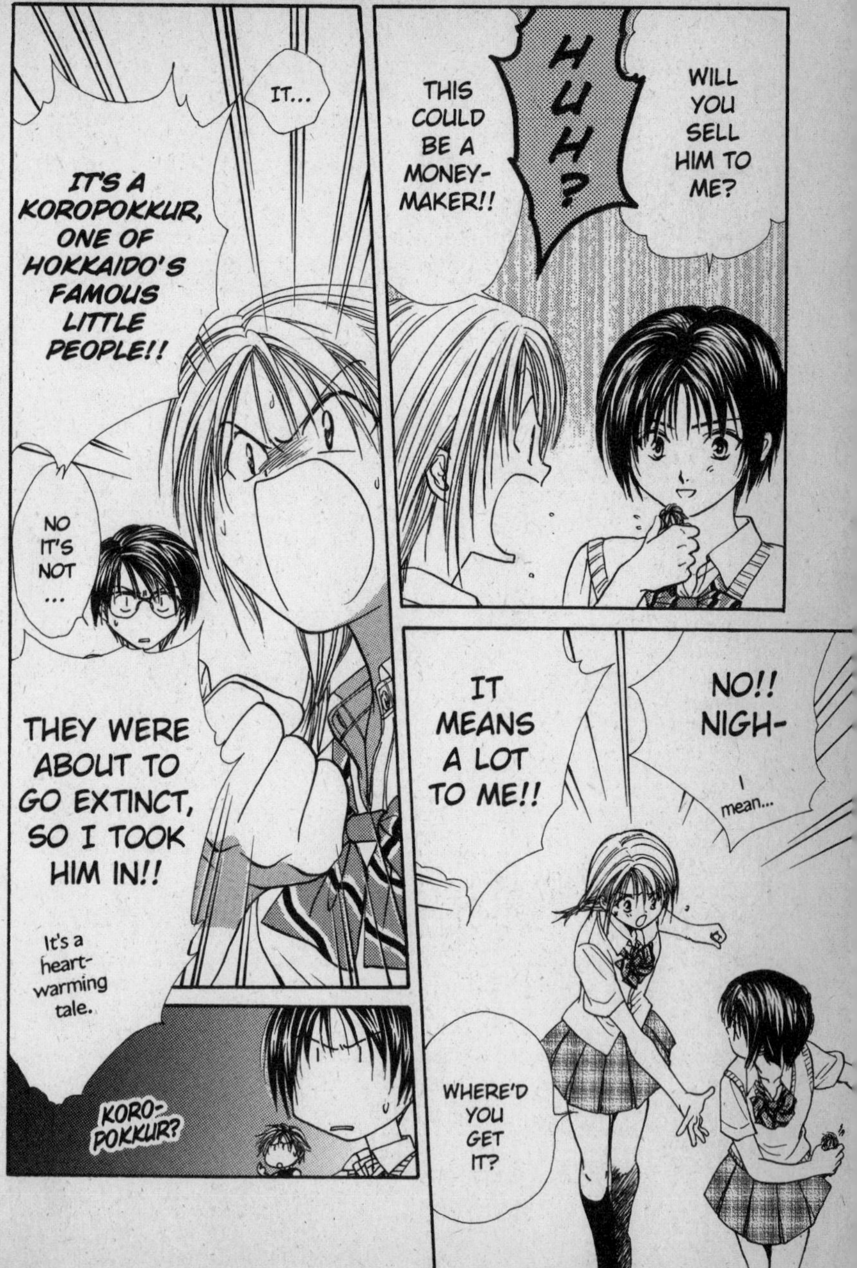

WILL YOU SELL HIM TO ME?
HUH?
THIS COULD BE A MONEY-MAKER!!
NO!! NIGH-
I mean...
IT MEANS A LOT TO ME!!
WHERE'D YOU GET IT?
IT...
IT'S A KOROPOKKUR, ONE OF HOKKAIDO'S FAMOUS LITTLE PEOPLE!!
NO IT'S NOT ...
THEY WERE ABOUT TO GO EXTINCT, SO I TOOK HIM IN!!
It's a heart-warming tale.
KORO-POKKUR?

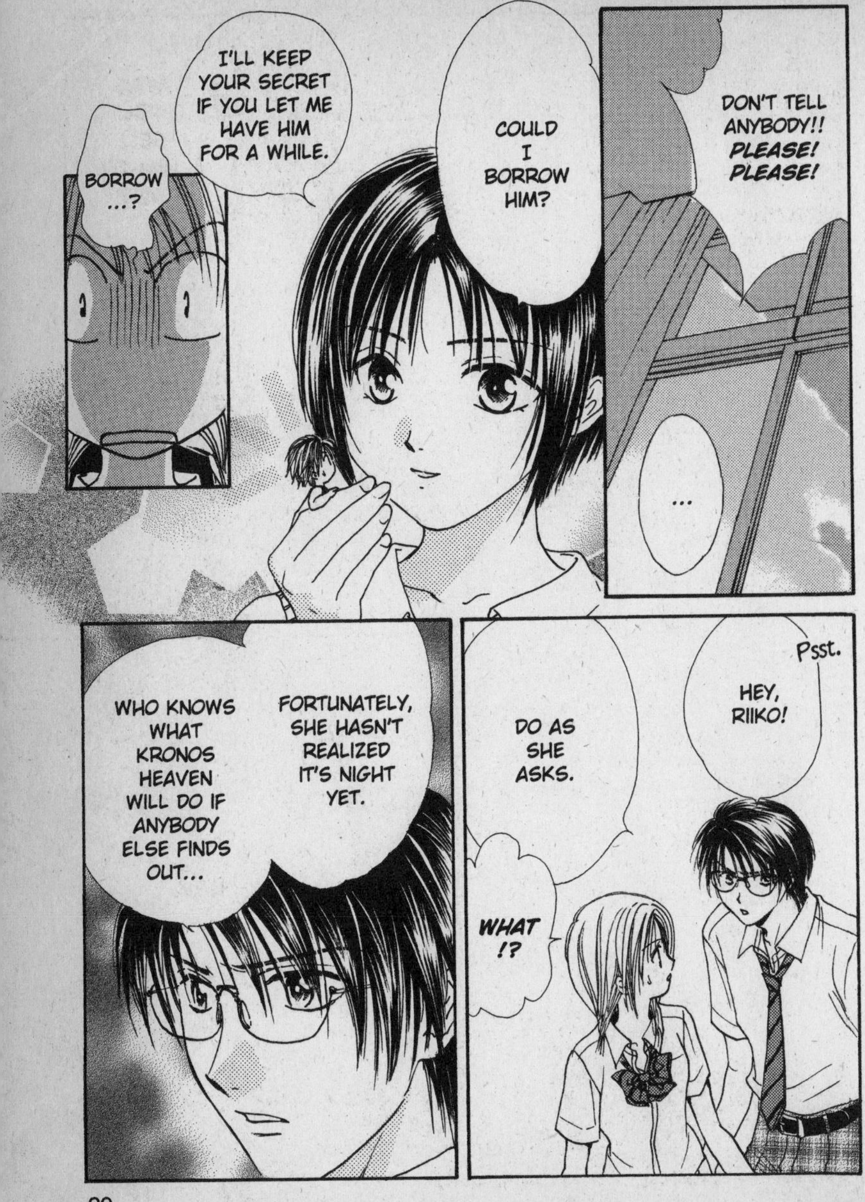
DON'T TELL ANYBODY!! PLEASE! PLEASE!
...
COULD I BORROW HIM?
I'LL KEEP YOUR SECRET IF YOU LET ME HAVE HIM FOR A WHILE.
BORROW ...?
Psst.
HEY, RIIKO!
DO AS SHE ASKS.
WHAT !?
FORTUNATELY, SHE HASN'T REALIZED IT'S NIGHT YET.
WHO KNOWS WHAT KRONOS HEAVEN WILL DO IF ANYBODY ELSE FINDS OUT...

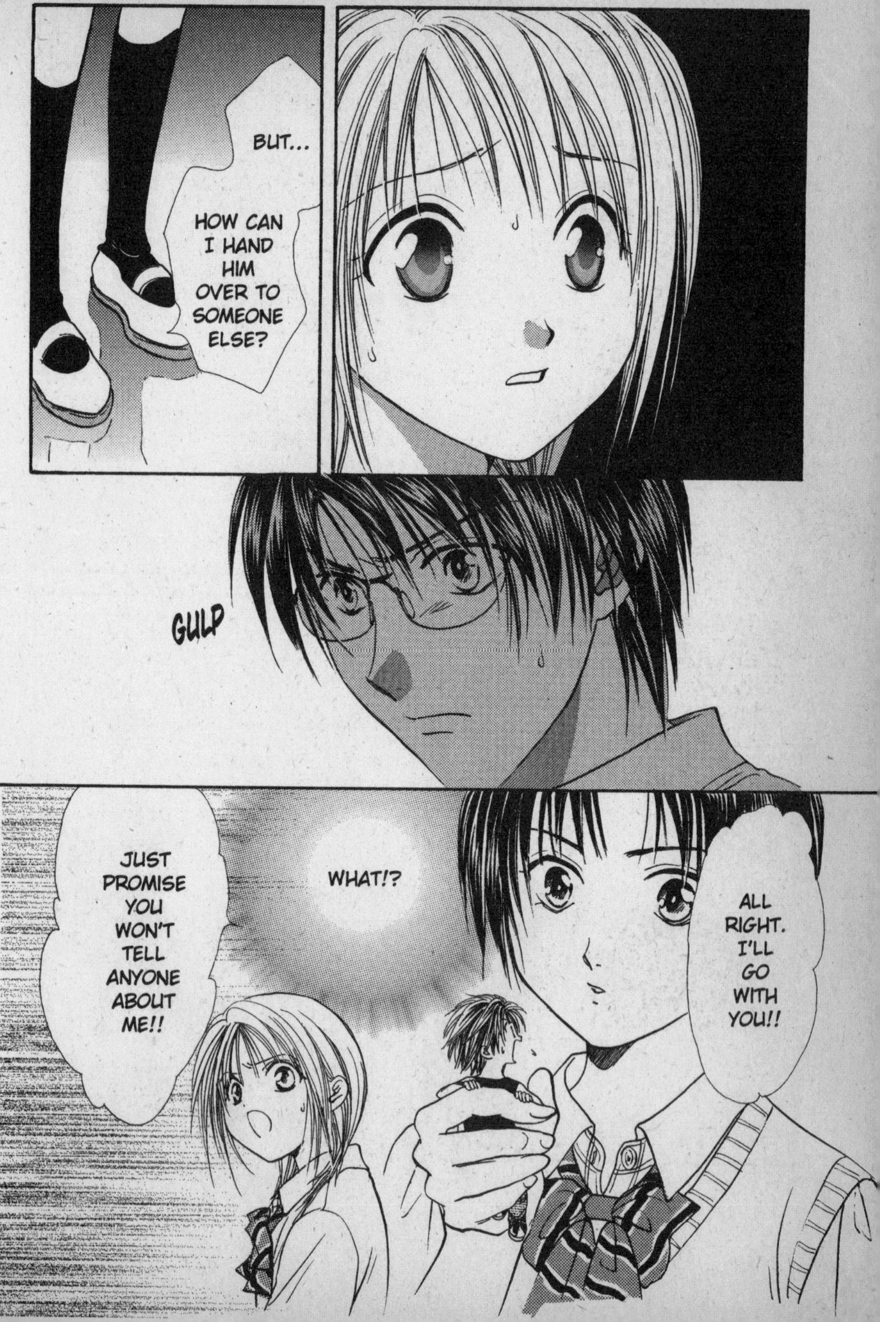
BUT...
HOW CAN I HAND HIM OVER TO SOMEONE ELSE?
GULP
ALL RIGHT. I'LL GO WITH YOU!!
WHAT!?
JUST PROMISE YOU WON'T TELL ANYONE ABOUT ME!!

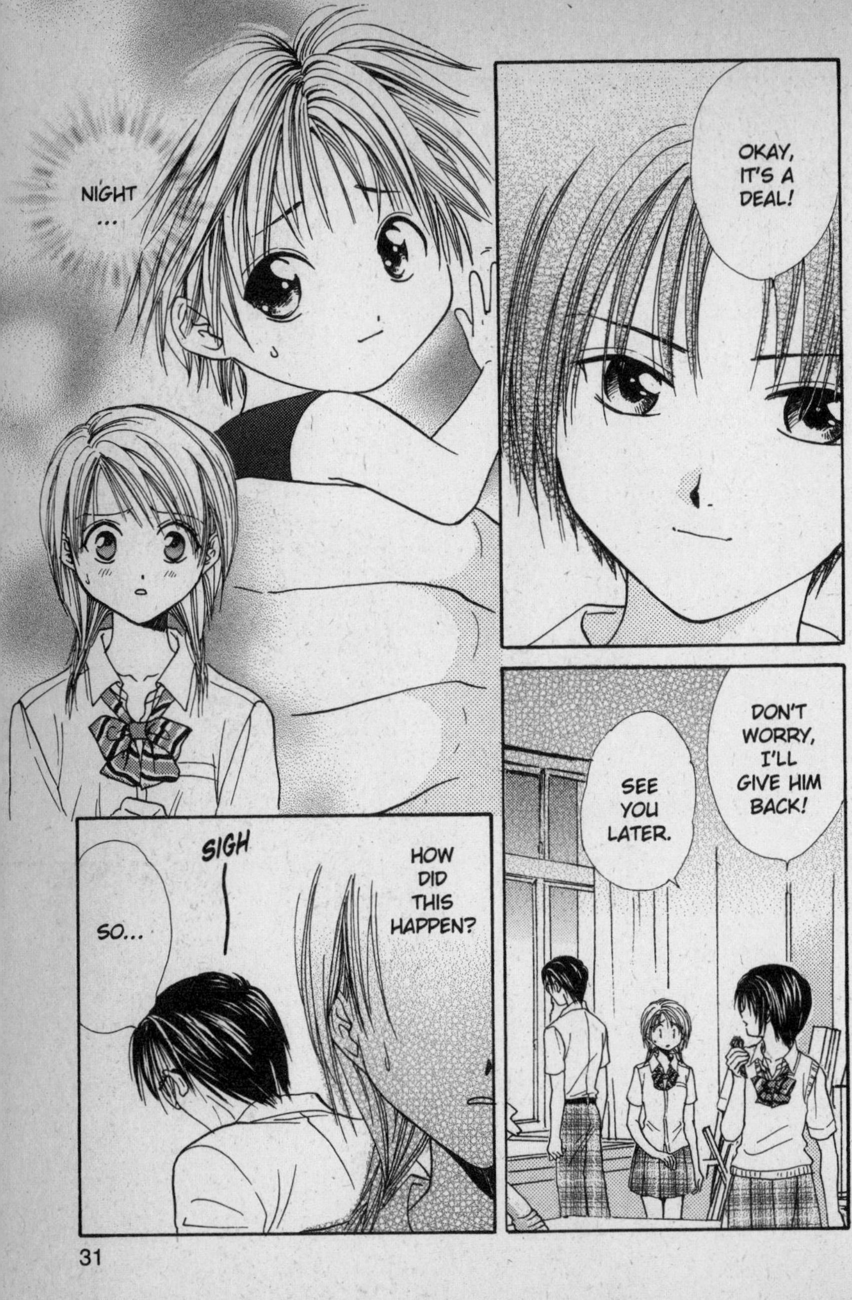
OKAY, IT'S A DEAL!
DON'T WORRY, I'LL GIVE HIM BACK!
SEE YOU LATER.
NIGHT ...
HOW DID THIS HAPPEN?
SIGH
SO...

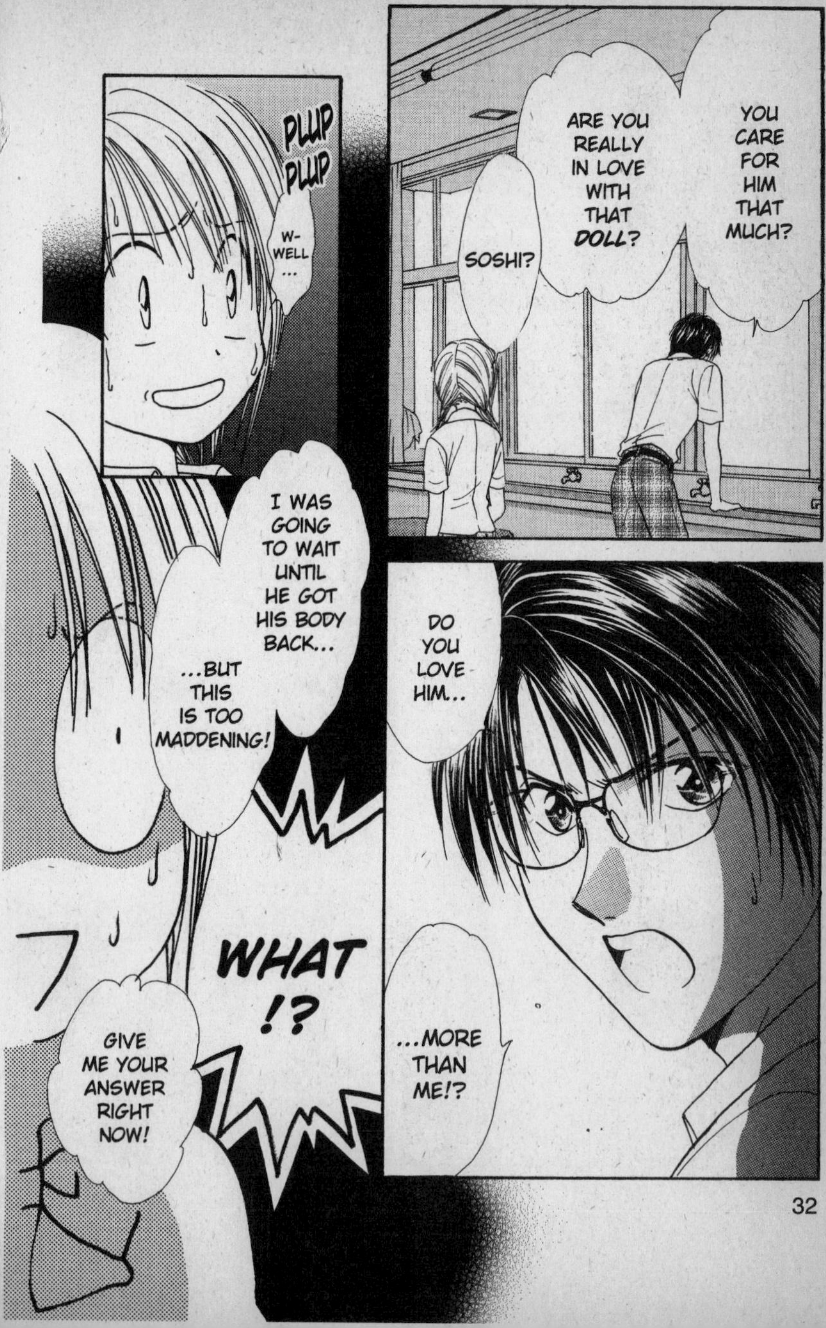
YOU CARE FOR HIM THAT MUCH?
ARE YOU REALLY IN LOVE WITH THAT DOLL?
SOSHI?
PLUP PLUP
W-WELL...
DO YOU LOVE HIM...
...MORE THAN ME!?
I WAS GOING TO WAIT UNTIL HE GOT HIS BODY BACK...
...BUT THIS IS TOO MADDENING!
WHAT!?
GIVE ME YOUR ANSWER RIGHT NOW!

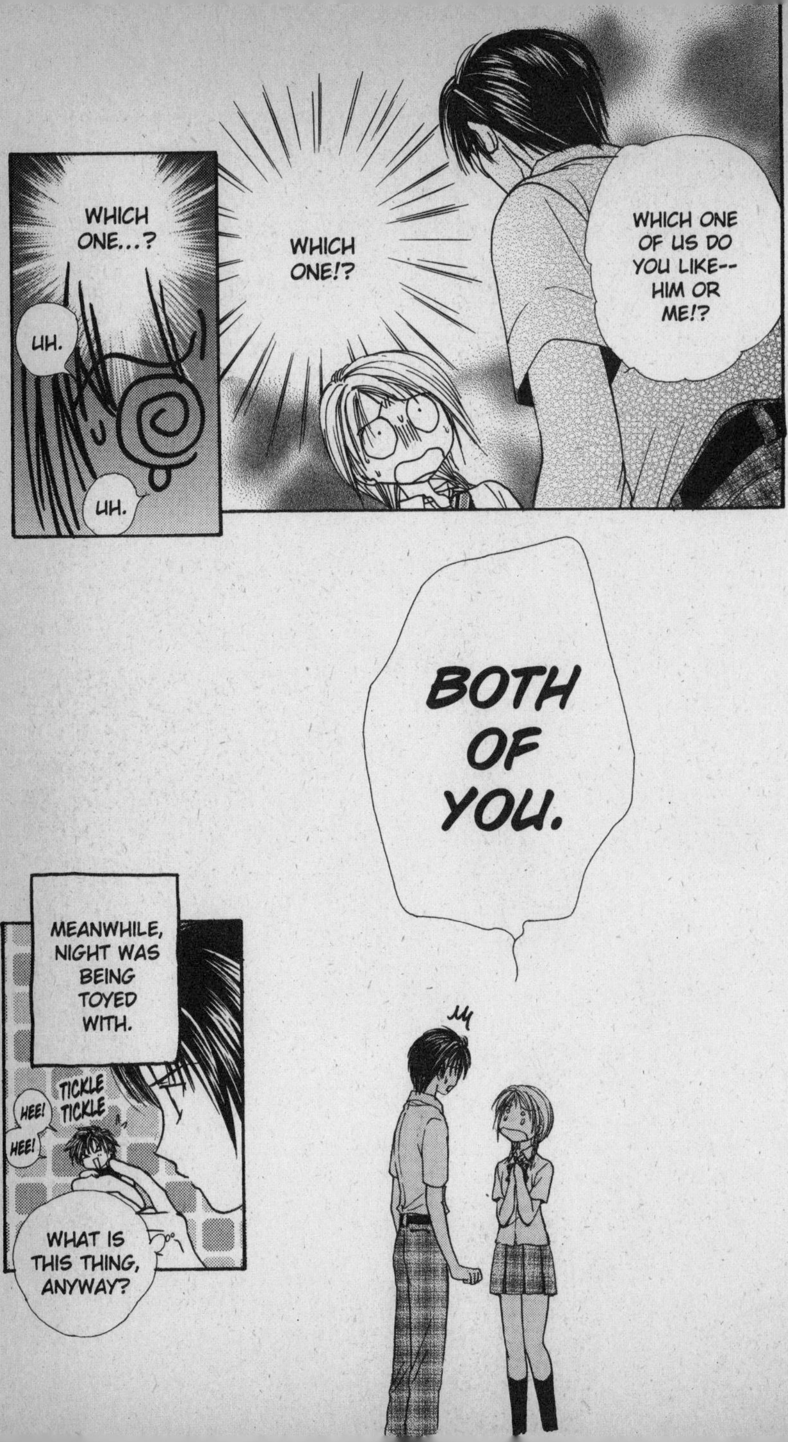
WHICH ONE OF US DO YOU LIKE-- HIM OR ME!?
WHICH ONE!?
WHICH ONE...?
UH.
UH.
BOTH OF YOU.
MEANWHILE, NIGHT WAS BEING TOYED WITH.
TICKLE TICKLE
HEE!
HEE!
WHAT IS THIS THING, ANYWAY?

Absolute Boyfriend

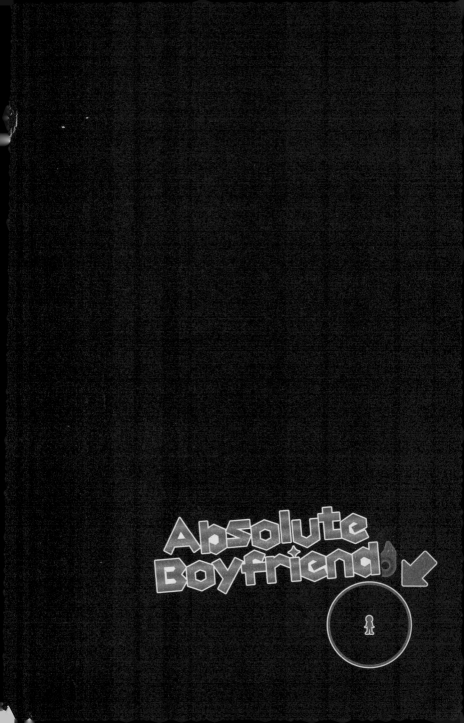

Act 26: Both

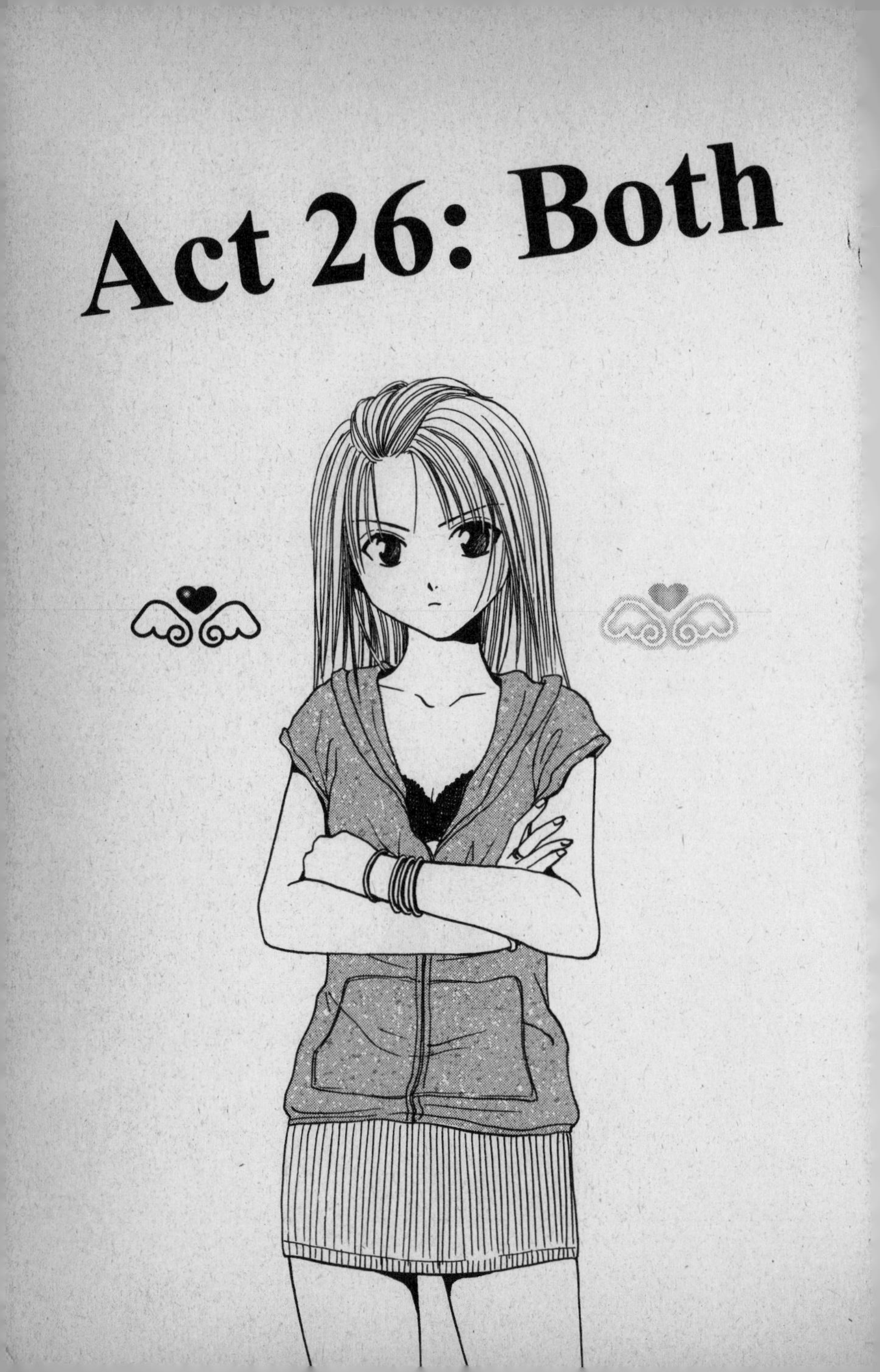

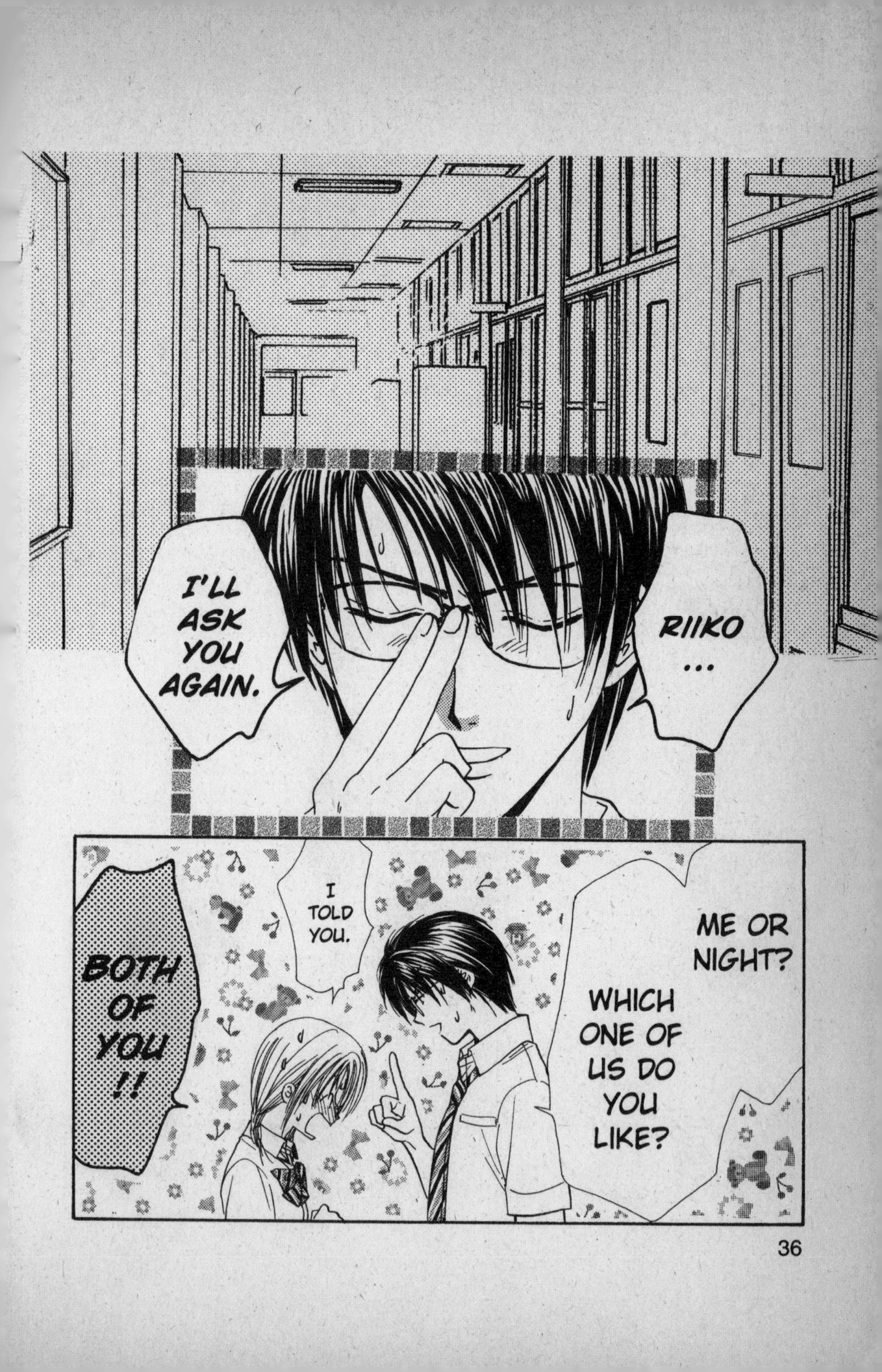
RIIKO...
I'LL ASK YOU AGAIN.
ME OR NIGHT?
WHICH ONE OF US DO YOU LIKE?
I TOLD YOU.
BOTH OF YOU!!

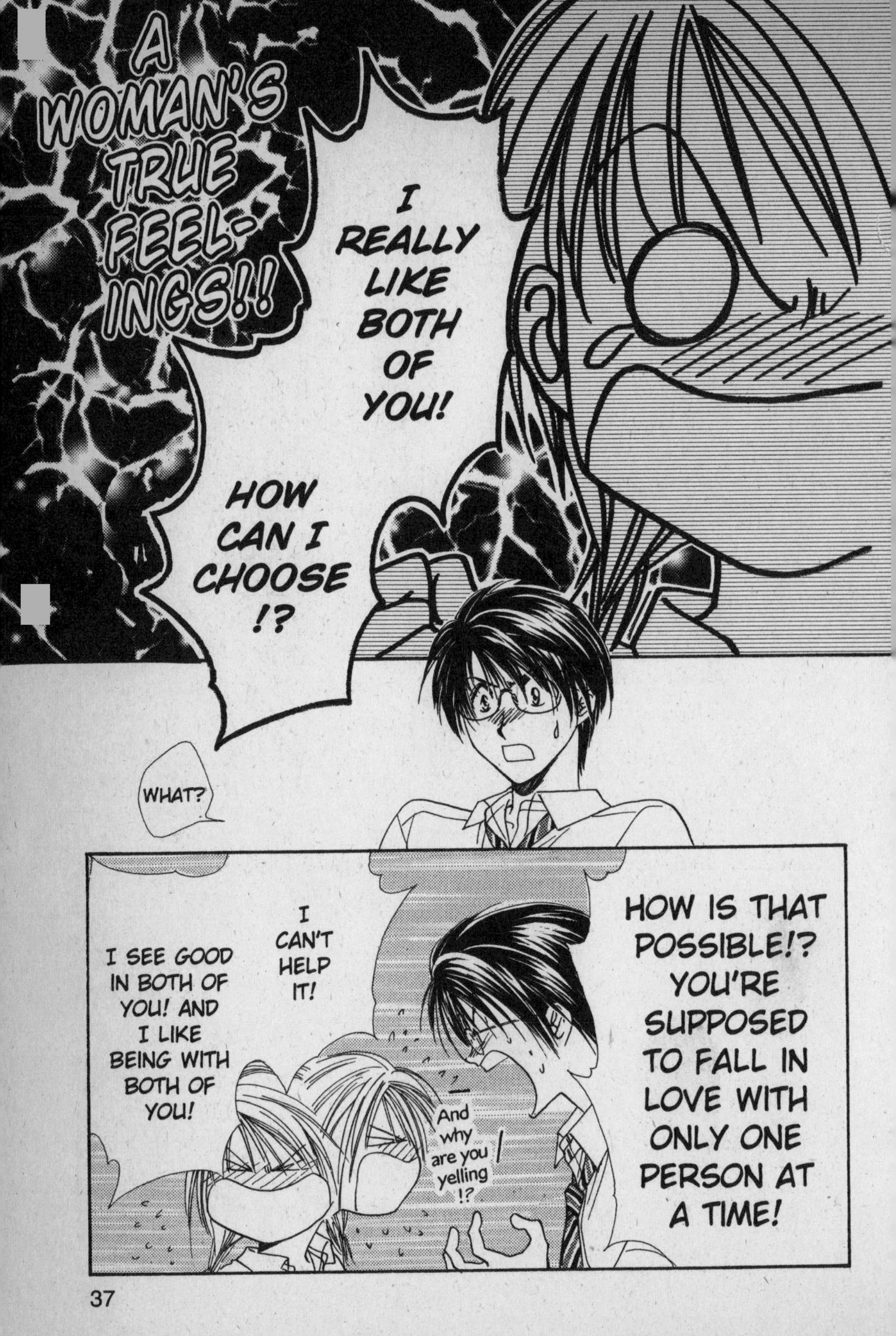

I REALLY LIKE BOTH OF YOU!
HOW CAN I CHOOSE!?
A WOMAN'S TRUE FEEL-INGS!!
WHAT?
HOW IS THAT POSSIBLE!? YOU'RE SUPPOSED TO FALL IN LOVE WITH ONLY ONE PERSON AT A TIME!
And why are you yelling!?
I CAN'T HELP IT!
I SEE GOOD IN BOTH OF YOU! AND I LIKE BEING WITH BOTH OF YOU!

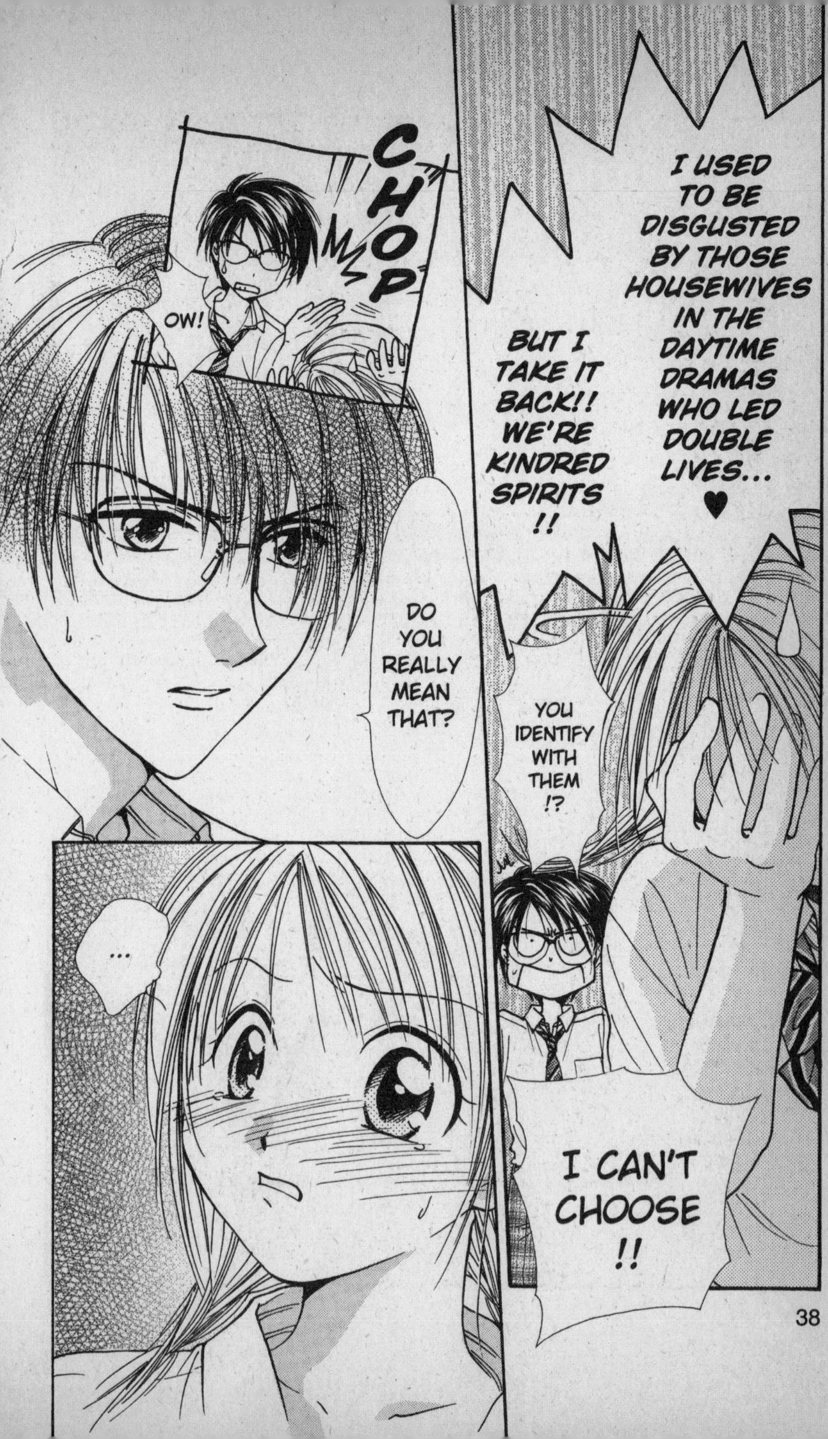
I USED TO BE DISGUSTED BY THOSE HOUSEWIVES IN THE DAYTIME DRAMAS WHO LED DOUBLE LIVES... ♥
BUT I TAKE IT BACK!! WE'RE KINDRED SPIRITS !!
YOU IDENTIFY WITH THEM !?
I CAN'T CHOOSE !!
CHOP
OW!
DO YOU REALLY MEAN THAT?
...

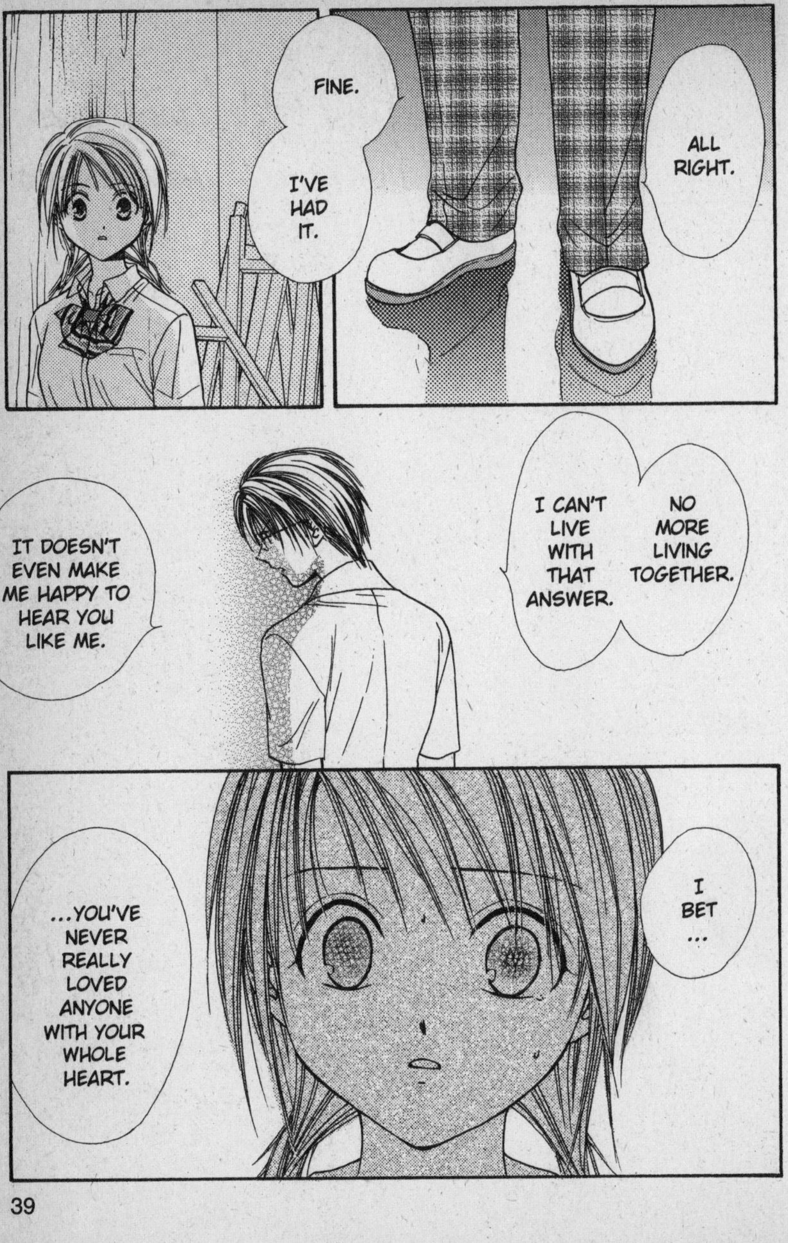
ALL RIGHT.
FINE.
I'VE HAD IT.
NO MORE LIVING TOGETHER.
I CAN'T LIVE WITH THAT ANSWER.
IT DOESN'T EVEN MAKE ME HAPPY TO HEAR YOU LIKE ME.
I BET ...
...YOU'VE NEVER REALLY LOVED ANYONE WITH YOUR WHOLE HEART.

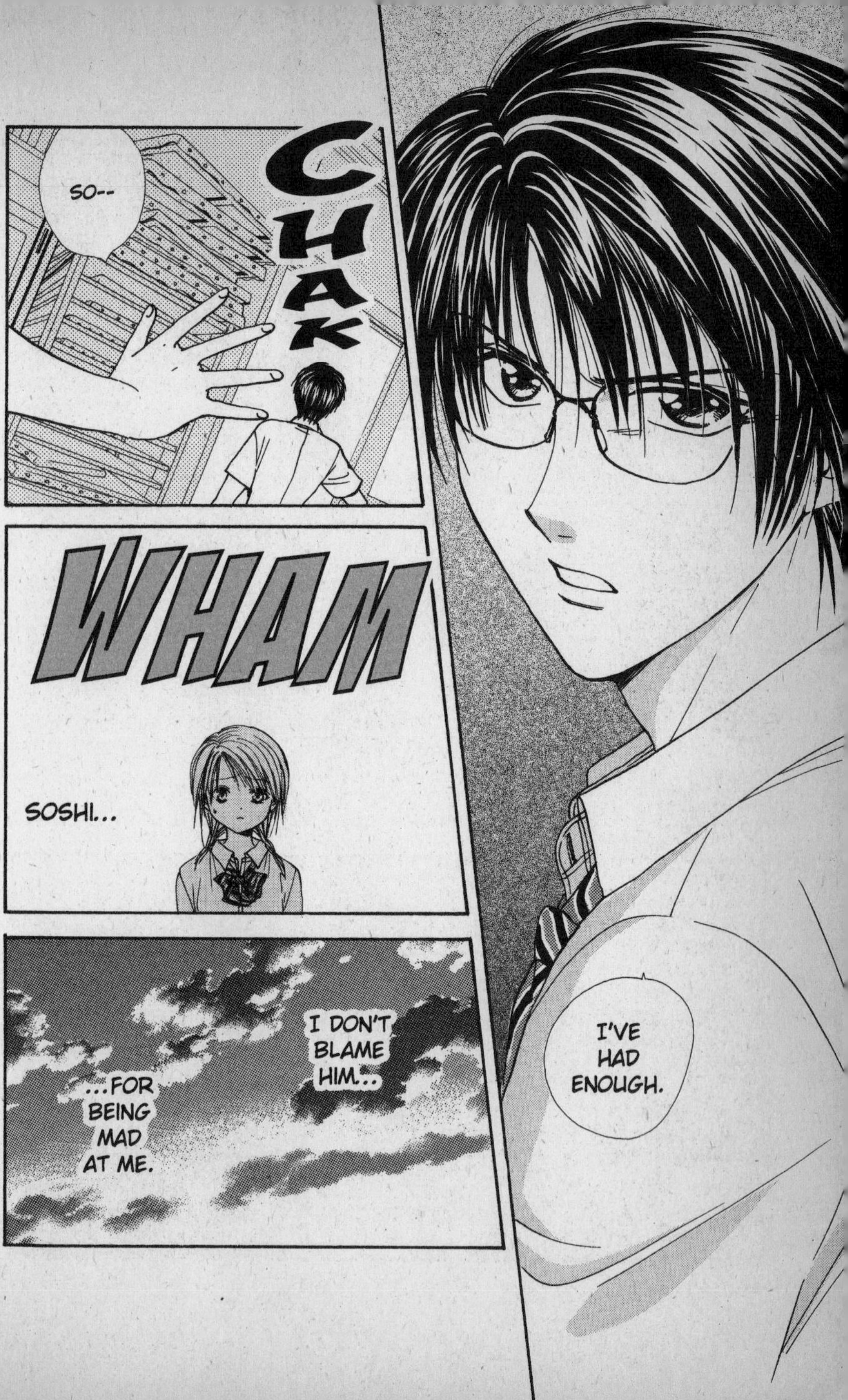
I'VE HAD ENOUGH.
SO--
CHAK
WHAM
SOSHI...
I DON'T BLAME HIM...
...FOR BEING MAD AT ME.

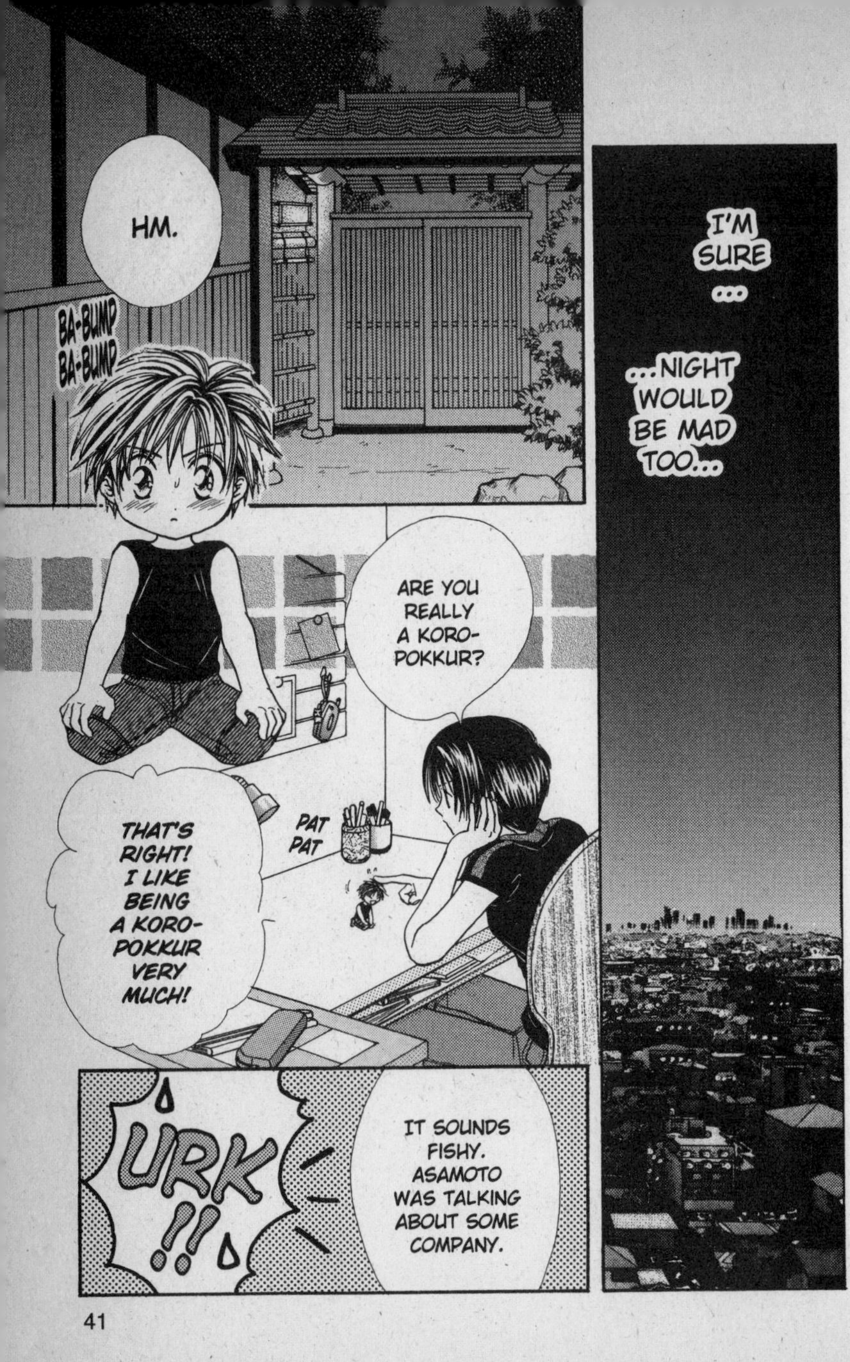
I'M SURE ...
...NIGHT WOULD BE MAD TOO...
HM.
BA-BUMP BA-BUMP
ARE YOU REALLY A KORO-POKKUR?
PAT PAT
THAT'S RIGHT! I LIKE BEING A KORO-POKKUR VERY MUCH!
IT SOUNDS FISHY. ASAMOTO WAS TALKING ABOUT SOME COMPANY.
URK!!!

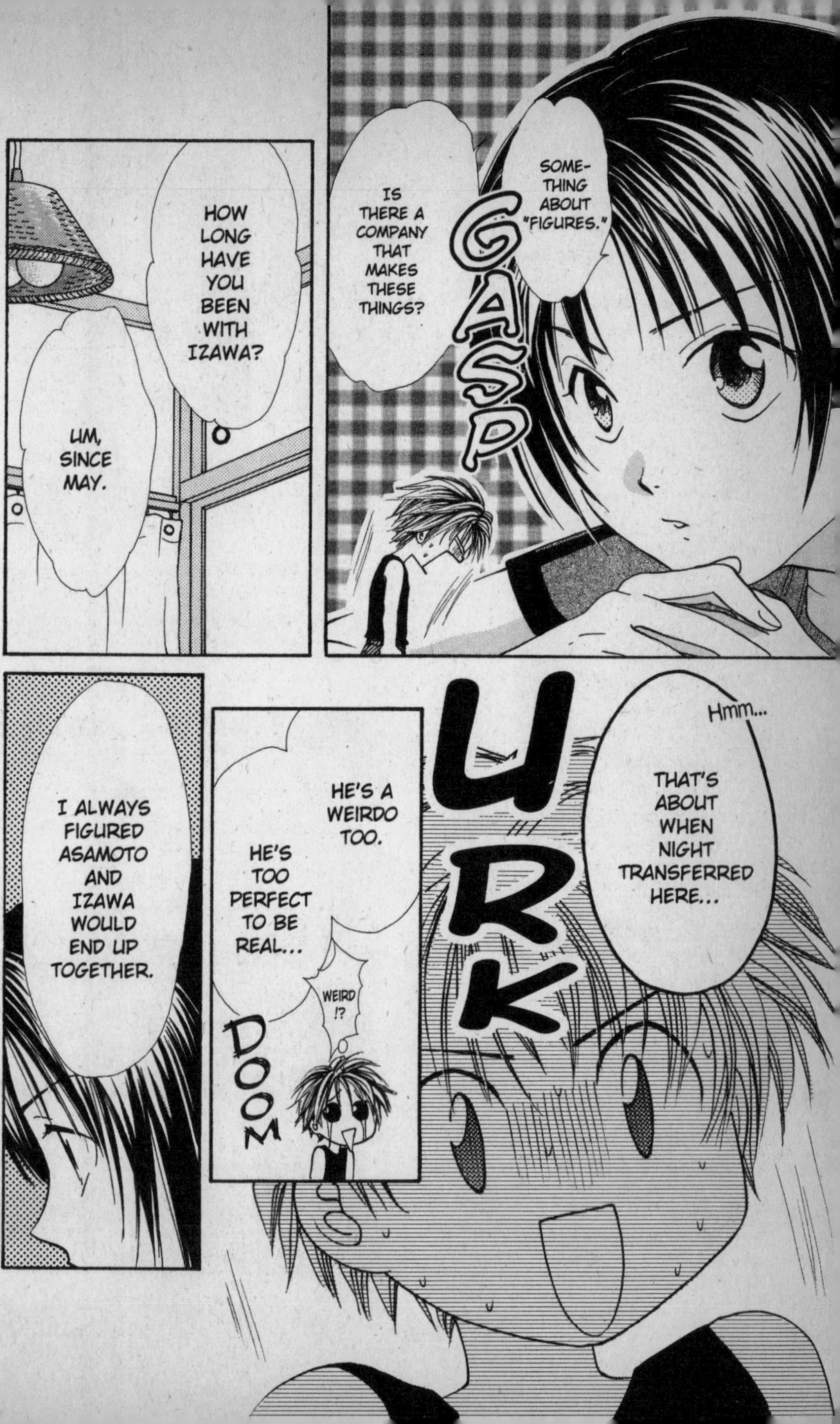
SOMETHING ABOUT "FIGURES."
IS THERE A COMPANY THAT MAKES THESE THINGS?
GASP
HOW LONG HAVE YOU BEEN WITH IZAWA?
UM, SINCE MAY.
Hmm...
THAT'S ABOUT WHEN NIGHT TRANSFERRED HERE...
URK
HE'S A WEIRDO TOO.
HE'S TOO PERFECT TO BE REAL...
WEIRD !?
DOOM
I ALWAYS FIGURED ASAMOTO AND IZAWA WOULD END UP TOGETHER.

I'd like to thank everyone who came to the autograph session in late August at the Animate store in Ikebukuro. (I'm sorry if you couldn't get tickets.)
I was delighted by all the nice presents. Too bad it was raining... At least it wasn't pouring.

It was actually the day after I turned in my work (the last chapter of *Absolute Boyfriend*, coincidentally!) so I had been feeling under the weather since that morning, and I was half-dead. (Then I was in a meeting until nighttime. Maybe I'm tougher than I think?)
I usually keel over for two days after my deadlines. It's really tough, but the moment I turn something in is always satisfying. Then I can go to bed and sleep away. I wish I could sleep for a whole year.
Or at least six months. That's my fantasy. I'd like to go to a tropical island and space out and just be lazy... Sigh...

Oh! Back to reality!
I was on a tropical island for a moment there. Well, that's how things are right now. I'm not making any sense!
There were a few guys at the autograph session. I wonder what aspects of my work they like?

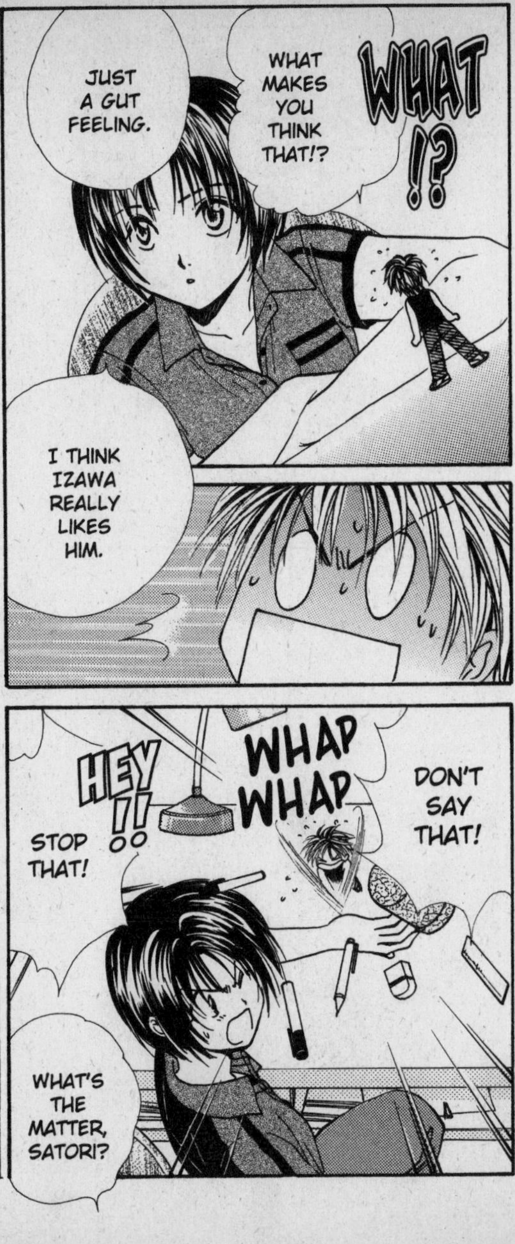
WHAT !?
WHAT MAKES YOU THINK THAT!?
JUST A GUT FEELING.
I THINK IZAWA REALLY LIKES HIM.
DON'T SAY THAT!
WHAP WHAP
HEY !!
STOP THAT!
WHAT'S THE MATTER, SATORI?

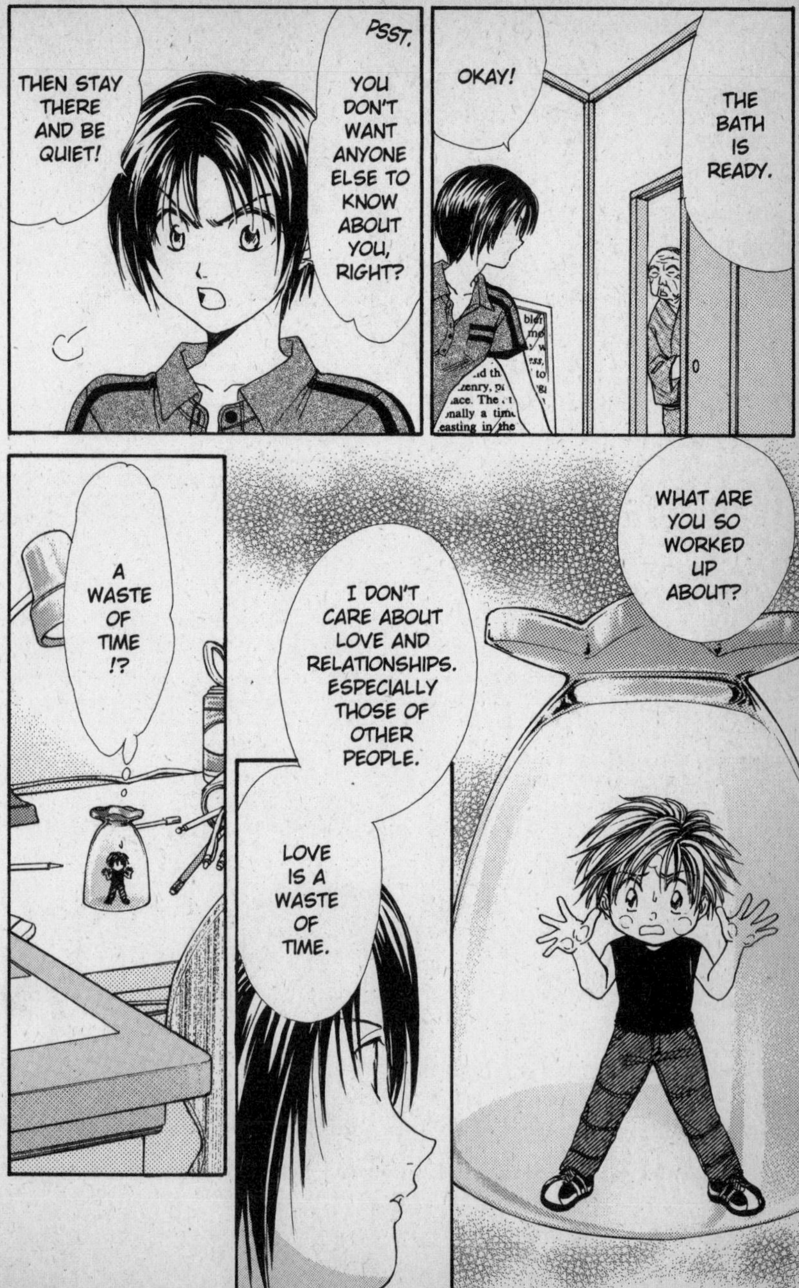
THE BATH IS READY.
OKAY!
PSST.
YOU DON'T WANT ANYONE ELSE TO KNOW ABOUT YOU, RIGHT?
THEN STAY THERE AND BE QUIET!
WHAT ARE YOU SO WORKED UP ABOUT?
I DON'T CARE ABOUT LOVE AND RELATIONSHIPS. ESPECIALLY THOSE OF OTHER PEOPLE.
LOVE IS A WASTE OF TIME.
A WASTE OF TIME !?

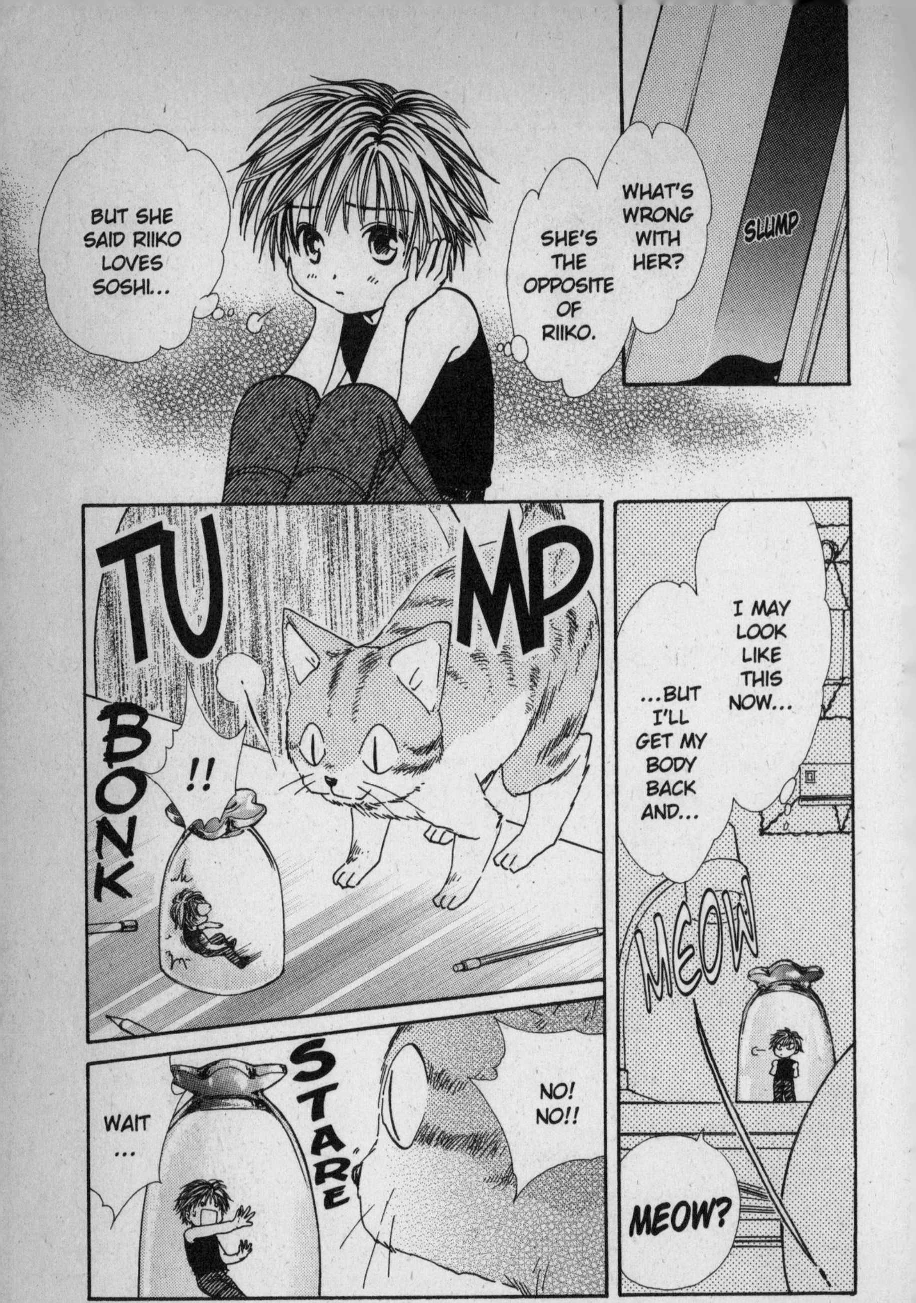
SLUMP
WHAT'S WRONG WITH HER?
SHE'S THE OPPOSITE OF RIIKO.
BUT SHE SAID RIIKO LOVES SOSHI...
I MAY LOOK LIKE THIS NOW...
...BUT I'LL GET MY BODY BACK AND...
MEOW
MEOW?
TUMP
!!
BONK
NO! NO!!
STARE
WAIT ...

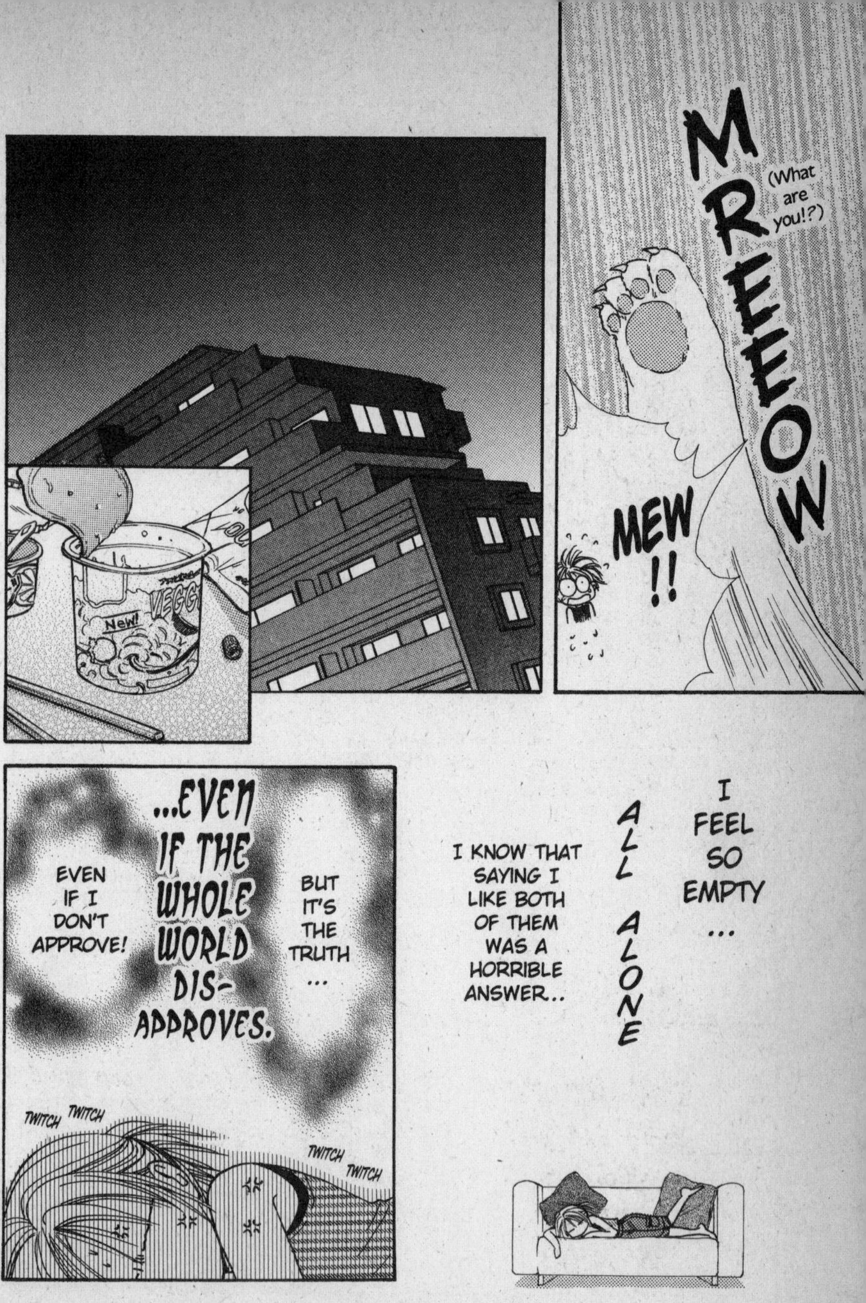
MREEEOW
(What are you!?)
MEW!!
New!
I FEEL SO EMPTY...
ALL ALONE
I KNOW THAT SAYING I LIKE BOTH OF THEM WAS A HORRIBLE ANSWER...
BUT IT'S THE TRUTH...
...EVEN IF THE WHOLE WORLD DIS-APPROVES.
EVEN IF I DON'T APPROVE!
TWITCH TWITCH
TWITCH TWITCH

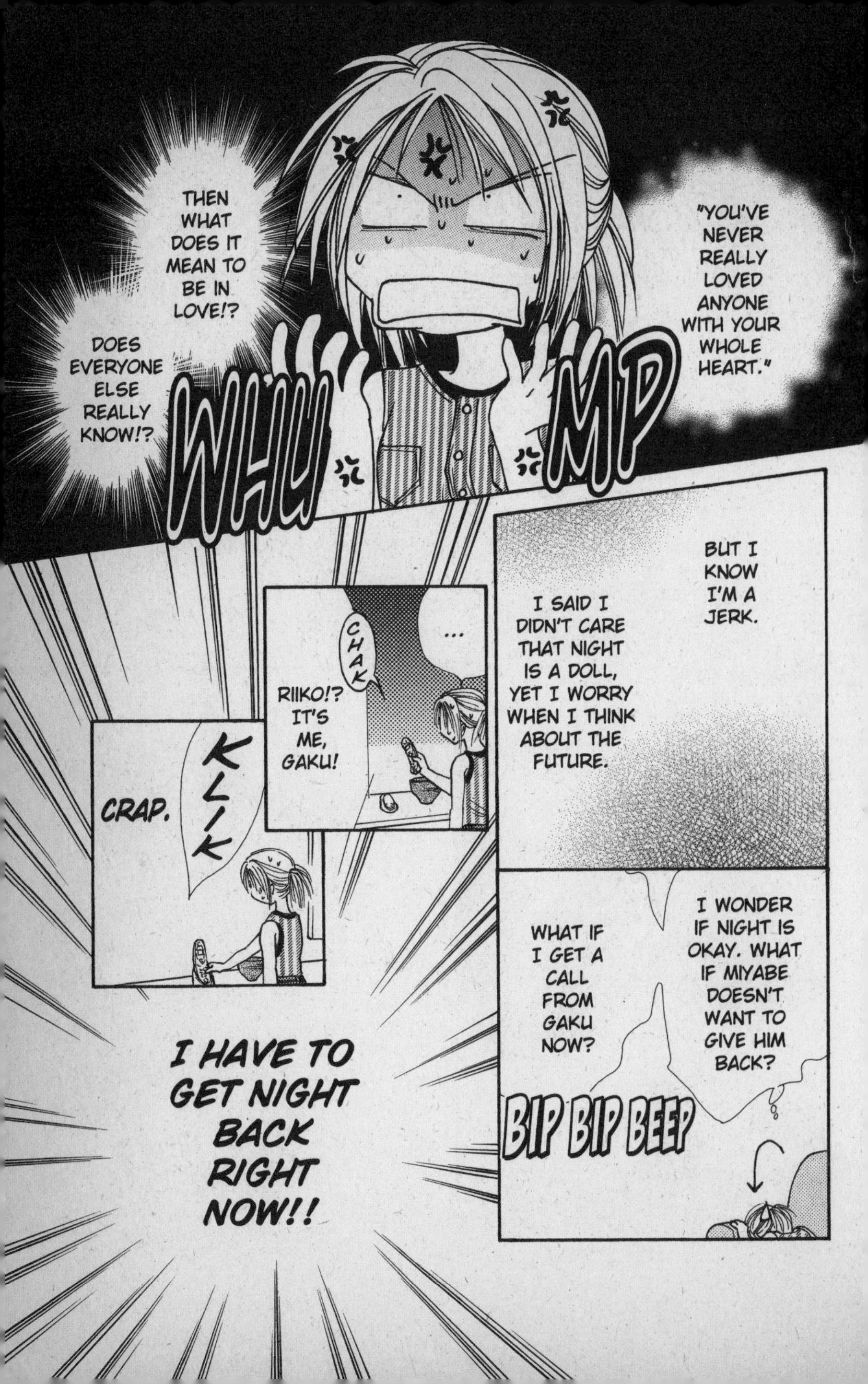
"YOU'VE NEVER REALLY LOVED ANYONE WITH YOUR WHOLE HEART."
THEN WHAT DOES IT MEAN TO BE IN LOVE!?
DOES EVERYONE ELSE REALLY KNOW!?
WHUMP
BUT I KNOW I'M A JERK.
I SAID I DIDN'T CARE THAT NIGHT IS A DOLL, YET I WORRY WHEN I THINK ABOUT THE FUTURE.
I WONDER IF NIGHT IS OKAY. WHAT IF MIYABE DOESN'T WANT TO GIVE HIM BACK?
WHAT IF I GET A CALL FROM GAKU NOW?
BIP BIP BEEP
...
CHAK
RIIKO!? IT'S ME, GAKU!
KLIK
CRAP.
I HAVE TO GET NIGHT BACK RIGHT NOW!!

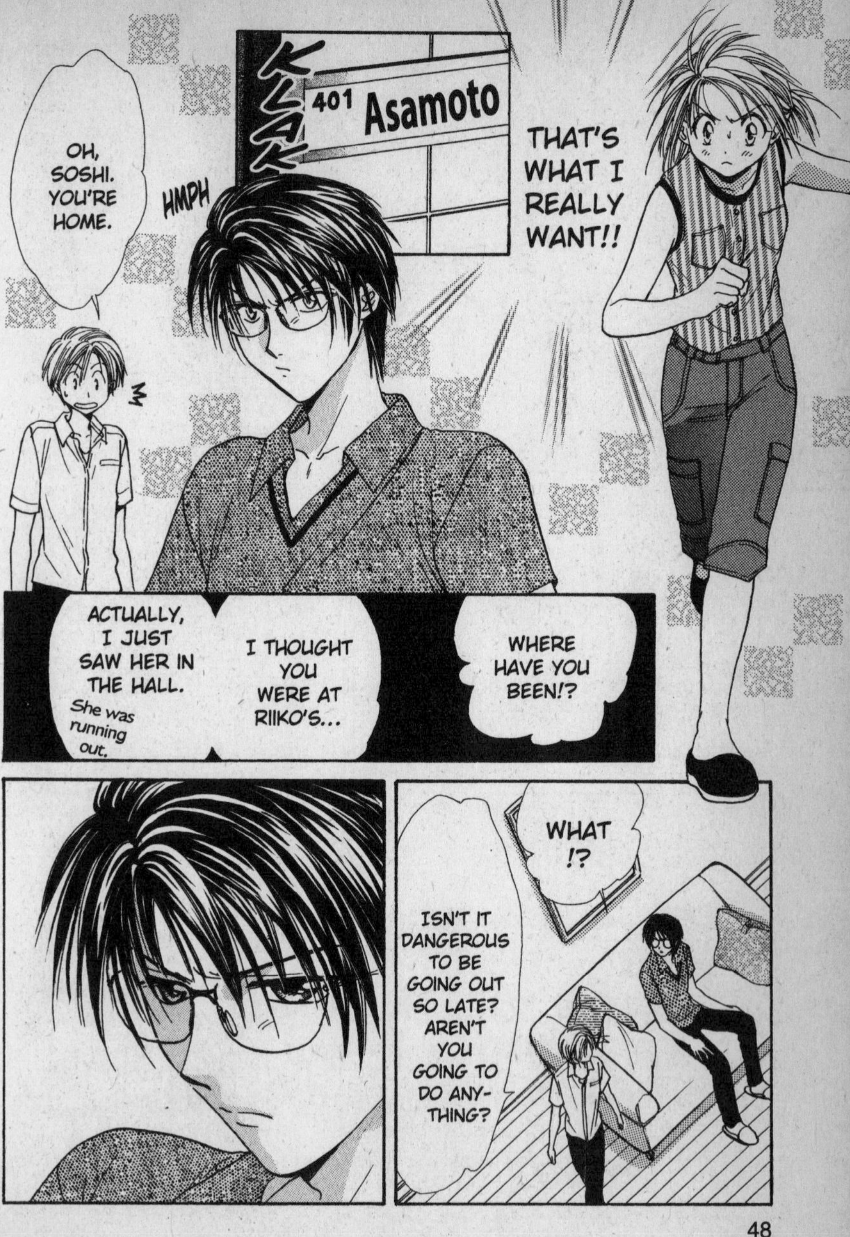
THAT'S WHAT I REALLY WANT!!
401 Asamoto
KLAK
HMPH
OH, SOSHI. YOU'RE HOME.
WHERE HAVE YOU BEEN!?
I THOUGHT YOU WERE AT RIIKO'S...
ACTUALLY, I JUST SAW HER IN THE HALL.
She was running out.
WHAT!?
ISN'T IT DANGEROUS TO BE GOING OUT SO LATE? AREN'T YOU GOING TO DO ANY-THING?

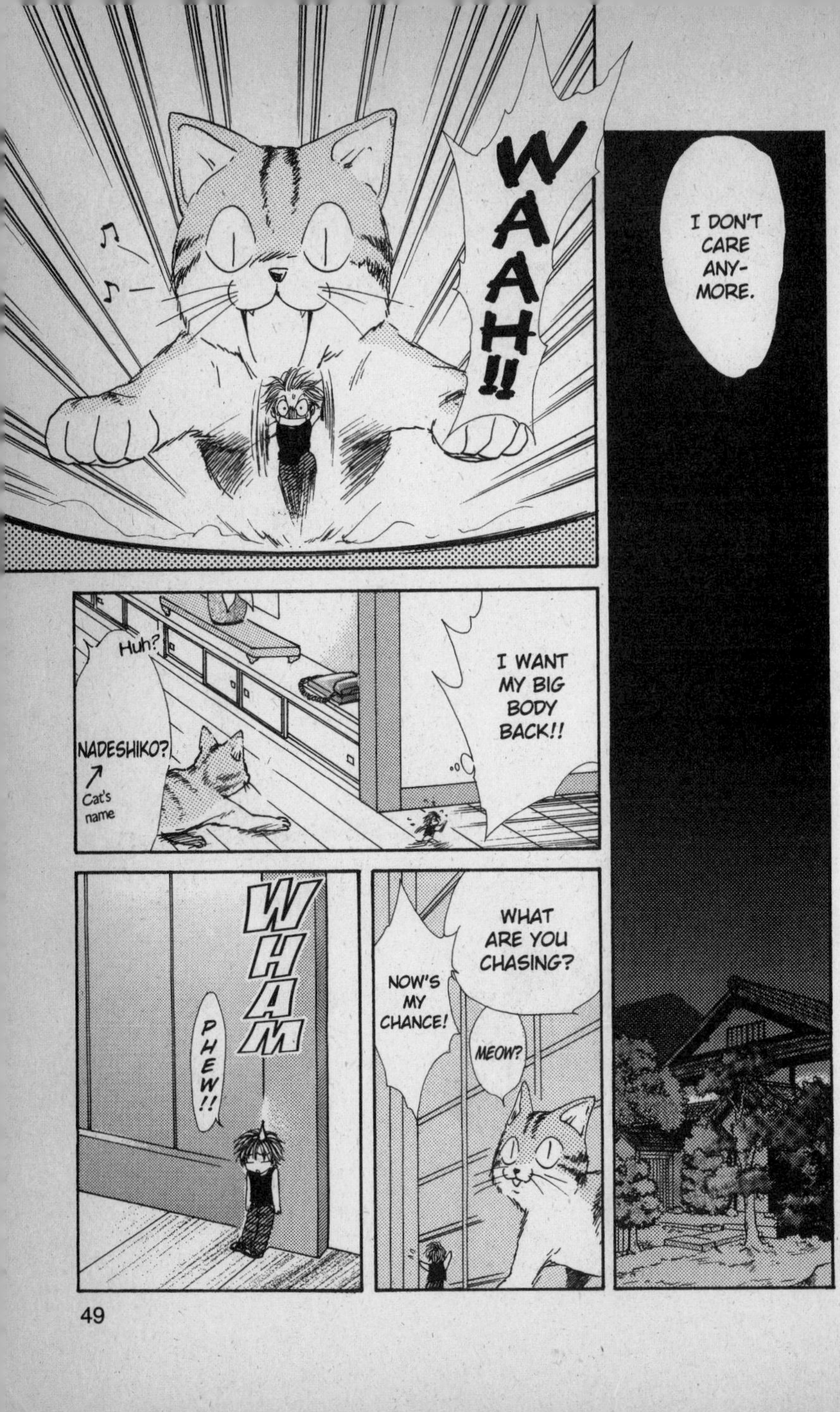
I DON'T CARE ANY-MORE.
WAAAH!!
I WANT MY BIG BODY BACK!!
Huh?
NADESHIKO?
Cat's name
WHAT ARE YOU CHASING?
NOW'S MY CHANCE!
MEOW?
WHAM
PHEW!!

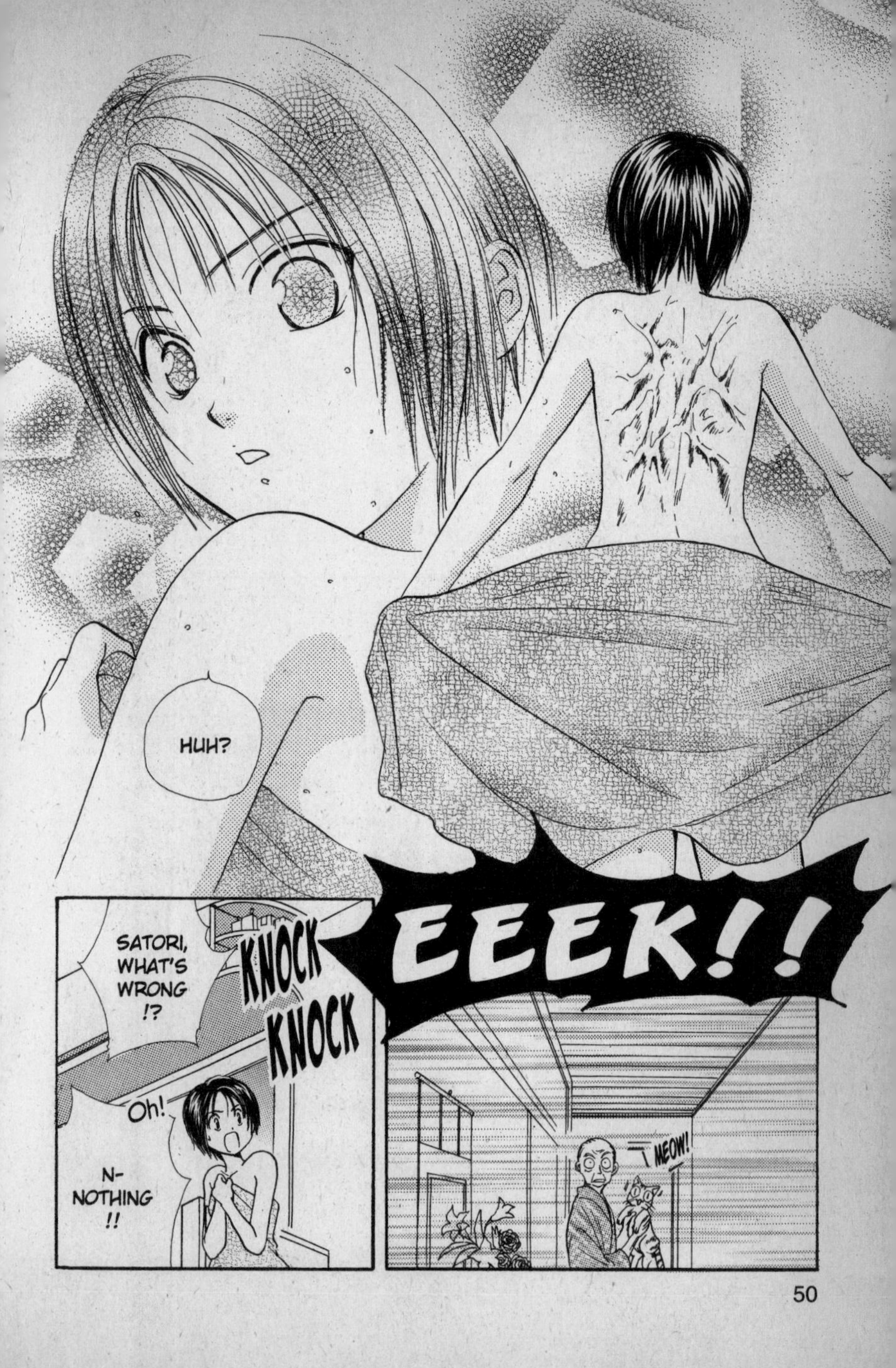
HUH?
EEEK!!
MEOW!
KNOCK KNOCK
SATORI, WHAT'S WRONG !?
Oh!
N-NOTHING !!

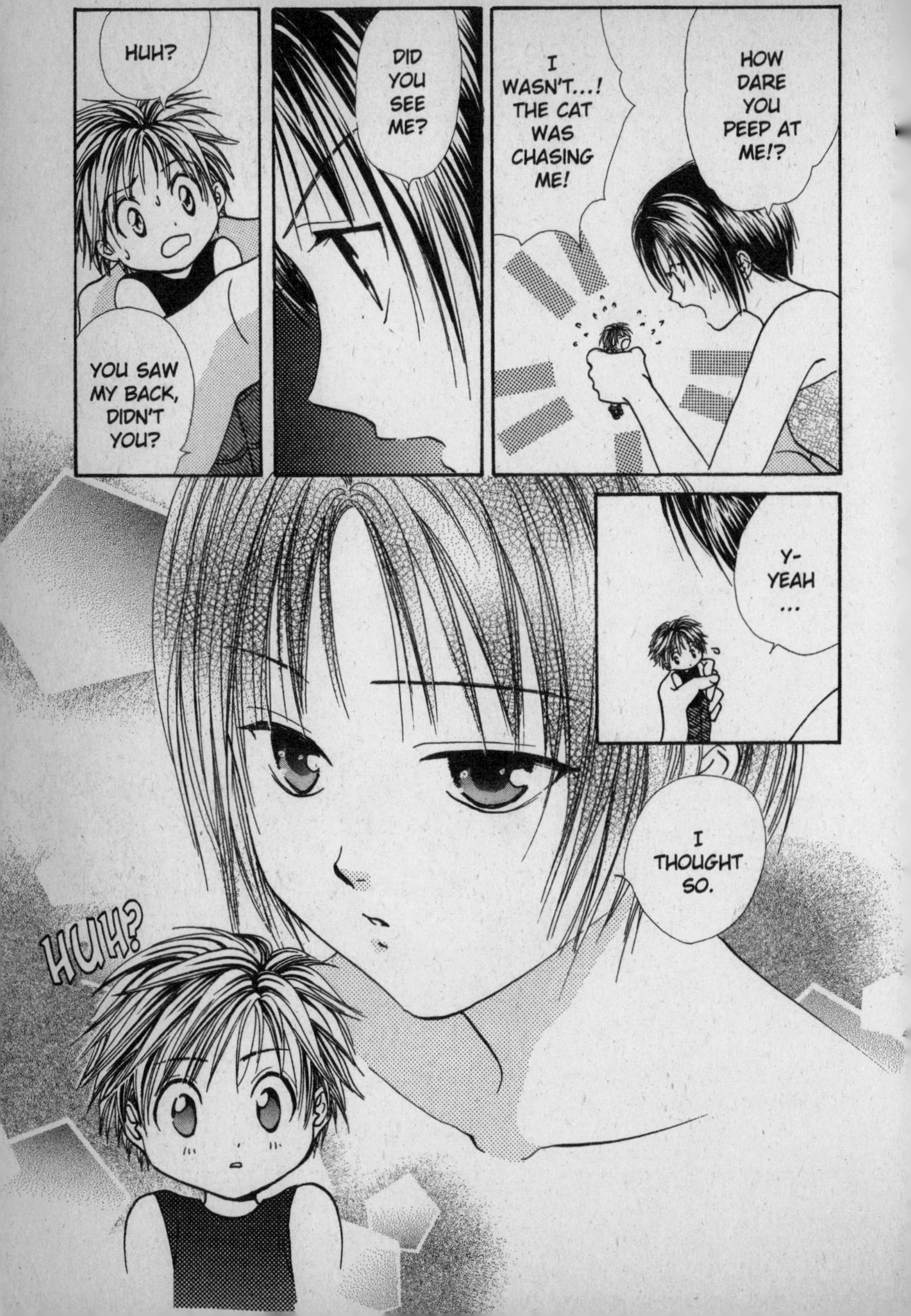
HOW DARE YOU PEEP AT ME!?
I WASN'T...! THE CAT WAS CHASING ME!
DID YOU SEE ME?
HUH?
YOU SAW MY BACK, DIDN'T YOU?
Y-YEAH...
I THOUGHT SO.
HUH?

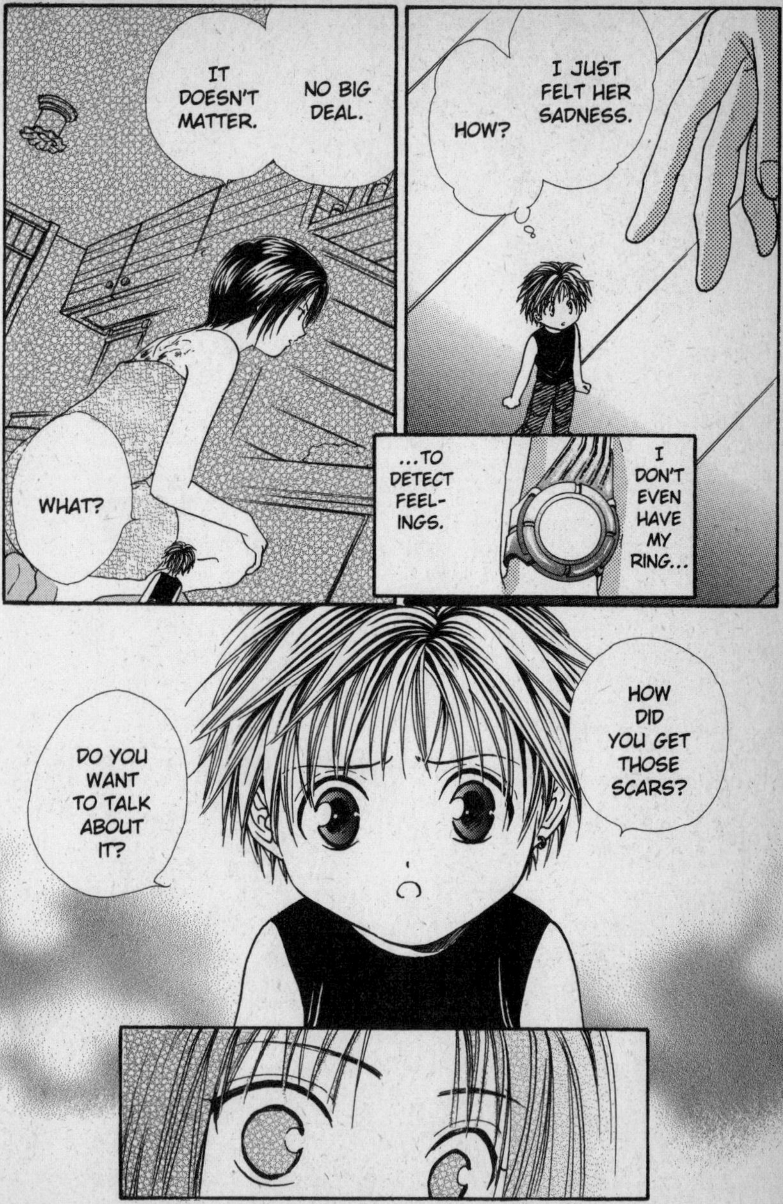
I JUST FELT HER SADNESS.
HOW?
I DON'T EVEN HAVE MY RING...
...TO DETECT FEEL-INGS.
NO BIG DEAL.
IT DOESN'T MATTER.
WHAT?
HOW DID YOU GET THOSE SCARS?
DO YOU WANT TO TALK ABOUT IT?

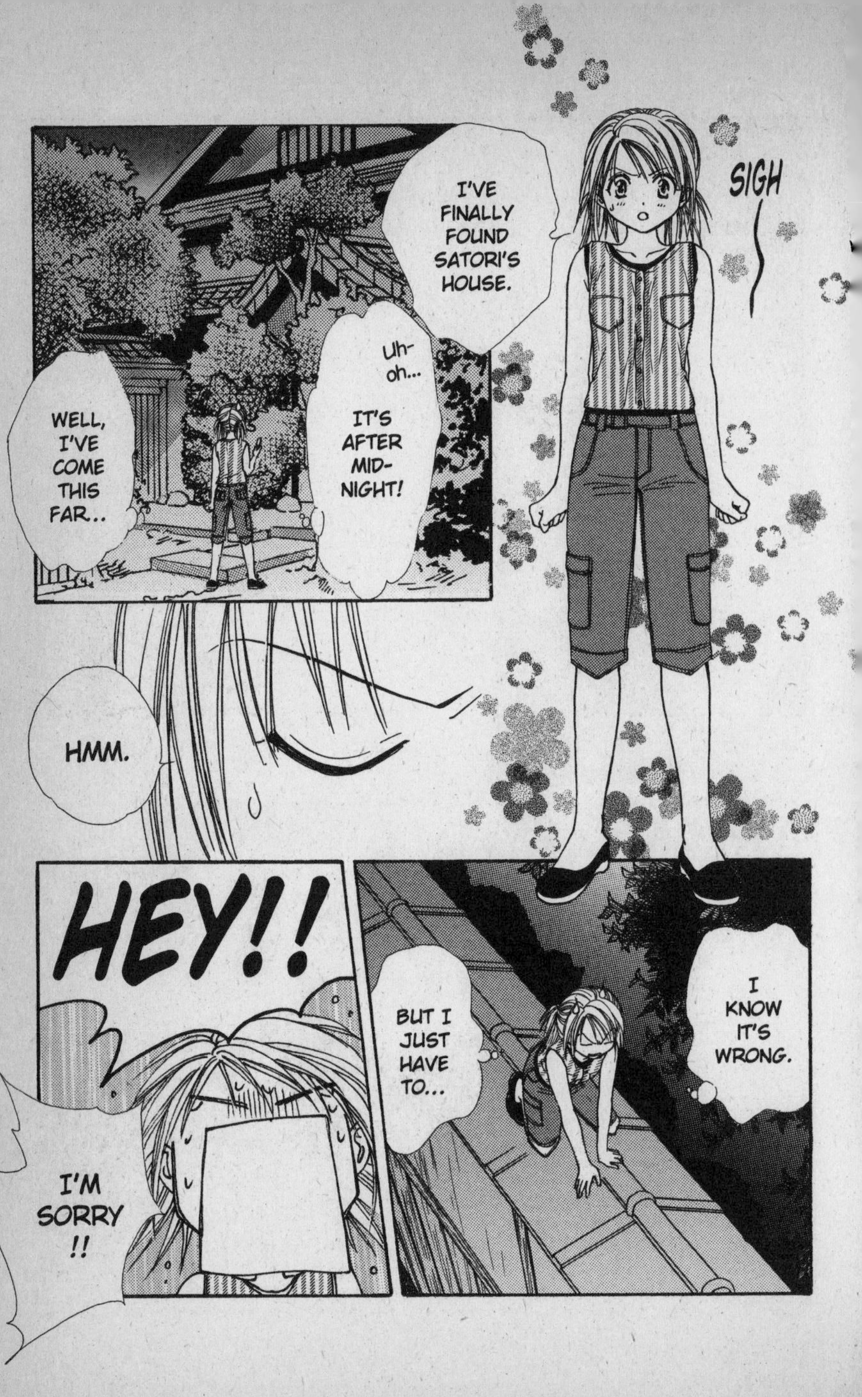
SIGH
I'VE FINALLY FOUND SATORI'S HOUSE.
Uh-oh...
IT'S AFTER MID-NIGHT!
WELL, I'VE COME THIS FAR..
HMM.
I KNOW IT'S WRONG.
BUT I JUST HAVE TO...
HEY!!
I'M SORRY !!

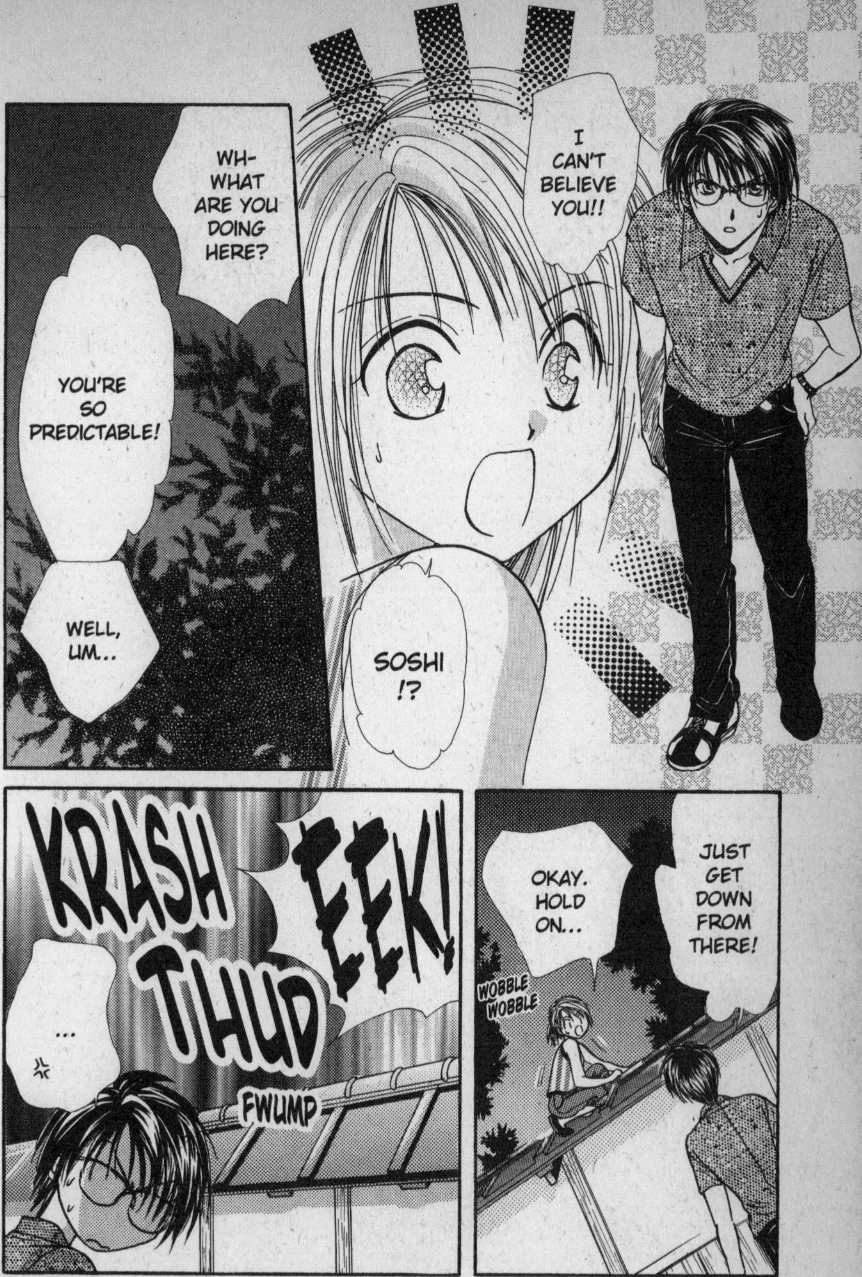
I CAN'T BELIEVE YOU!!
SOSHI !?
WH- WHAT ARE YOU DOING HERE?
YOU'RE SO PREDICTABLE!
WELL, UM...
JUST GET DOWN FROM THERE!
OKAY. HOLD ON...
WOBBLE WOBBLE
EEK!
KRASH THUD
FWUMP
...

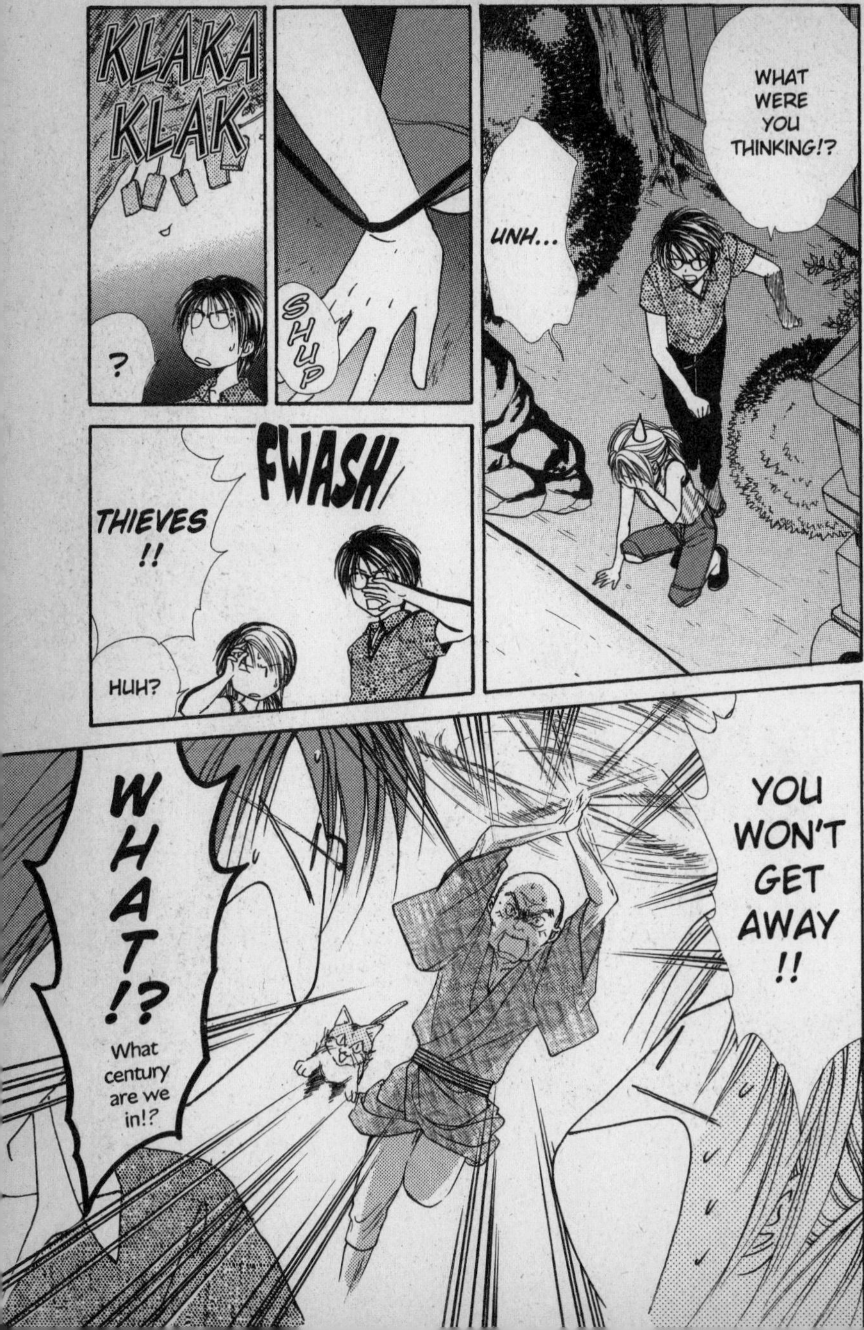

WHAT WERE YOU THINKING!?
UNH...
SHUP
KLAKA KLAK
?
FWASH
THIEVES!!
HUH?
YOU WON'T GET AWAY!!
WHAT!?
What century are we in!?

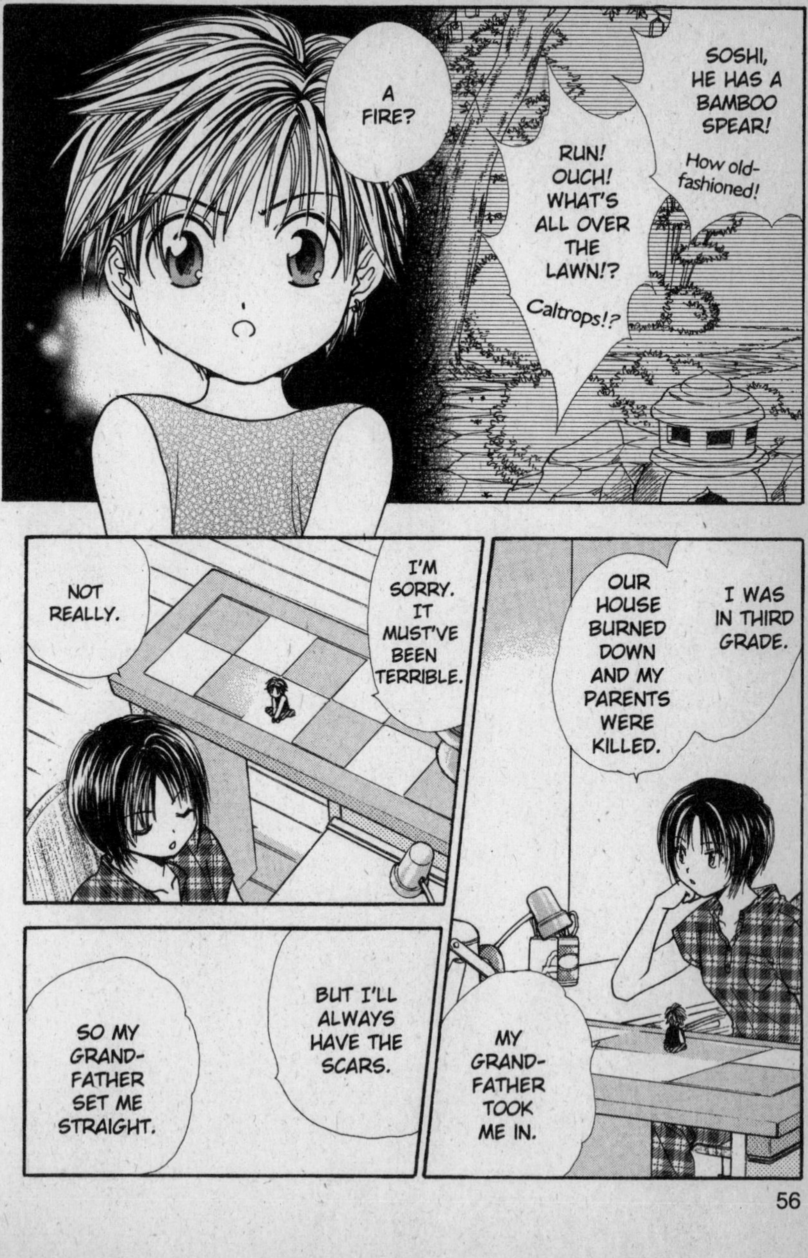
SOSHI, HE HAS A BAMBOO SPEAR!
How old-fashioned!
RUN! OUCH! WHAT'S ALL OVER THE LAWN!?
Caltrops!?
A FIRE?
I WAS IN THIRD GRADE.
OUR HOUSE BURNED DOWN AND MY PARENTS WERE KILLED.
MY GRAND-FATHER TOOK ME IN.
I'M SORRY. IT MUST'VE BEEN TERRIBLE.
NOT REALLY.
BUT I'LL ALWAYS HAVE THE SCARS.
SO MY GRAND-FATHER SET ME STRAIGHT.

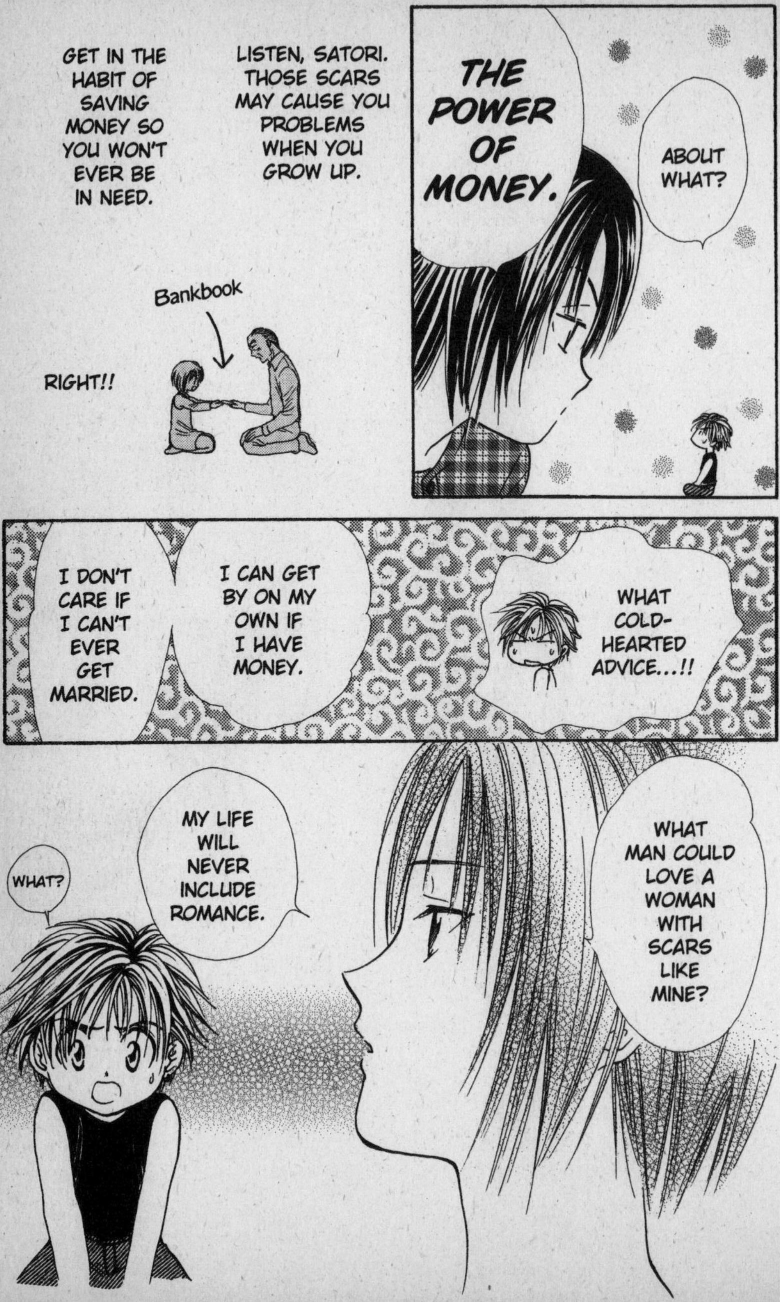
ABOUT WHAT?
THE POWER OF MONEY.
LISTEN, SATORI. THOSE SCARS MAY CAUSE YOU PROBLEMS WHEN YOU GROW UP.
GET IN THE HABIT OF SAVING MONEY SO YOU WON'T EVER BE IN NEED.
Bankbook
RIGHT!!
WHAT COLD-HEARTED ADVICE...!!
I CAN GET BY ON MY OWN IF I HAVE MONEY.
I DON'T CARE IF I CAN'T EVER GET MARRIED.
WHAT MAN COULD LOVE A WOMAN WITH SCARS LIKE MINE?
MY LIFE WILL NEVER INCLUDE ROMANCE.
WHAT?

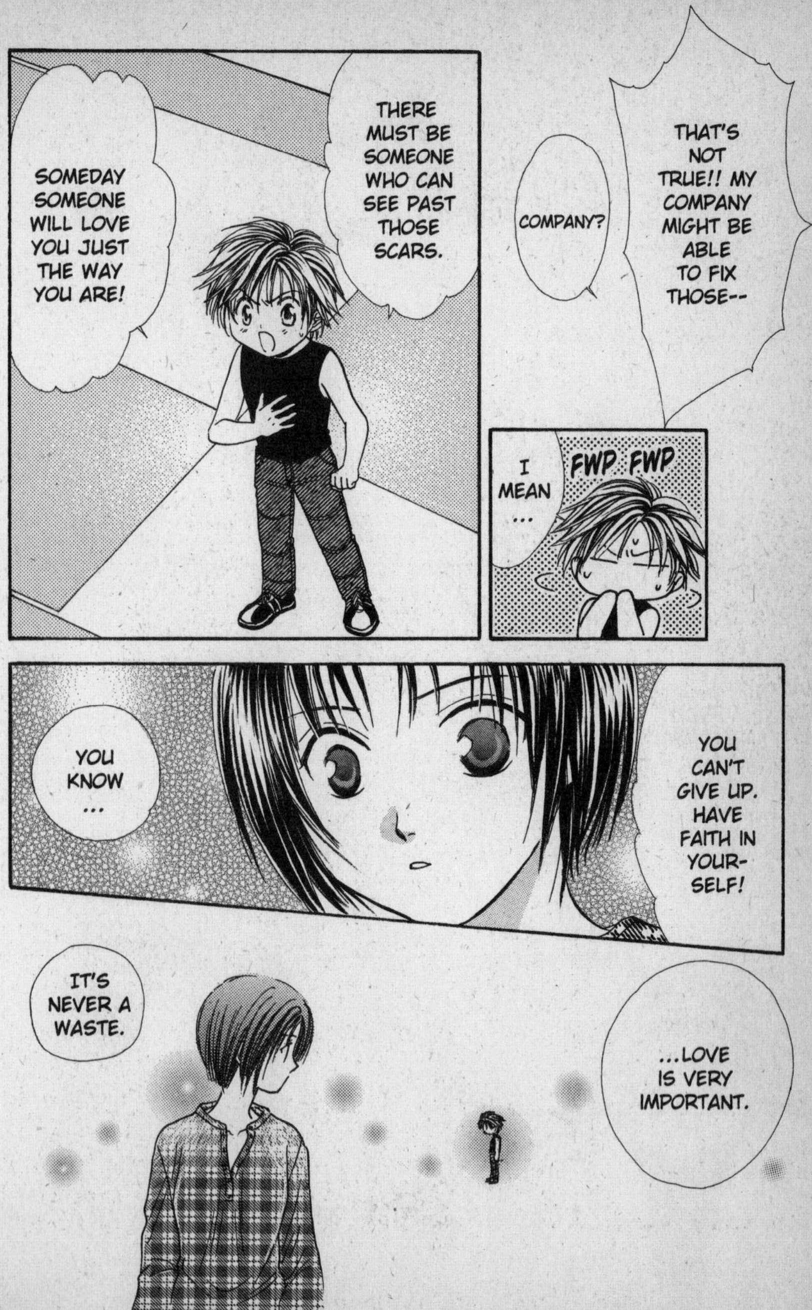
THAT'S NOT TRUE!! MY COMPANY MIGHT BE ABLE TO FIX THOSE--
COMPANY?
FWP FWP
I MEAN ...
THERE MUST BE SOMEONE WHO CAN SEE PAST THOSE SCARS.
SOMEDAY SOMEONE WILL LOVE YOU JUST THE WAY YOU ARE!
YOU CAN'T GIVE UP. HAVE FAITH IN YOUR-SELF!
YOU KNOW ...
...LOVE IS VERY IMPORTANT.
IT'S NEVER A WASTE.

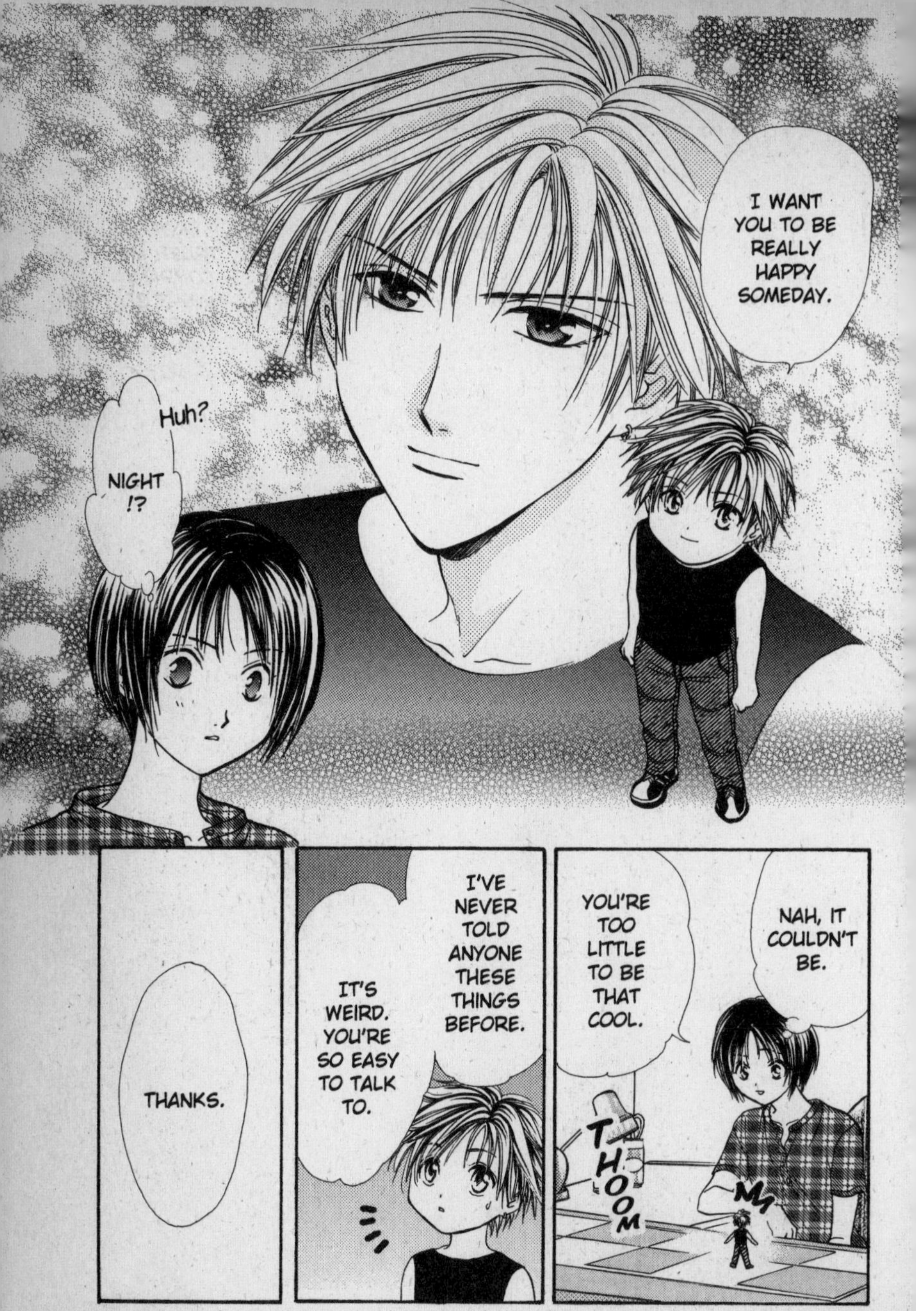
I WANT YOU TO BE REALLY HAPPY SOMEDAY.
Huh?
NIGHT!?
NAH, IT COULDN'T BE.
YOU'RE TOO LITTLE TO BE THAT COOL.
THOOM
MM
I'VE NEVER TOLD ANYONE THESE THINGS BEFORE.
IT'S WEIRD. YOU'RE SO EASY TO TALK TO.
THANKS.

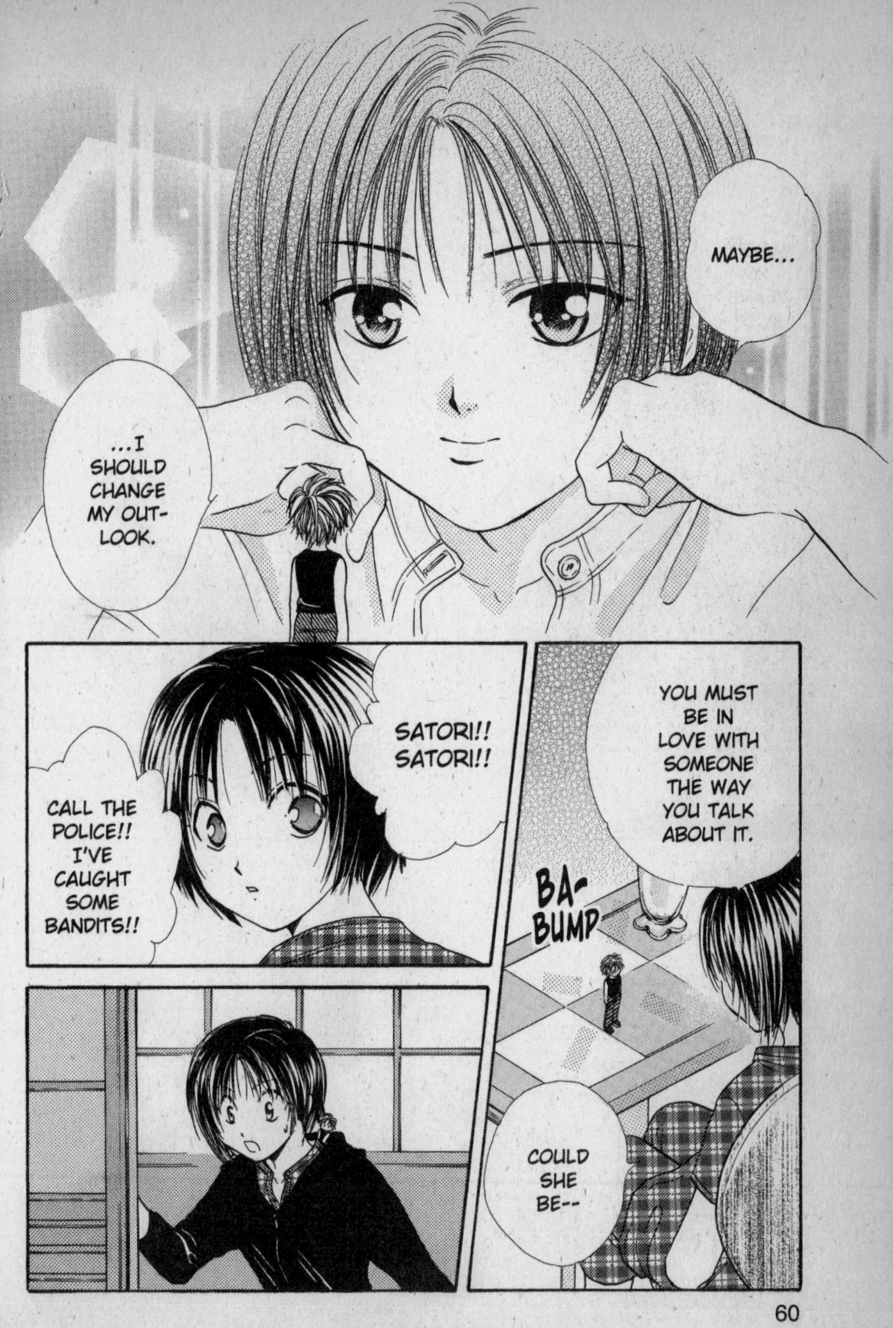
MAYBE...
...I SHOULD CHANGE MY OUT-LOOK.
YOU MUST BE IN LOVE WITH SOMEONE THE WAY YOU TALK ABOUT IT.
BA-BUMP
COULD SHE BE--
SATORI!! SATORI!!
CALL THE POLICE!! I'VE CAUGHT SOME BANDITS!!

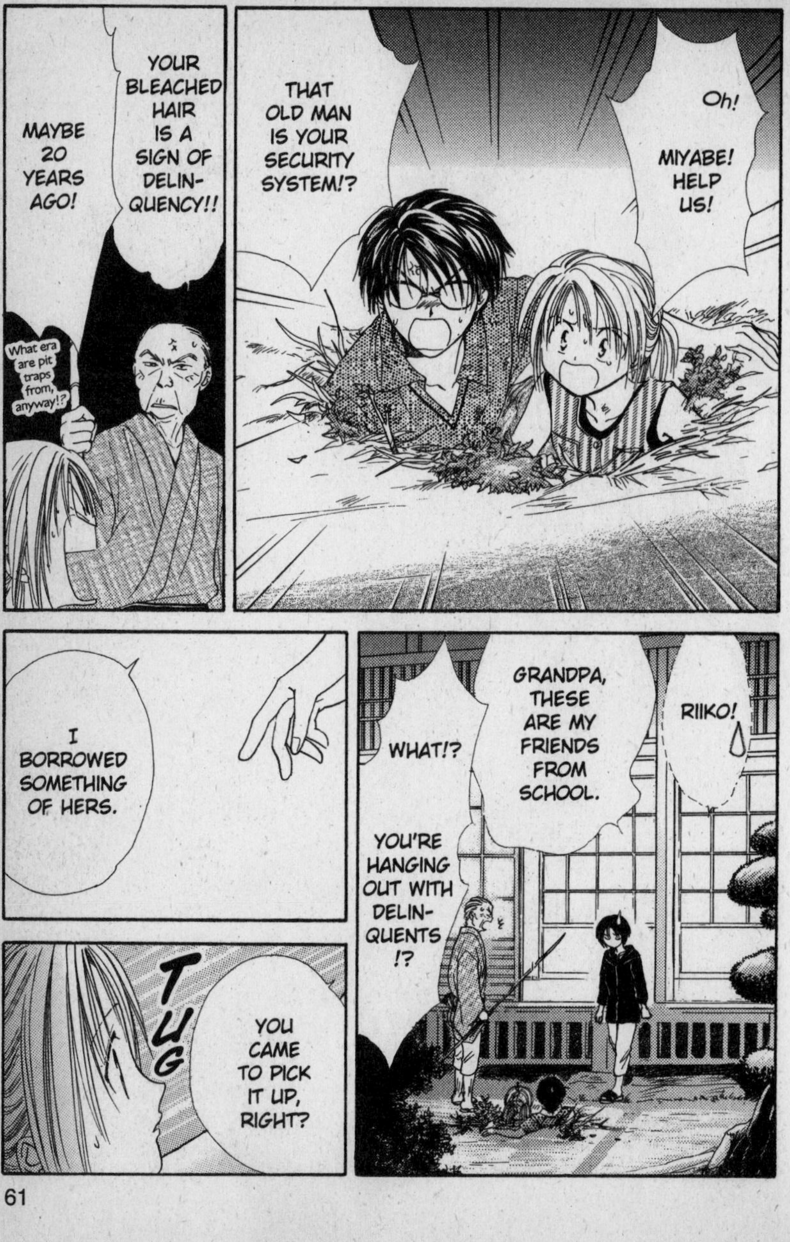
Oh!
MIYABE! HELP US!
THAT OLD MAN IS YOUR SECURITY SYSTEM!?
YOUR BLEACHED HAIR IS A SIGN OF DELIN-QUENCY!!
MAYBE 20 YEARS AGO!
What era are pit traps from, anyway!?
RIIKO!
GRANDPA, THESE ARE MY FRIENDS FROM SCHOOL.
WHAT!?
YOU'RE HANGING OUT WITH DELIN-QUENTS !?
I BORROWED SOMETHING OF HERS.
TUG
YOU CAME TO PICK IT UP, RIGHT?

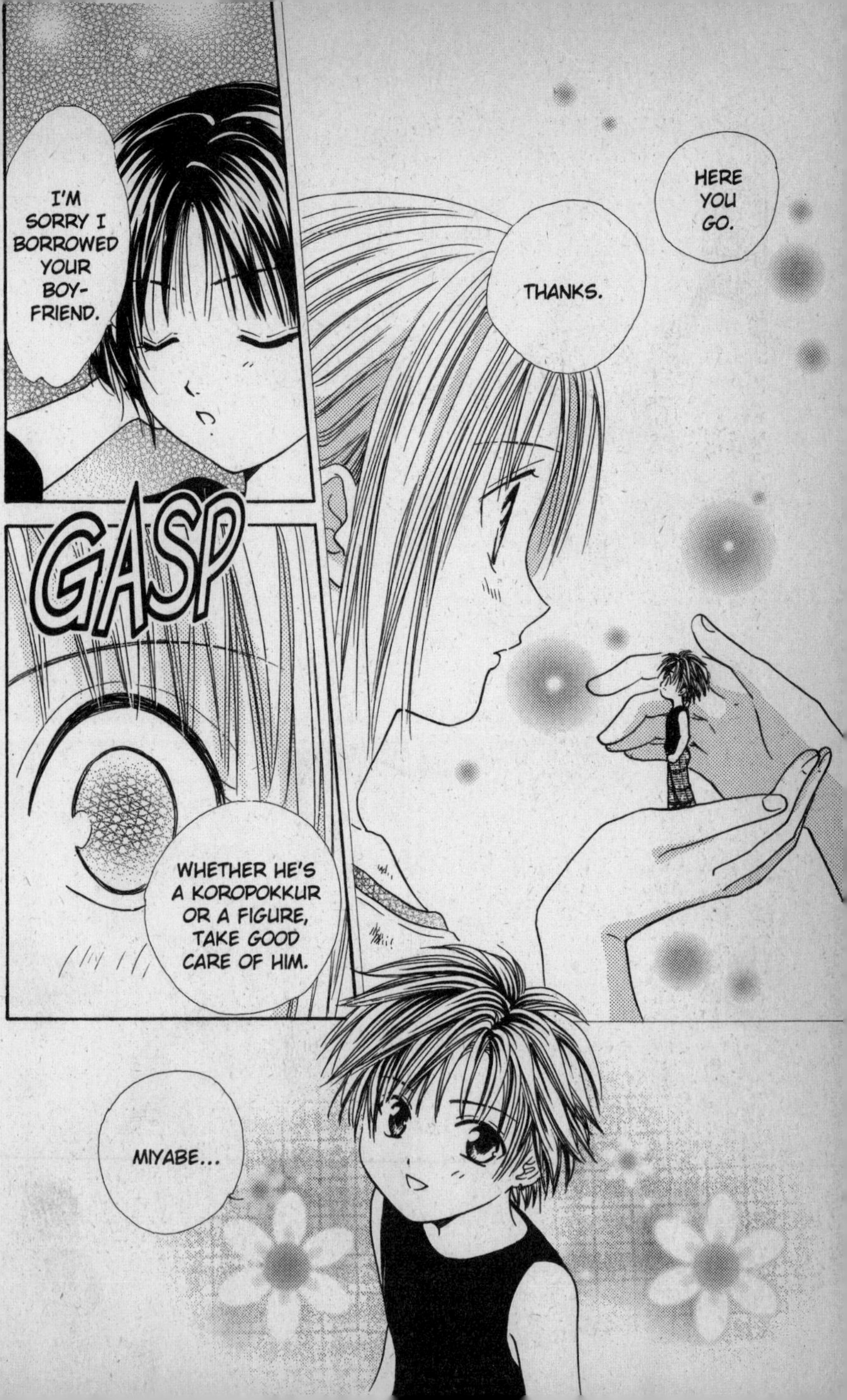
HERE YOU GO.
THANKS.
I'M SORRY I BORROWED YOUR BOY-FRIEND.
GASP
WHETHER HE'S A KOROPOKKUR OR A FIGURE, TAKE GOOD CARE OF HIM.
MIYABE...

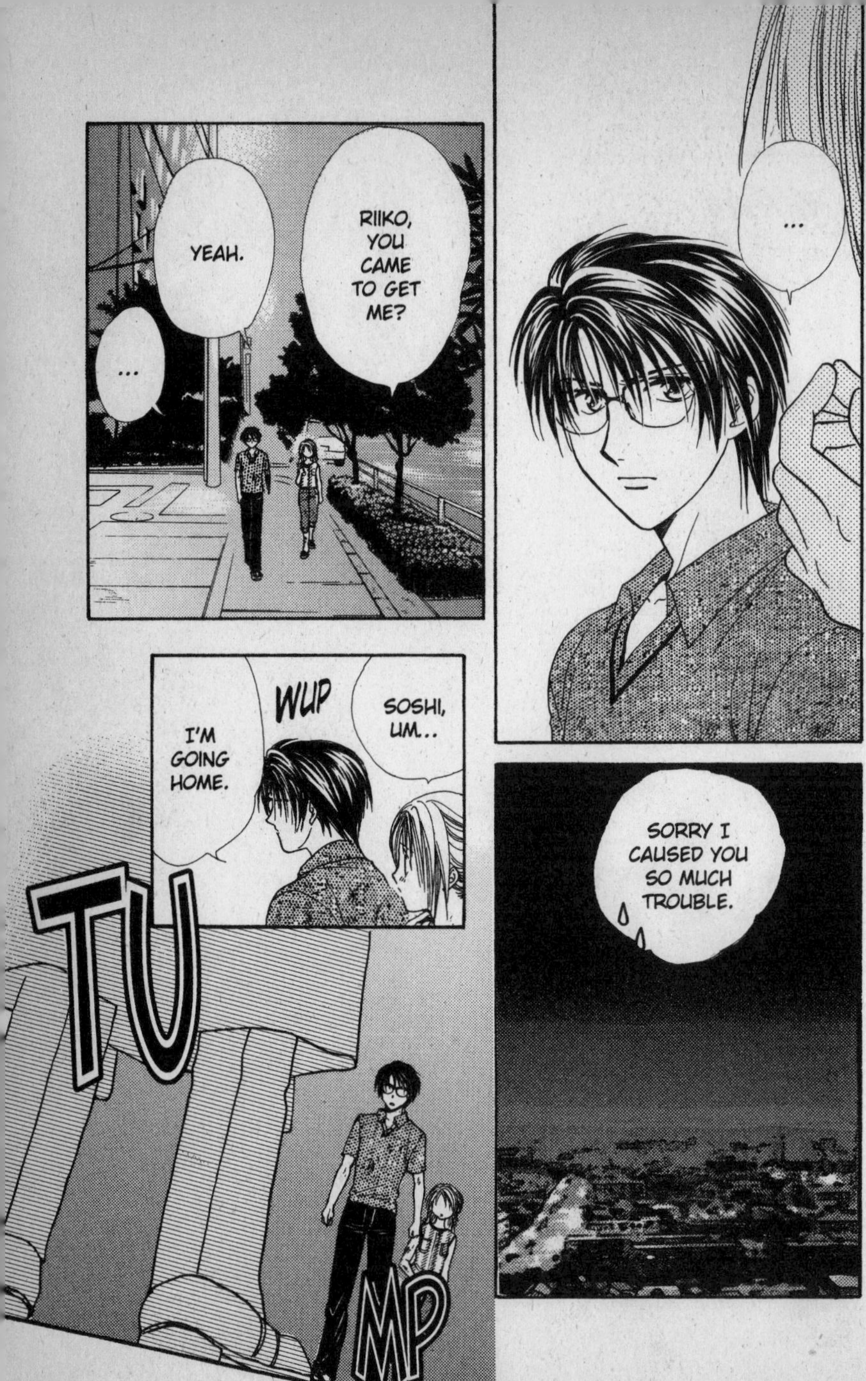
...
RIIKO, YOU CAME TO GET ME?
YEAH.
...
SORRY I CAUSED YOU SO MUCH TROUBLE.
SOSHI, UM...
WUP
I'M GOING HOME.
TUMP

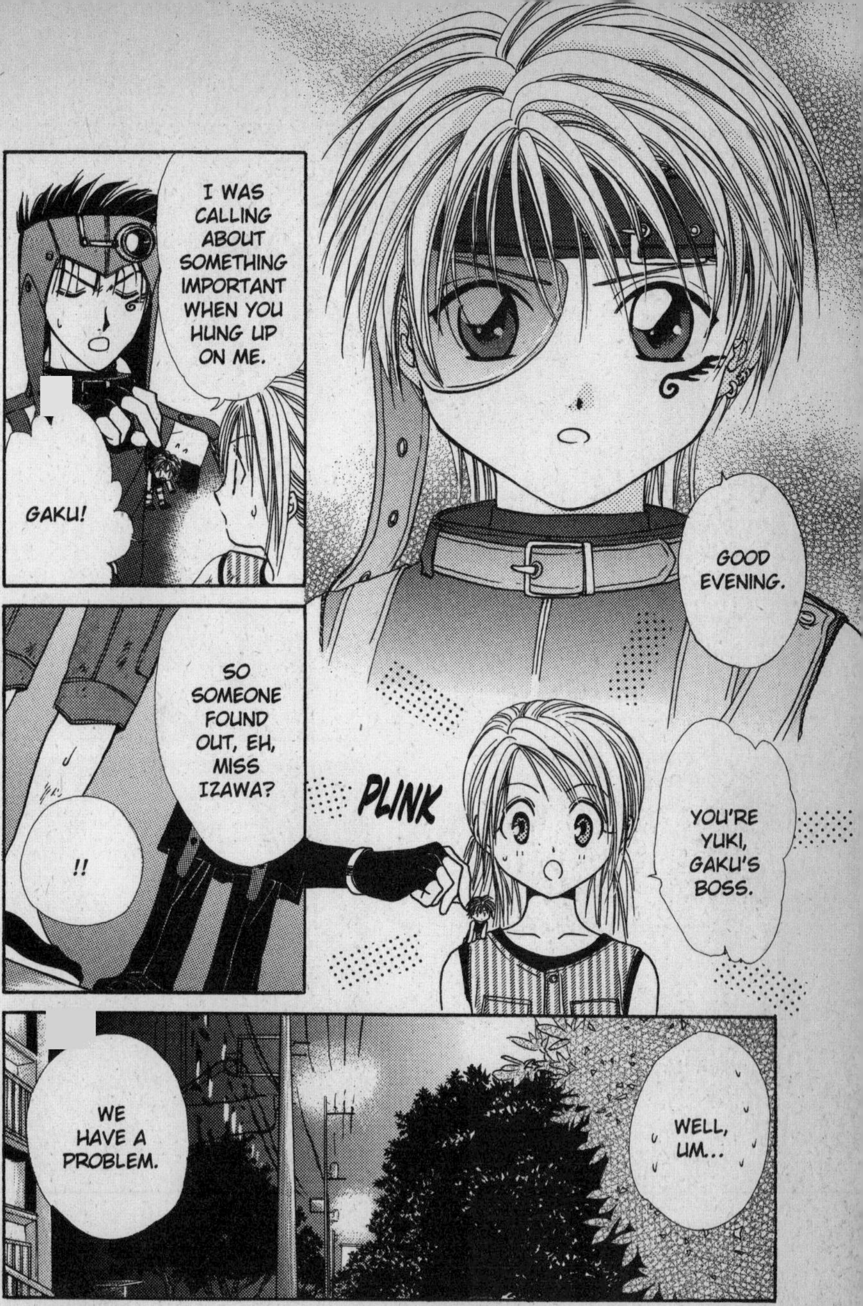
GOOD EVENING.
YOU'RE YUKI, GAKU'S BOSS.
I WAS CALLING ABOUT SOMETHING IMPORTANT WHEN YOU HUNG UP ON ME.
GAKU!
SO SOMEONE FOUND OUT, EH, MISS IZAWA?
PLINK
!!
WELL, UM..
WE HAVE A PROBLEM.

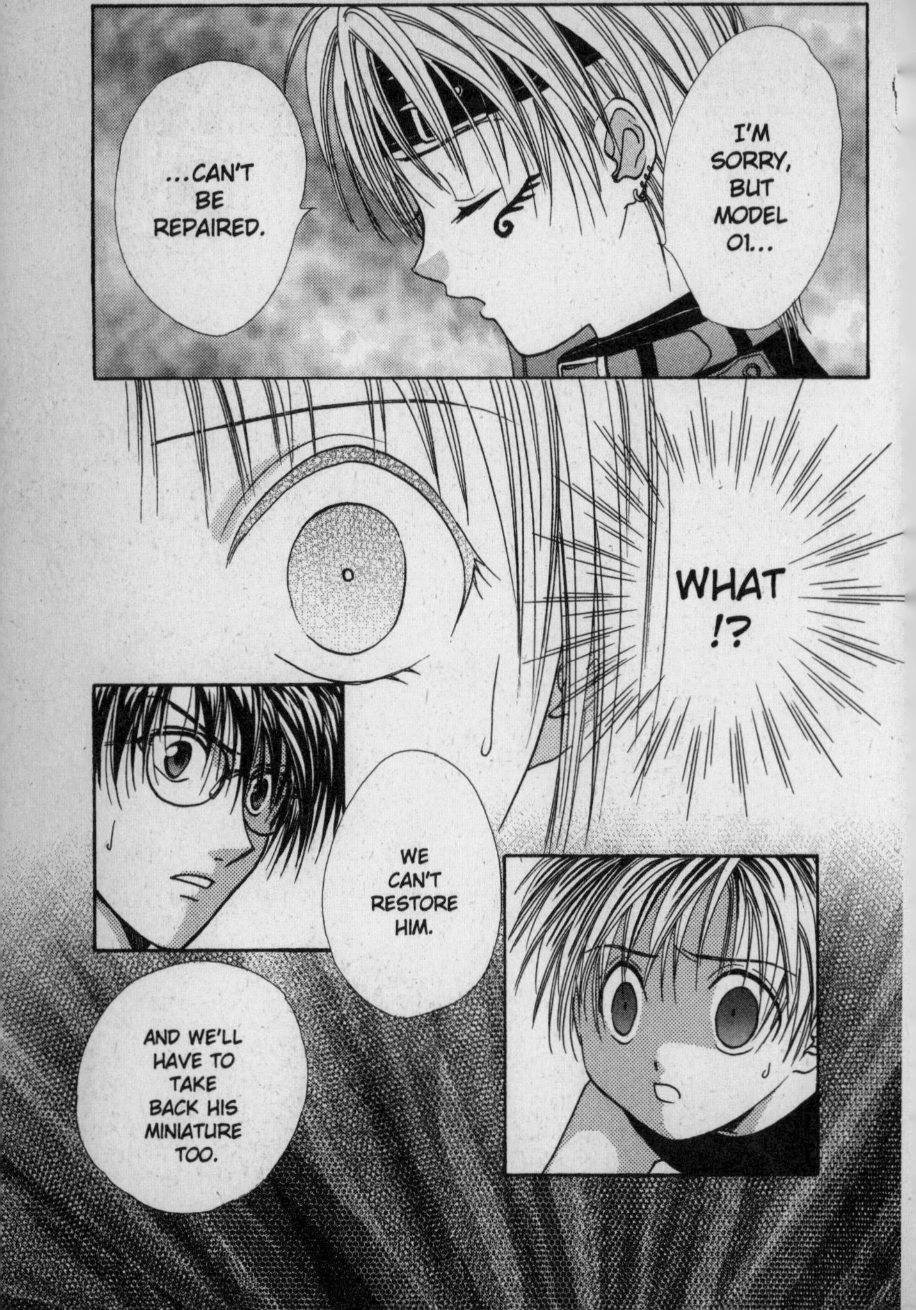
I'M SORRY, BUT MODEL 01...
...CAN'T BE REPAIRED.
WHAT!?
WE CAN'T RESTORE HIM.
AND WE'LL HAVE TO TAKE BACK HIS MINIATURE TOO.

Absolute Boyfriend

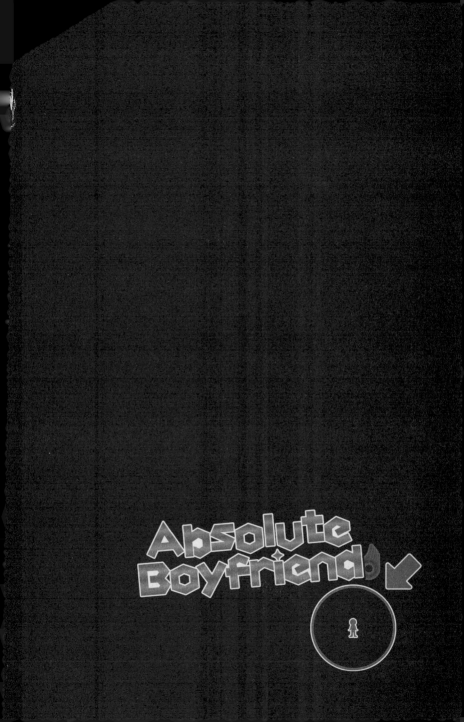

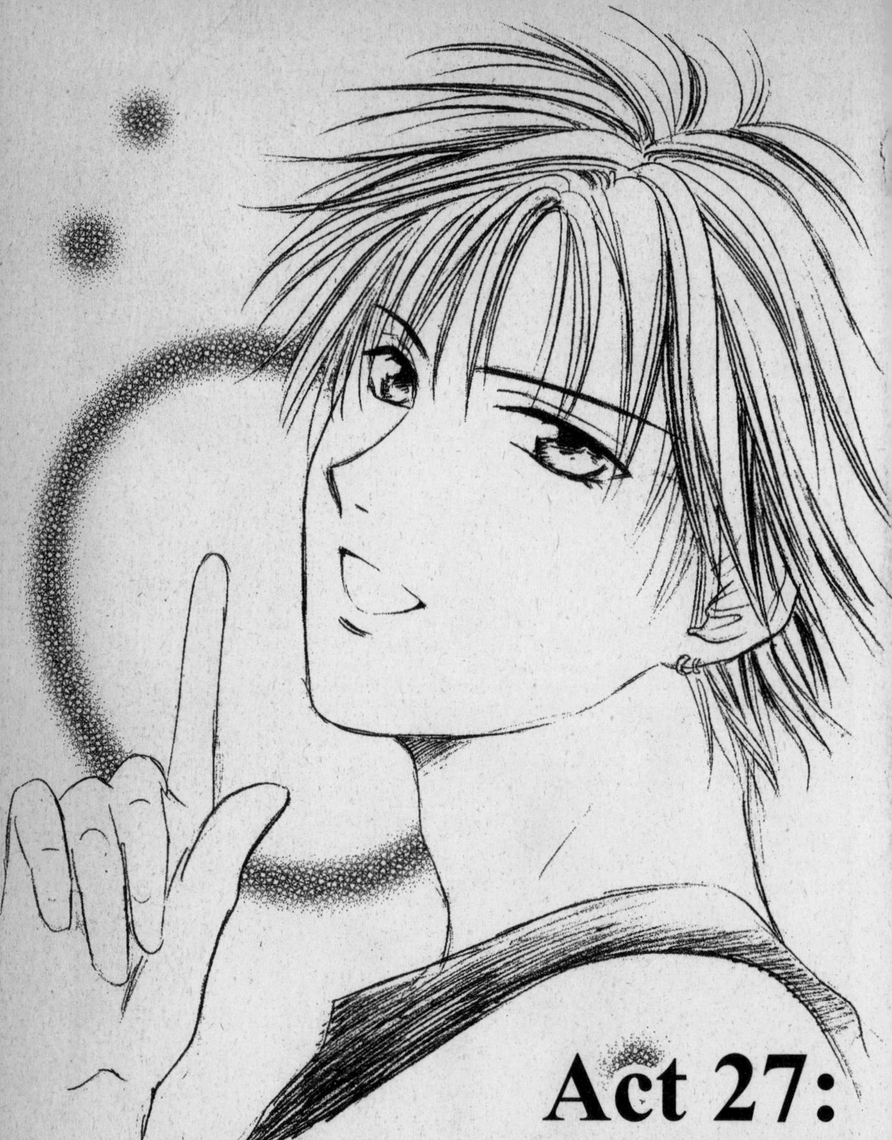

Act 27: My Love for You

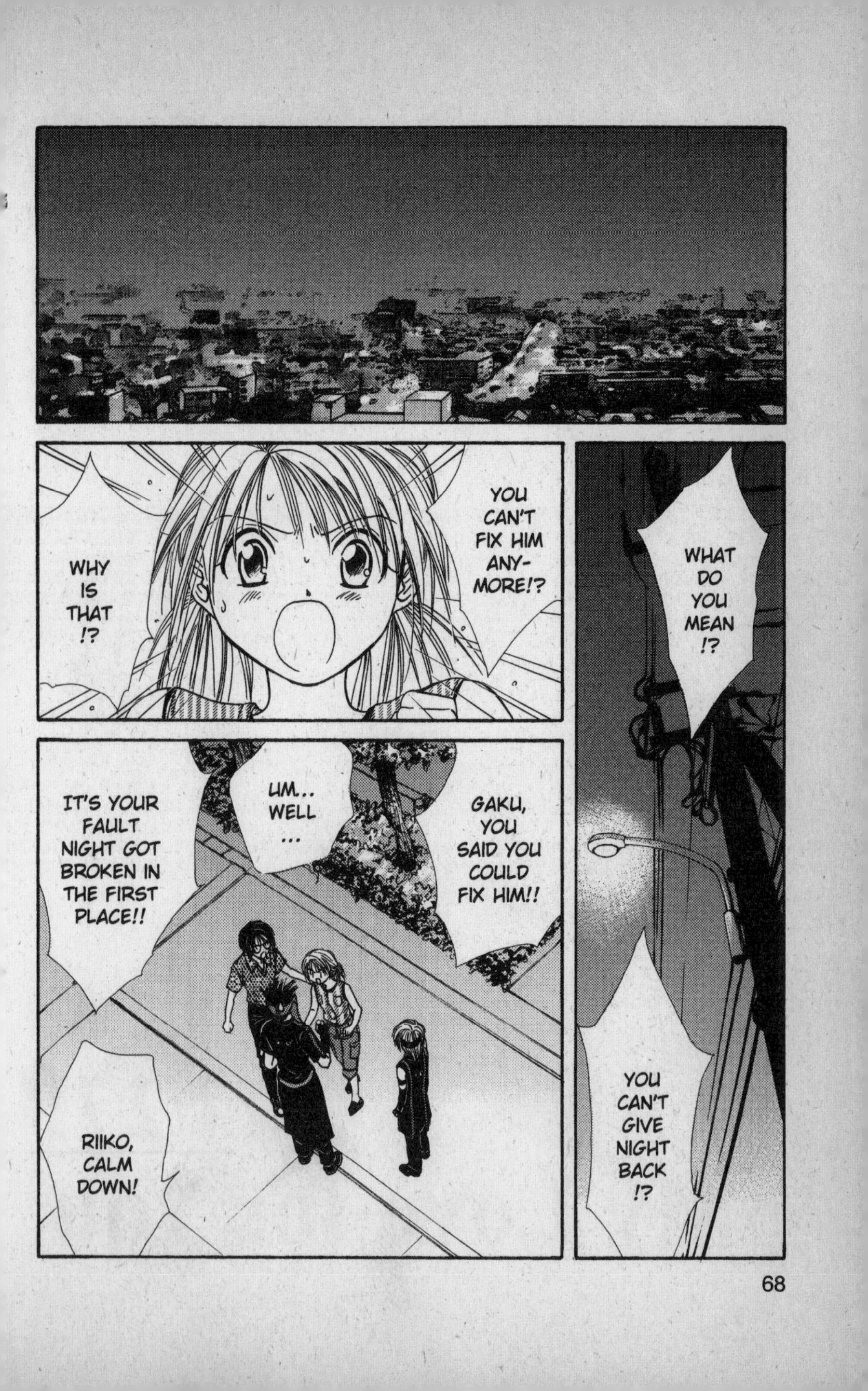
WHAT DO YOU MEAN!?
YOU CAN'T GIVE NIGHT BACK!?
YOU CAN'T FIX HIM ANY-MORE!?
WHY IS THAT!?
GAKU, YOU SAID YOU COULD FIX HIM!!
UM... WELL...
IT'S YOUR FAULT NIGHT GOT BROKEN IN THE FIRST PLACE!!
RIIKO, CALM DOWN!

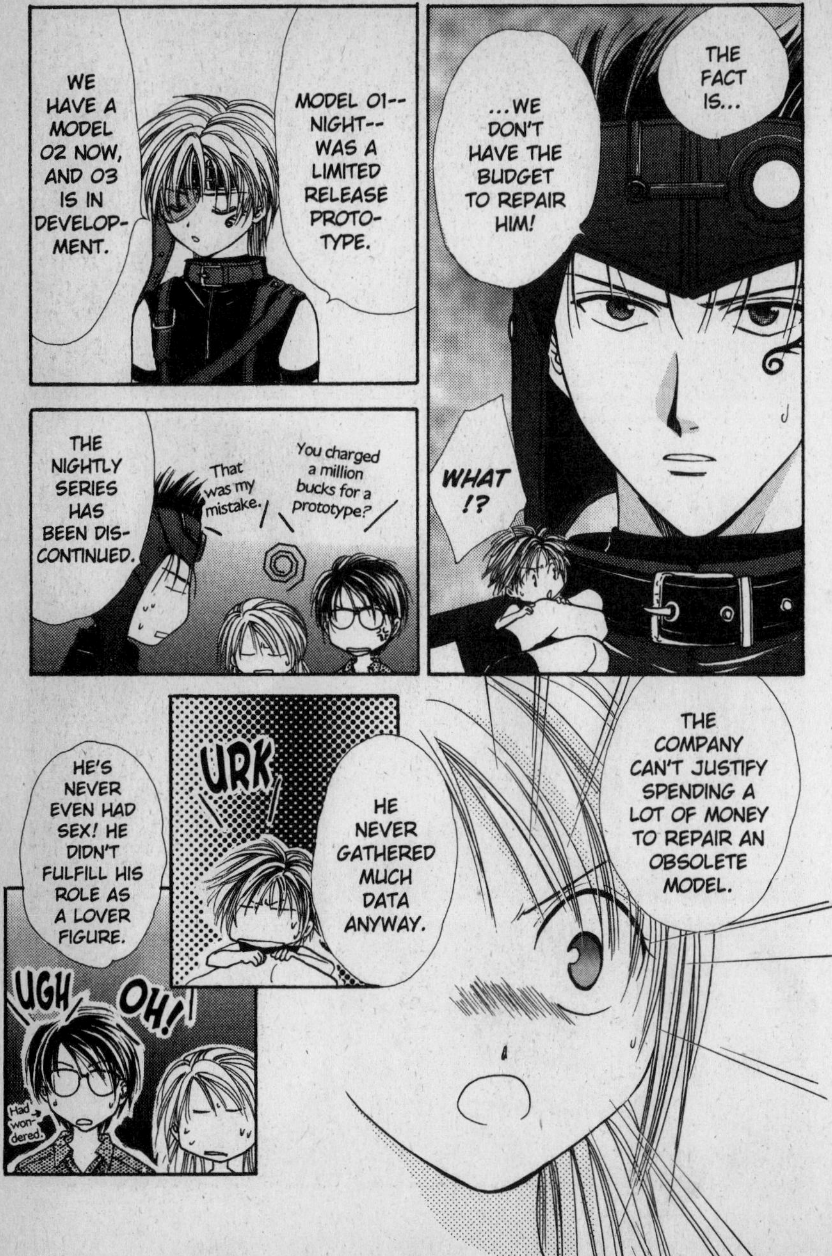
THE FACT IS...
...WE DON'T HAVE THE BUDGET TO REPAIR HIM!
WHAT!?
MODEL 01--NIGHT--WAS A LIMITED RELEASE PROTOTYPE.
WE HAVE A MODEL 02 NOW, AND 03 IS IN DEVELOPMENT.
THE NIGHTLY SERIES HAS BEEN DISCONTINUED.
You charged a million bucks for a prototype?
That was my mistake.
THE COMPANY CAN'T JUSTIFY SPENDING A LOT OF MONEY TO REPAIR AN OBSOLETE MODEL.
HE NEVER GATHERED MUCH DATA ANYWAY.
URK
HE'S NEVER EVEN HAD SEX! HE DIDN'T FULFILL HIS ROLE AS A LOVER FIGURE.
OH!
UGH
Had wondered.

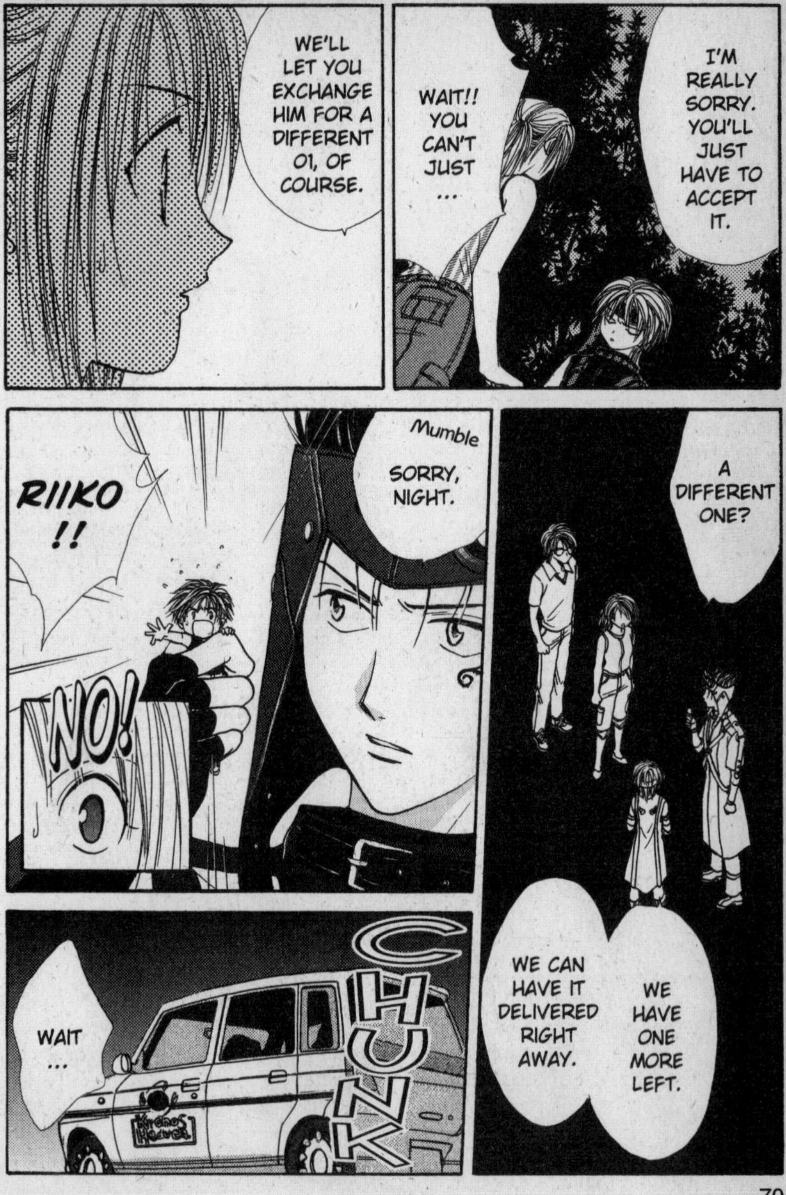
I'M REALLY SORRY. YOU'LL JUST HAVE TO ACCEPT IT.
WAIT!! YOU CAN'T JUST ...
WE'LL LET YOU EXCHANGE HIM FOR A DIFFERENT 01, OF COURSE.
A DIFFERENT ONE?
WE HAVE ONE MORE LEFT.
WE CAN HAVE IT DELIVERED RIGHT AWAY.
Mumble
SORRY, NIGHT.
RIIKO !!
NO!
CHUNK
WAIT ...

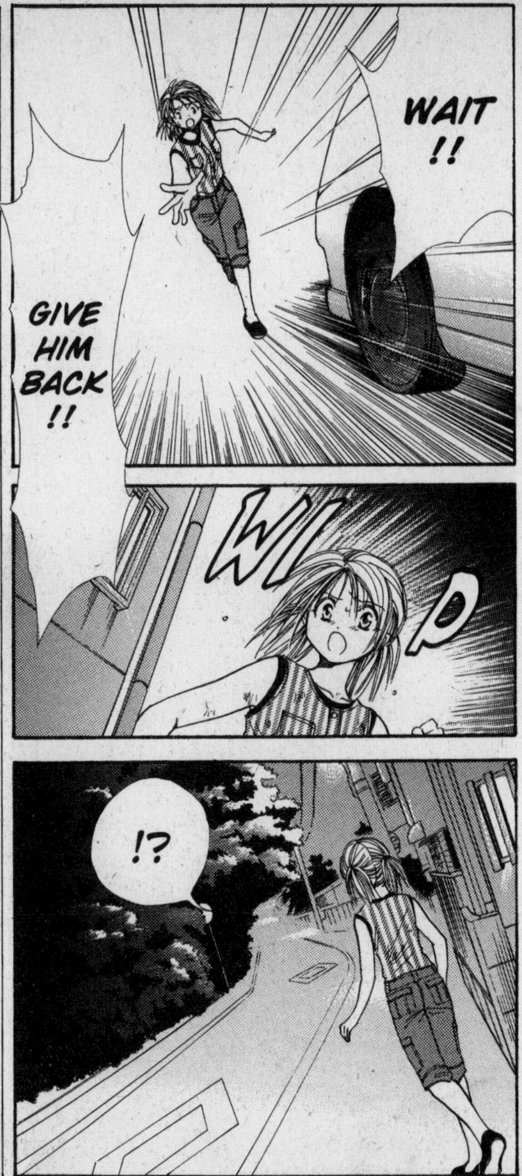
WAIT !!
GIVE HIM BACK !!
WHIP
!?

Living in my dreams ...

*I'm so tired.

A hot springs ...

A lush forest ...

A deep blue sea...

Then ...

...having fun drawing manga.

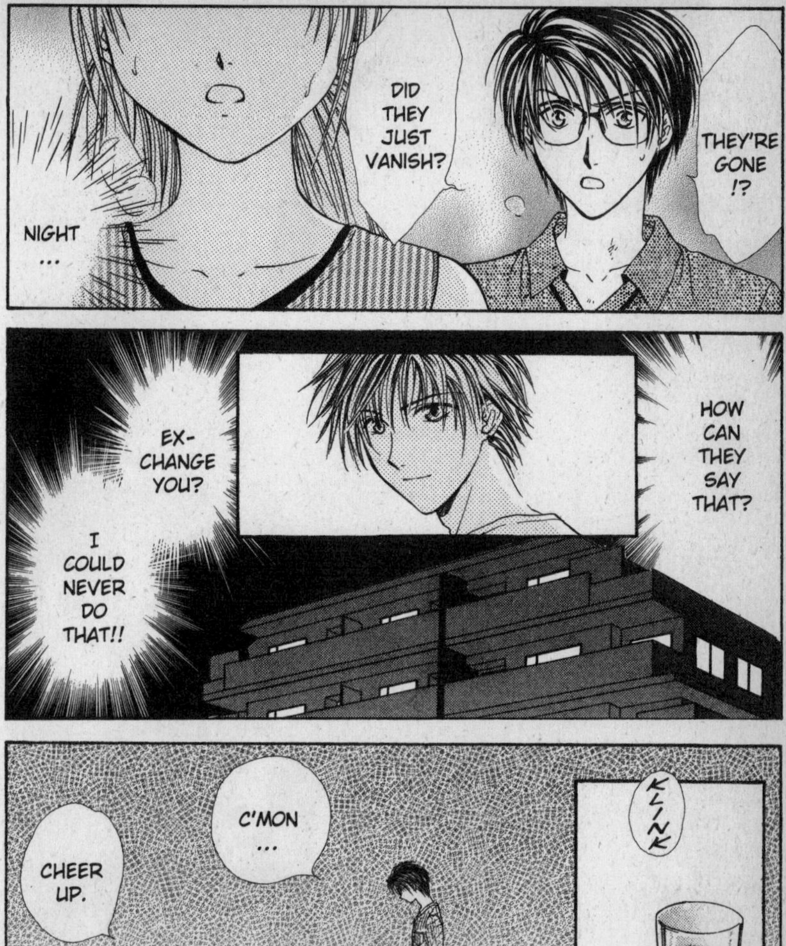
THEY'RE GONE !?
DID THEY JUST VANISH?
NIGHT ...
HOW CAN THEY SAY THAT?
EX-CHANGE YOU?
I COULD NEVER DO THAT!!
KLINK
HERE, RIIKO.
C'MON ...
CHEER UP.

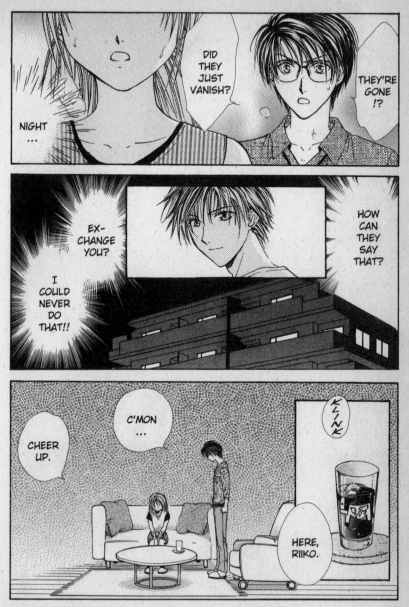

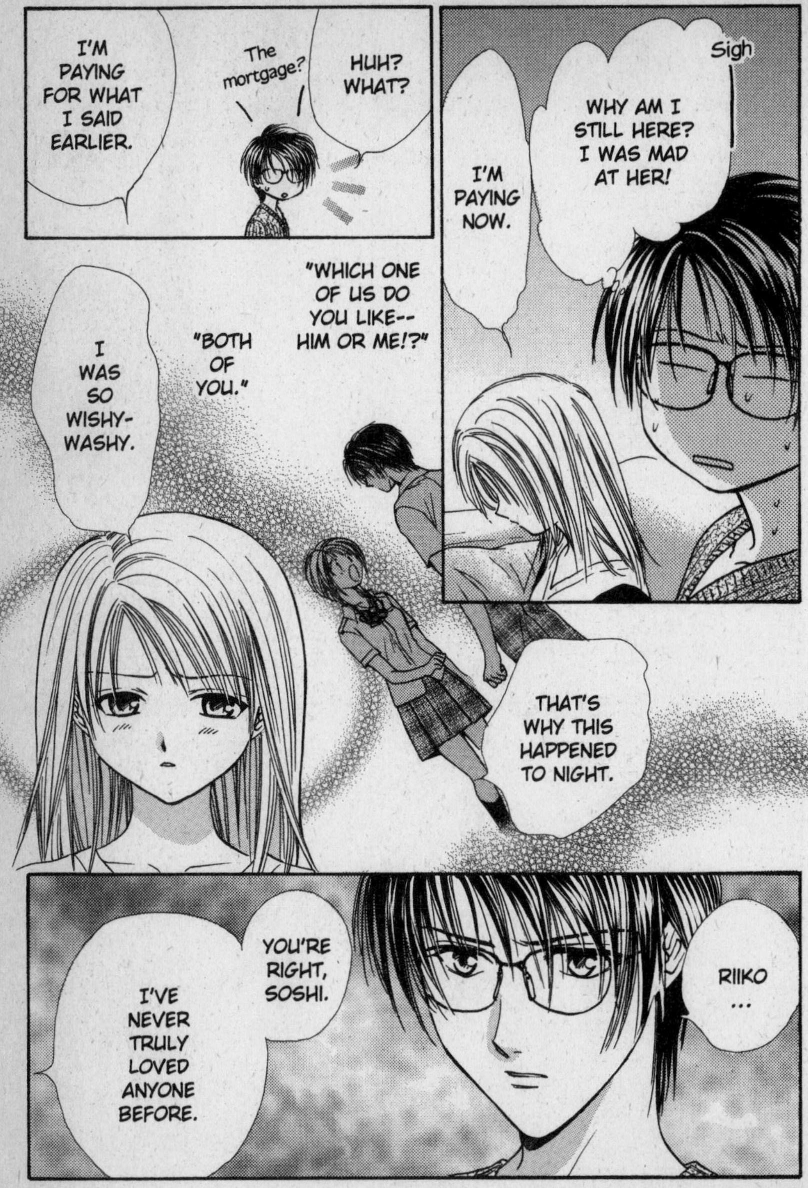
Sigh
WHY AM I STILL HERE? I WAS MAD AT HER!
I'M PAYING NOW.
HUH? WHAT?
The mortgage?
I'M PAYING FOR WHAT I SAID EARLIER.
"WHICH ONE OF US DO YOU LIKE--HIM OR ME!?"
"BOTH OF YOU."
I WAS SO WISHY-WASHY.
THAT'S WHY THIS HAPPENED TO NIGHT.
RIIKO...
YOU'RE RIGHT, SOSHI.
I'VE NEVER TRULY LOVED ANYONE BEFORE.

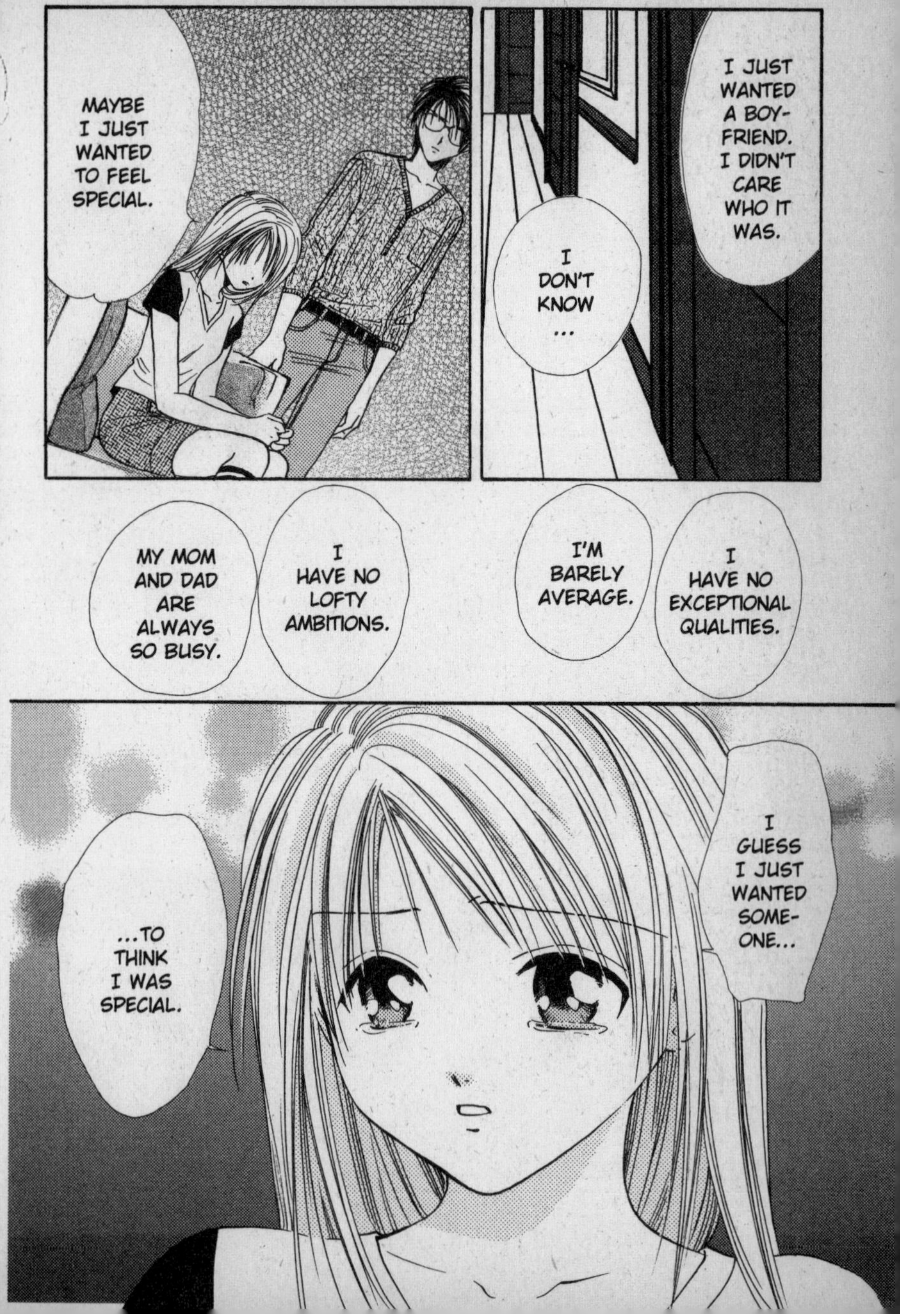
I JUST WANTED A BOY-FRIEND. I DIDN'T CARE WHO IT WAS.
I DON'T KNOW ...
MAYBE I JUST WANTED TO FEEL SPECIAL.
I HAVE NO EXCEPTIONAL QUALITIES.
I'M BARELY AVERAGE.
I HAVE NO LOFTY AMBITIONS.
MY MOM AND DAD ARE ALWAYS SO BUSY.
I GUESS I JUST WANTED SOME-ONE...
...TO THINK I WAS SPECIAL.

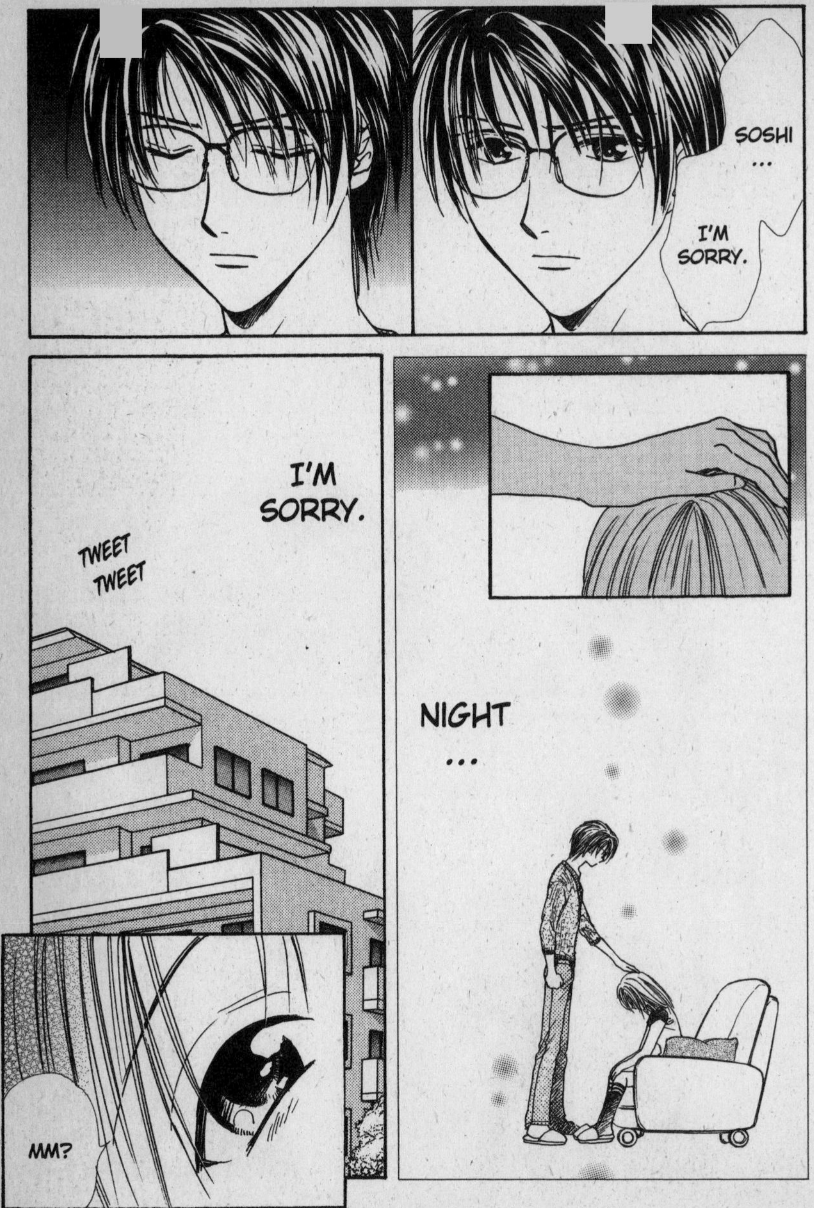
SOSHI ...
I'M SORRY.
NIGHT ...
I'M SORRY.
TWEET TWEET
MM?

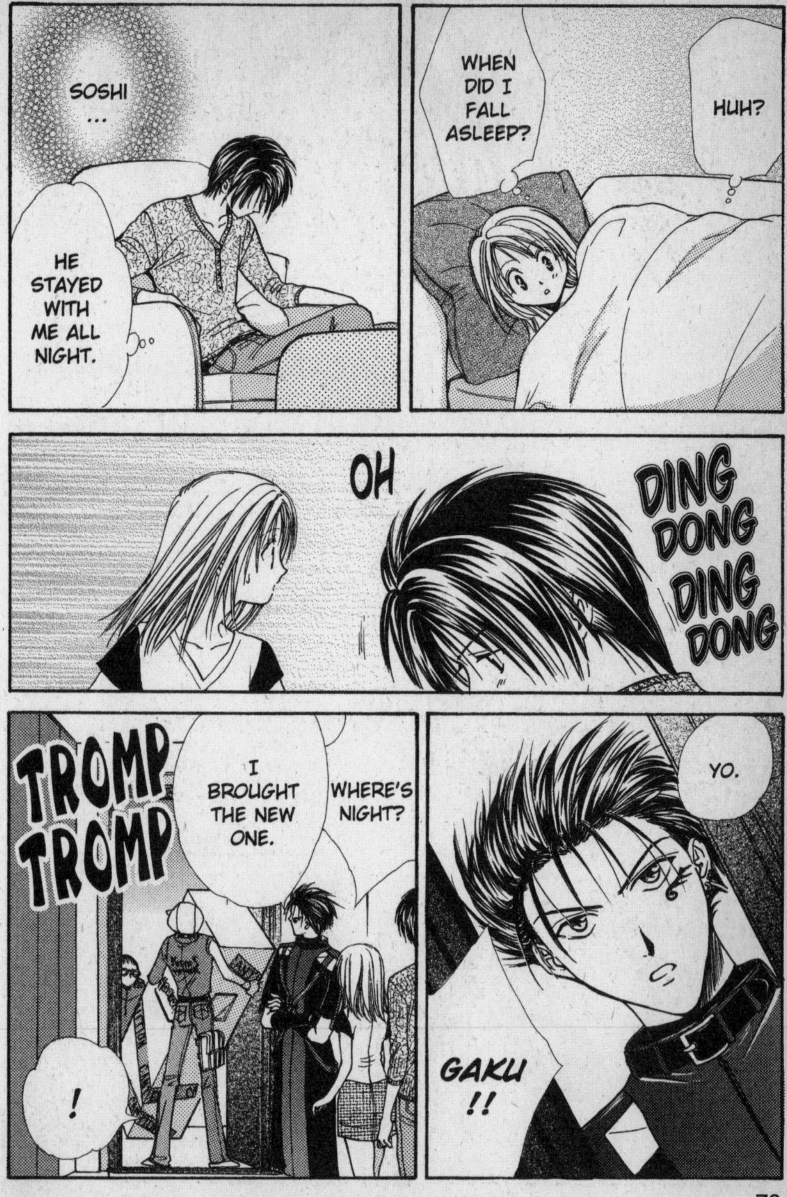
HUH?
WHEN DID I FALL ASLEEP?
SOSHI ...
HE STAYED WITH ME ALL NIGHT.
DING DONG DING DONG
OH
YO.
GAKU !!
WHERE'S NIGHT?
I BROUGHT THE NEW ONE.
TROMP TROMP
!

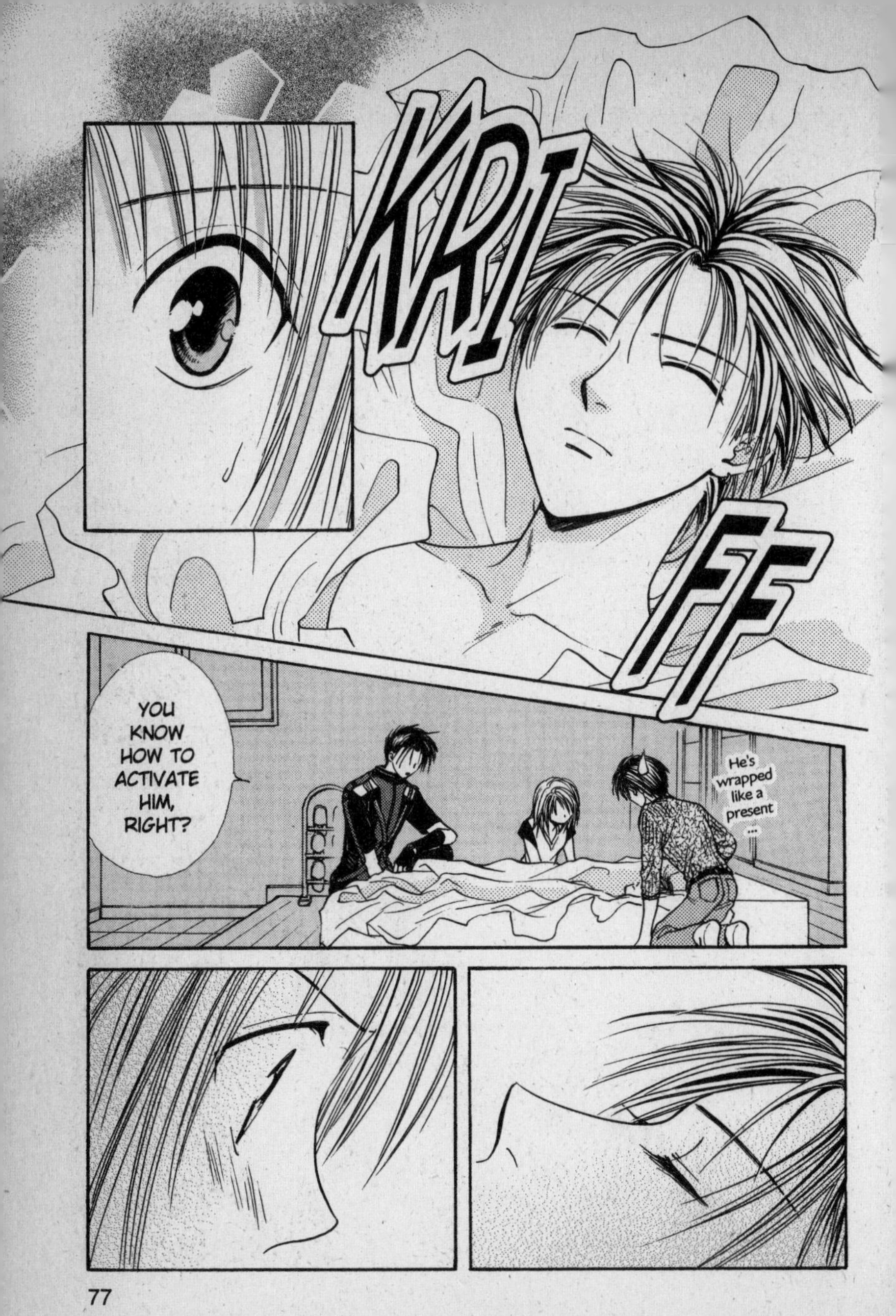
KARI
FF
He's wrapped like a present ...
YOU KNOW HOW TO ACTIVATE HIM, RIGHT?

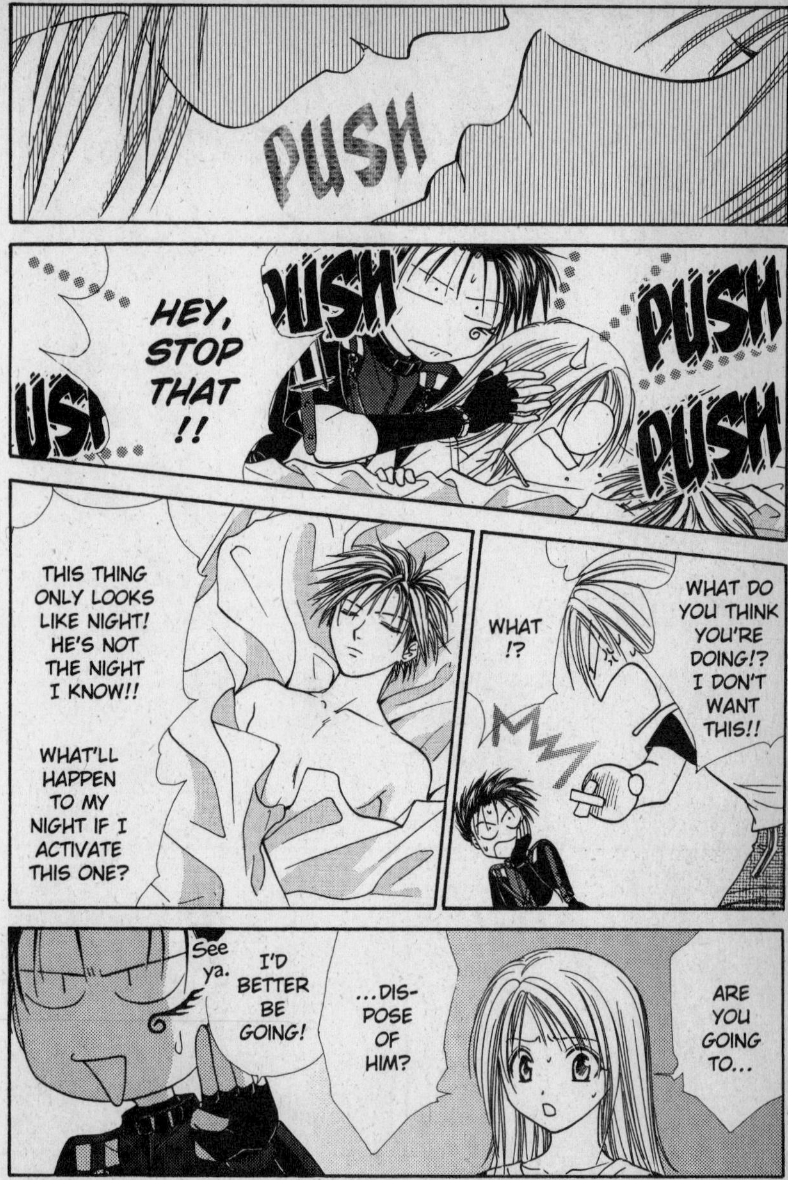
PUSH
PUSH
PUSH
HEY, STOP THAT!!
PUSH
WHAT DO YOU THINK YOU'RE DOING!? I DON'T WANT THIS!!
WHAT!?
THIS THING ONLY LOOKS LIKE NIGHT! HE'S NOT THE NIGHT I KNOW!!
WHAT'LL HAPPEN TO MY NIGHT IF I ACTIVATE THIS ONE?
ARE YOU GOING TO...
...DISPOSE OF HIM?
I'D BETTER BE GOING!
See ya.

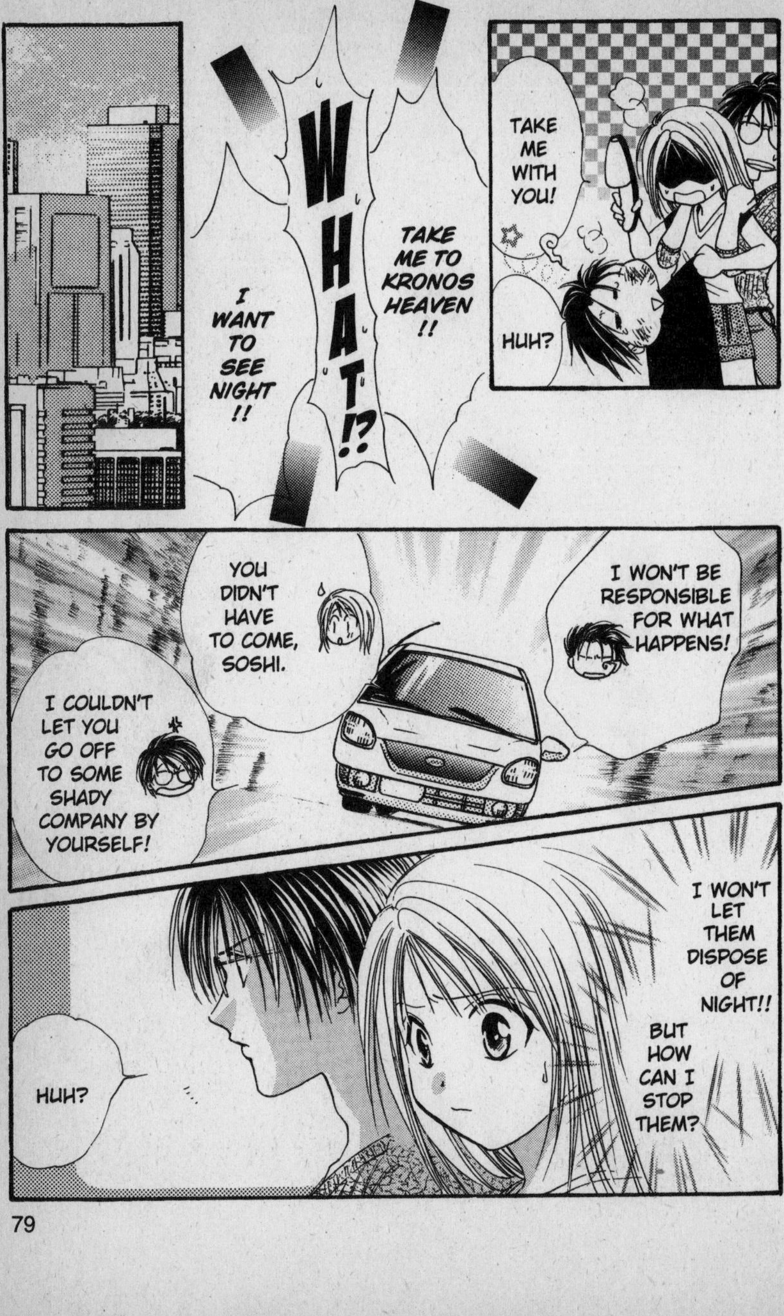
TAKE ME WITH YOU!
HUH?
WHAT!?
TAKE ME TO KRONOS HEAVEN!!
I WANT TO SEE NIGHT!!
I WON'T BE RESPONSIBLE FOR WHAT HAPPENS!
YOU DIDN'T HAVE TO COME, SOSHI.
I COULDN'T LET YOU GO OFF TO SOME SHADY COMPANY BY YOURSELF!
I WON'T LET THEM DISPOSE OF NIGHT!!
BUT HOW CAN I STOP THEM?
HUH?

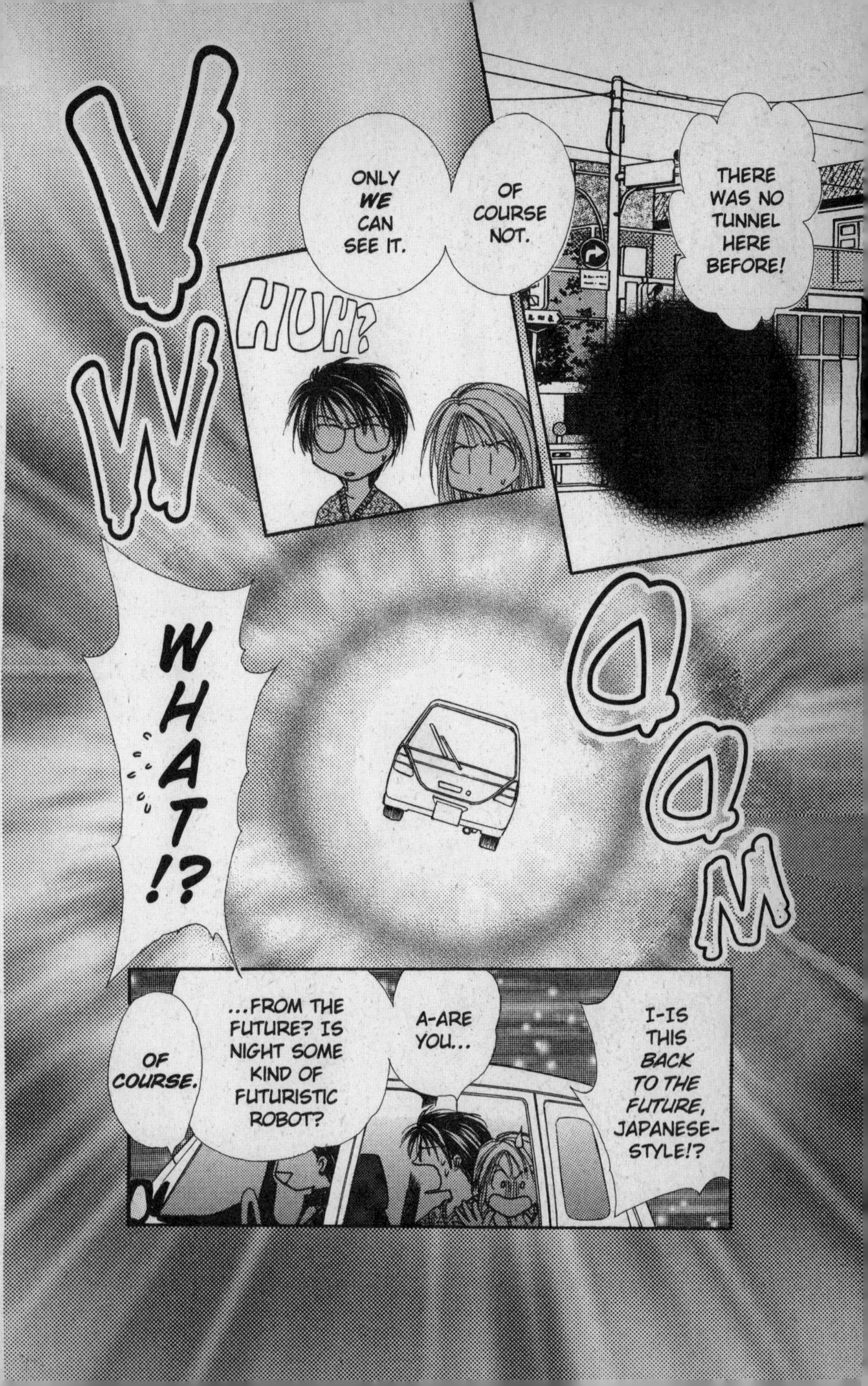

THERE WAS NO TUNNEL HERE BEFORE!
OF COURSE NOT.
ONLY WE CAN SEE IT.
HUH?
VWOOM
WHAT!?
I-IS THIS BACK TO THE FUTURE, JAPANESE-STYLE!?
A-ARE YOU...
...FROM THE FUTURE? IS NIGHT SOME KIND OF FUTURISTIC ROBOT?
OF COURSE.

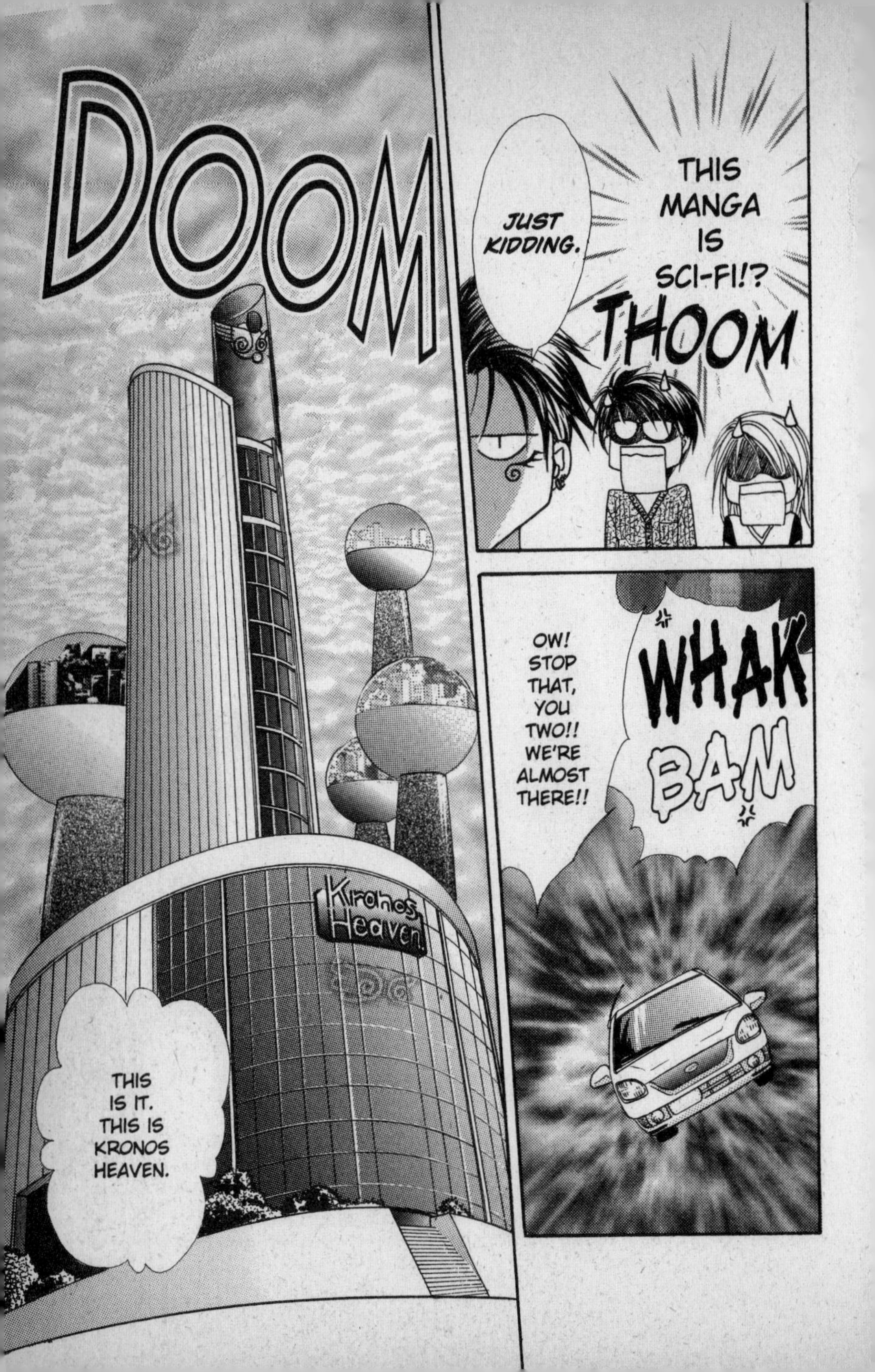
THIS MANGA IS SCI-FI!?
THOOM
JUST KIDDING.
WHAK
BAM
OW! STOP THAT, YOU TWO!! WE'RE ALMOST THERE!!
DOOM
Kronos Heaven
THIS IS IT. THIS IS KRONOS HEAVEN.

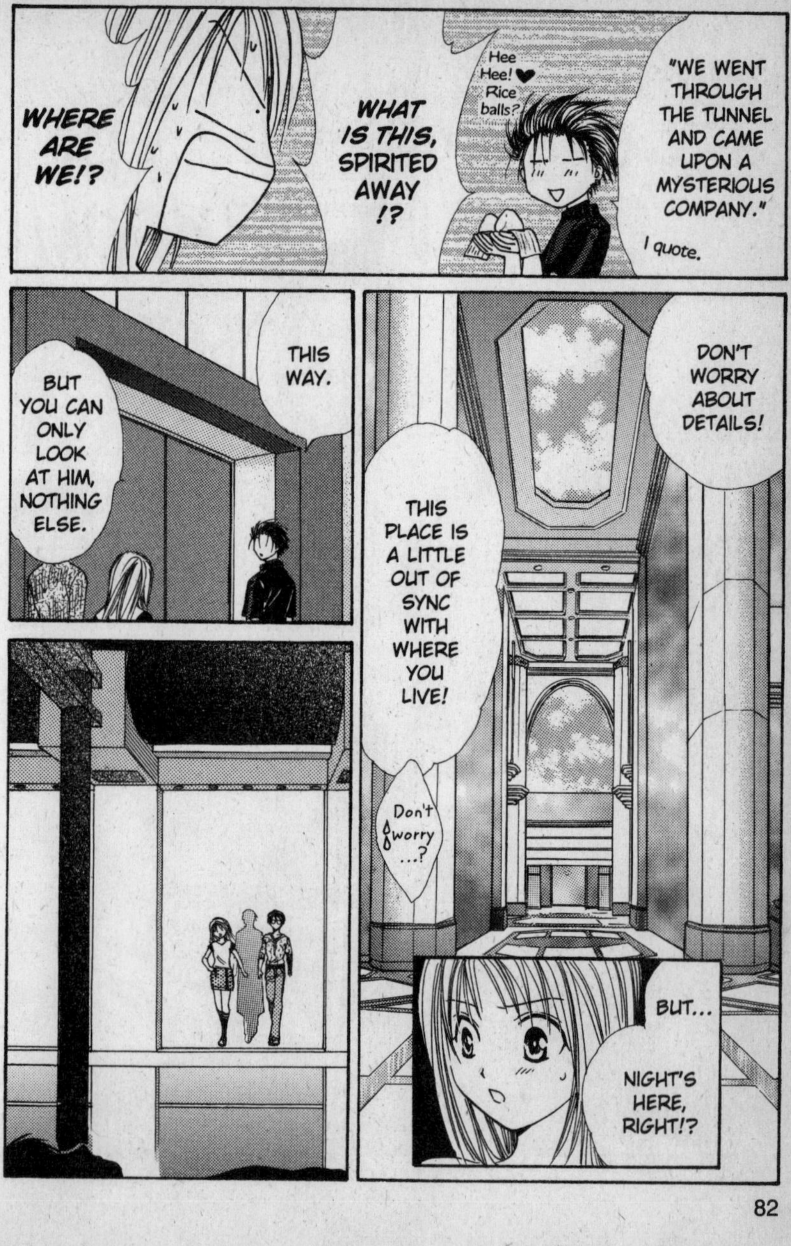
"WE WENT THROUGH THE TUNNEL AND CAME UPON A MYSTERIOUS COMPANY."
I quote.
Hee Hee! Rice balls?
WHAT IS THIS, SPIRITED AWAY!?
WHERE ARE WE!?
DON'T WORRY ABOUT DETAILS!
THIS PLACE IS A LITTLE OUT OF SYNC WITH WHERE YOU LIVE!
Don't worry...?
BUT...
NIGHT'S HERE, RIGHT!?
THIS WAY.
BUT YOU CAN ONLY LOOK AT HIM, NOTHING ELSE.

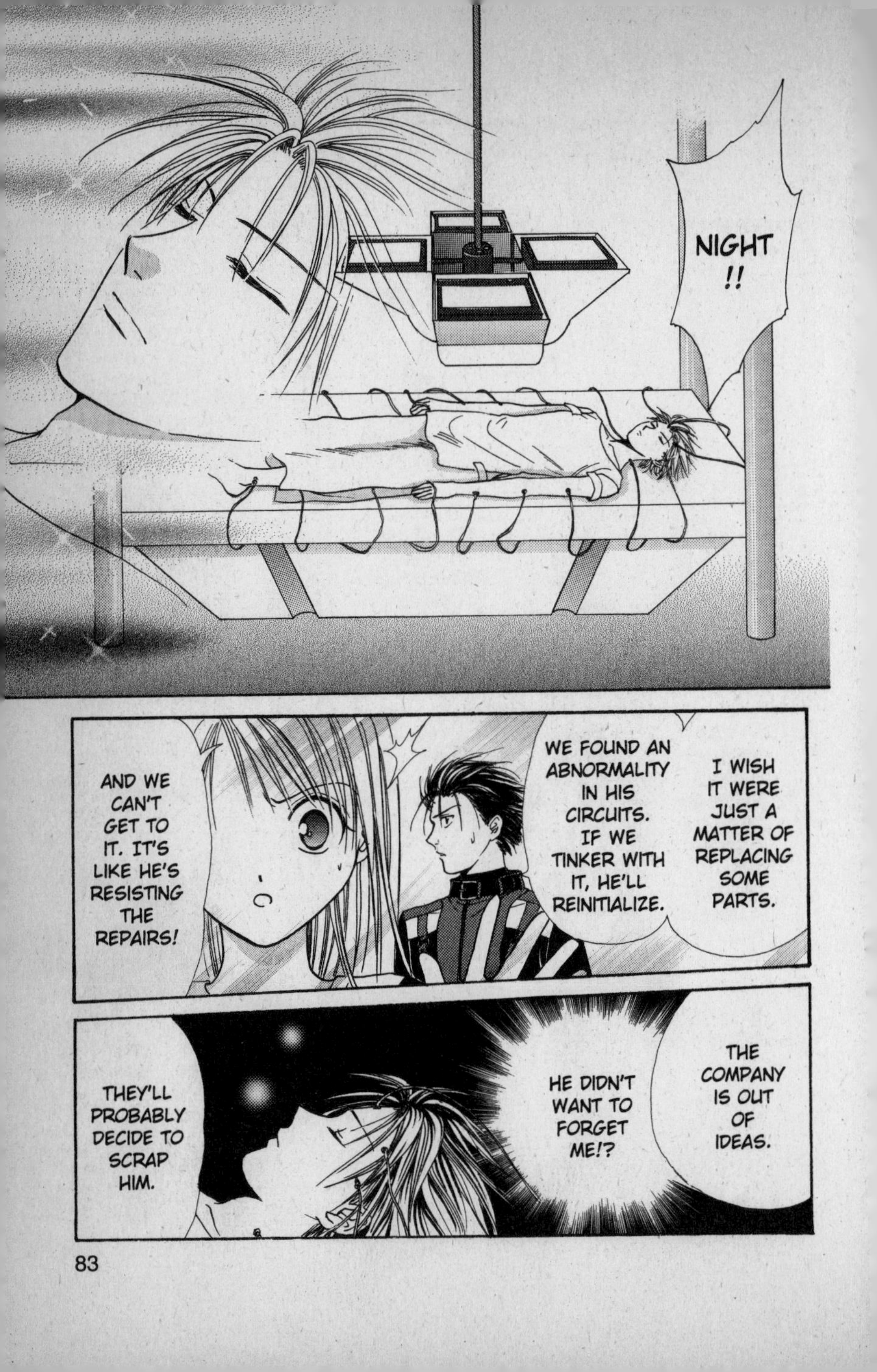
NIGHT!!
I WISH IT WERE JUST A MATTER OF REPLACING SOME PARTS.
WE FOUND AN ABNORMALITY IN HIS CIRCUITS. IF WE TINKER WITH IT, HE'LL REINITIALIZE.
AND WE CAN'T GET TO IT. IT'S LIKE HE'S RESISTING THE REPAIRS!
THE COMPANY IS OUT OF IDEAS.
HE DIDN'T WANT TO FORGET ME!?
THEY'LL PROBABLY DECIDE TO SCRAP HIM.

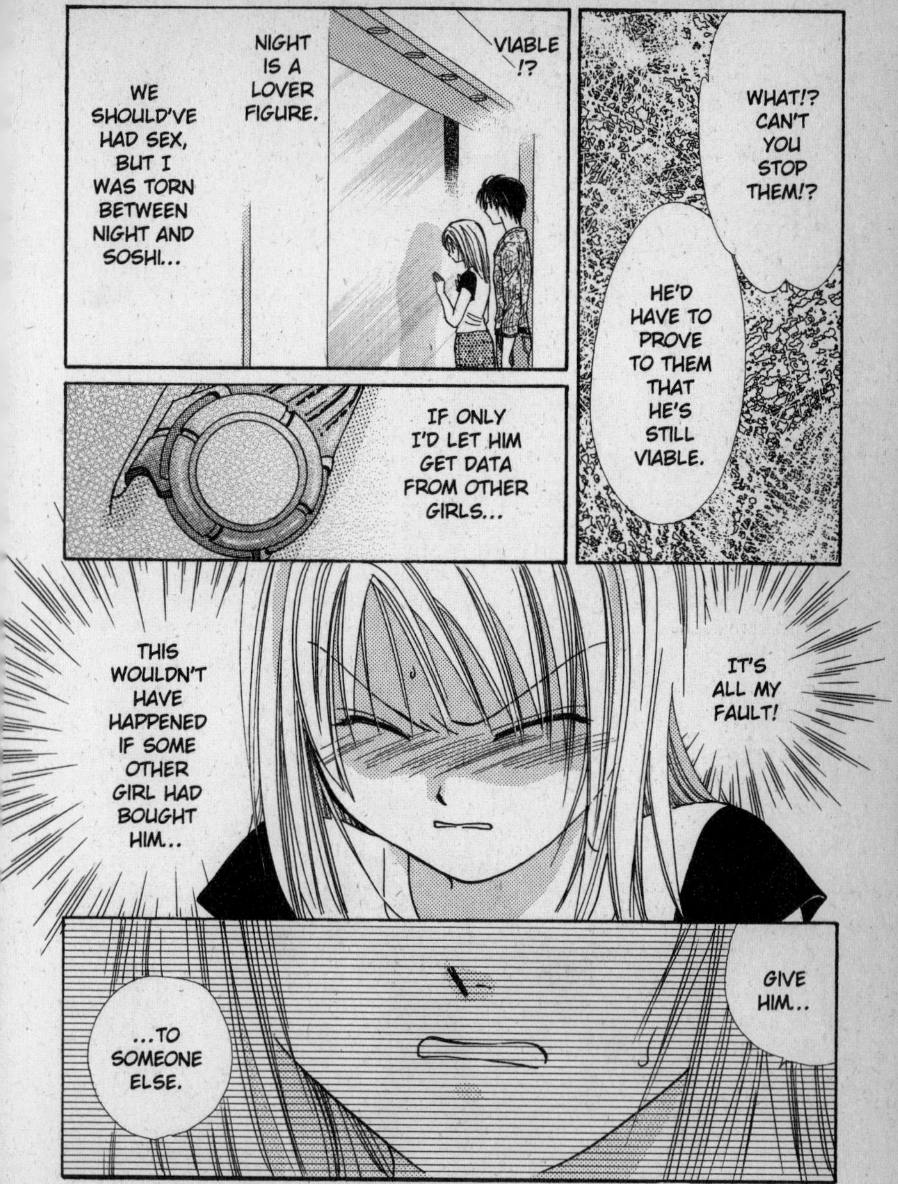
WHAT!? CAN'T YOU STOP THEM!?
HE'D HAVE TO PROVE TO THEM THAT HE'S STILL VIABLE.
VIABLE !?
NIGHT IS A LOVER FIGURE.
WE SHOULD'VE HAD SEX, BUT I WAS TORN BETWEEN NIGHT AND SOSHI...
IF ONLY I'D LET HIM GET DATA FROM OTHER GIRLS...
IT'S ALL MY FAULT!
THIS WOULDN'T HAVE HAPPENED IF SOME OTHER GIRL HAD BOUGHT HIM...
GIVE HIM..
...TO SOMEONE ELSE.

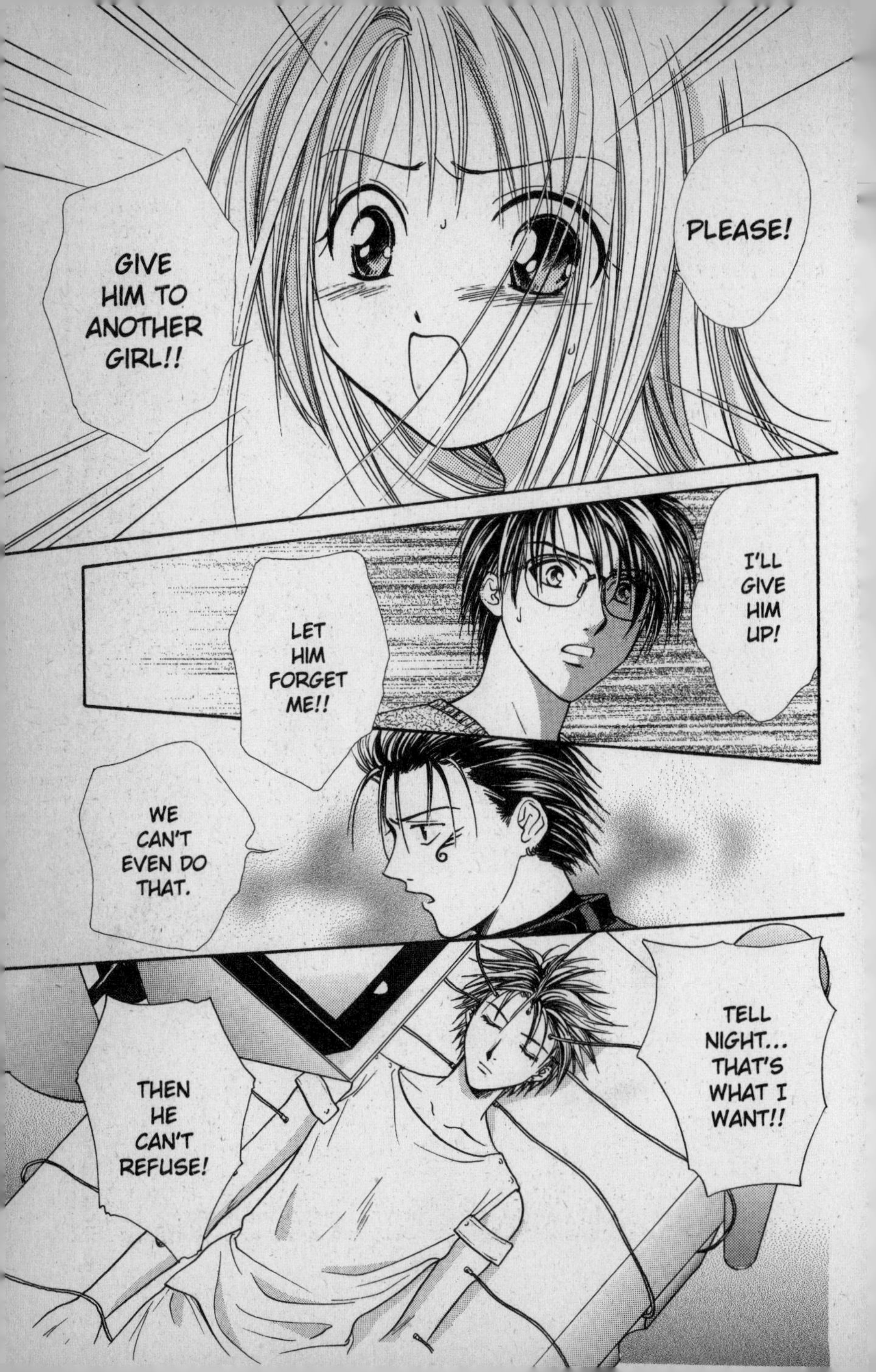
PLEASE!
GIVE HIM TO ANOTHER GIRL!!
I'LL GIVE HIM UP!
LET HIM FORGET ME!!
WE CAN'T EVEN DO THAT.
TELL NIGHT... THAT'S WHAT I WANT!!
THEN HE CAN'T REFUSE!

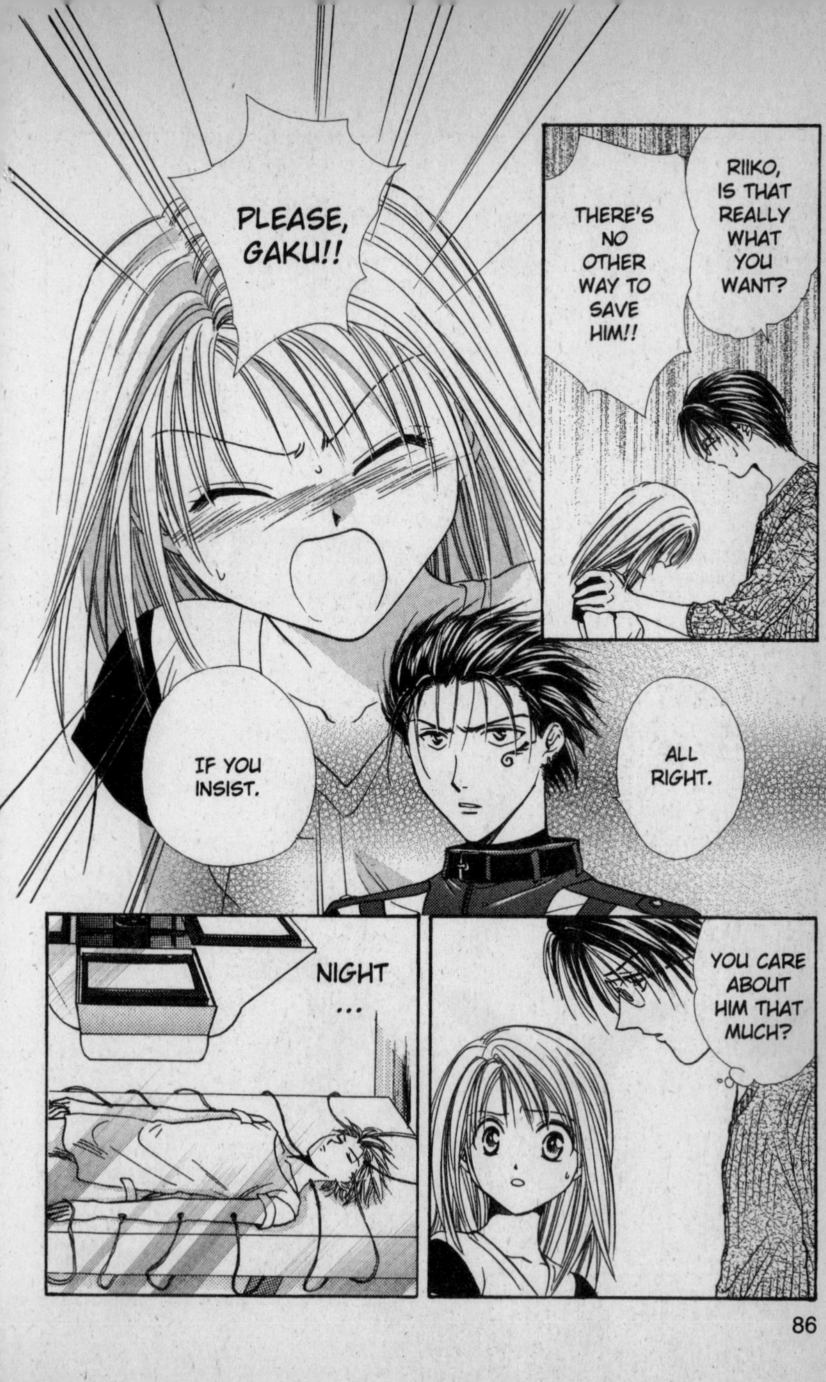
RIIKO, IS THAT REALLY WHAT YOU WANT?
THERE'S NO OTHER WAY TO SAVE HIM!!
PLEASE, GAKU!!
ALL RIGHT.
IF YOU INSIST.
YOU CARE ABOUT HIM THAT MUCH?
NIGHT ...

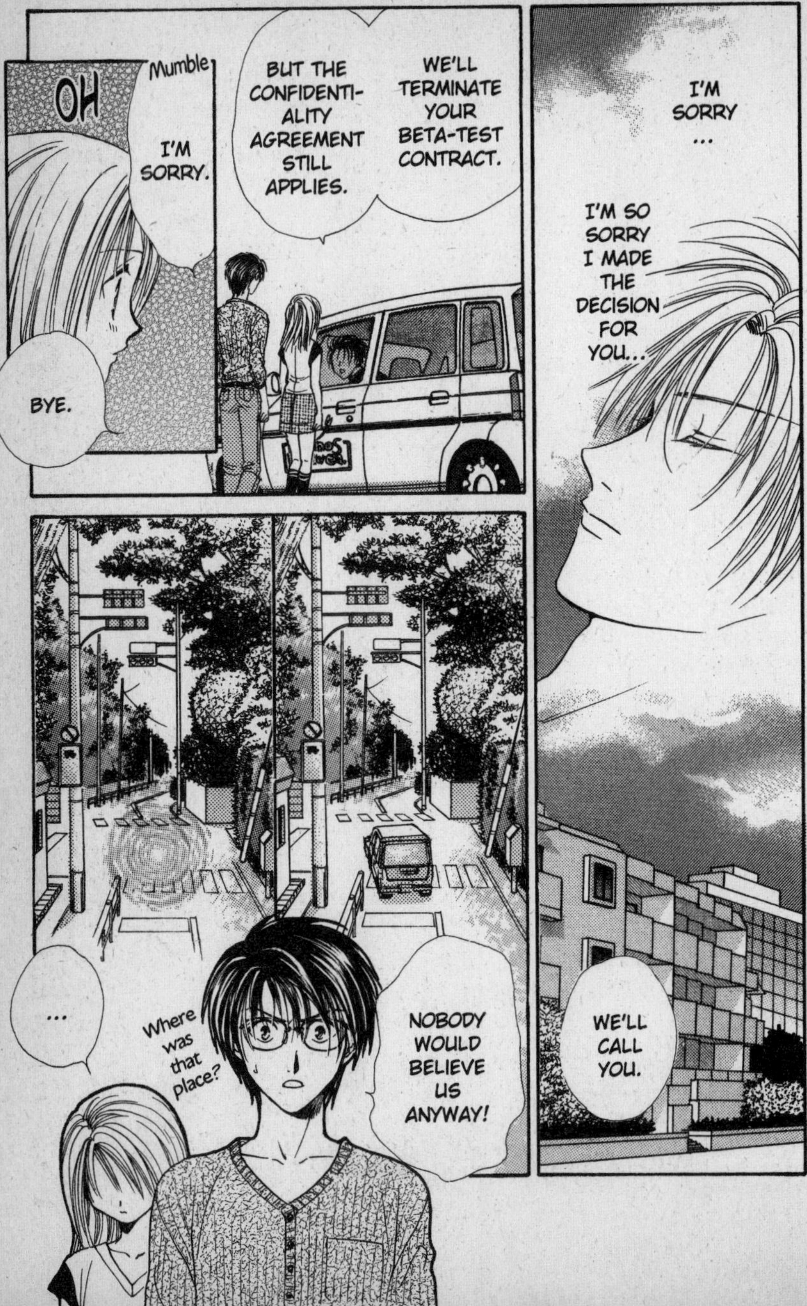
I'M SORRY ...
I'M SO SORRY I MADE THE DECISION FOR YOU...
WE'LL CALL YOU.
WE'LL TERMINATE YOUR BETA-TEST CONTRACT.
BUT THE CONFIDENTIALITY AGREEMENT STILL APPLIES.
Mumble
I'M SORRY.
OH
BYE.
NOBODY WOULD BELIEVE US ANYWAY!
Where was that place?
...

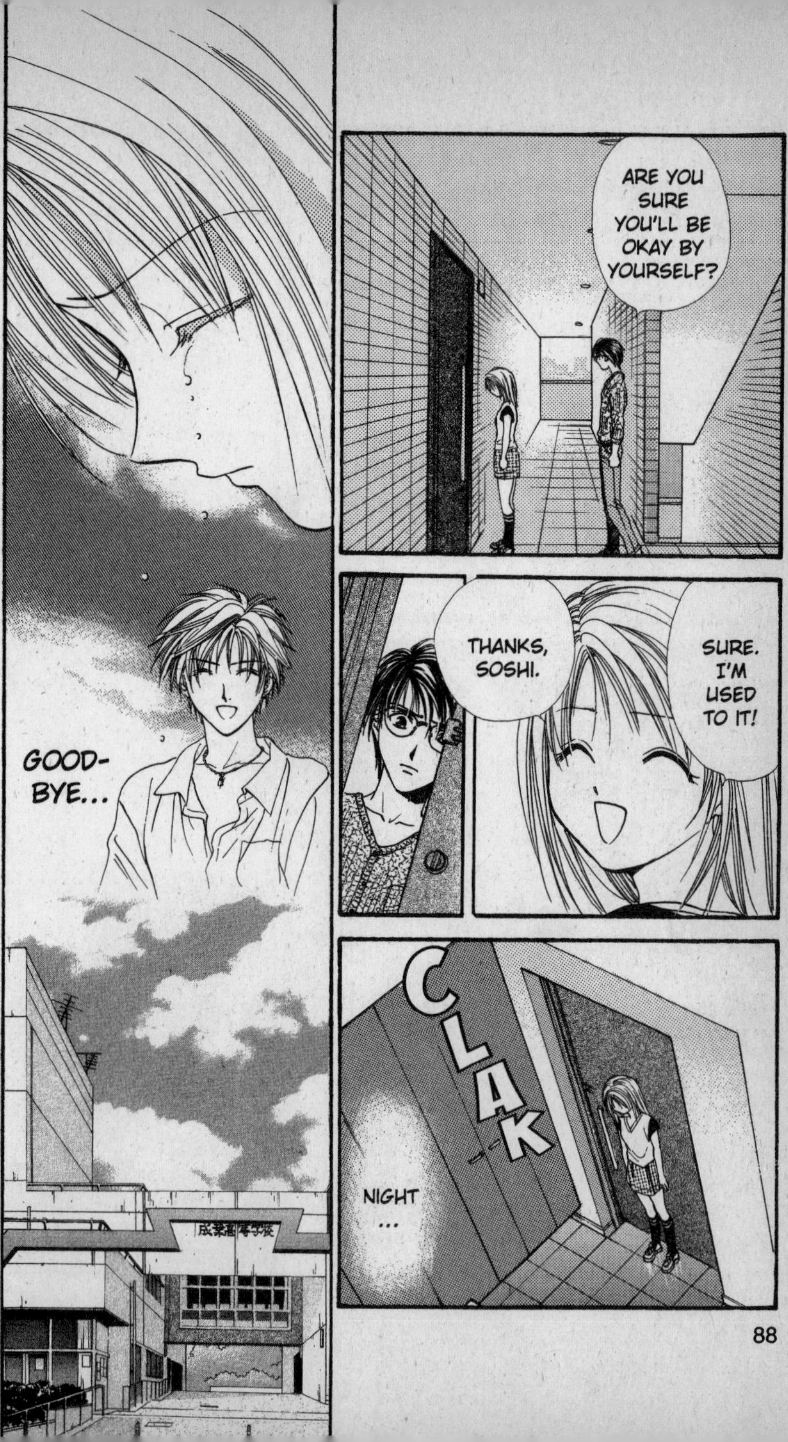
ARE YOU SURE YOU'LL BE OKAY BY YOURSELF?
SURE. I'M USED TO IT!
THANKS, SOSHI.
CLAK
NIGHT ...
GOOD-BYE...

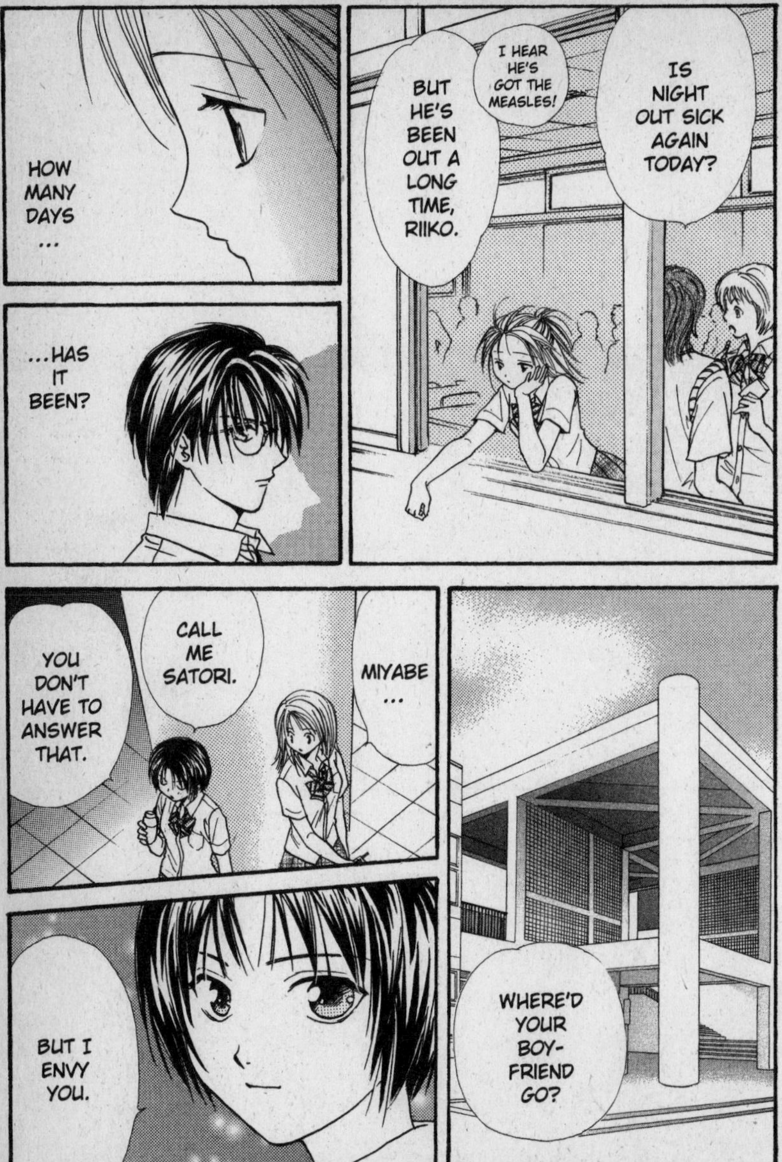
IS NIGHT OUT SICK AGAIN TODAY?
I HEAR HE'S GOT THE MEASLES!
BUT HE'S BEEN OUT A LONG TIME, RIIKO.
HOW MANY DAYS ...
...HAS IT BEEN?
WHERE'D YOUR BOY-FRIEND GO?
MIYABE ...
CALL ME SATORI.
YOU DON'T HAVE TO ANSWER THAT.
BUT I ENVY YOU.

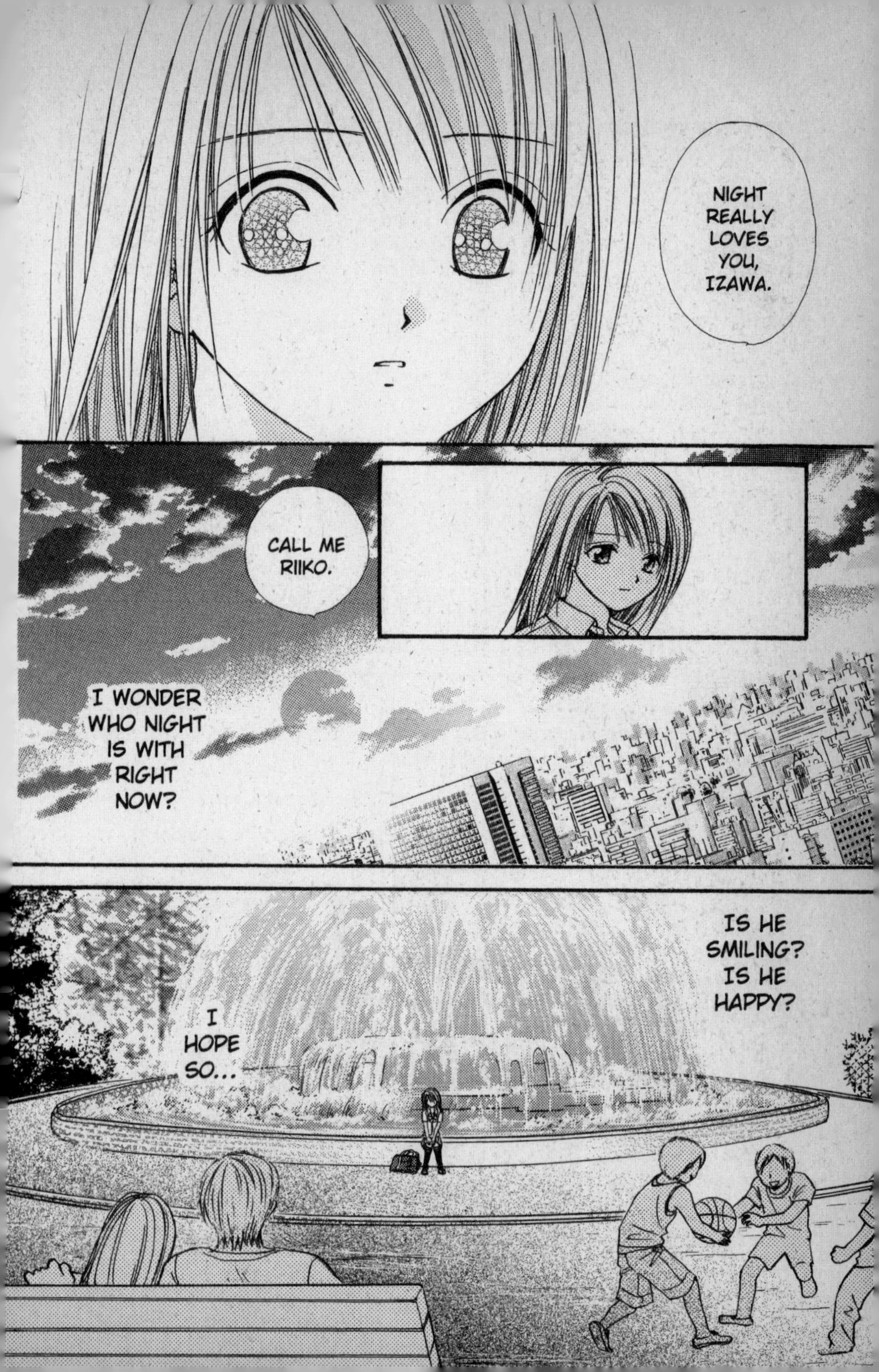
NIGHT REALLY LOVES YOU, IZAWA.
CALL ME RIIKO.
I WONDER WHO NIGHT IS WITH RIGHT NOW?
IS HE SMILING? IS HE HAPPY?
I HOPE SO...

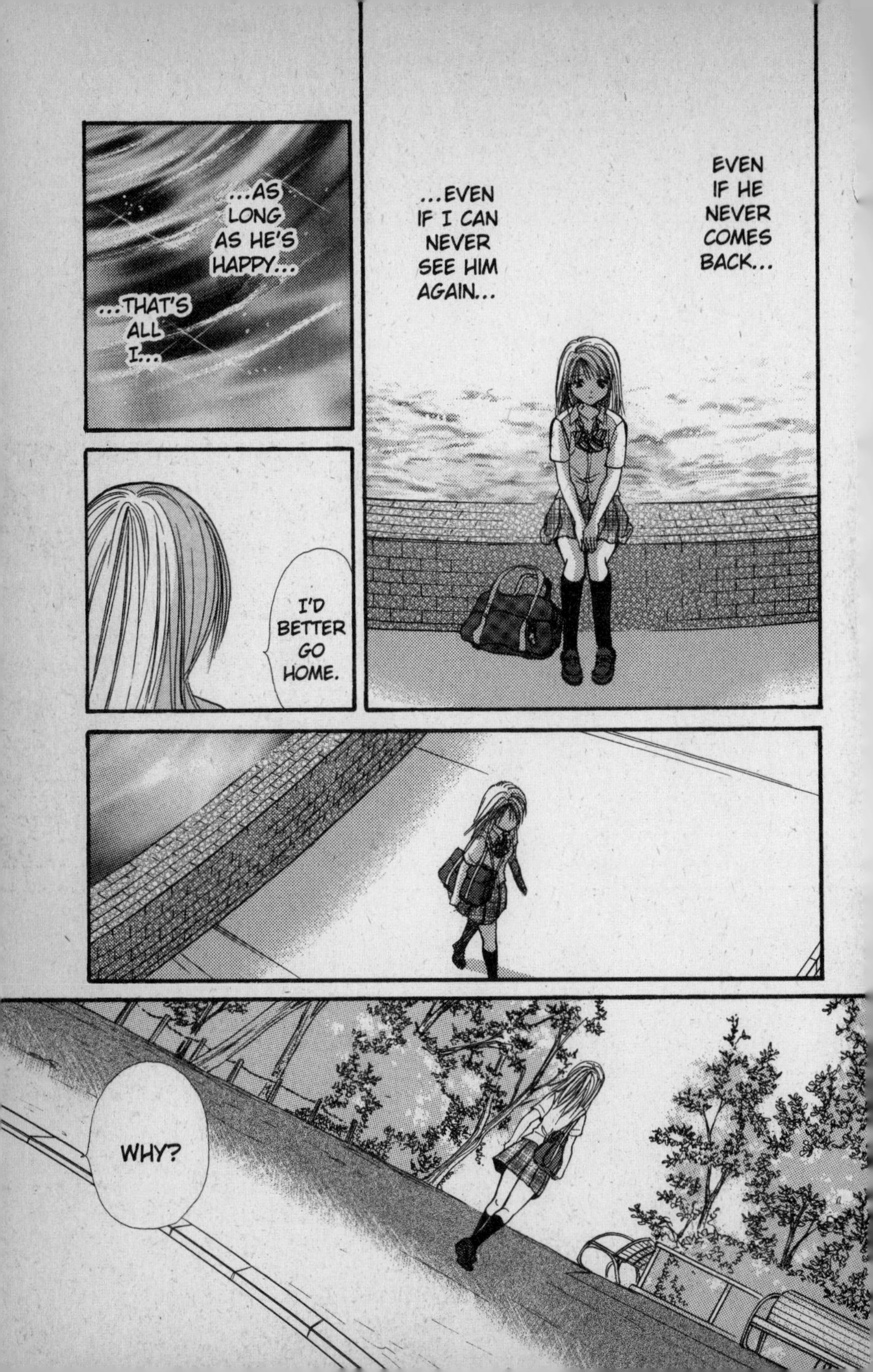
EVEN IF HE NEVER COMES BACK...
...EVEN IF I CAN NEVER SEE HIM AGAIN...
...AS LONG AS HE'S HAPPY...
...THAT'S ALL I...
I'D BETTER GO HOME.
WHY?

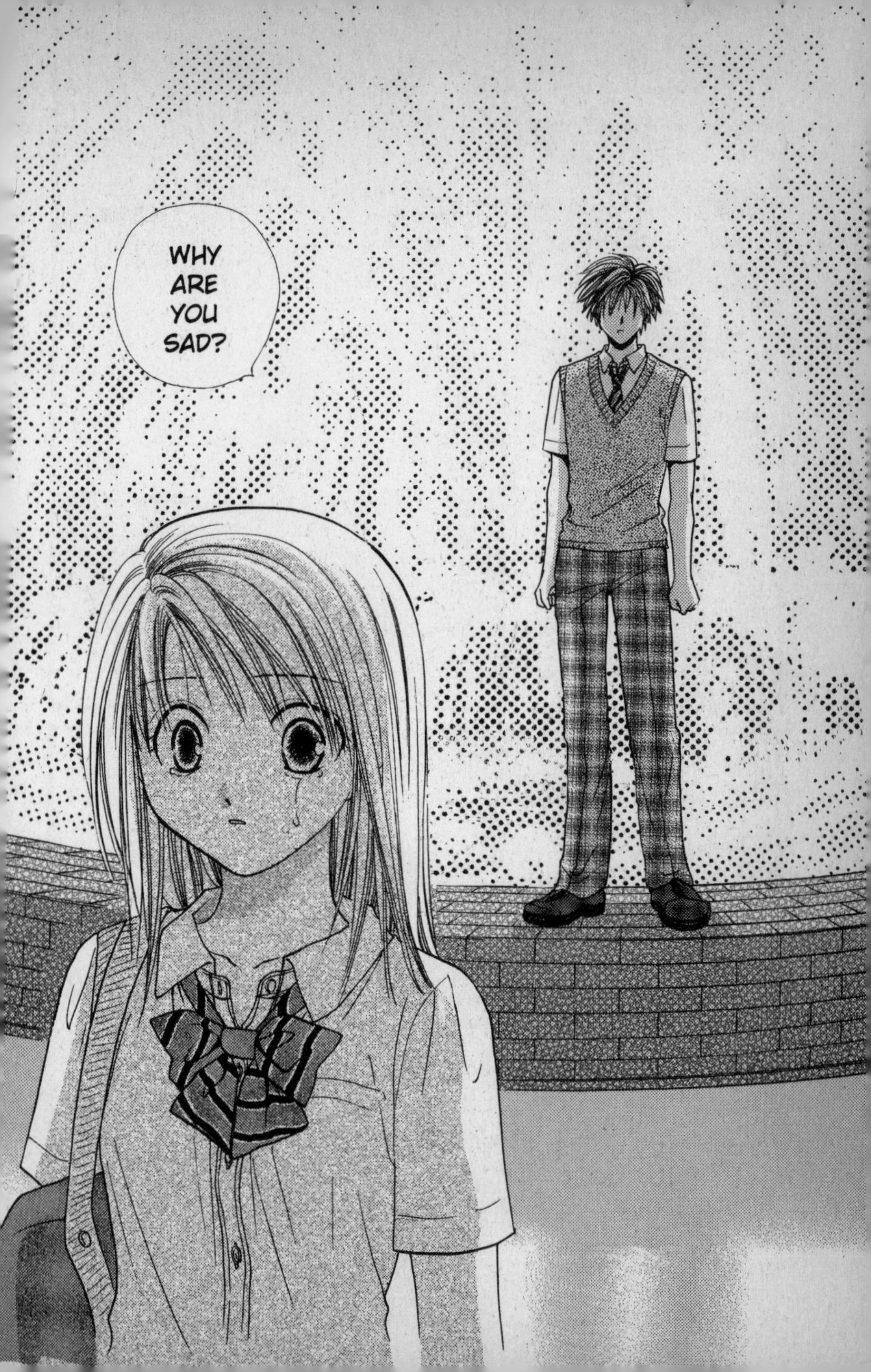
WHY ARE YOU SAD?

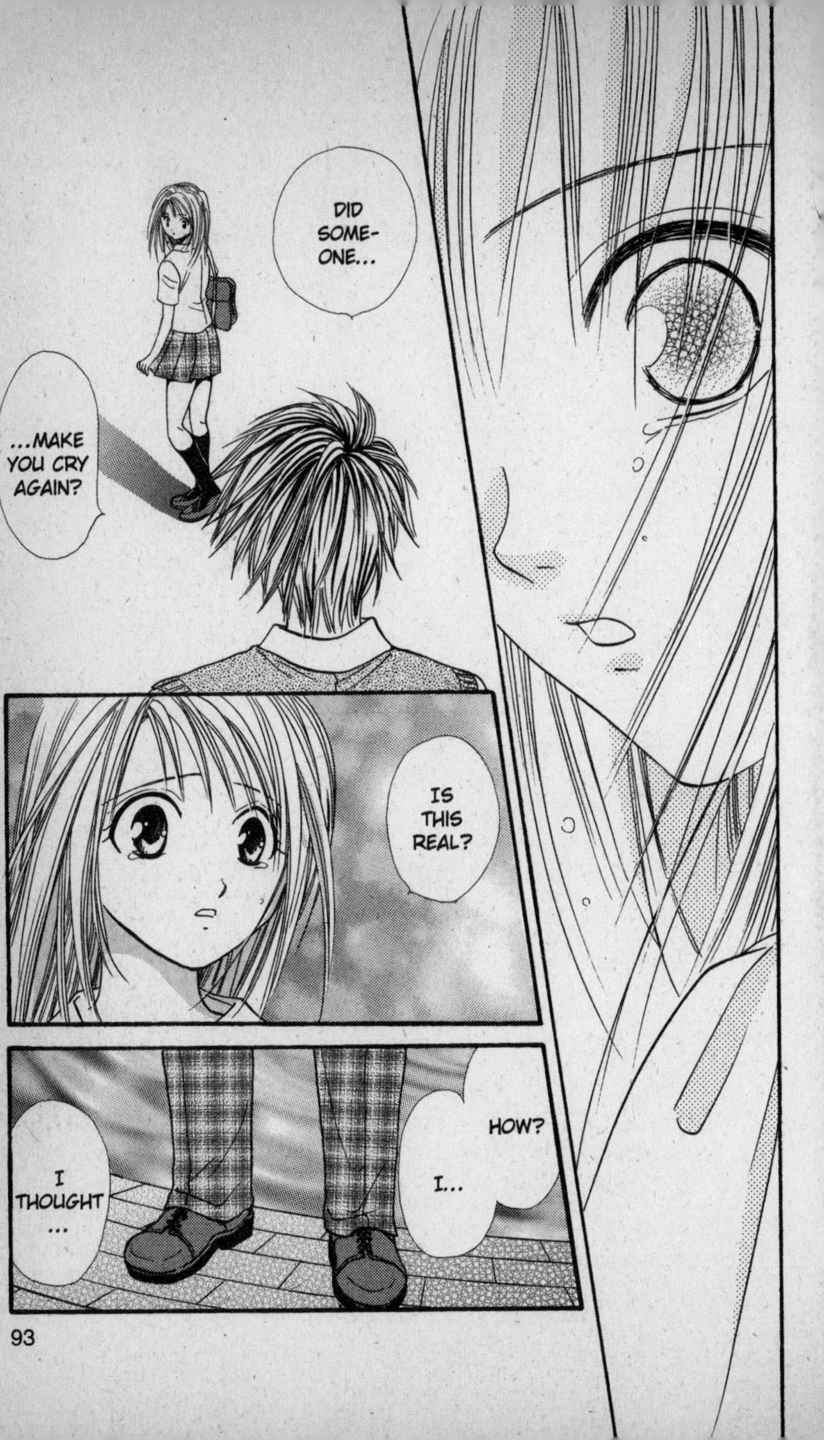
DID SOME-ONE...
...MAKE YOU CRY AGAIN?
IS THIS REAL?
HOW?
I...
I THOUGHT...

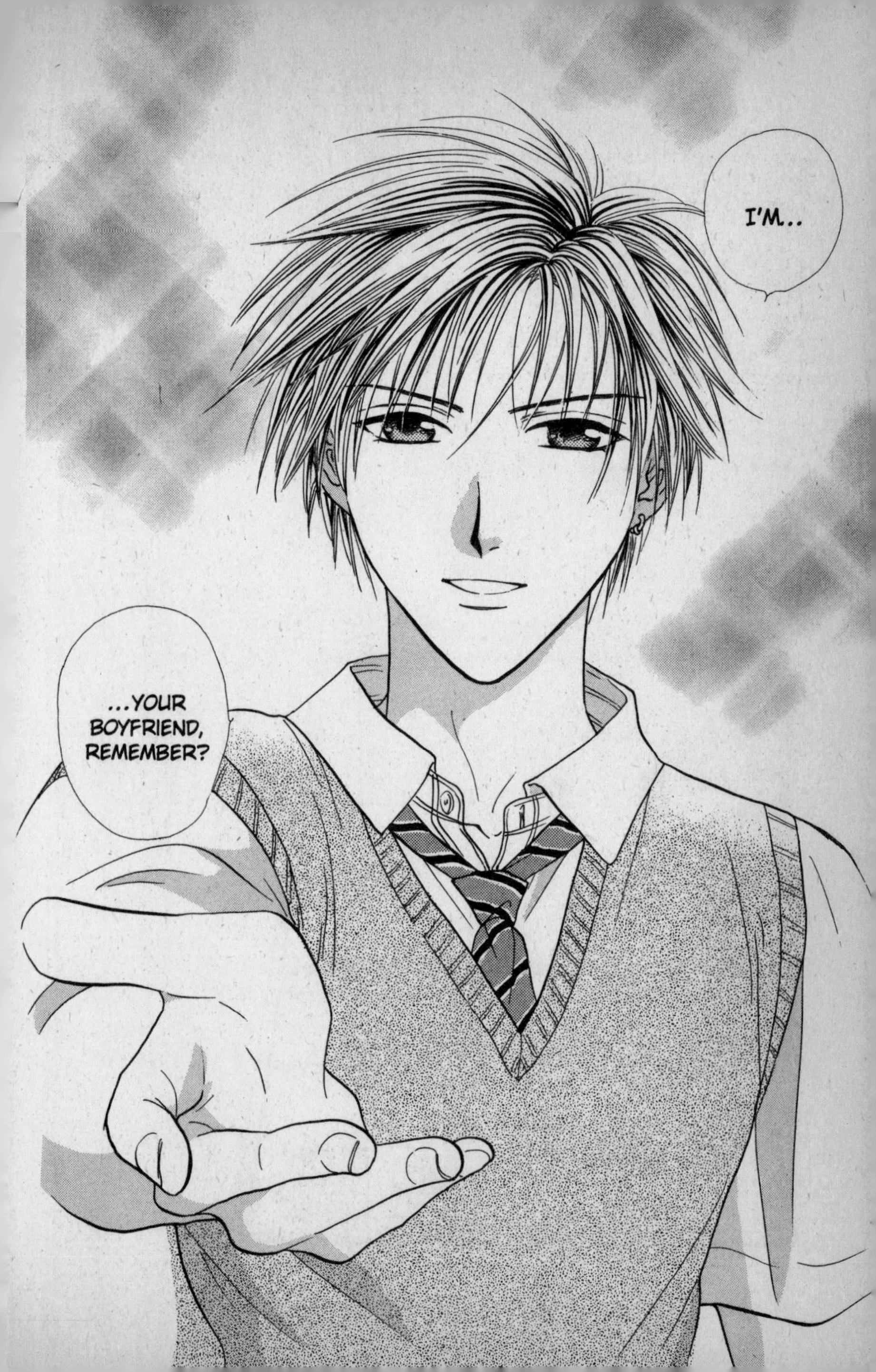
I'M...
...YOUR BOYFRIEND, REMEMBER?

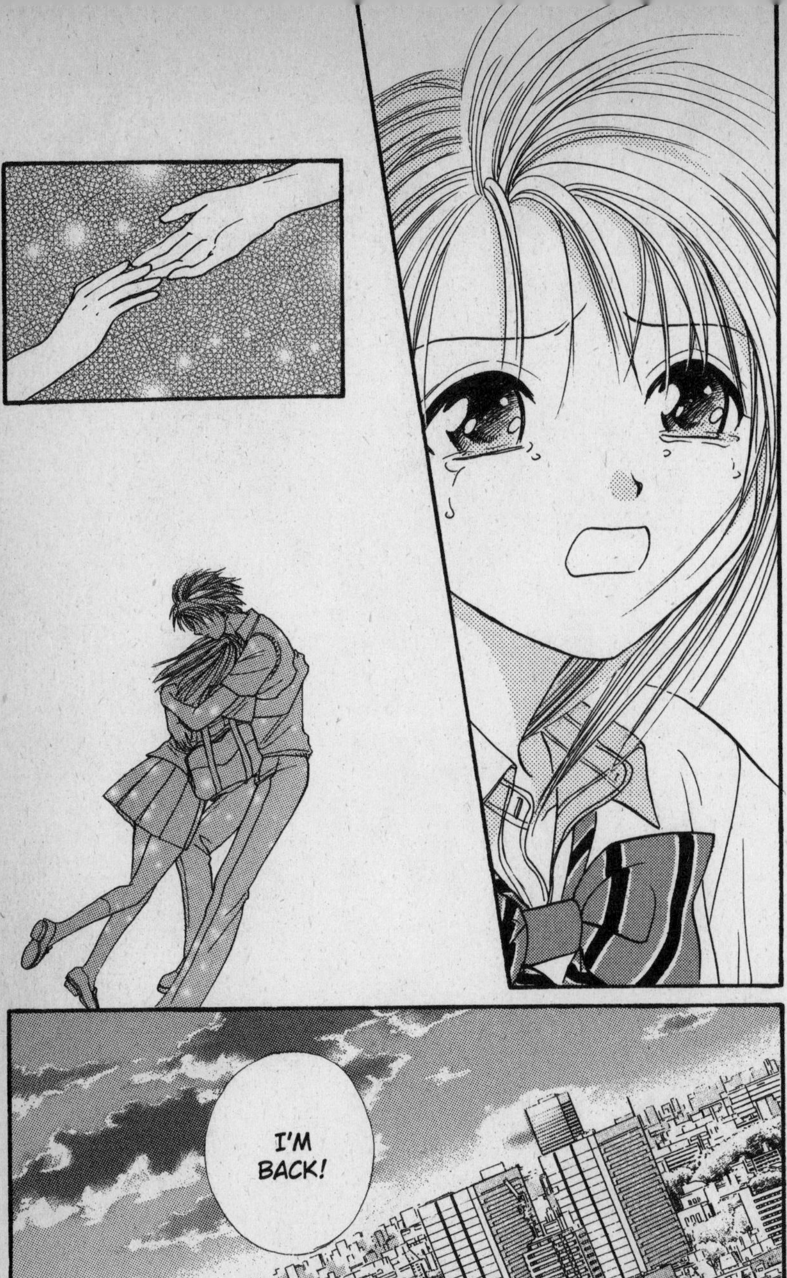
I'M BACK!

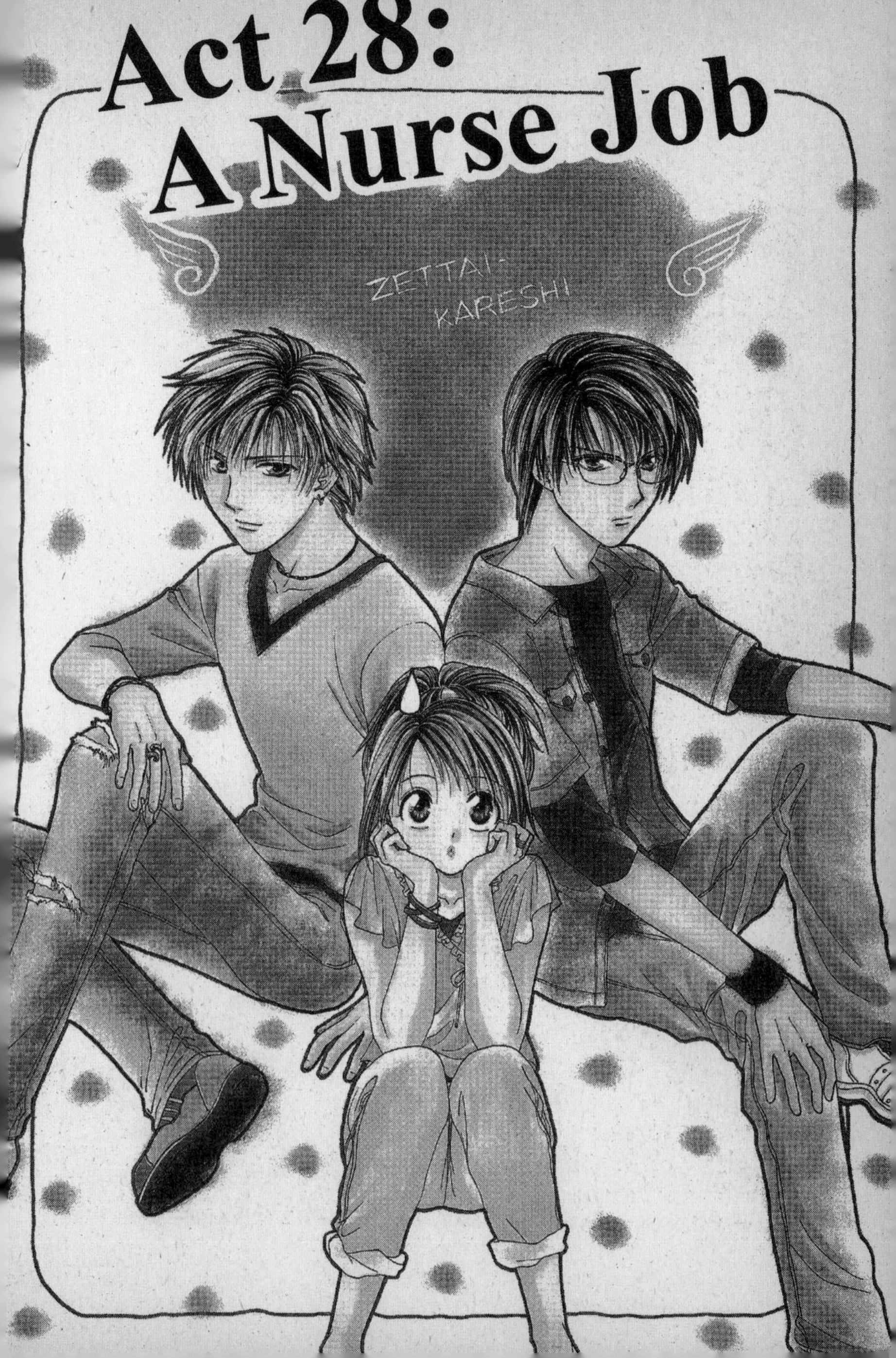
Act 28:
A Nurse Job
ZETTAI-
KARESHI

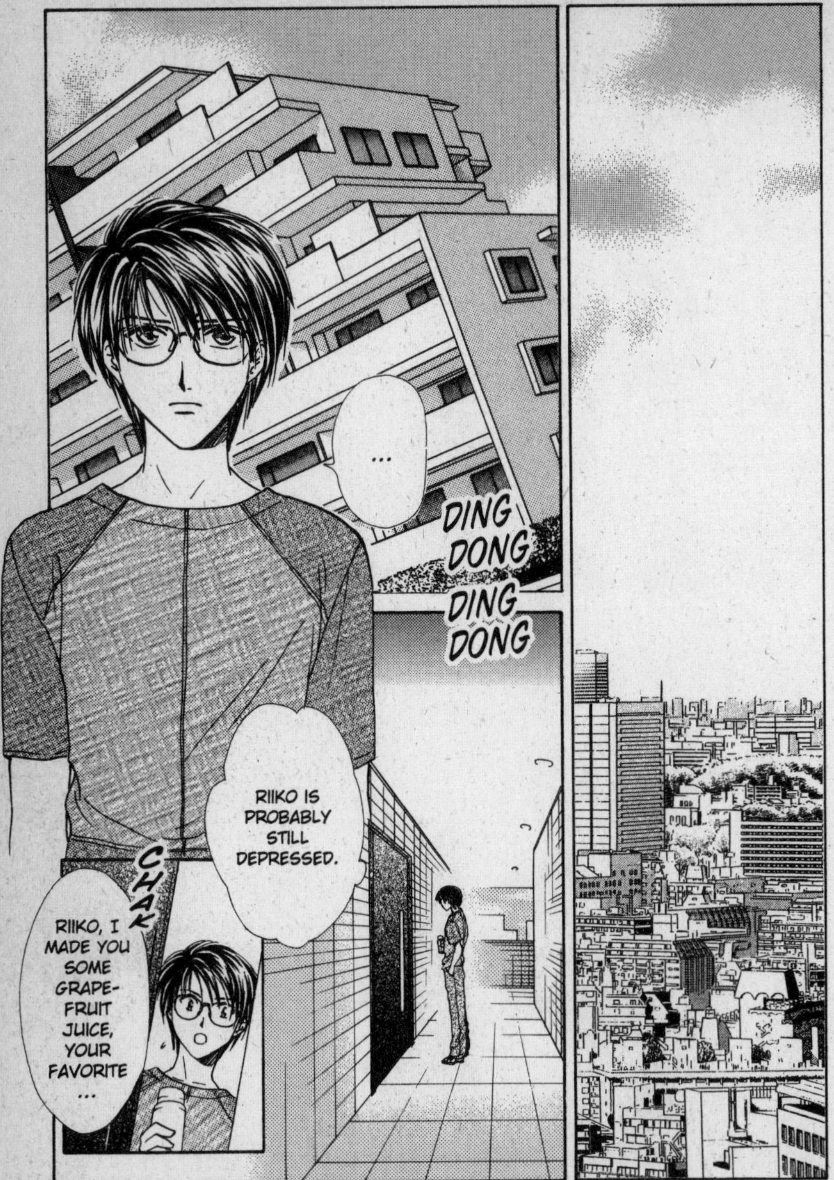
...
DING DONG DING DONG
RIIKO IS PROBABLY STILL DEPRESSED.
CHAK
RIIKO, I MADE YOU SOME GRAPEFRUIT JUICE, YOUR FAVORITE ...

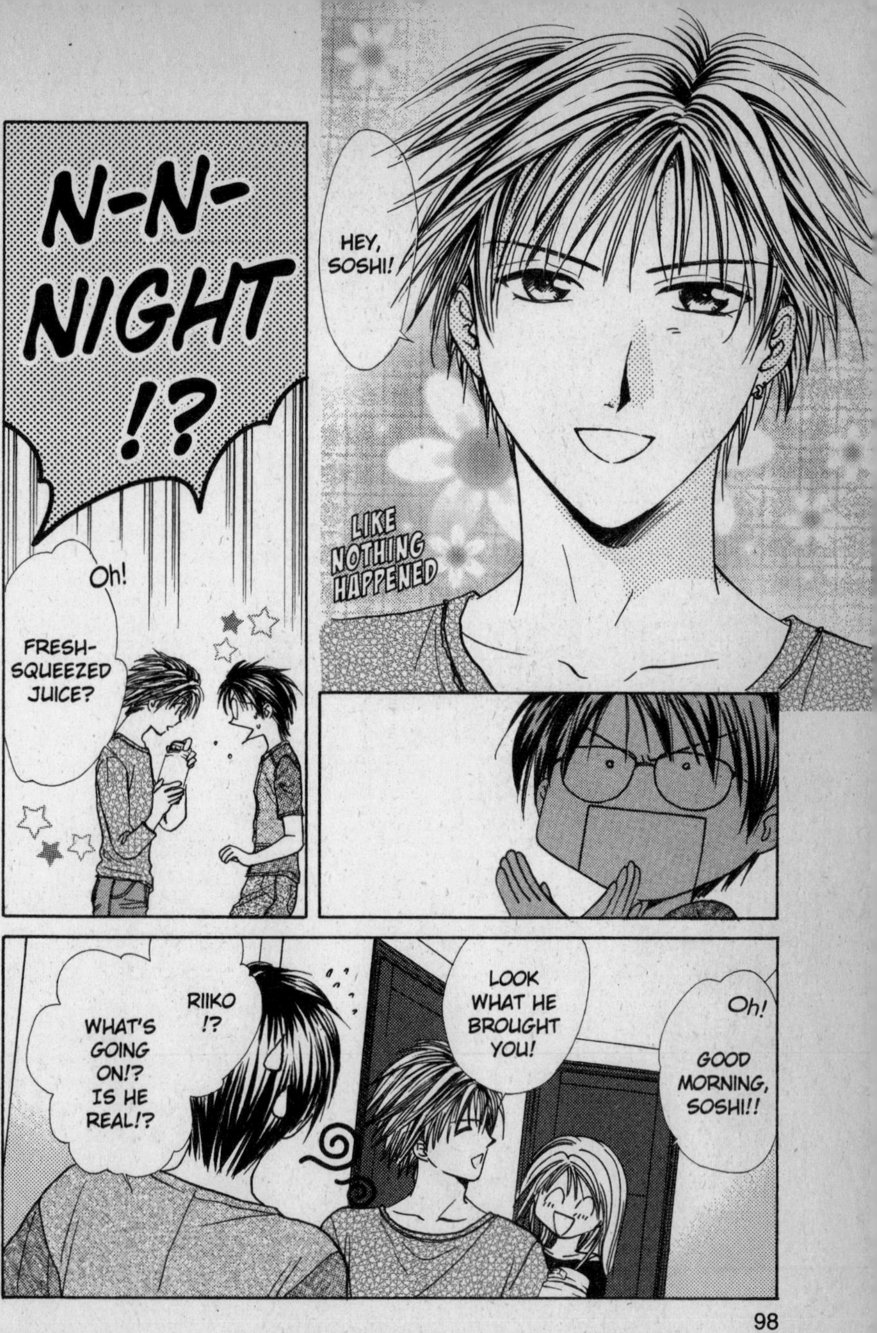
HEY, SOSHI!
LIKE NOTHING HAPPENED
N-N-NIGHT!?
Oh!
FRESH-SQUEEZED JUICE?
Oh!
GOOD MORNING, SOSHI!!
LOOK WHAT HE BROUGHT YOU!
RIIKO!?
WHAT'S GOING ON!? IS HE REAL!?

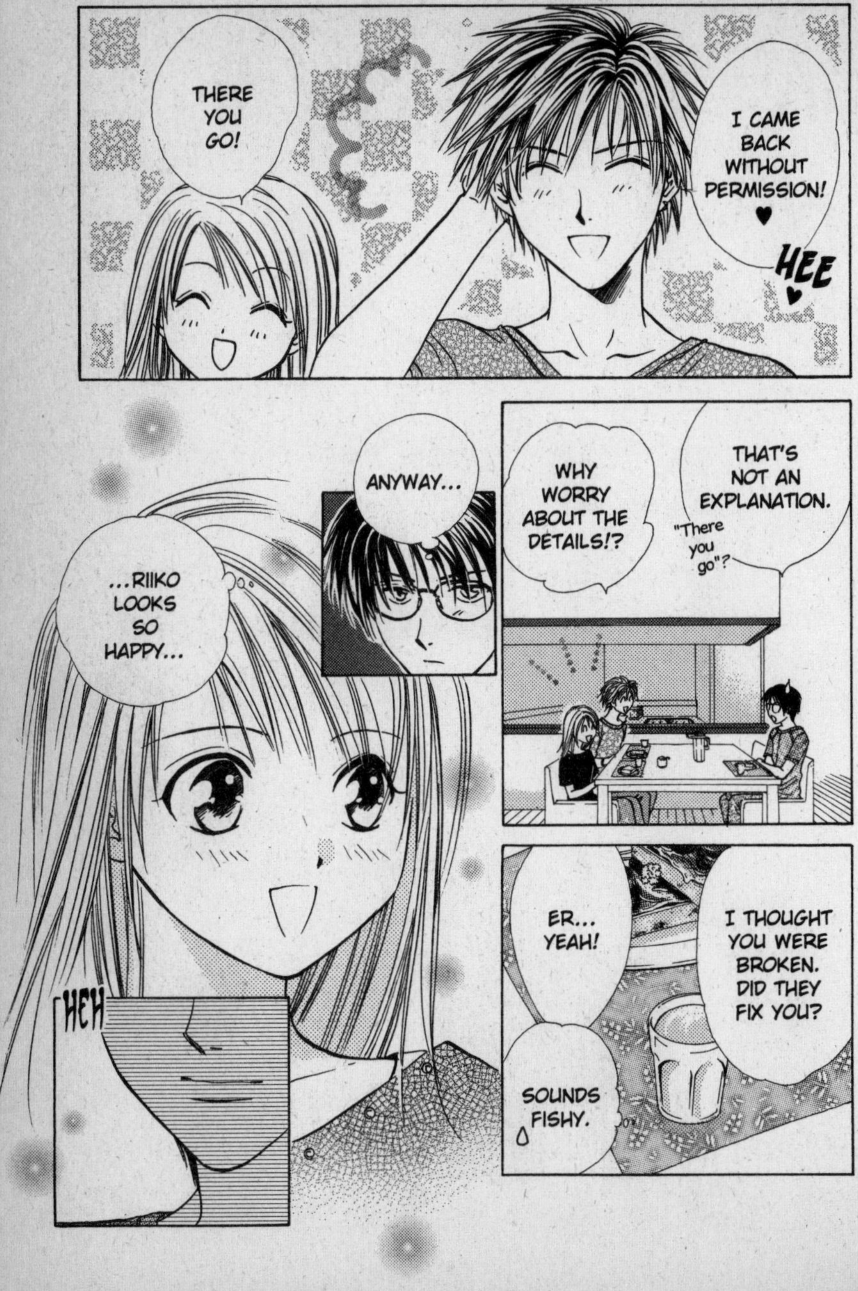
I CAME BACK WITHOUT PERMISSION! ♥
HEE ♥
THERE YOU GO!
THAT'S NOT AN EXPLANATION.
"There you go"?
WHY WORRY ABOUT THE DETAILS!?
I THOUGHT YOU WERE BROKEN. DID THEY FIX YOU?
ER... YEAH!
SOUNDS FISHY.
ANYWAY...
...RIIKO LOOKS SO HAPPY...
HEH

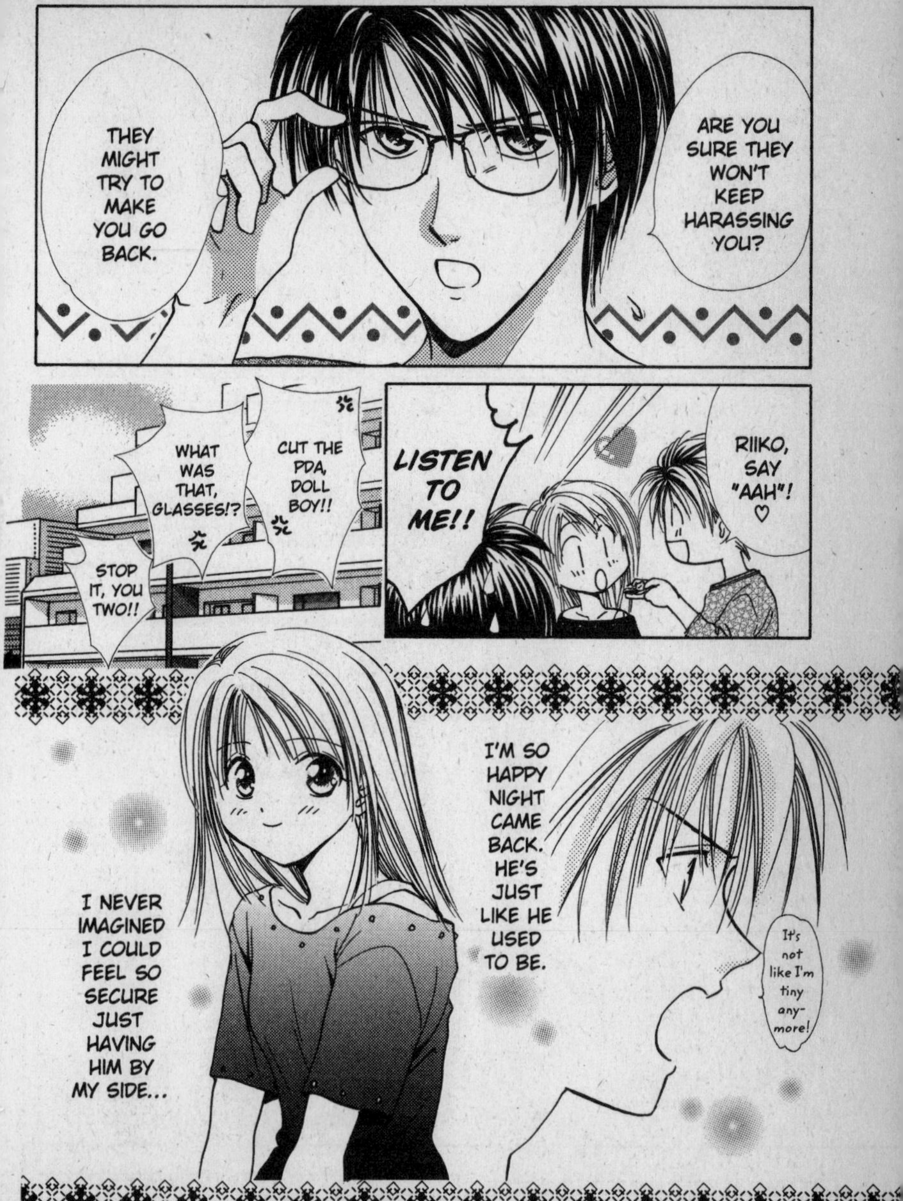
ARE YOU SURE THEY WON'T KEEP HARASSING YOU?
THEY MIGHT TRY TO MAKE YOU GO BACK.
RIIKO, SAY "AAH"! ♡
LISTEN TO ME!!
CUT THE PDA, DOLL BOY!!
WHAT WAS THAT, GLASSES!?
STOP IT, YOU TWO!!
It's not like I'm tiny any-more!
I'M SO HAPPY NIGHT CAME BACK. HE'S JUST LIKE HE USED TO BE.
I NEVER IMAGINED I COULD FEEL SO SECURE JUST HAVING HIM BY MY SIDE...

Night's the most popular character in *Absolute Boyfriend*, but women in their twenties and people who like guys with glasses prefer Soshi. Surprisingly, Yuki (seen here ↘) is also pretty popular! Maybe it's because he's a cute little kid. As you will see in the following pages, at Kronos Heaven, the higher up in the company people are, the younger they are, for some reason. My assistants wonder if they're really middle-aged on the inside. Does that mean Yuki is in his thirties? I don't know... The company is just a gag. It's lots of fun drawing Yuki. Gaku was actually supposed to be a little kid at first. I didn't want to waste the idea, so I used it for Yuki. But now that he's so popular, I wish I'd made Gaku a kid too!

If you like little boys, let me know! (That sounded weird.) Well, Gaku is popular, in his own way. He's probably the most popular here at work. We're all grownups, of course. And Gaku, being 25 years old, is just right.

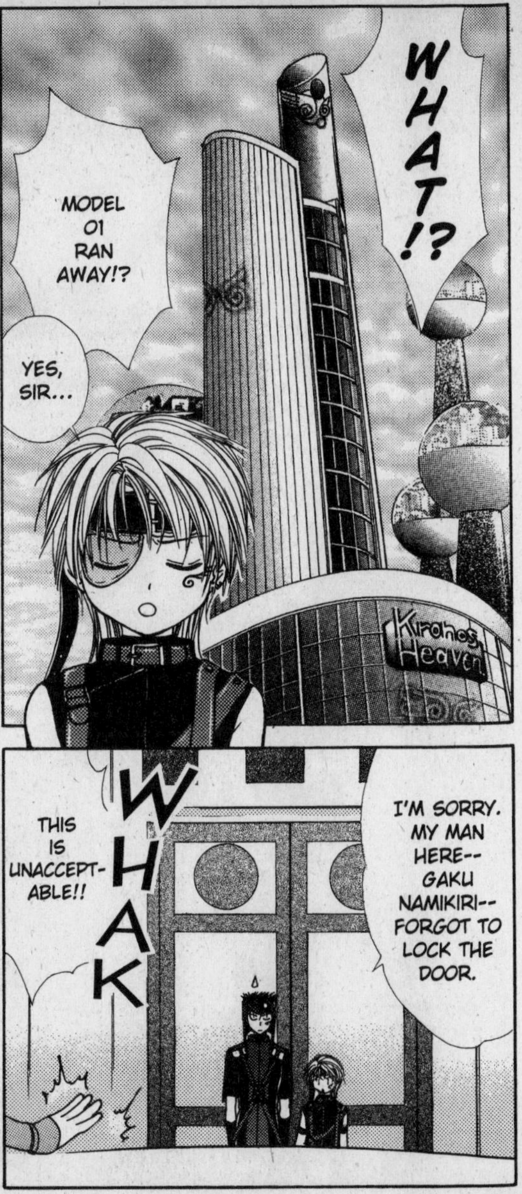
WHAT!?
MODEL 01 RAN AWAY!?
YES, SIR...
Kronos Heaven
I'M SORRY. MY MAN HERE--GAKU NAMIKIRI--FORGOT TO LOCK THE DOOR.
WHAK
THIS IS UNACCEPTABLE!!

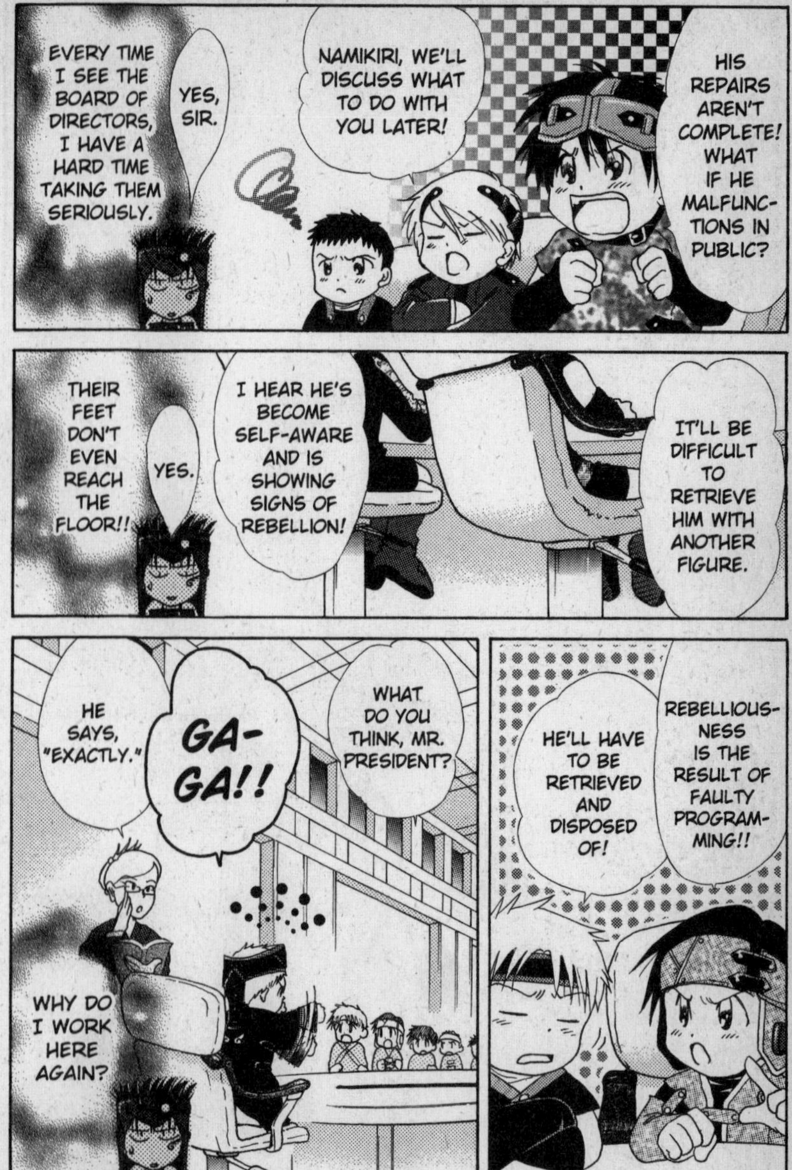
HIS REPAIRS AREN'T COMPLETE! WHAT IF HE MALFUNCTIONS IN PUBLIC?
NAMIKIRI, WE'LL DISCUSS WHAT TO DO WITH YOU LATER!
YES, SIR.
EVERY TIME I SEE THE BOARD OF DIRECTORS, I HAVE A HARD TIME TAKING THEM SERIOUSLY.
IT'LL BE DIFFICULT TO RETRIEVE HIM WITH ANOTHER FIGURE.
I HEAR HE'S BECOME SELF-AWARE AND IS SHOWING SIGNS OF REBELLION!
YES.
THEIR FEET DON'T EVEN REACH THE FLOOR!!
REBELLIOUSNESS IS THE RESULT OF FAULTY PROGRAMMING!!
HE'LL HAVE TO BE RETRIEVED AND DISPOSED OF!
WHAT DO YOU THINK, MR. PRESIDENT?
GA-GA!!
HE SAYS, "EXACTLY."
WHY DO I WORK HERE AGAIN?

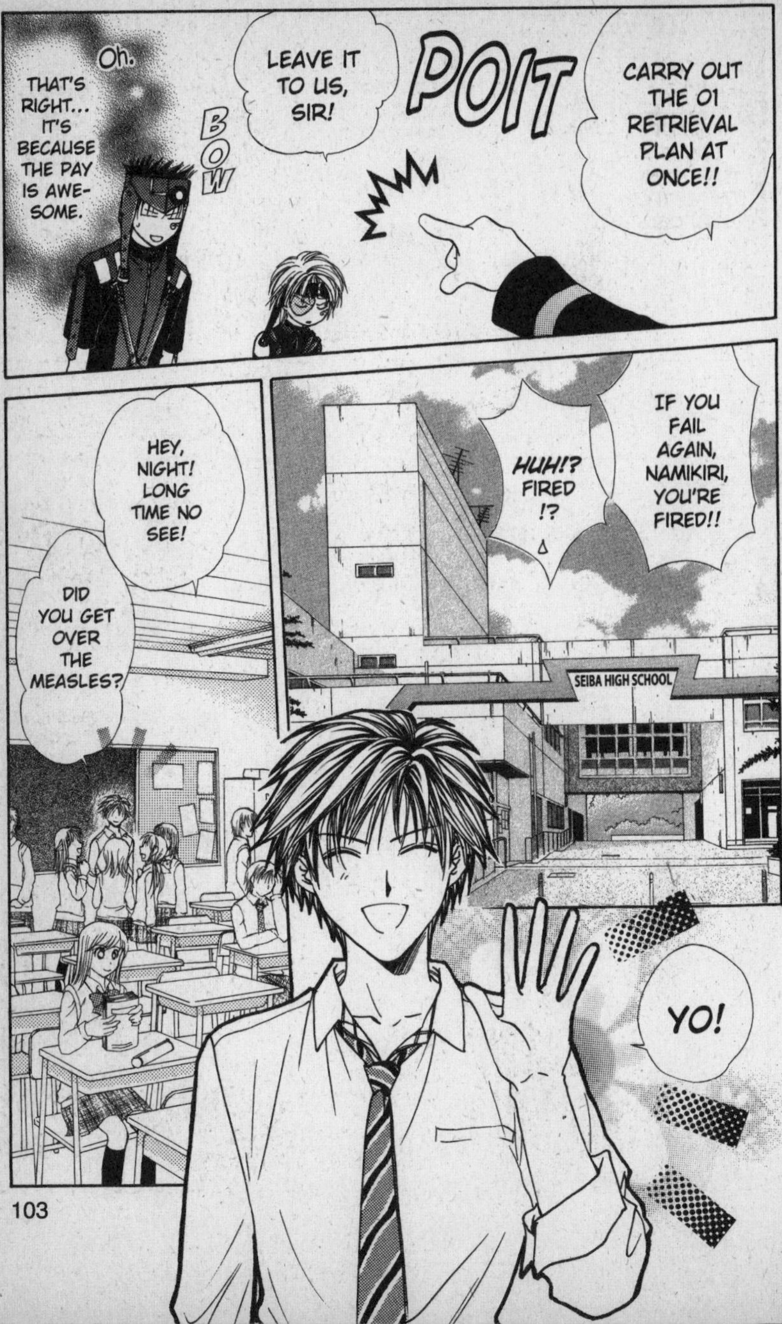
CARRY OUT THE 01 RETRIEVAL PLAN AT ONCE!!
POIT
LEAVE IT TO US, SIR!
BOW
Oh.
THAT'S RIGHT... IT'S BECAUSE THE PAY IS AWESOME.
IF YOU FAIL AGAIN, NAMIKIRI, YOU'RE FIRED!!
HUH!? FIRED!?
SEIBA HIGH SCHOOL
HEY, NIGHT! LONG TIME NO SEE!
DID YOU GET OVER THE MEASLES?
YO!

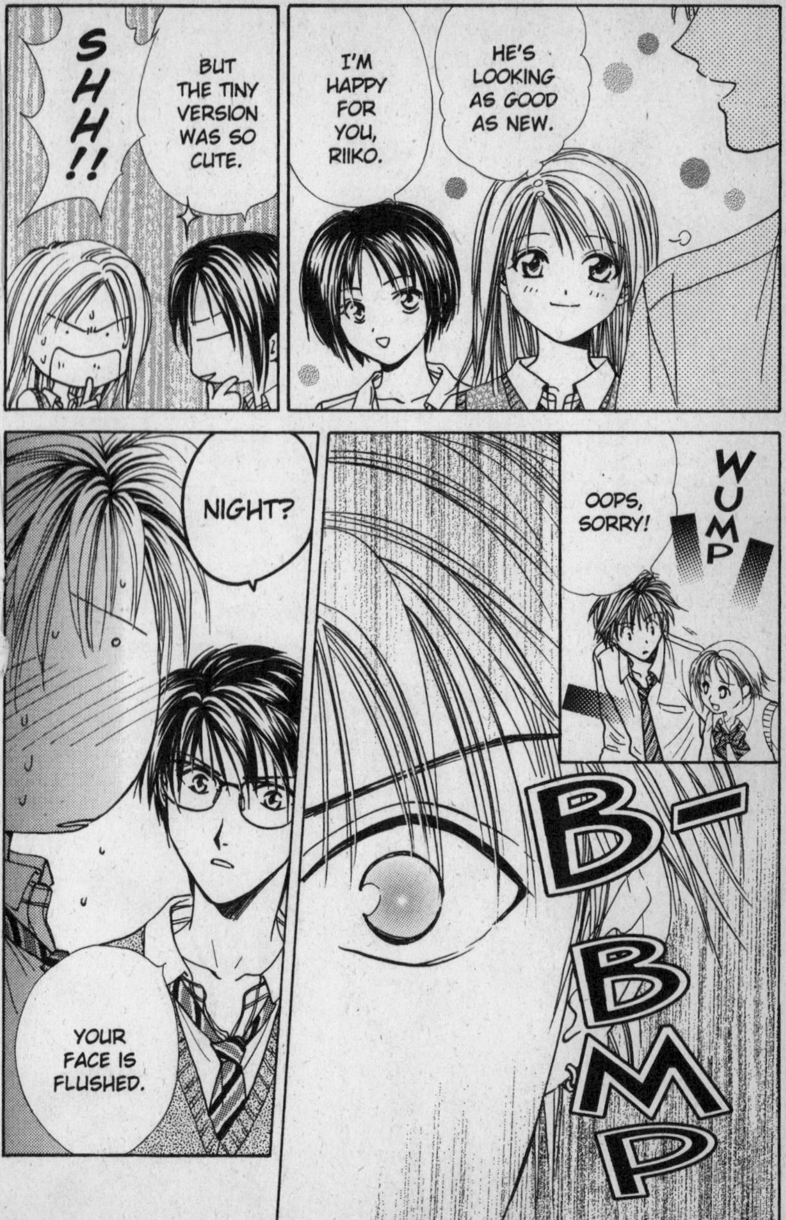

HE'S LOOKING AS GOOD AS NEW.
I'M HAPPY FOR YOU, RIIKO.
BUT THE TINY VERSION WAS SO CUTE.
SHH!!
WUMP
OOPS, SORRY!
B-BMP
NIGHT?
YOUR FACE IS FLUSHED.

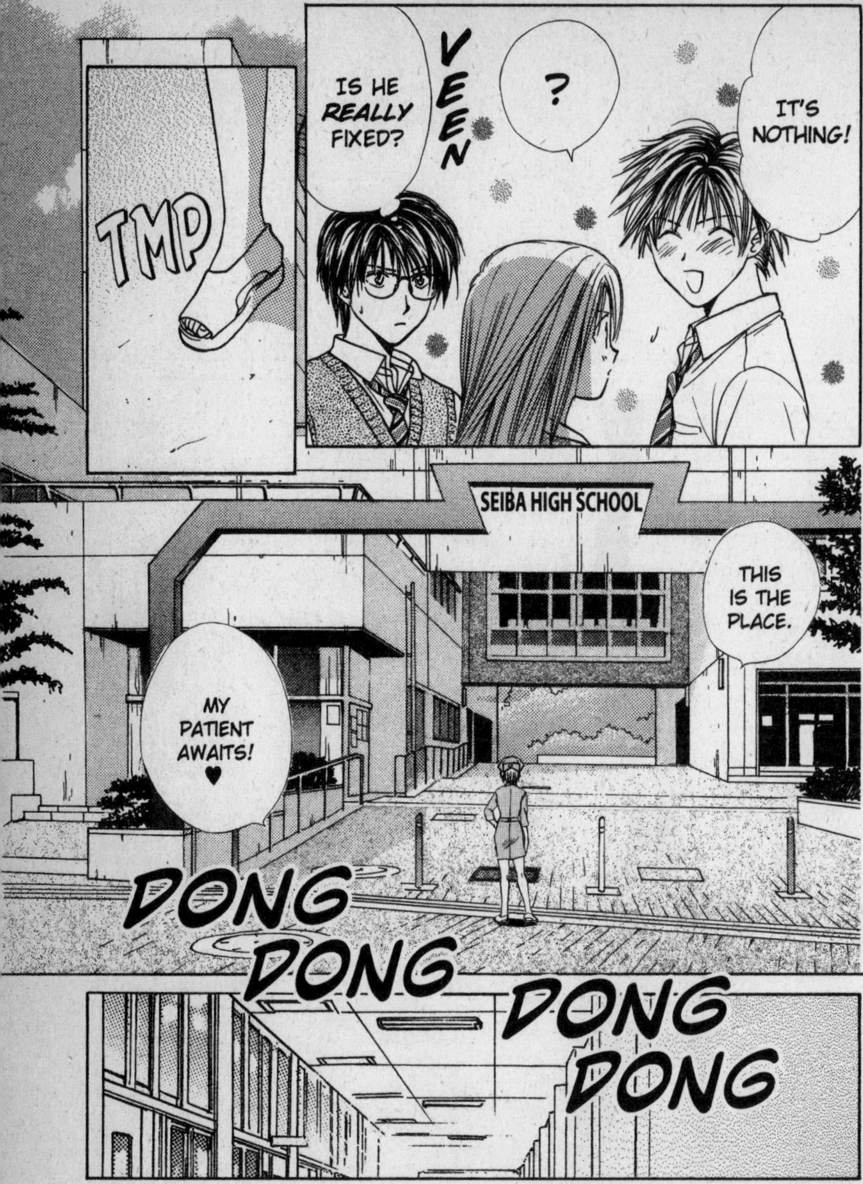
IT'S NOTHING!
?
VEEN
IS HE REALLY FIXED?
TMP
SEIBA HIGH SCHOOL
THIS IS THE PLACE.
MY PATIENT AWAITS! ♥
DONG DONG
DONG DONG

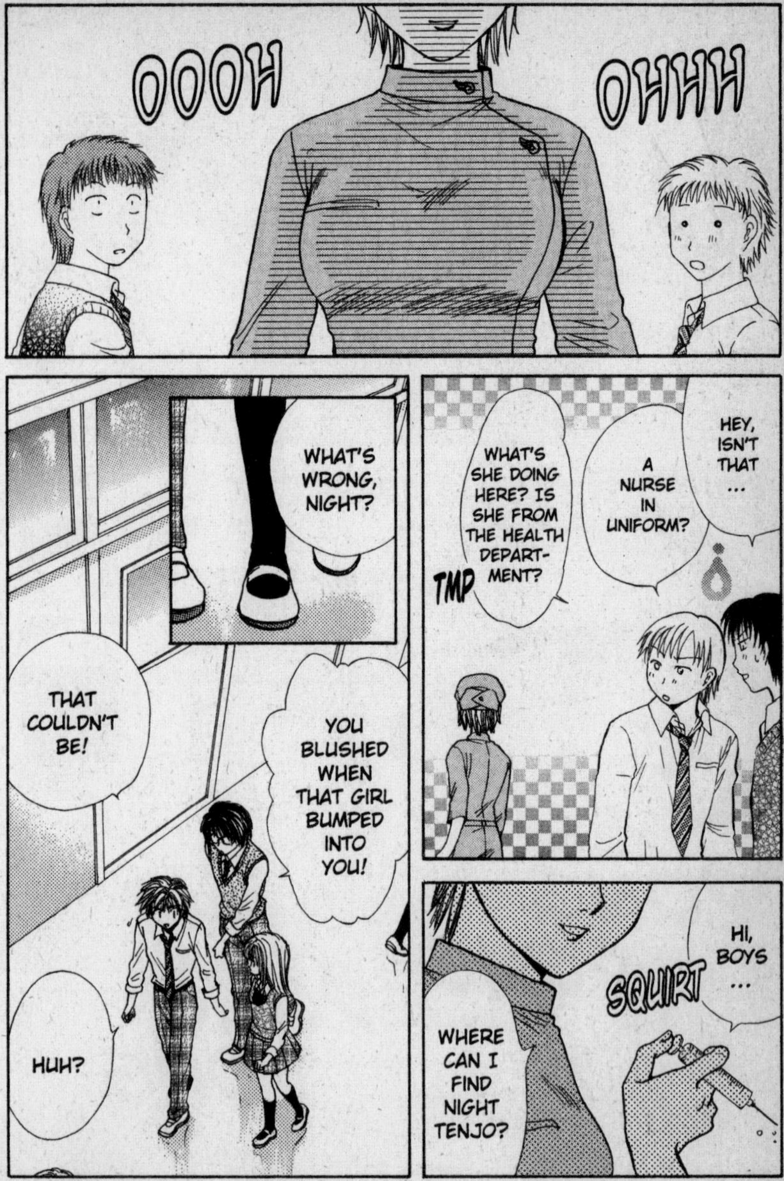
OHHH
OOOH
HEY, ISN'T THAT ...
A NURSE IN UNIFORM?
WHAT'S SHE DOING HERE? IS SHE FROM THE HEALTH DEPART-MENT?
TMP
HI, BOYS ...
SQUIRT
WHERE CAN I FIND NIGHT TENJO?
WHAT'S WRONG, NIGHT?
YOU BLUSHED WHEN THAT GIRL BUMPED INTO YOU!
THAT COULDN'T BE!
HUH?

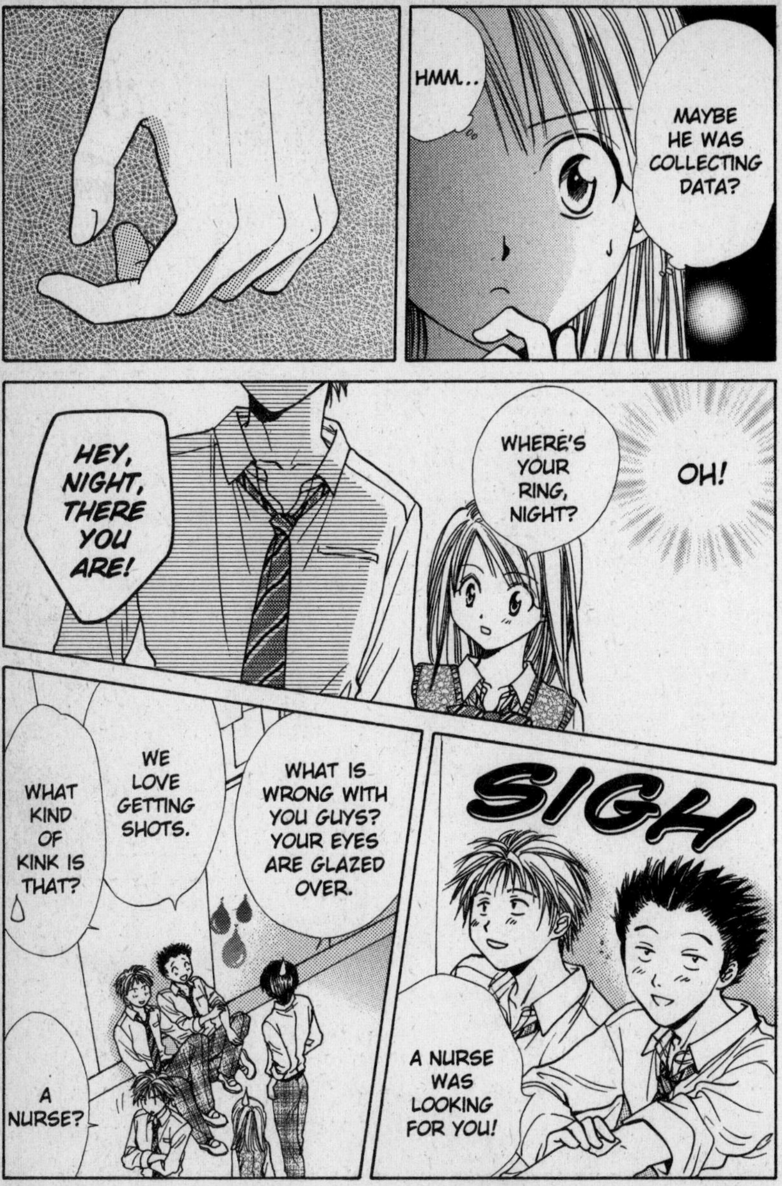
MAYBE HE WAS COLLECTING DATA?
HMM...
OH!
WHERE'S YOUR RING, NIGHT?
HEY, NIGHT, THERE YOU ARE!
SIGH
A NURSE WAS LOOKING FOR YOU!
WHAT IS WRONG WITH YOU GUYS? YOUR EYES ARE GLAZED OVER.
WE LOVE GETTING SHOTS.
WHAT KIND OF KINK IS THAT?
A NURSE?

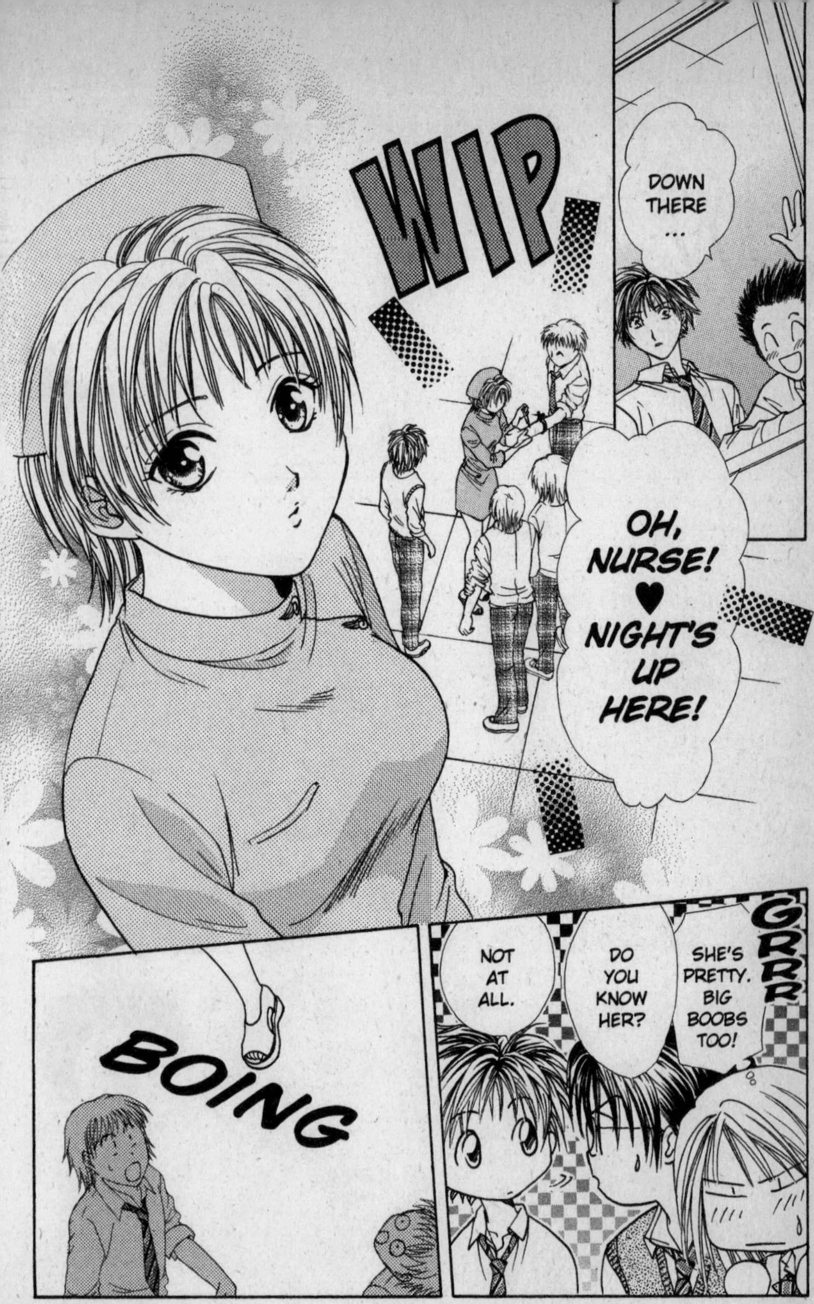
DOWN THERE ...
WIP
OH, NURSE! ♥ NIGHT'S UP HERE!
GRRR
SHE'S PRETTY. BIG BOOBS TOO!
DO YOU KNOW HER?
NOT AT ALL.
BOING

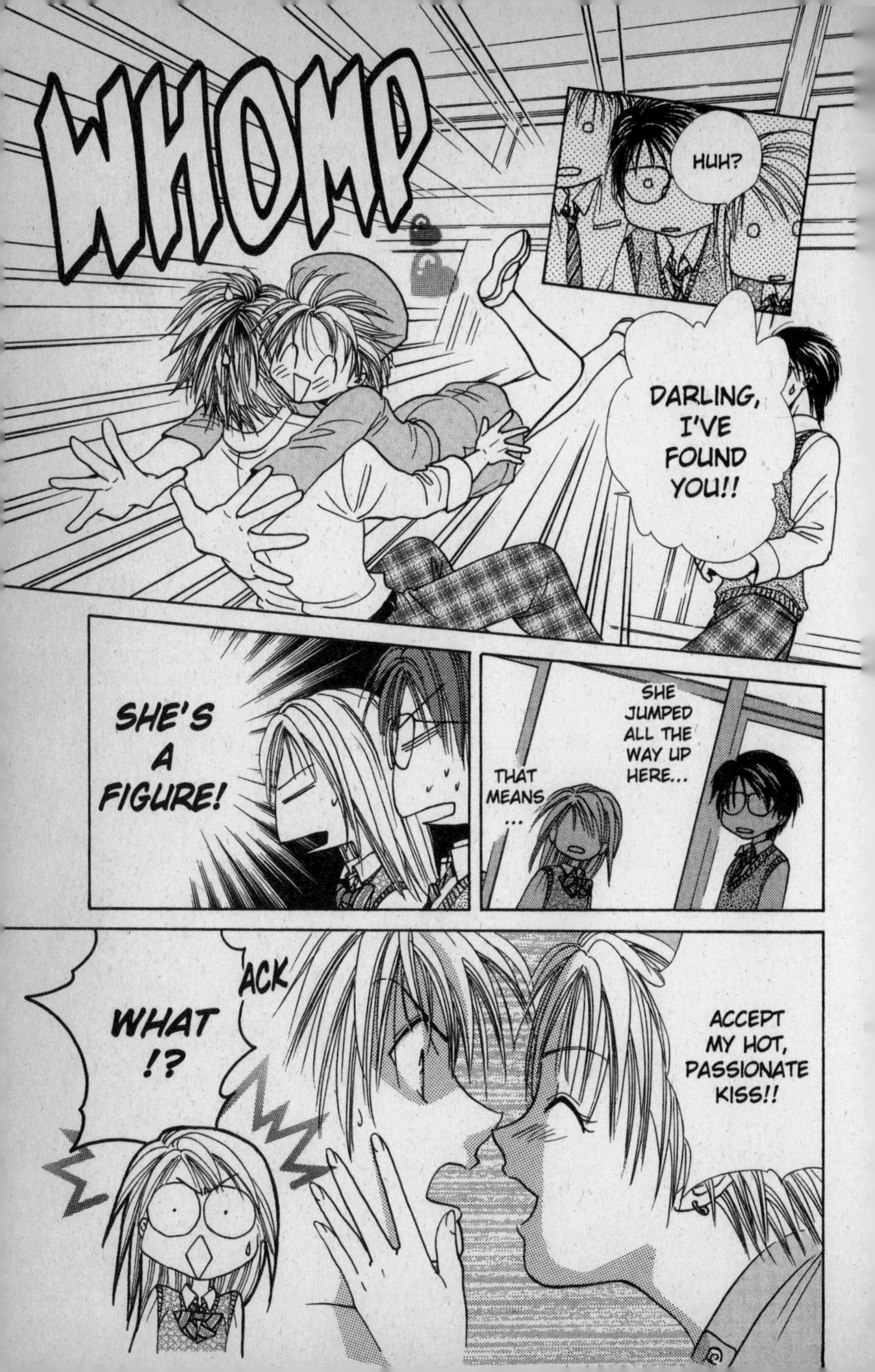
HUH?
WHOMP
DARLING, I'VE FOUND YOU!!
SHE JUMPED ALL THE WAY UP HERE...
THAT MEANS...
SHE'S A FIGURE!
ACCEPT MY HOT, PASSIONATE KISS!!
ACK
WHAT!?

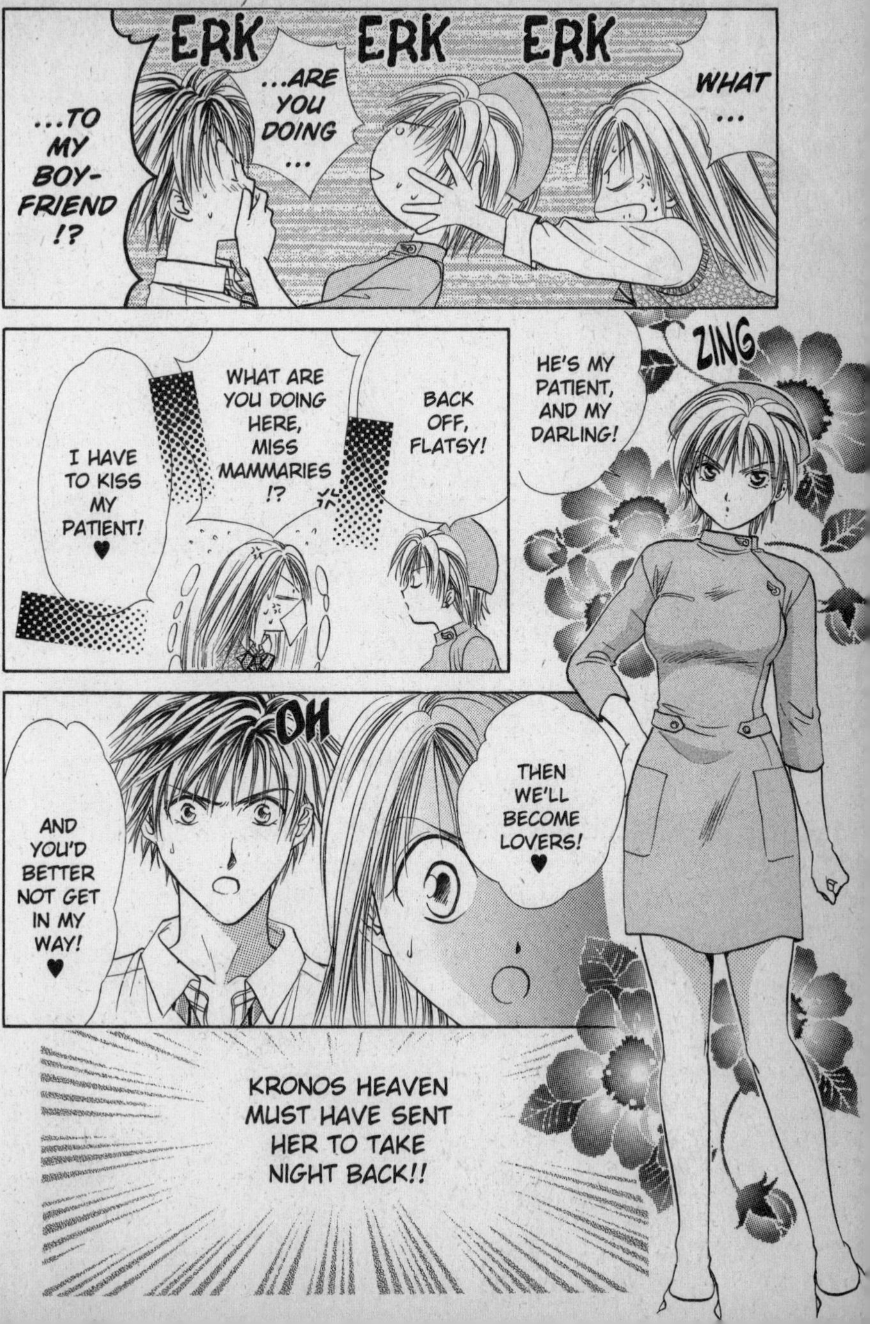
ERK ERK ERK
WHAT...
...ARE YOU DOING...
...TO MY BOY-FRIEND!?
ZING
HE'S MY PATIENT, AND MY DARLING!
BACK OFF, FLATSY!
WHAT ARE YOU DOING HERE, MISS MAMMARIES!?
I HAVE TO KISS MY PATIENT! ♥
OH
THEN WE'LL BECOME LOVERS! ♥
AND YOU'D BETTER NOT GET IN MY WAY! ♥
KRONOS HEAVEN MUST HAVE SENT HER TO TAKE NIGHT BACK!!

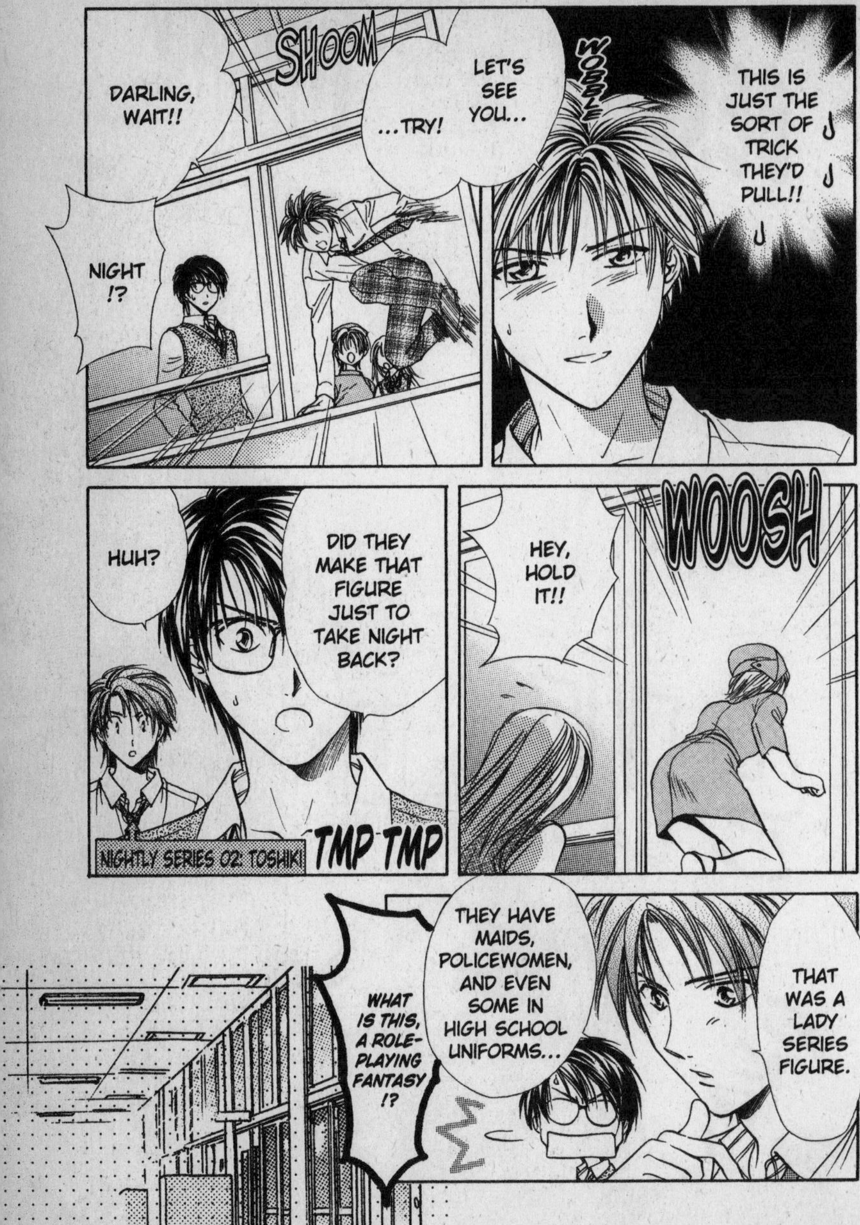
WOBBLE
THIS IS JUST THE SORT OF TRICK THEY'D PULL!!
SHOOM
LET'S SEE YOU...
...TRY!
DARLING, WAIT!!
NIGHT !?
WOOSH
HEY, HOLD IT!!
DID THEY MAKE THAT FIGURE JUST TO TAKE NIGHT BACK?
HUH?
TMP TMP
NIGHTLY SERIES 02: TOSHIKI
THAT WAS A LADY SERIES FIGURE.
THEY HAVE MAIDS, POLICEWOMEN, AND EVEN SOME IN HIGH SCHOOL UNIFORMS...
WHAT IS THIS, A ROLE-PLAYING FANTASY !?

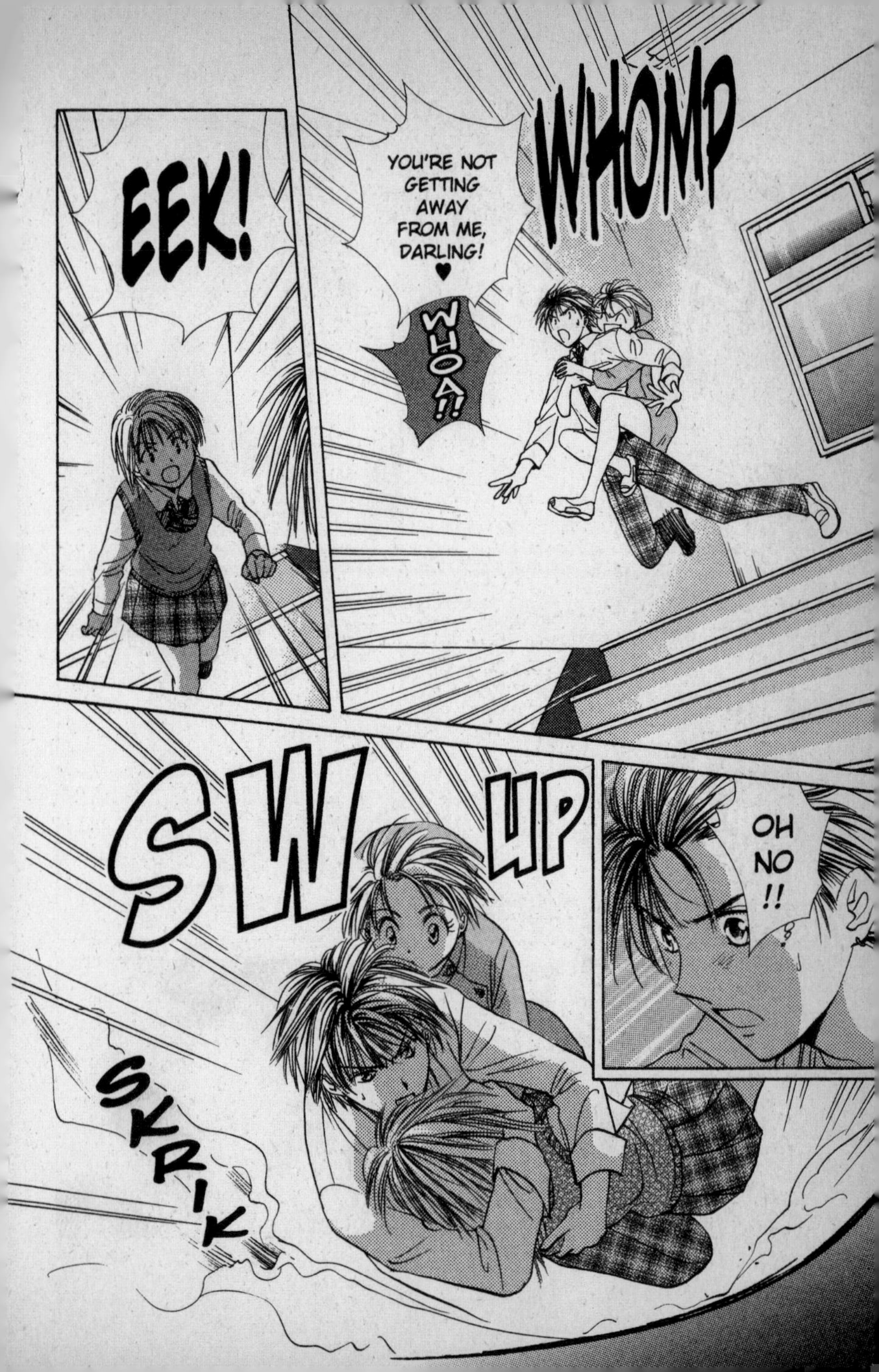
WHOMP
YOU'RE NOT GETTING AWAY FROM ME, DARLING! ♥
WHOA!!
EEK!
OH NO !!
SW UP
SKRIK

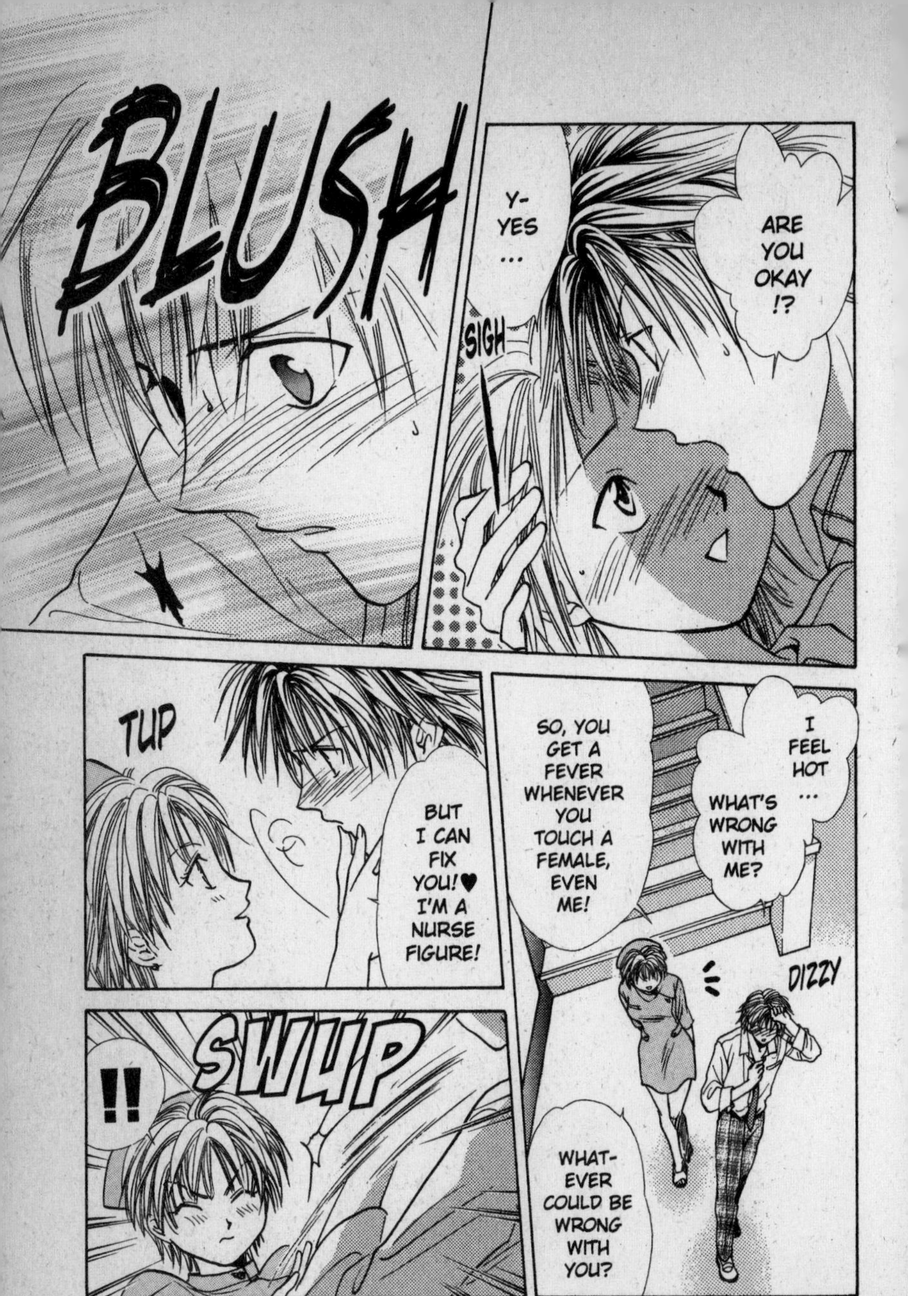
ARE YOU OKAY !?
Y- YES ...
SIGH
BLUSH
I FEEL HOT ...
WHAT'S WRONG WITH ME?
SO, YOU GET A FEVER WHENEVER YOU TOUCH A FEMALE, EVEN ME!
DIZZY
WHAT-EVER COULD BE WRONG WITH YOU?
BUT I CAN FIX YOU!♥ I'M A NURSE FIGURE!
TUP
SWUP
!!

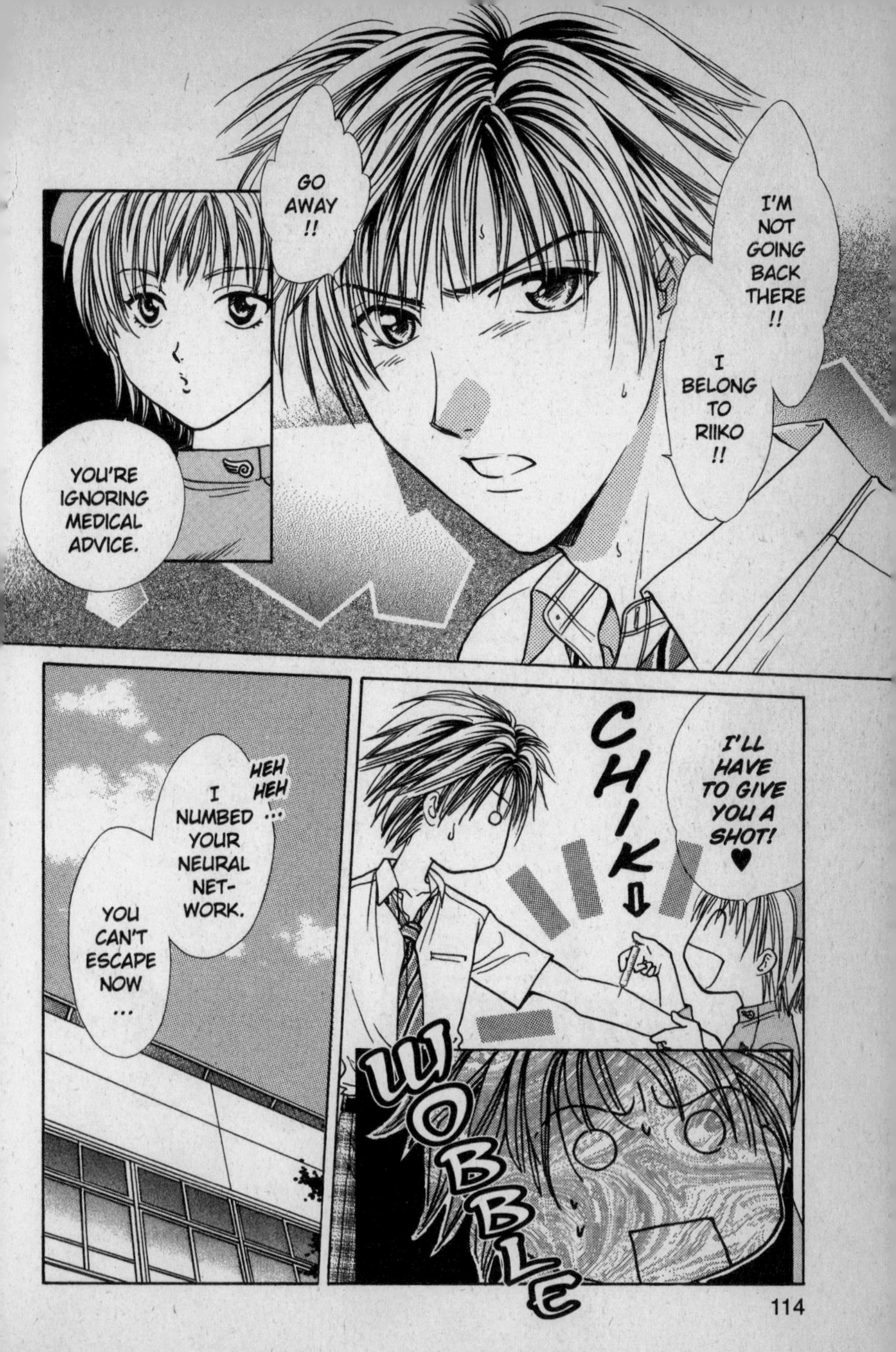
I'M NOT GOING BACK THERE !!
I BELONG TO RIIKO !!
GO AWAY !!
YOU'RE IGNORING MEDICAL ADVICE.
I'LL HAVE TO GIVE YOU A SHOT! ♥
CHIK
WOBBLE
HEH HEH ...
I NUMBED YOUR NEURAL NET-WORK.
YOU CAN'T ESCAPE NOW ...

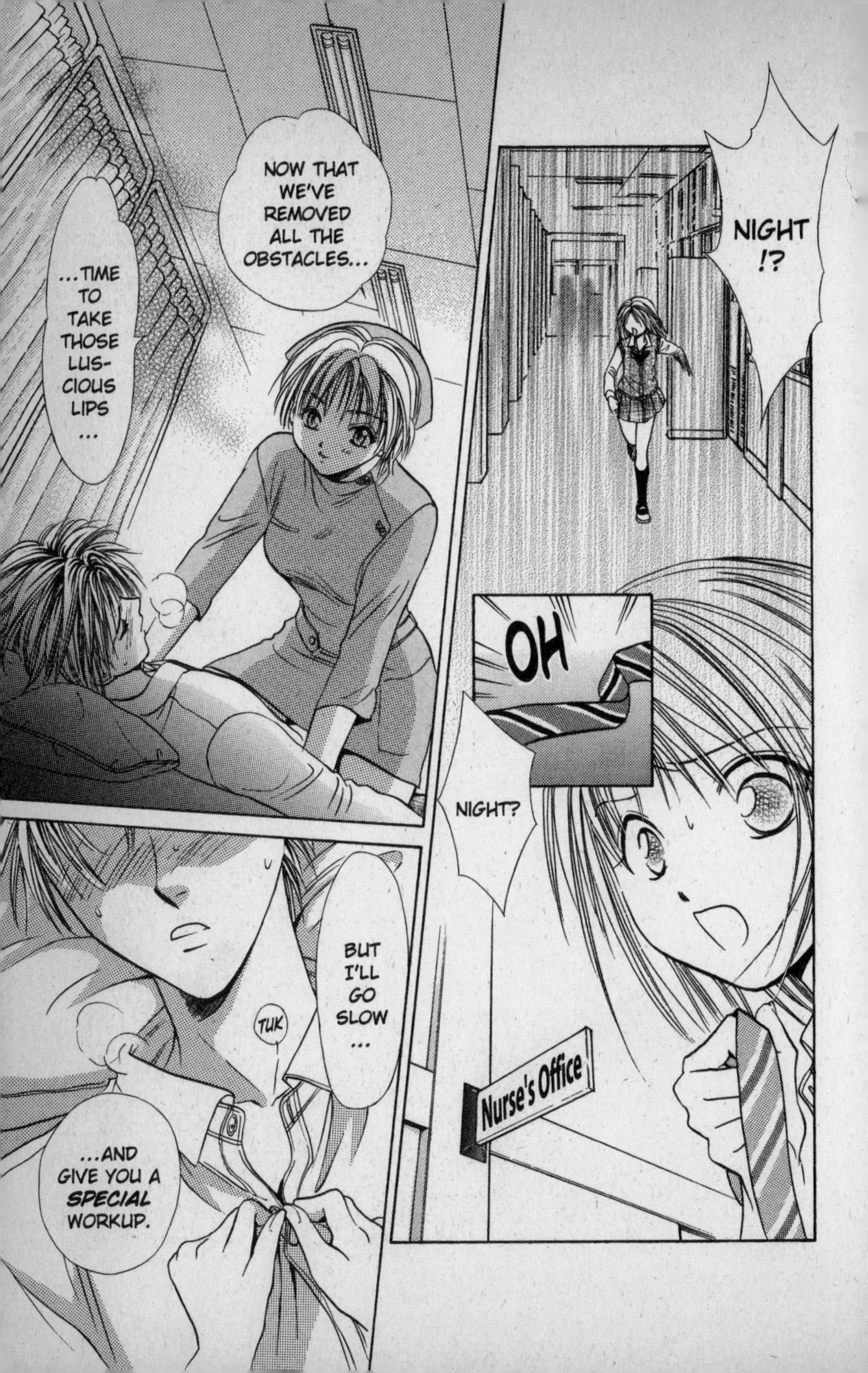
NIGHT !?
OH
NIGHT?
Nurse's Office
NOW THAT WE'VE REMOVED ALL THE OBSTACLES...
...TIME TO TAKE THOSE LUS-CIOUS LIPS ...
BUT I'LL GO SLOW ...
TUK
...AND GIVE YOU A *SPECIAL* WORKUP.

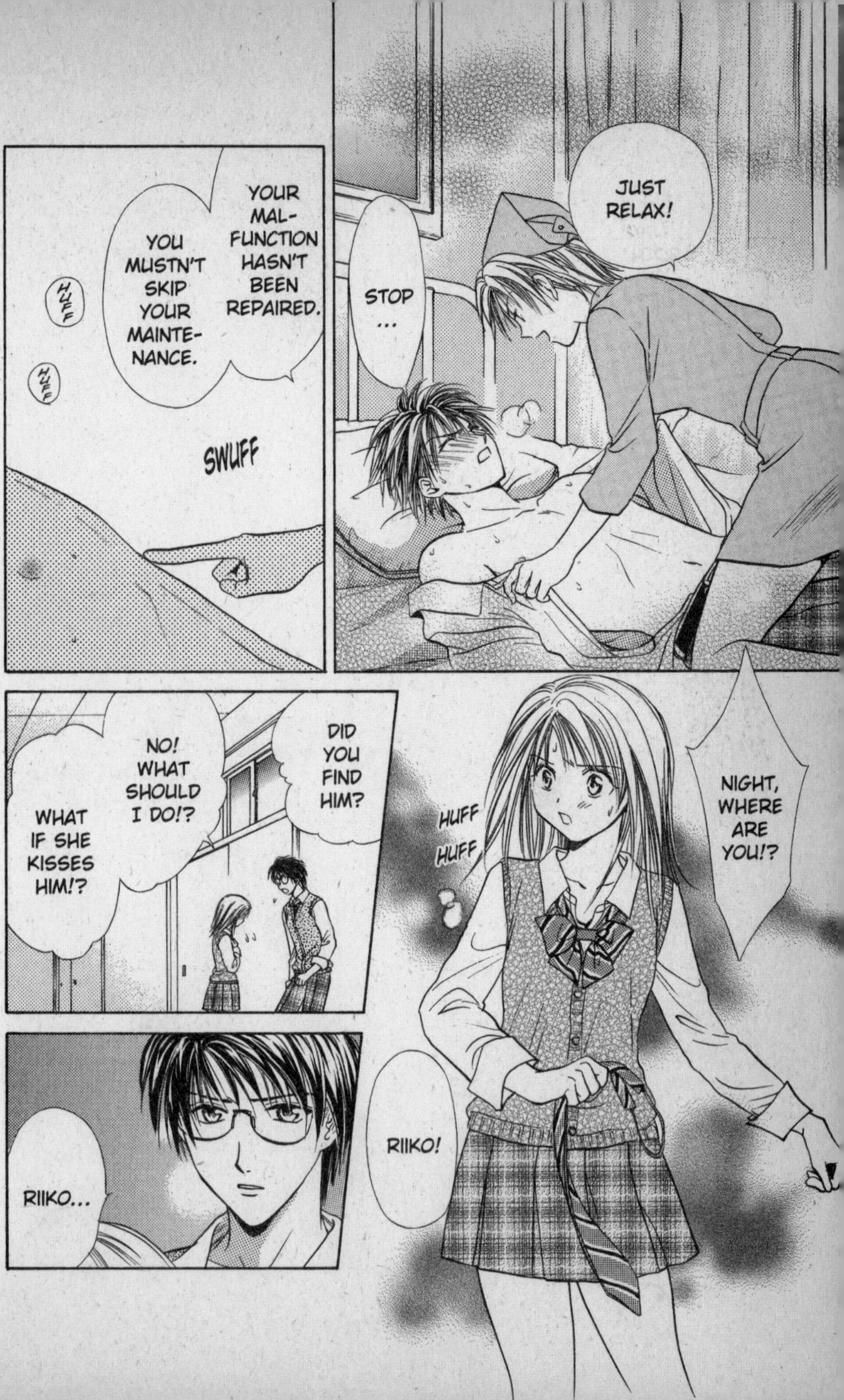
JUST RELAX!
STOP...
YOUR MAL-FUNCTION HASN'T BEEN REPAIRED.
YOU MUSTN'T SKIP YOUR MAINTE-NANCE.
HUFF
HUFF
SWUFF
NIGHT, WHERE ARE YOU!?
HUFF
HUFF
RIIKO!
DID YOU FIND HIM?
NO! WHAT SHOULD I DO!?
WHAT IF SHE KISSES HIM!?
RIIKO...

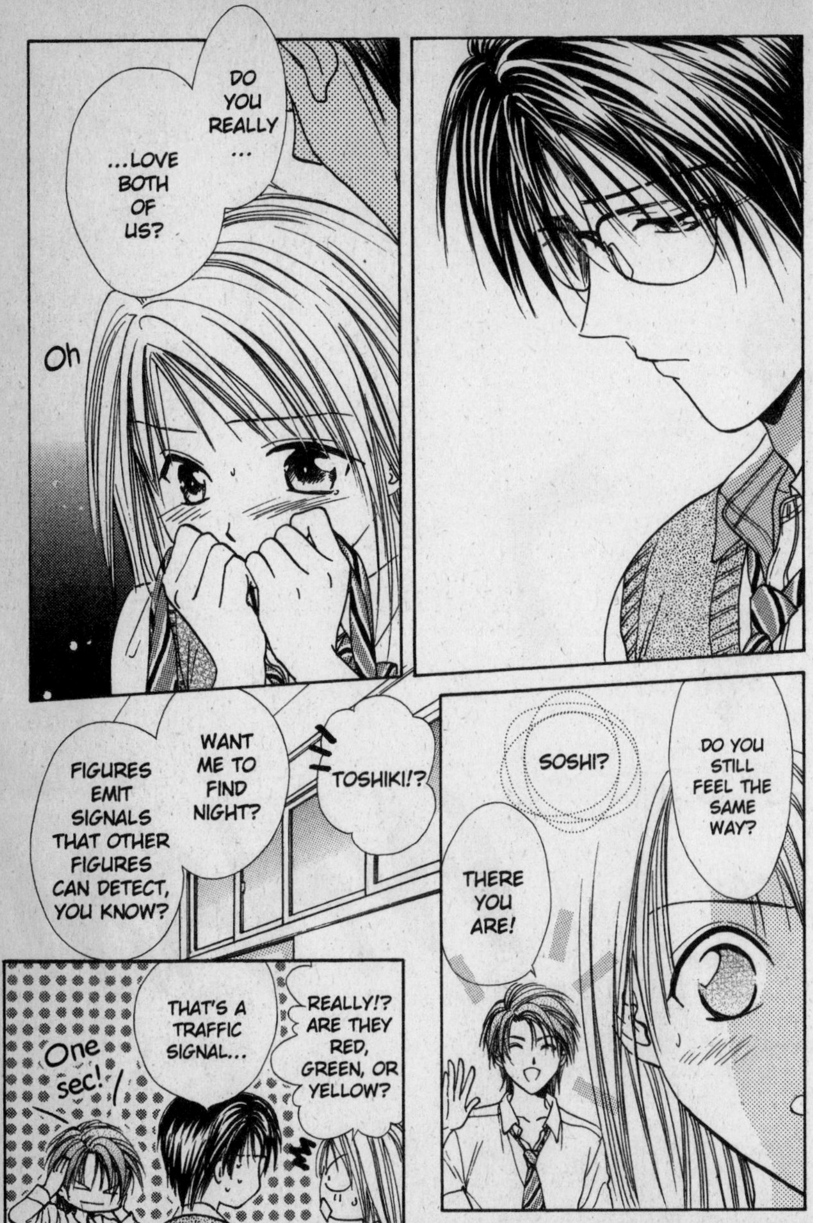
DO YOU REALLY ...
...LOVE BOTH OF US?
Oh
DO YOU STILL FEEL THE SAME WAY?
SOSHI?
THERE YOU ARE!
TOSHIKI!?
WANT ME TO FIND NIGHT?
FIGURES EMIT SIGNALS THAT OTHER FIGURES CAN DETECT, YOU KNOW?
REALLY!? ARE THEY RED, GREEN, OR YELLOW?
THAT'S A TRAFFIC SIGNAL...
One sec!

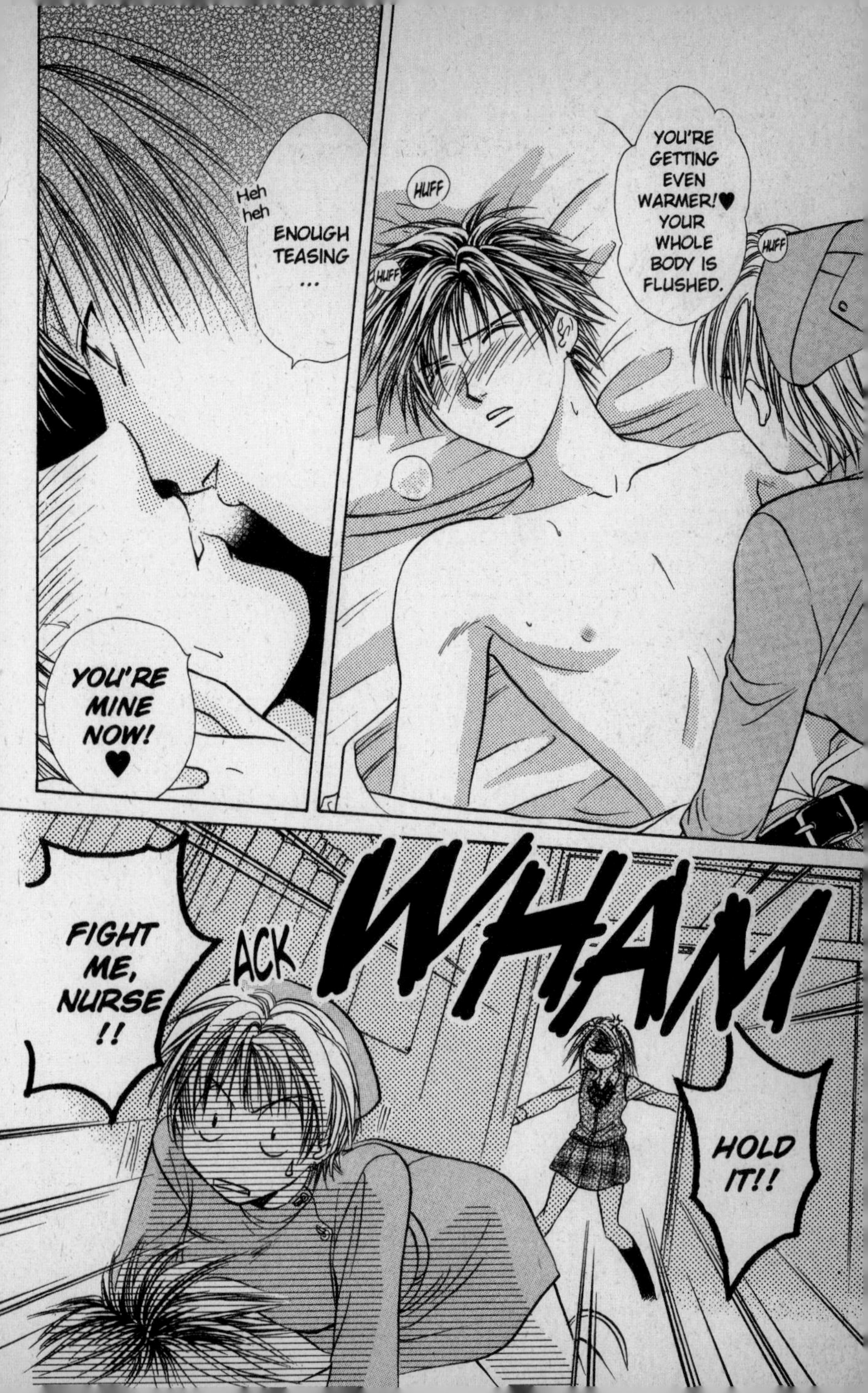

YOU'RE GETTING EVEN WARMER! ♥ YOUR WHOLE BODY IS FLUSHED.
HUFF
HUFF
HUFF
Heh heh
ENOUGH TEASING ...
YOU'RE MINE NOW! ♥
WHAM
HOLD IT!!
ACK
FIGHT ME, NURSE!!

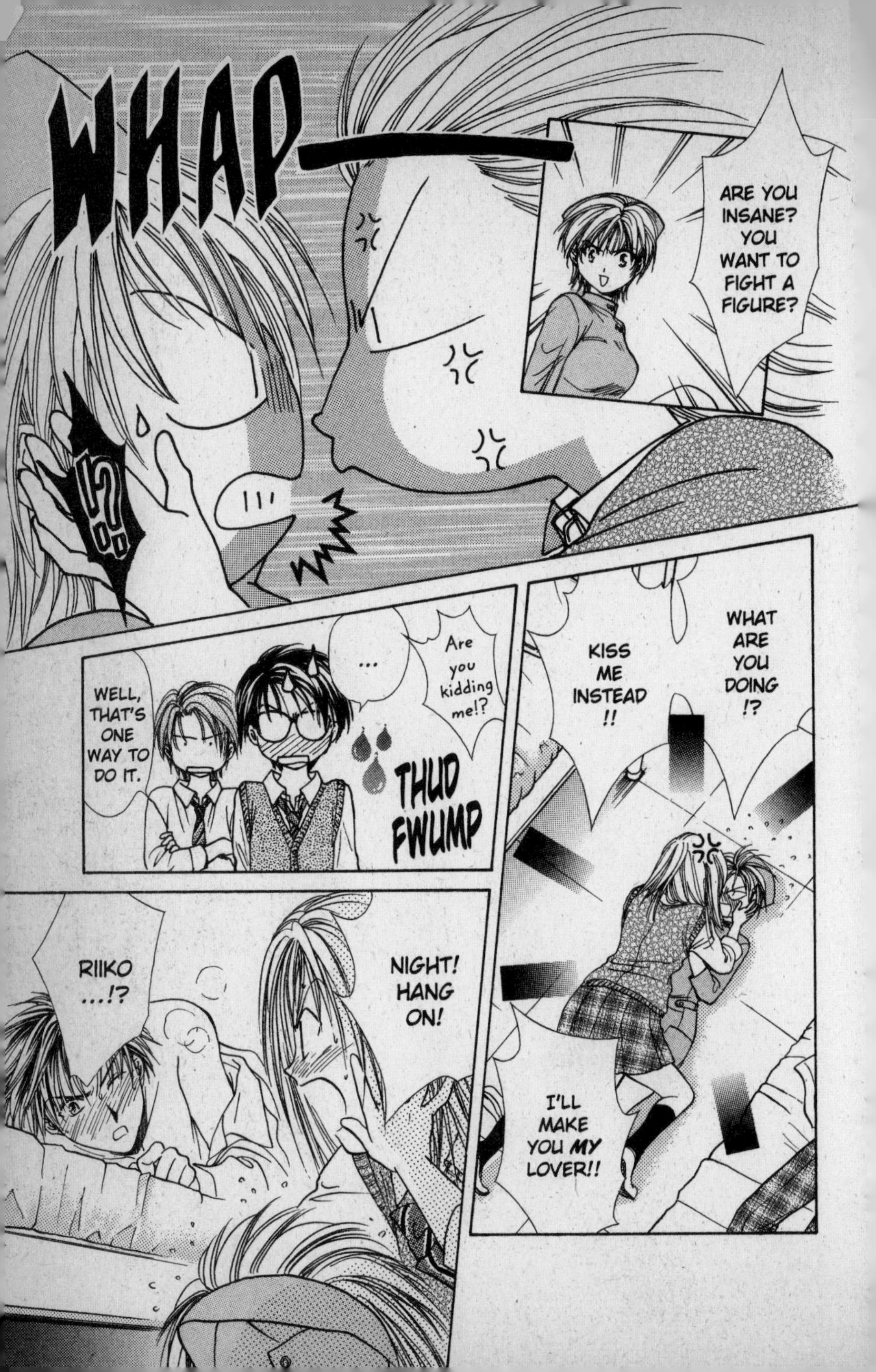
ARE YOU INSANE? YOU WANT TO FIGHT A FIGURE?
WHAP
!?
WHAT ARE YOU DOING !?
KISS ME INSTEAD !!
I'LL MAKE YOU MY LOVER!!
Are you kidding me!?
...
WELL, THAT'S ONE WAY TO DO IT.
THUD
FWUMP
NIGHT! HANG ON!
RIIKO ...!?

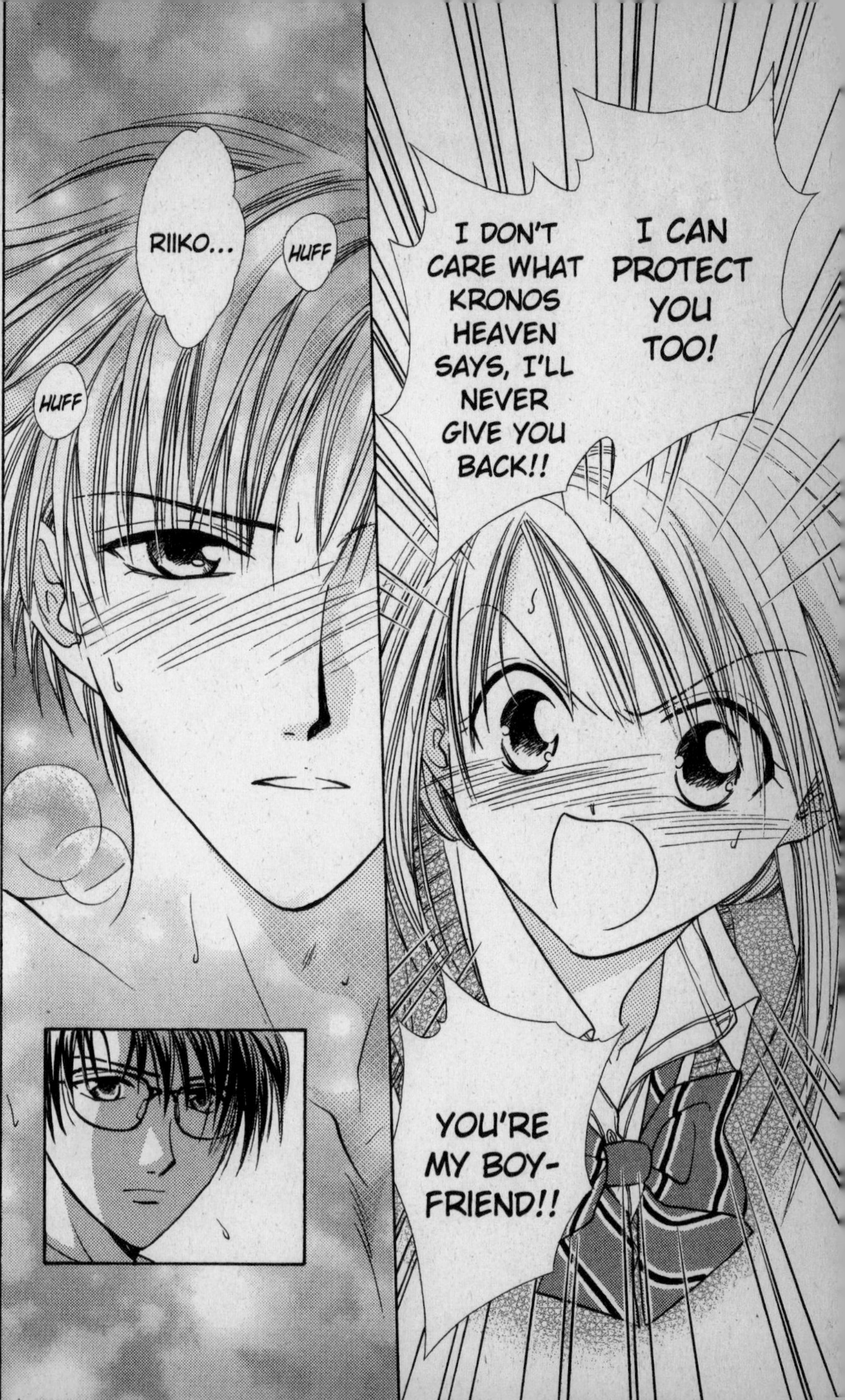
I CAN PROTECT YOU TOO!
I DON'T CARE WHAT KRONOS HEAVEN SAYS, I'LL NEVER GIVE YOU BACK!!
YOU'RE MY BOY-FRIEND!!
HUFF
RIIKO...
HUFF

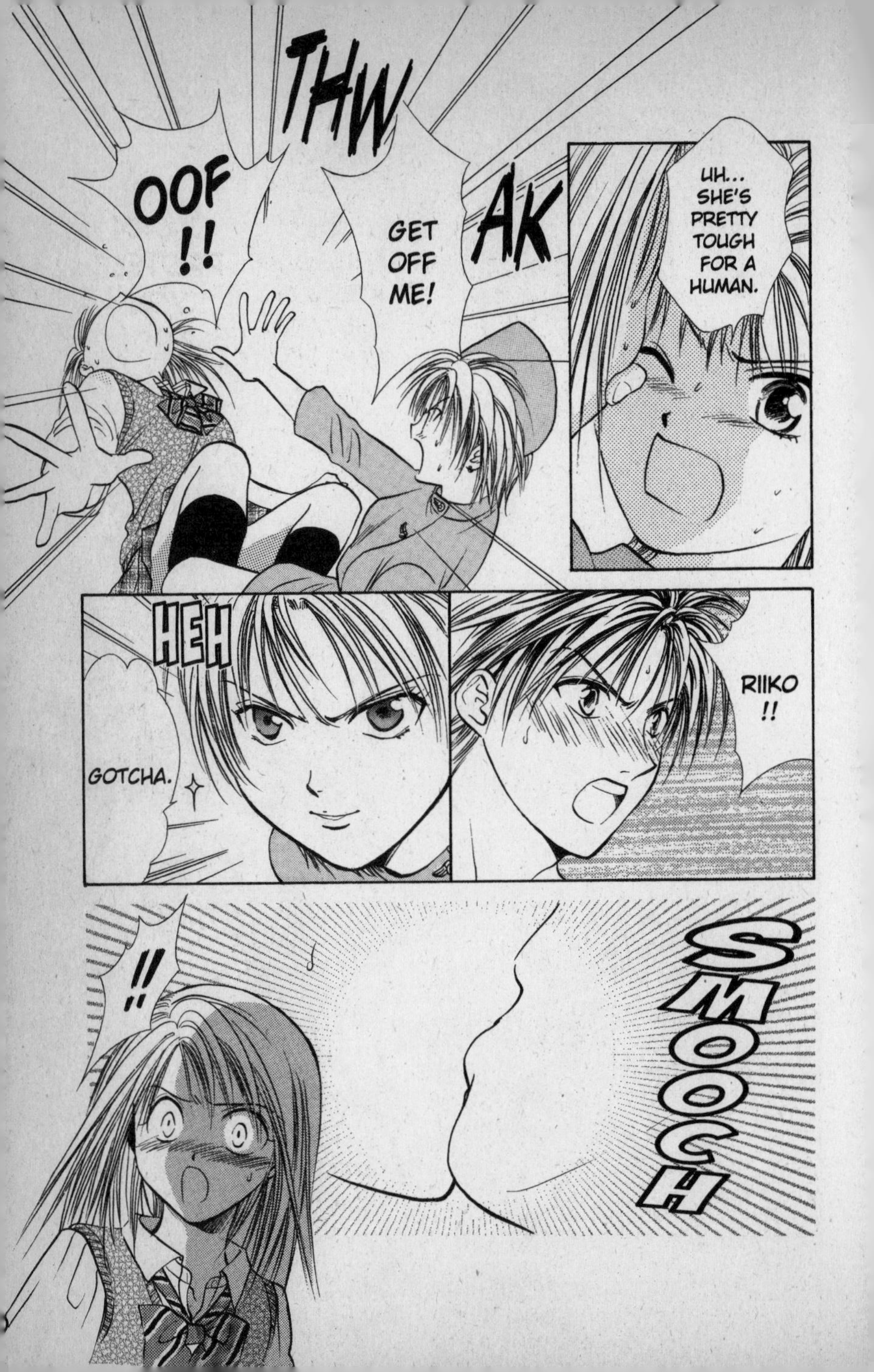
THWAK
GET OFF ME!
OOF!!
UH... SHE'S PRETTY TOUGH FOR A HUMAN.
RIIKO!!
HEH
GOTCHA.
SMOOCH
!!

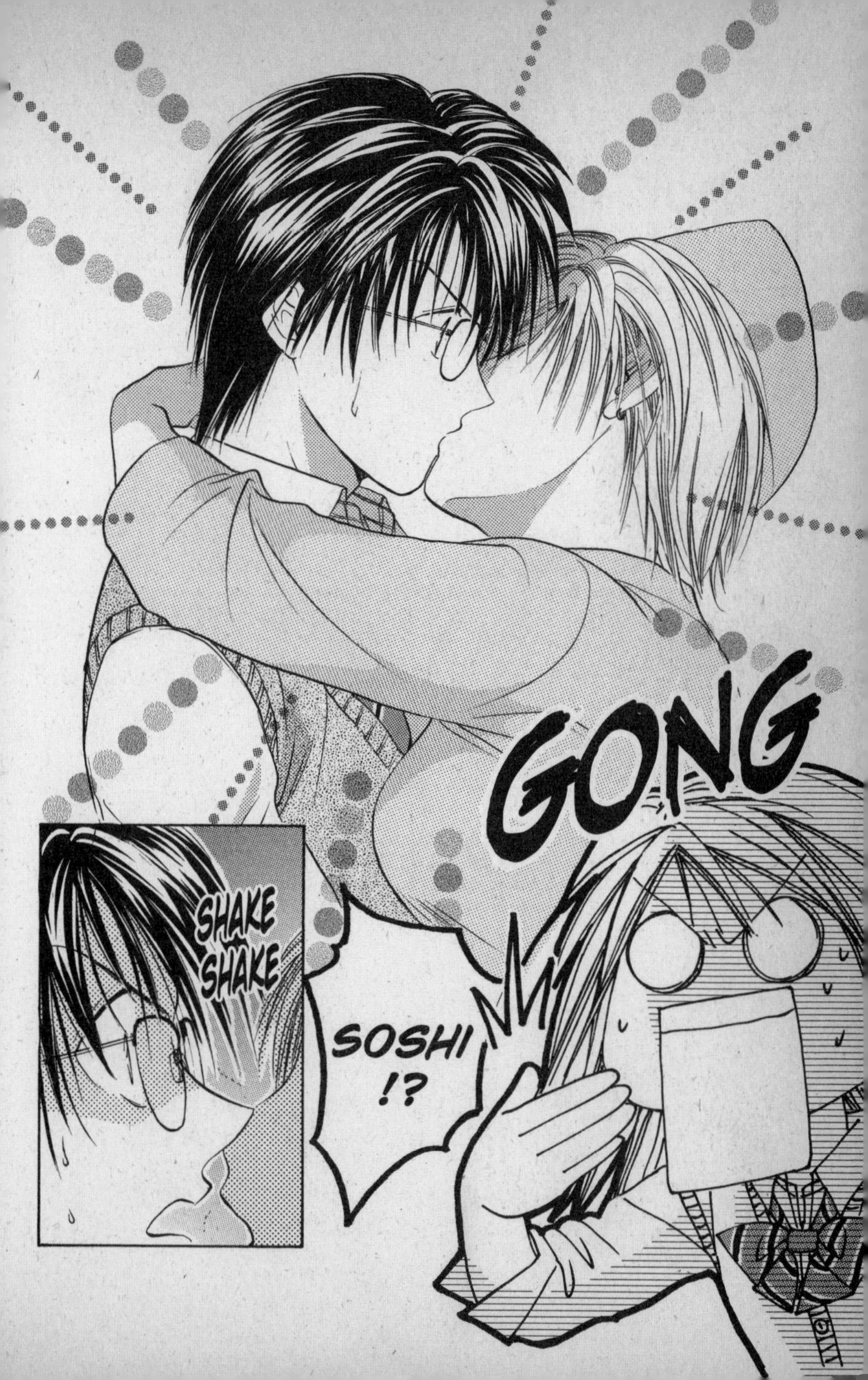
GONG
SOSHI !?
SHAKE SHAKE

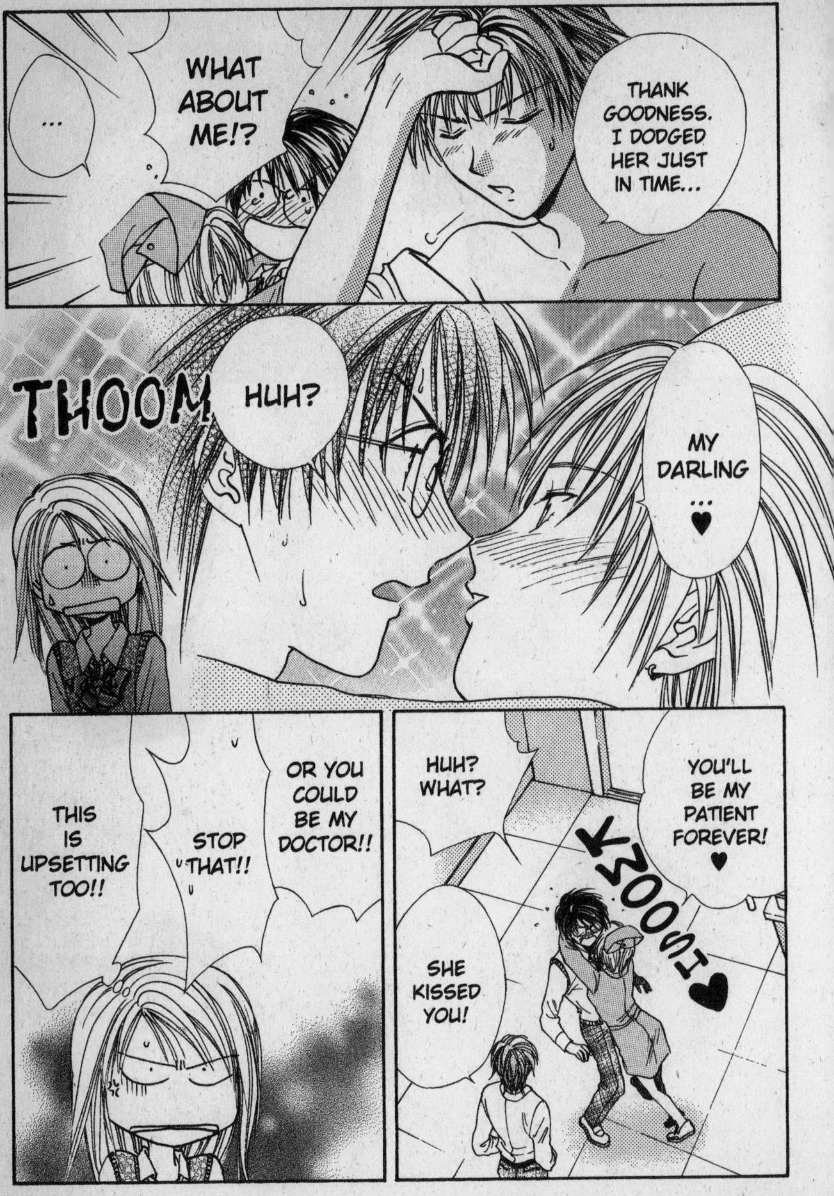
THANK GOODNESS. I DODGED HER JUST IN TIME...
WHAT ABOUT ME!?
...
MY DARLING ... ♥
HUH?
THOOM
YOU'LL BE MY PATIENT FOREVER! ♥
HUH? WHAT?
SHE KISSED YOU!
OR YOU COULD BE MY DOCTOR!!
STOP THAT!!
THIS IS UPSETTING TOO!!

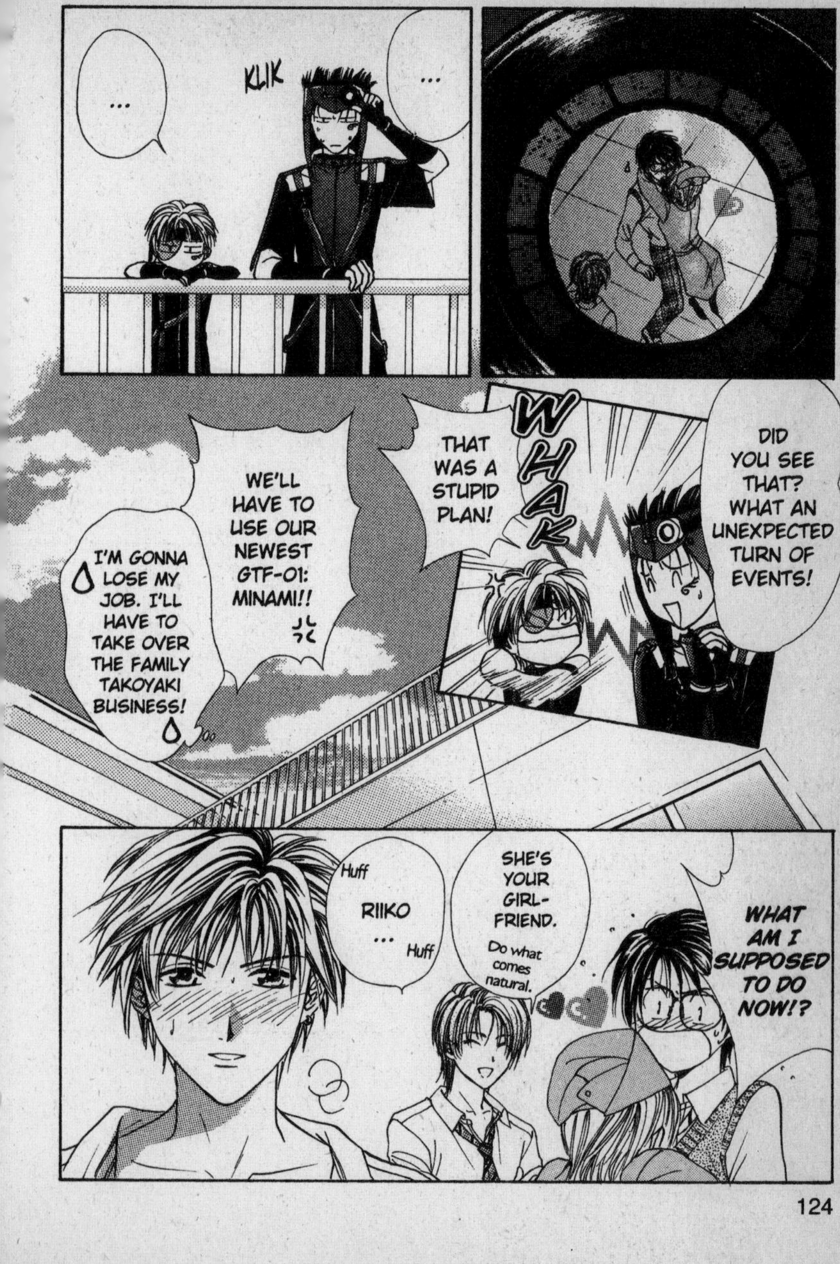
...
KLIK
...
DID YOU SEE THAT? WHAT AN UNEXPECTED TURN OF EVENTS!
WHAK
THAT WAS A STUPID PLAN!
WE'LL HAVE TO USE OUR NEWEST GTF-01: MINAMI!!
I'M GONNA LOSE MY JOB. I'LL HAVE TO TAKE OVER THE FAMILY TAKOYAKI BUSINESS!
WHAT AM I SUPPOSED TO DO NOW!?
SHE'S YOUR GIRL-FRIEND.
Do what comes natural.
Huff
RIIKO ...
Huff

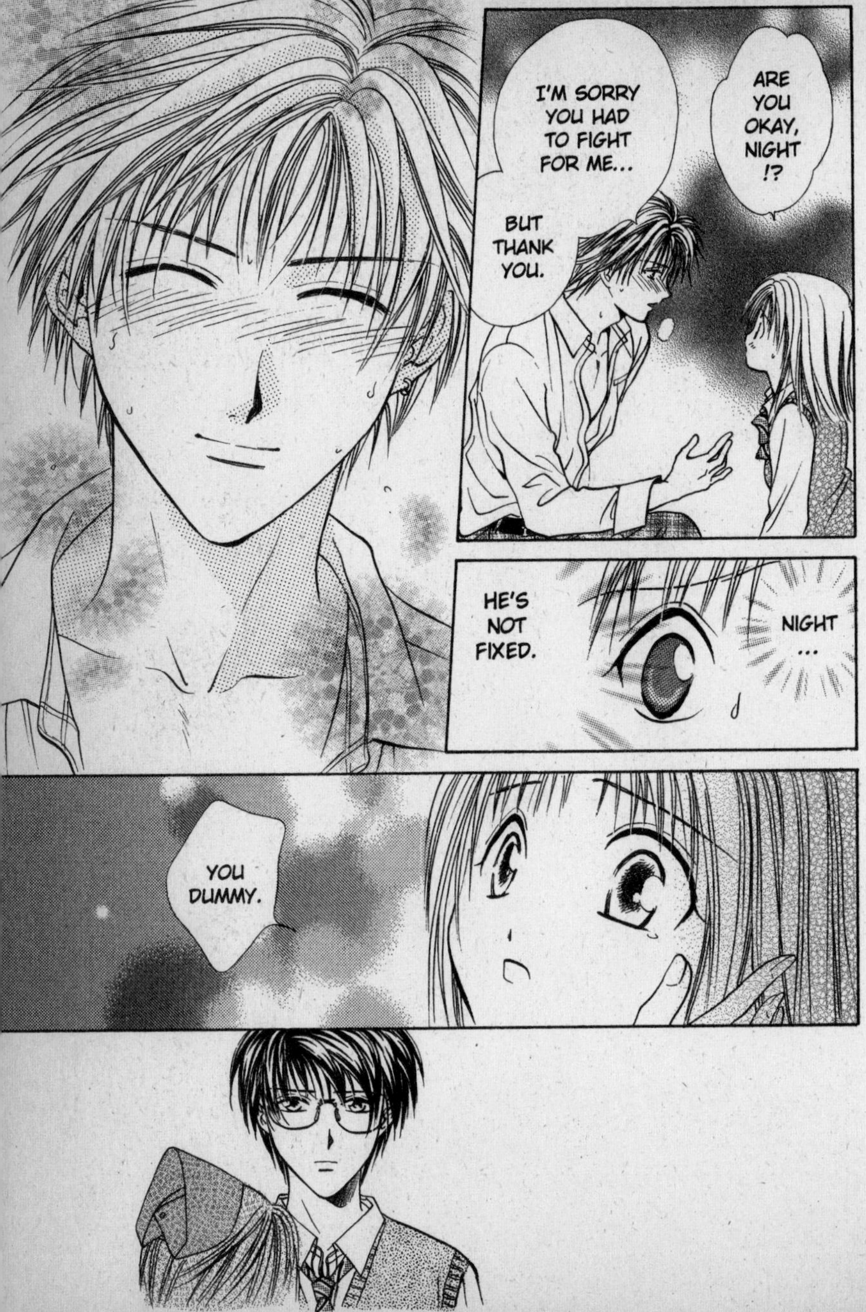
ARE YOU OKAY, NIGHT!?
I'M SORRY YOU HAD TO FIGHT FOR ME...
BUT THANK YOU.
NIGHT...
HE'S NOT FIXED.
YOU DUMMY.

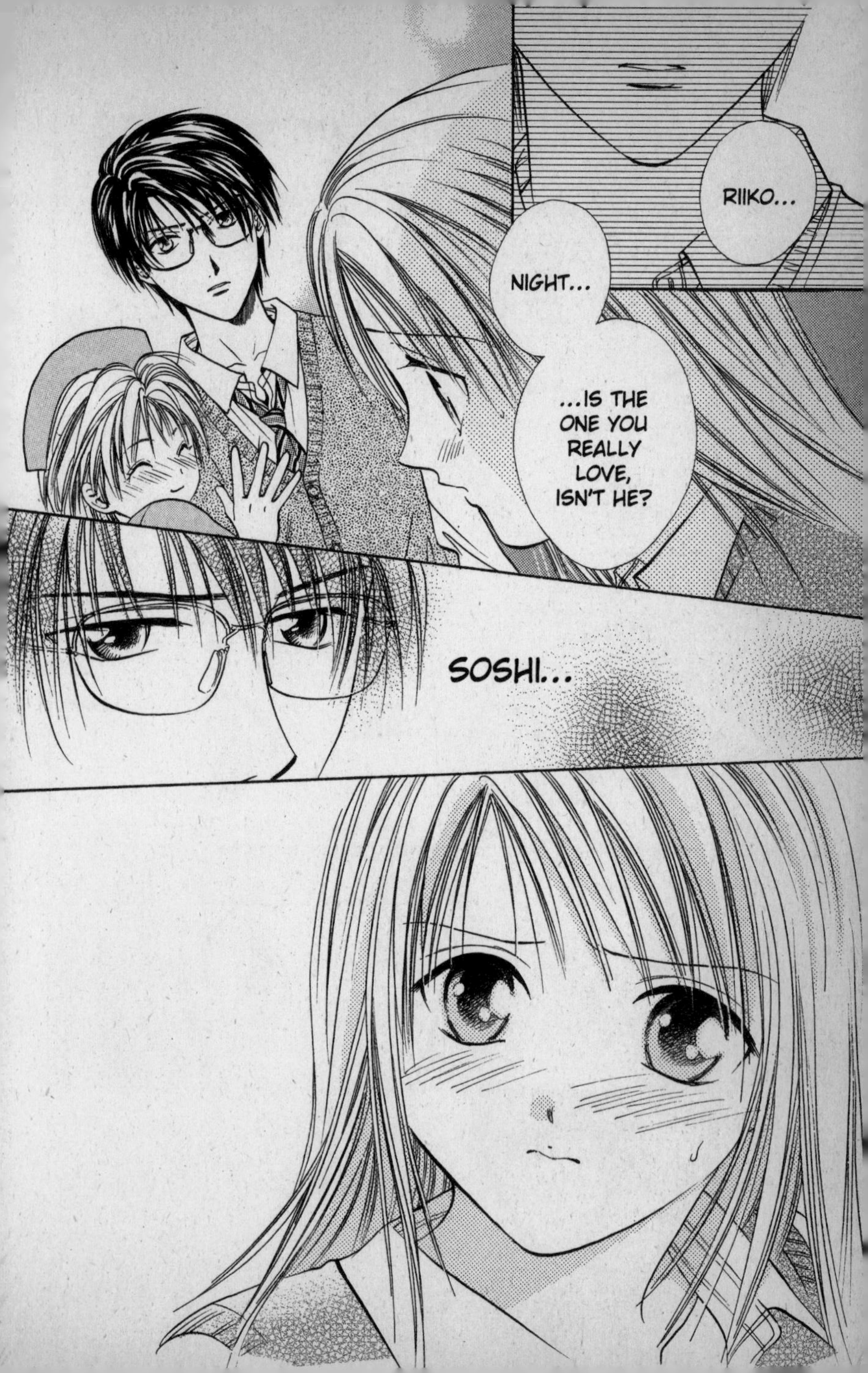
RIIKO...
NIGHT...
...IS THE ONE YOU REALLY LOVE, ISN'T HE?
SOSHI...

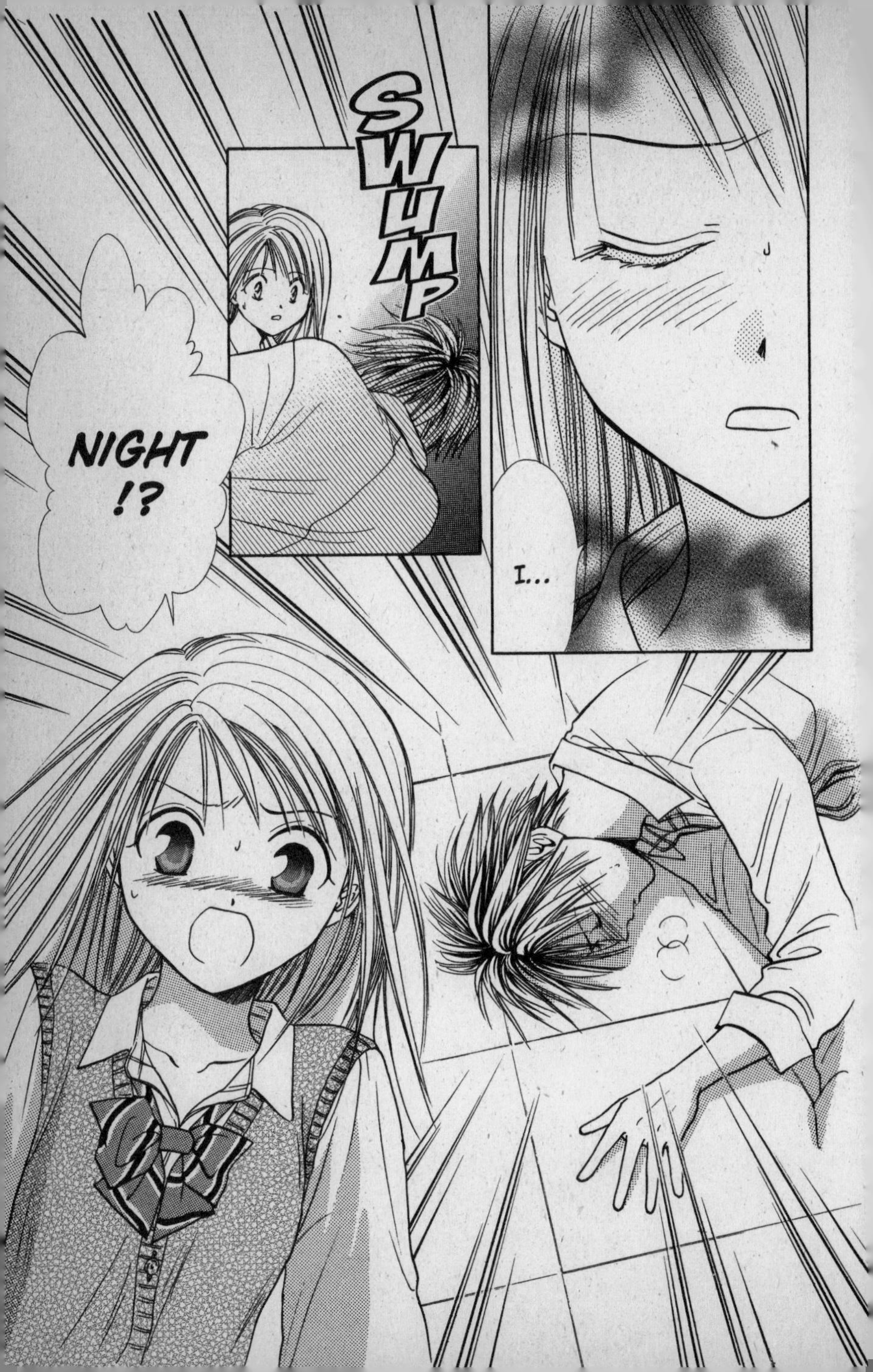
I...
SWUMP
NIGHT !?

Absolute Boyfriend

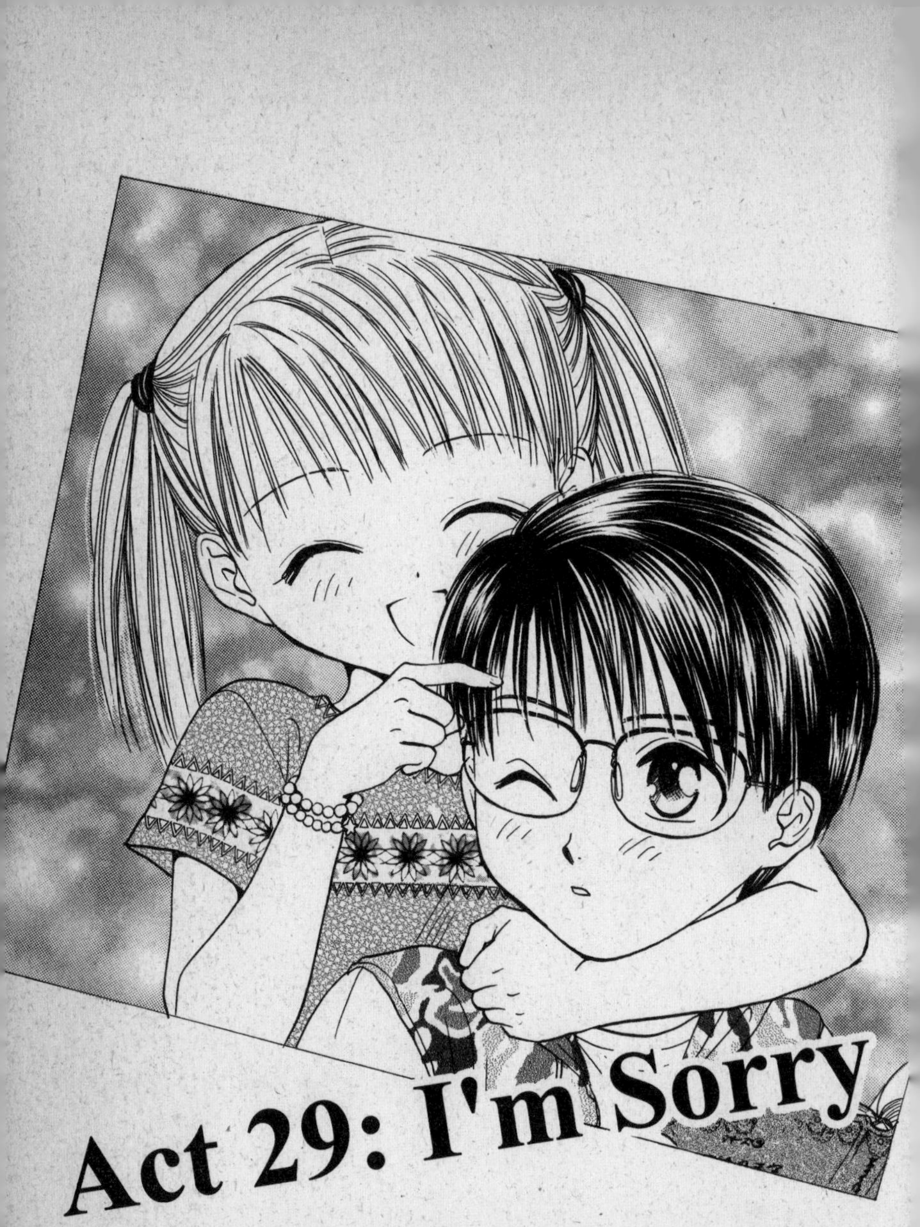

Act 29: I'm Sorry

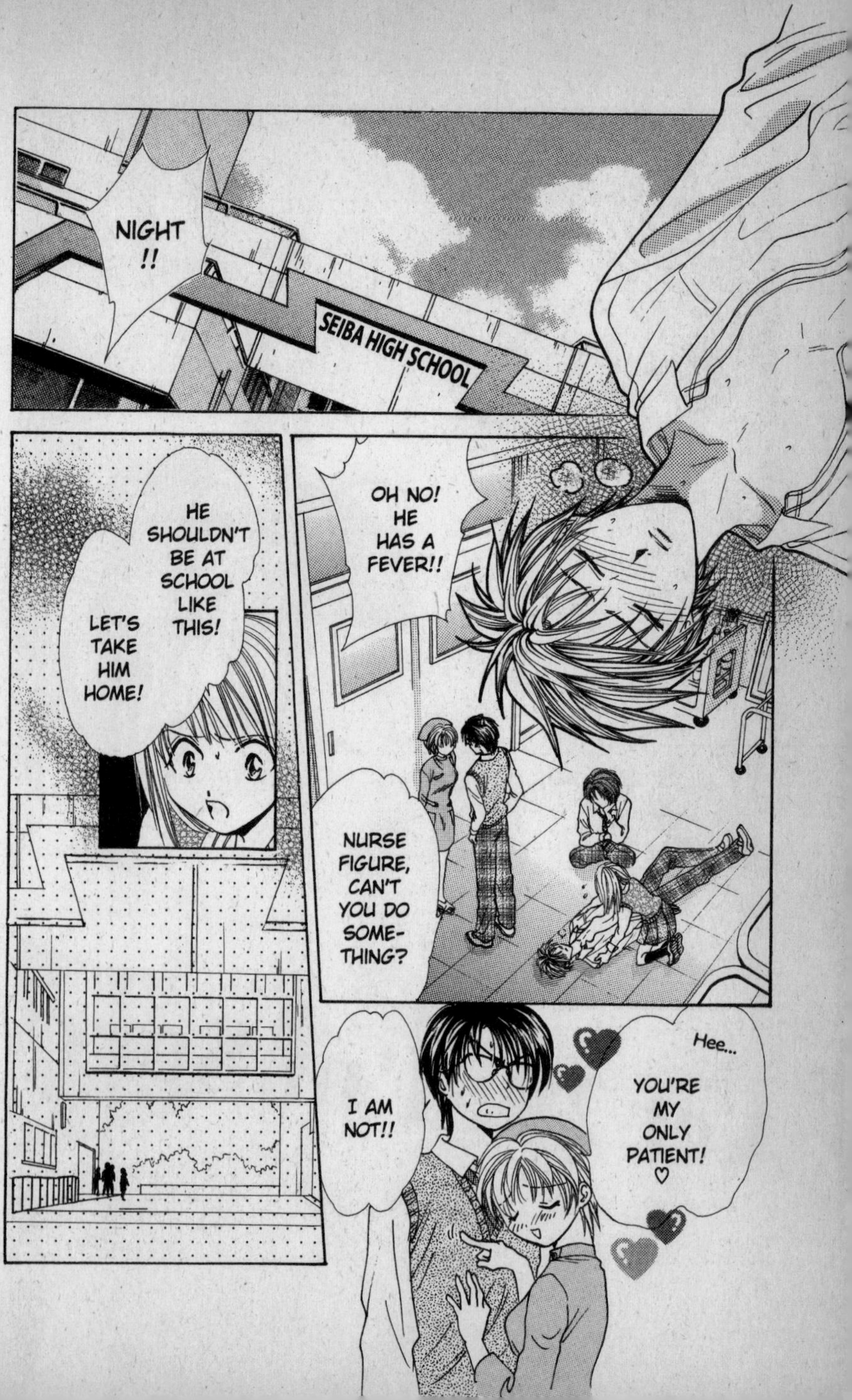
NIGHT!!
SEIBA HIGH SCHOOL
OH NO! HE HAS A FEVER!!
NURSE FIGURE, CAN'T YOU DO SOME-THING?
HE SHOULDN'T BE AT SCHOOL LIKE THIS!
LET'S TAKE HIM HOME!
Hee...
YOU'RE MY ONLY PATIENT! ♡
I AM NOT!!

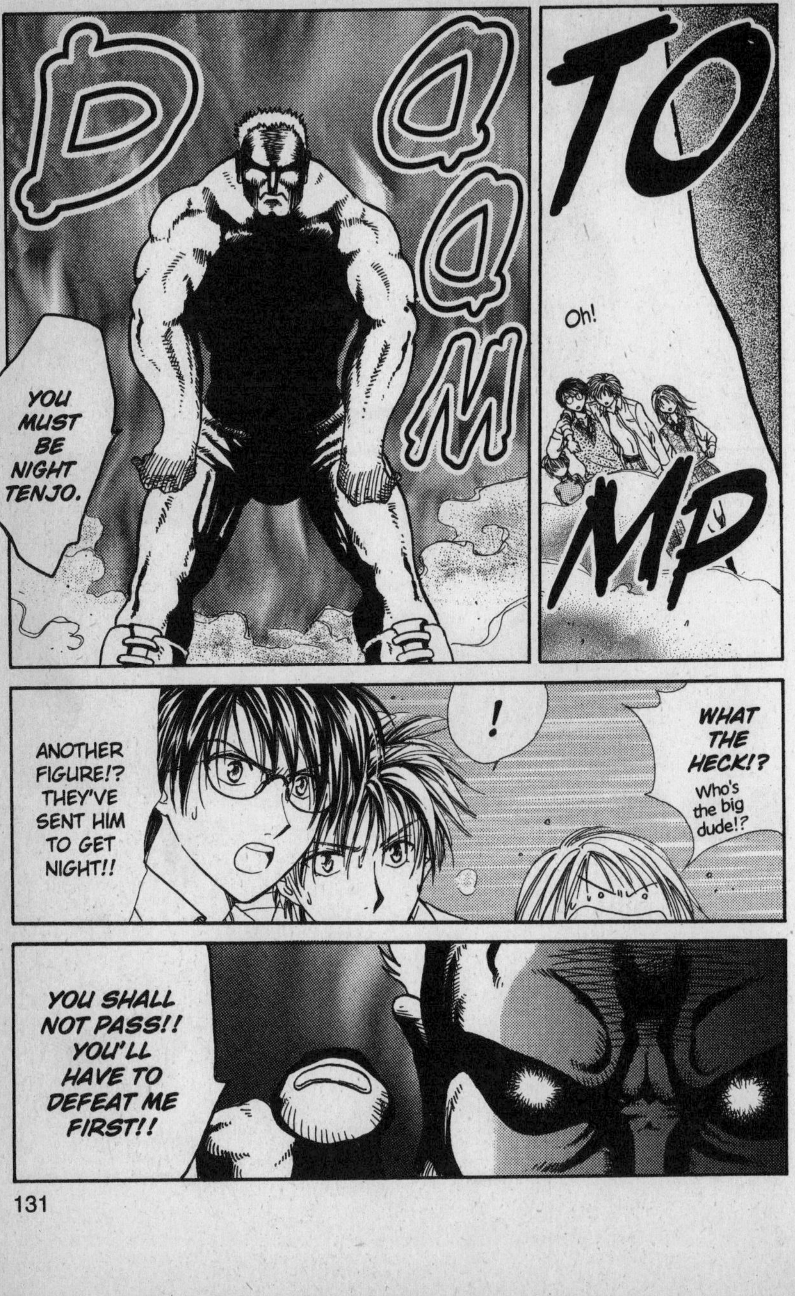
TO
Oh!
MP
DOOM
YOU MUST BE NIGHT TENJO.
WHAT THE HECK!?
Who's the big dude!?
!
ANOTHER FIGURE!? THEY'VE SENT HIM TO GET NIGHT!!
YOU SHALL NOT PASS!! YOU'LL HAVE TO DEFEAT ME FIRST!!

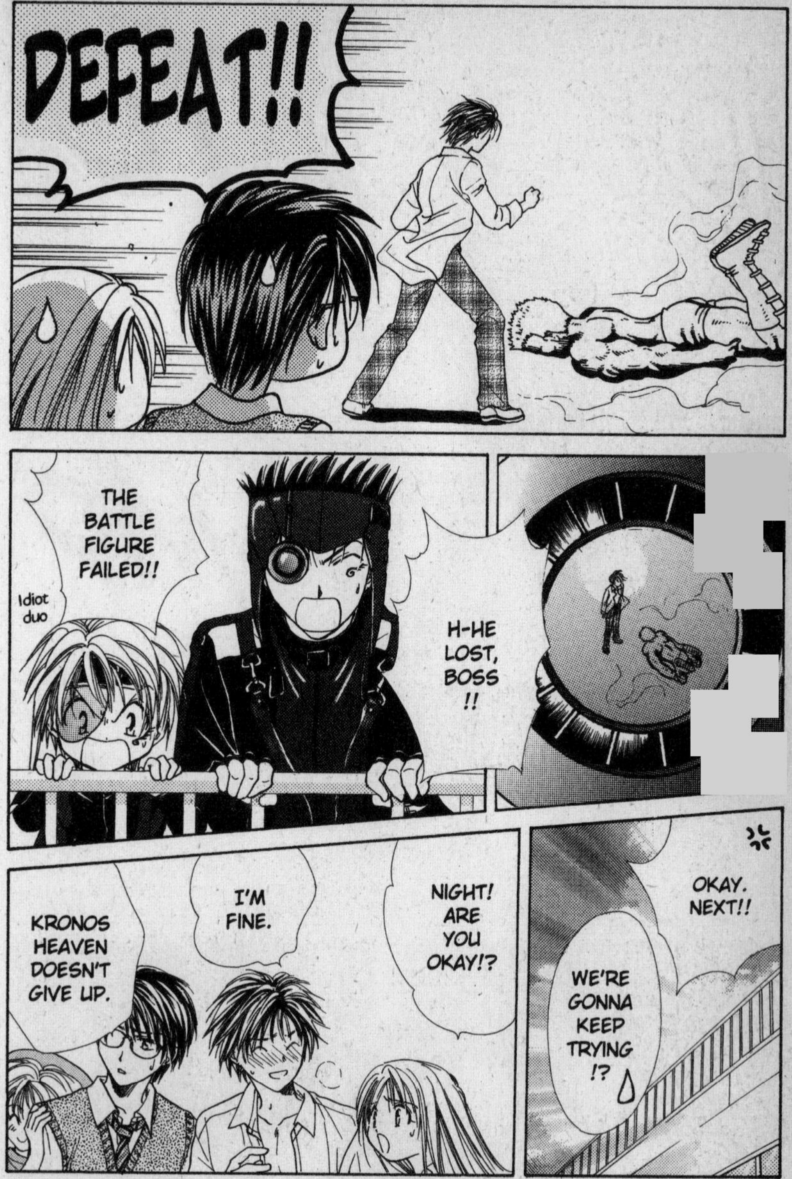
DEFEAT!!
H-HE LOST, BOSS!!
THE BATTLE FIGURE FAILED!!
Idiot duo
OKAY. NEXT!!
WE'RE GONNA KEEP TRYING!?
NIGHT! ARE YOU OKAY!?
I'M FINE.
KRONOS HEAVEN DOESN'T GIVE UP.

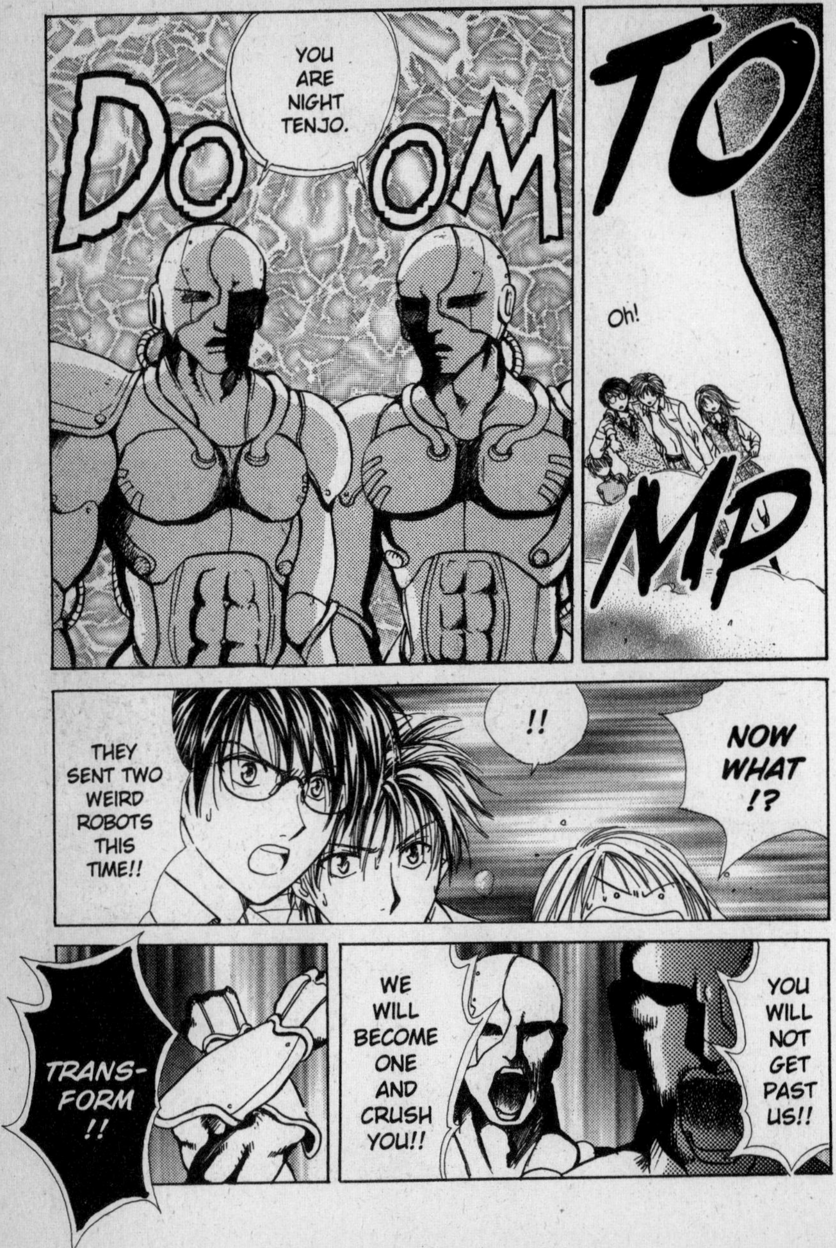
TO
MP
Oh!
YOU ARE NIGHT TENJO.
DO OM
NOW WHAT!?
!!
THEY SENT TWO WEIRD ROBOTS THIS TIME!!
YOU WILL NOT GET PAST US!!
WE WILL BECOME ONE AND CRUSH YOU!!
TRANS-FORM!!

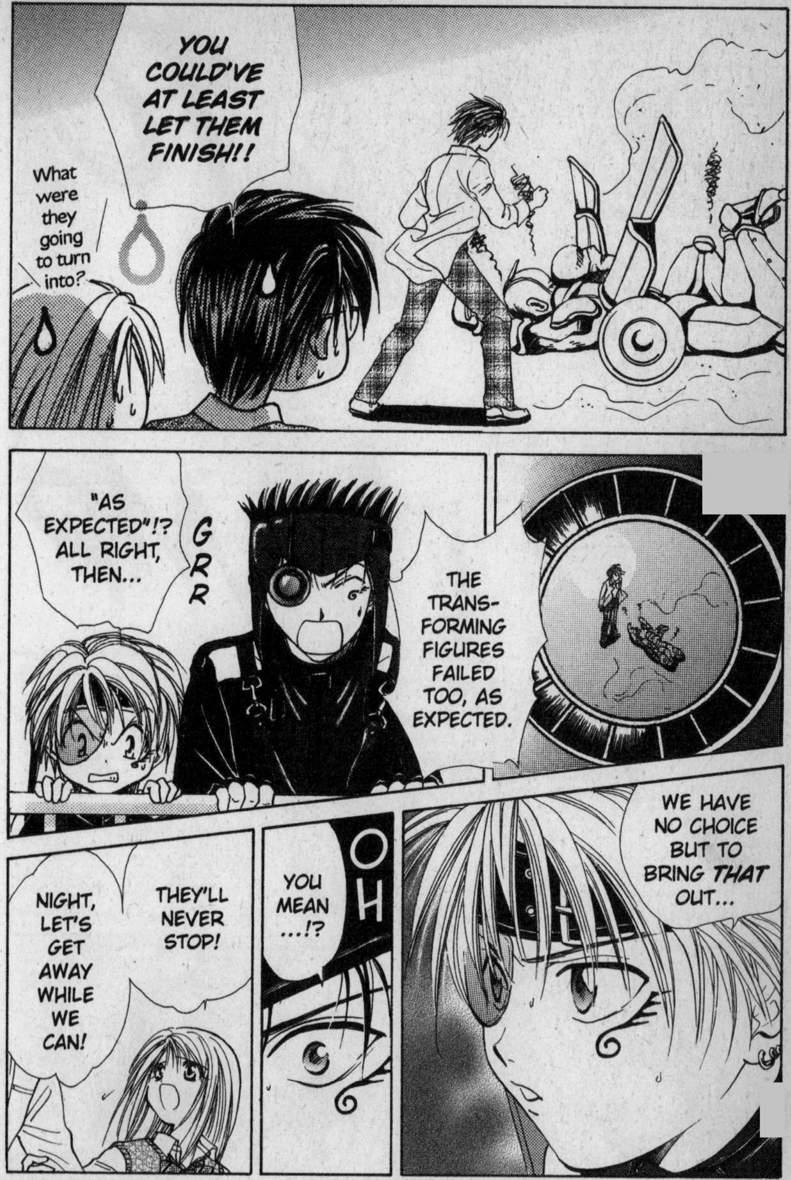
YOU COULD'VE AT LEAST LET THEM FINISH!!
What were they going to turn into?
THE TRANS-FORMING FIGURES FAILED TOO, AS EXPECTED.
"AS EXPECTED"!? ALL RIGHT, THEN...
GRR
WE HAVE NO CHOICE BUT TO BRING *THAT* OUT...
OH
YOU MEAN ...!?
THEY'LL NEVER STOP!
NIGHT, LET'S GET AWAY WHILE WE CAN!

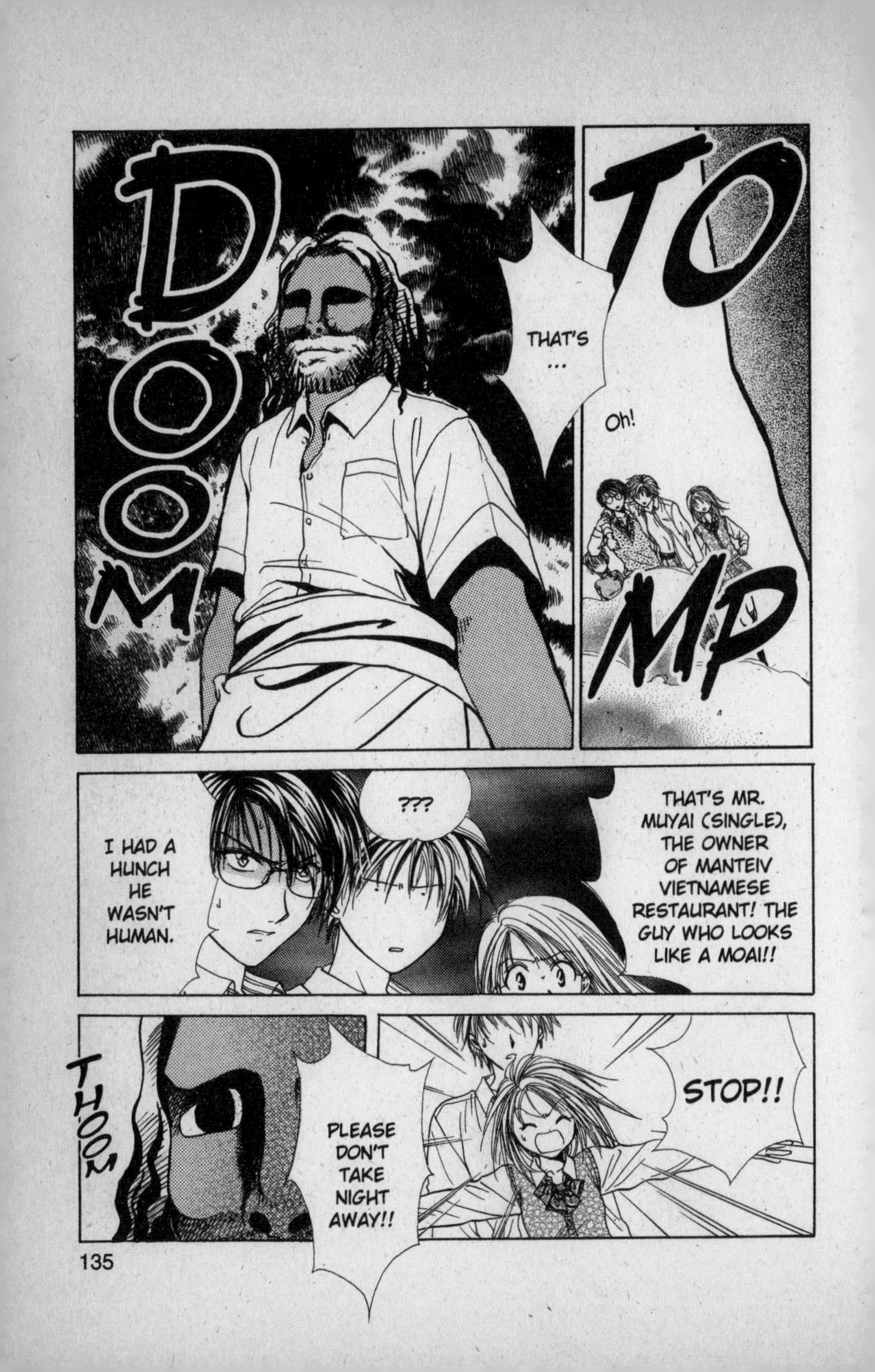

TO
THAT'S ...
Oh!
MP
DOOOM
THAT'S MR. MUYAI (SINGLE), THE OWNER OF MANTEIV VIETNAMESE RESTAURANT! THE GUY WHO LOOKS LIKE A MOAI!!
???
I HAD A HUNCH HE WASN'T HUMAN.
STOP!!
PLEASE DON'T TAKE NIGHT AWAY!!
THOOM

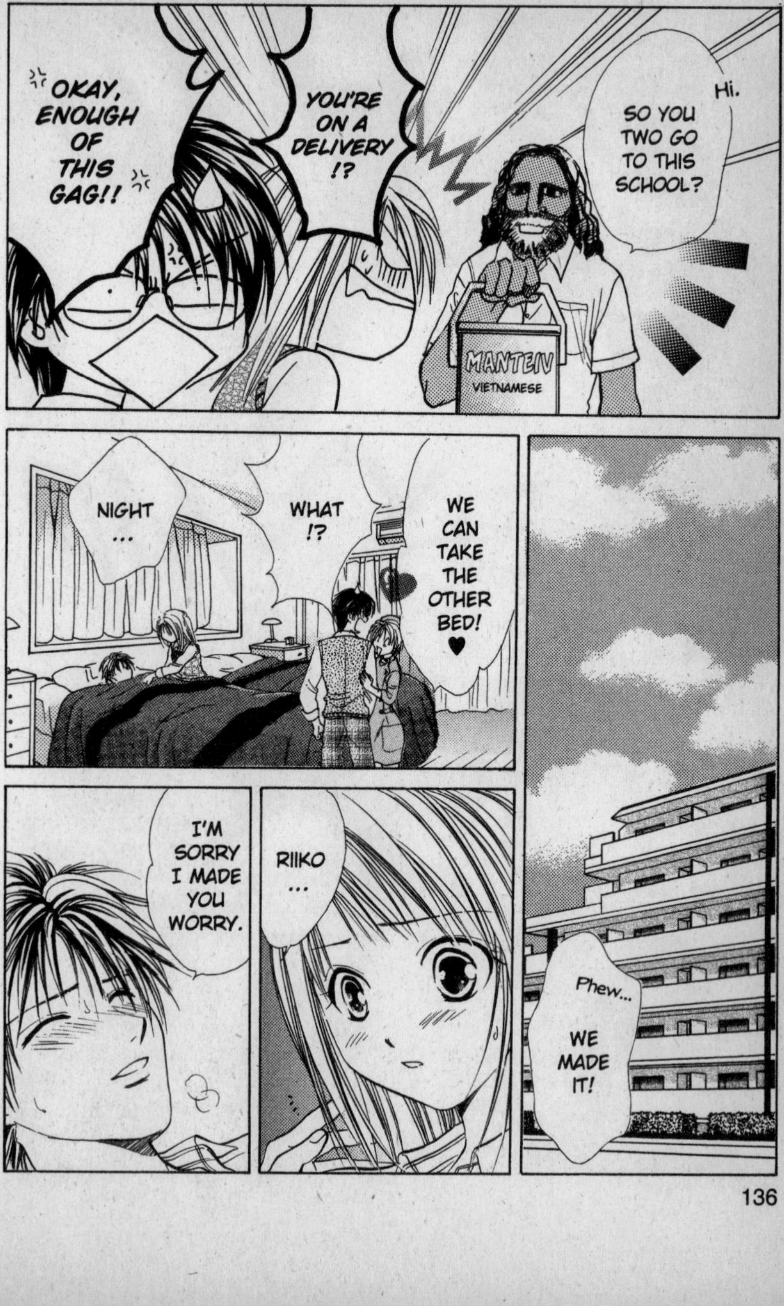
Hi.
SO YOU TWO GO TO THIS SCHOOL?
MANTEIV
VIETNAMESE
YOU'RE ON A DELIVERY!?
OKAY, ENOUGH OF THIS GAG!!
Phew...
WE MADE IT!
WE CAN TAKE THE OTHER BED! ♥
WHAT!?
NIGHT...
RIIKO...
I'M SORRY I MADE YOU WORRY.

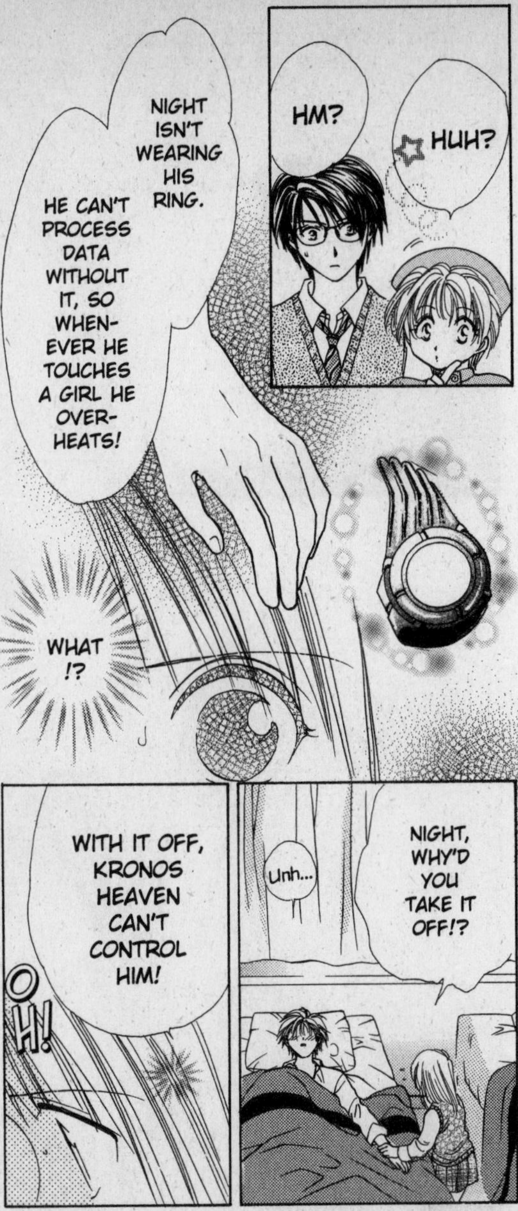
HUH?
HM?
NIGHT ISN'T WEARING HIS RING.
HE CAN'T PROCESS DATA WITHOUT IT, SO WHENEVER HE TOUCHES A GIRL HE OVERHEATS!
WHAT!?
NIGHT, WHY'D YOU TAKE IT OFF!?
Unh...
WITH IT OFF, KRONOS HEAVEN CAN'T CONTROL HIM!
OH!

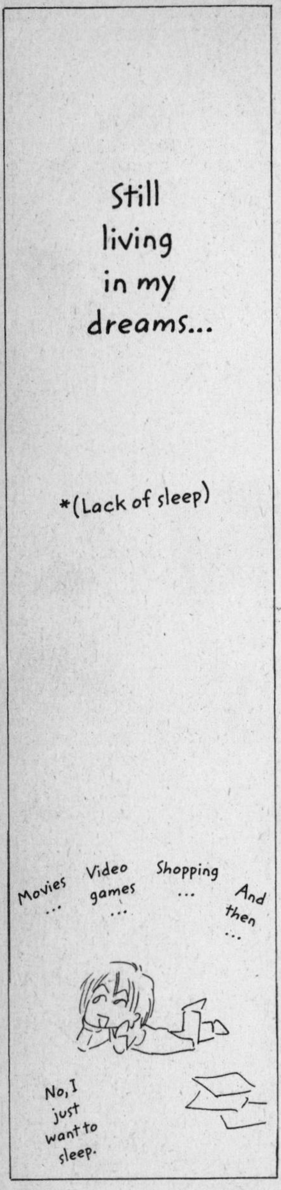
Still living in my dreams...
*(Lack of sleep)
Movies...
Video games...
Shopping...
And then...
No, I just want to sleep.

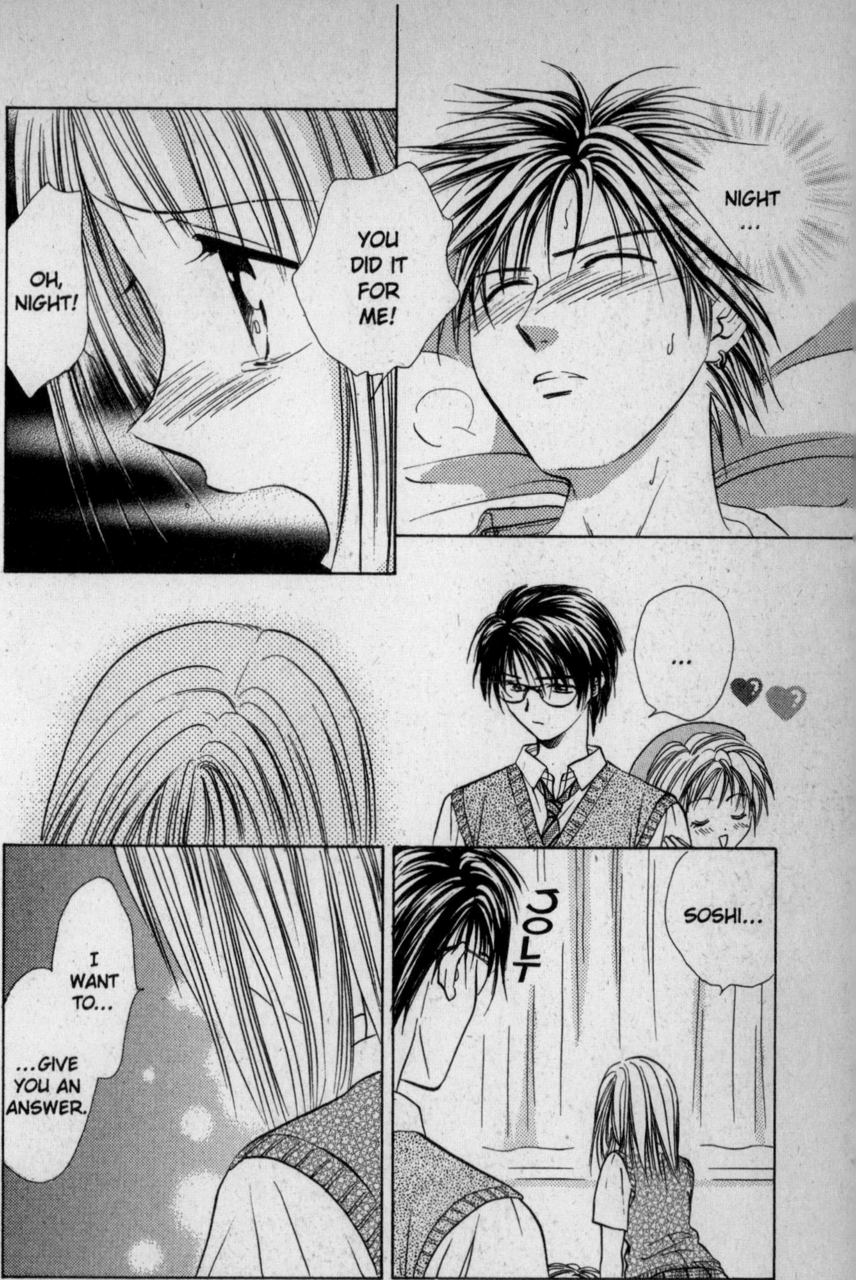
NIGHT ...
YOU DID IT FOR ME!
OH, NIGHT!
...
SOSHI...
JOLT
I WANT TO...
...GIVE YOU AN ANSWER.

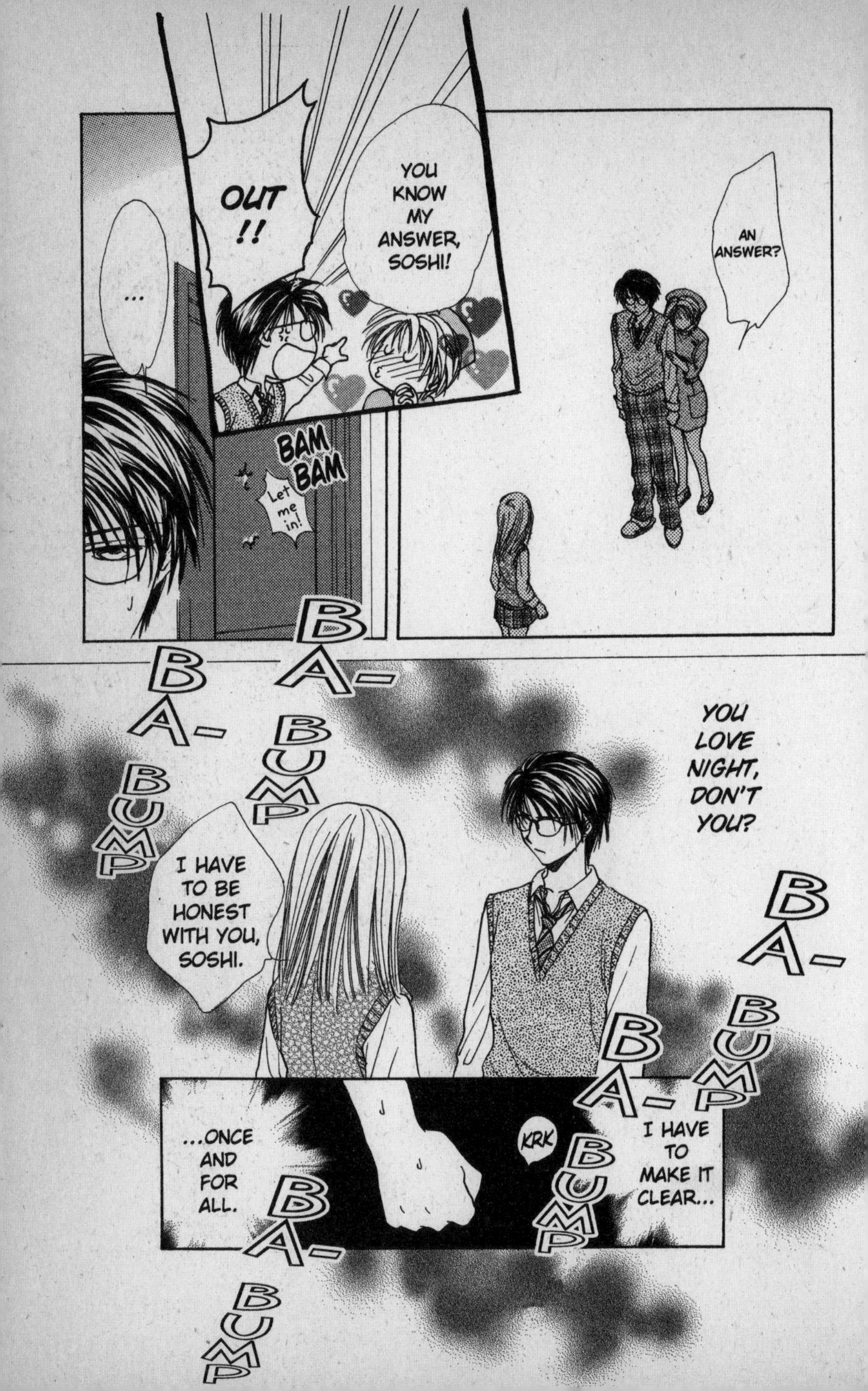
AN ANSWER?
YOU KNOW MY ANSWER, SOSHI!
OUT!!
...
BAM BAM
Let me in!
BA-BUMP
BA-BUMP
YOU LOVE NIGHT, DON'T YOU?
I HAVE TO BE HONEST WITH YOU, SOSHI.
BA-BUMP
BA-BUMP
I HAVE TO MAKE IT CLEAR...
KRK
...ONCE AND FOR ALL.
BA-BUMP

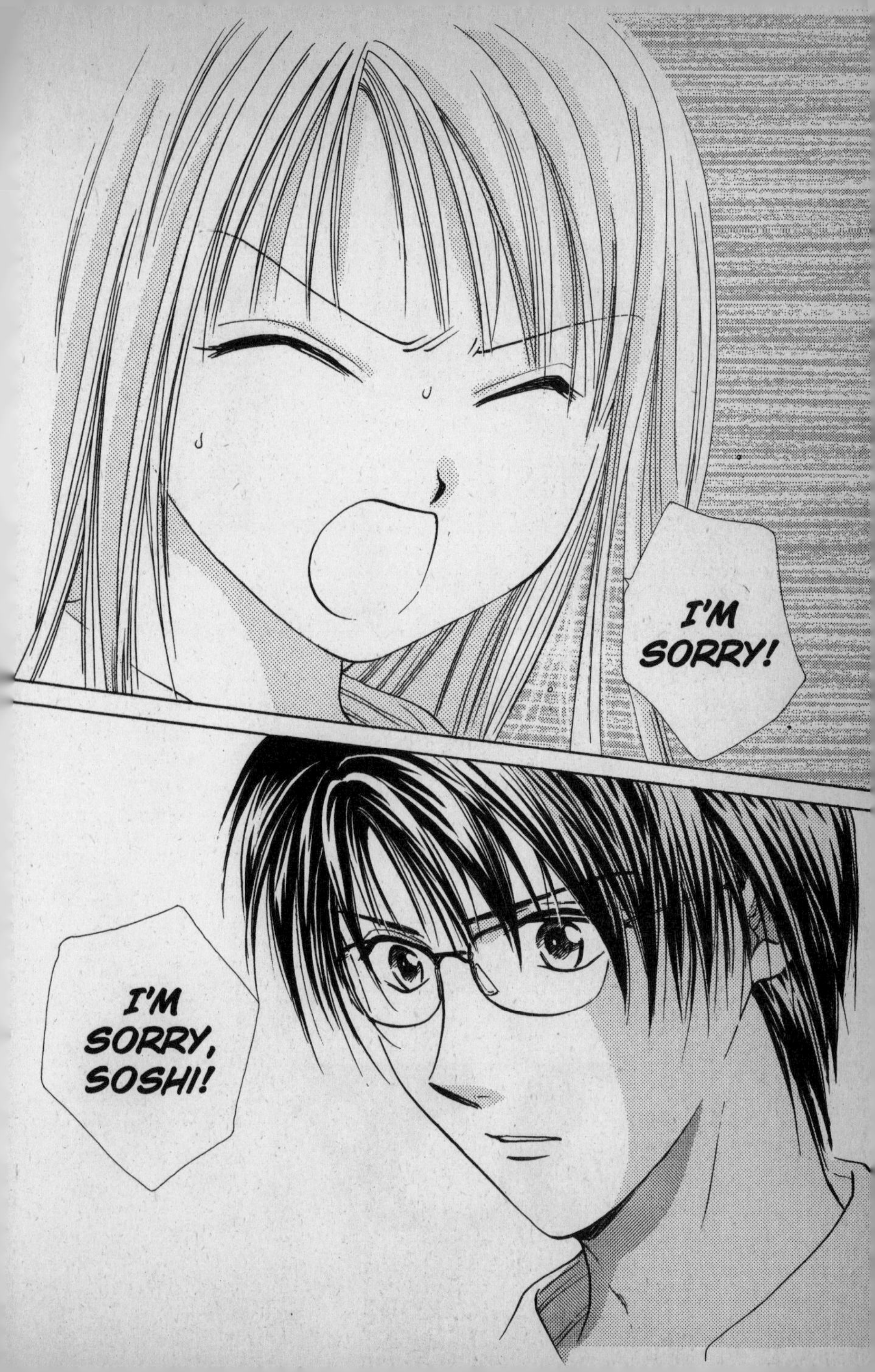
I'M SORRY!
I'M SORRY, SOSHI!

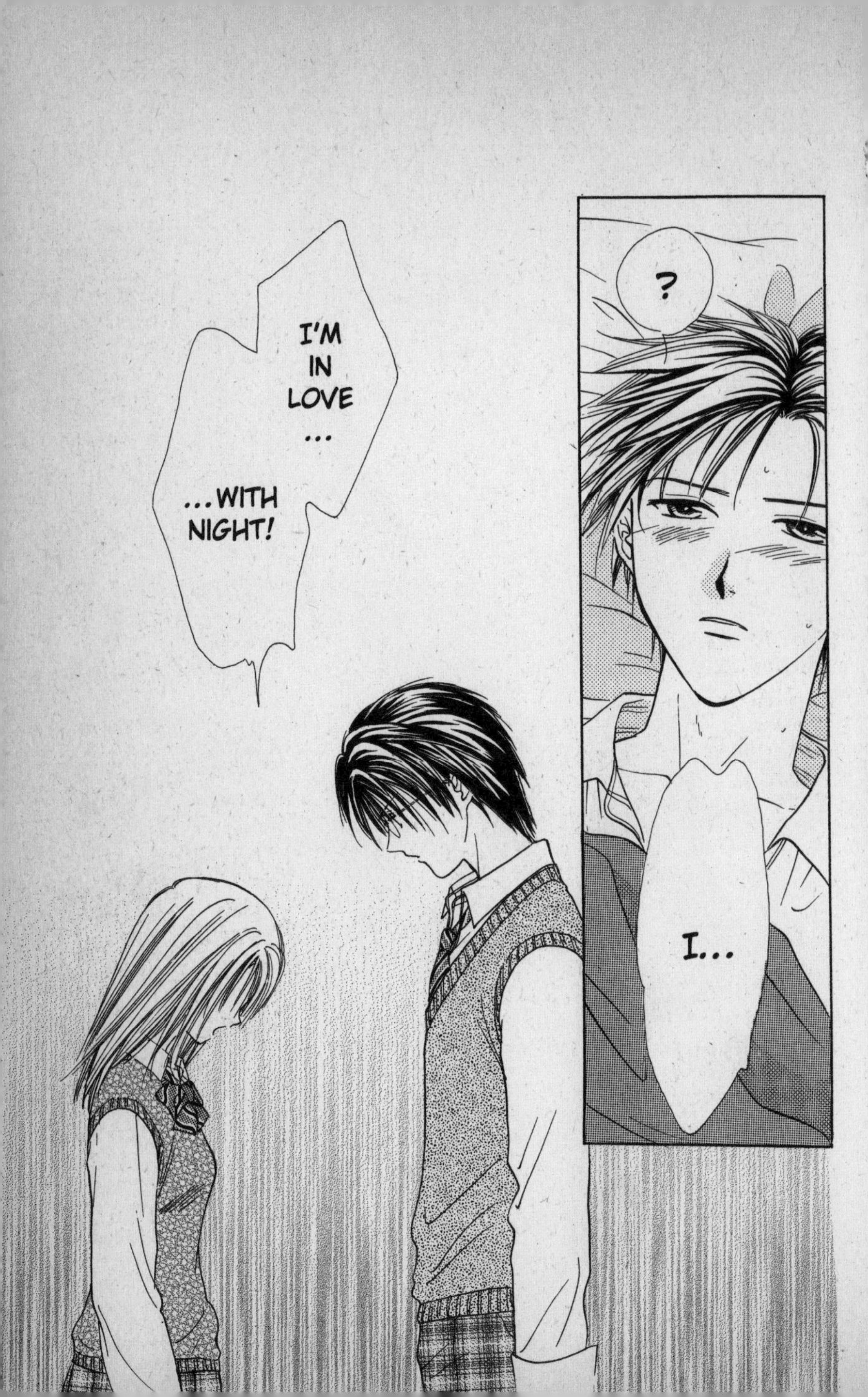
?
I...
I'M IN LOVE ...
...WITH NIGHT!

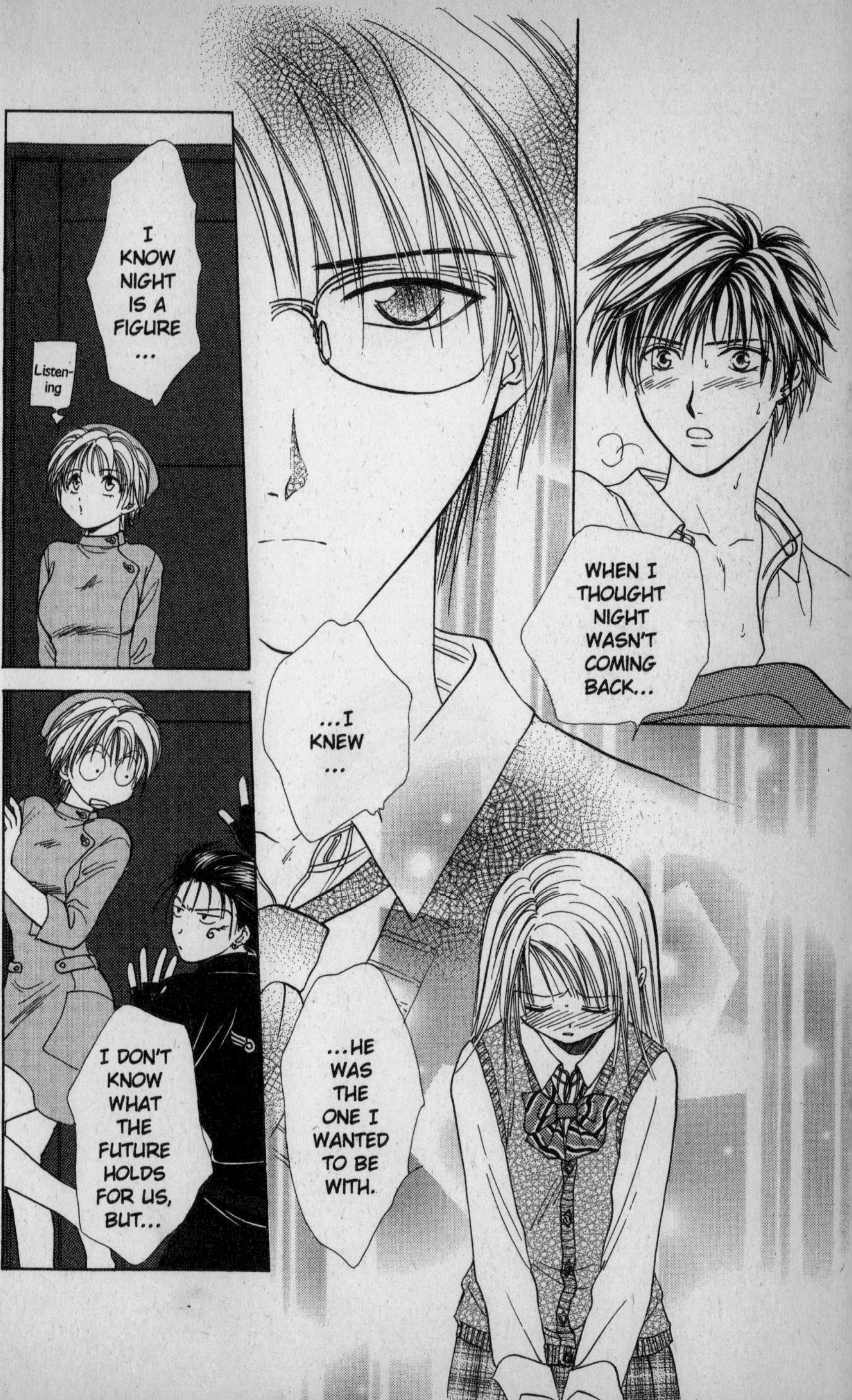
WHEN I THOUGHT NIGHT WASN'T COMING BACK...
...I KNEW...
...HE WAS THE ONE I WANTED TO BE WITH.
I KNOW NIGHT IS A FIGURE...
Listen-ing
I DON'T KNOW WHAT THE FUTURE HOLDS FOR US, BUT...

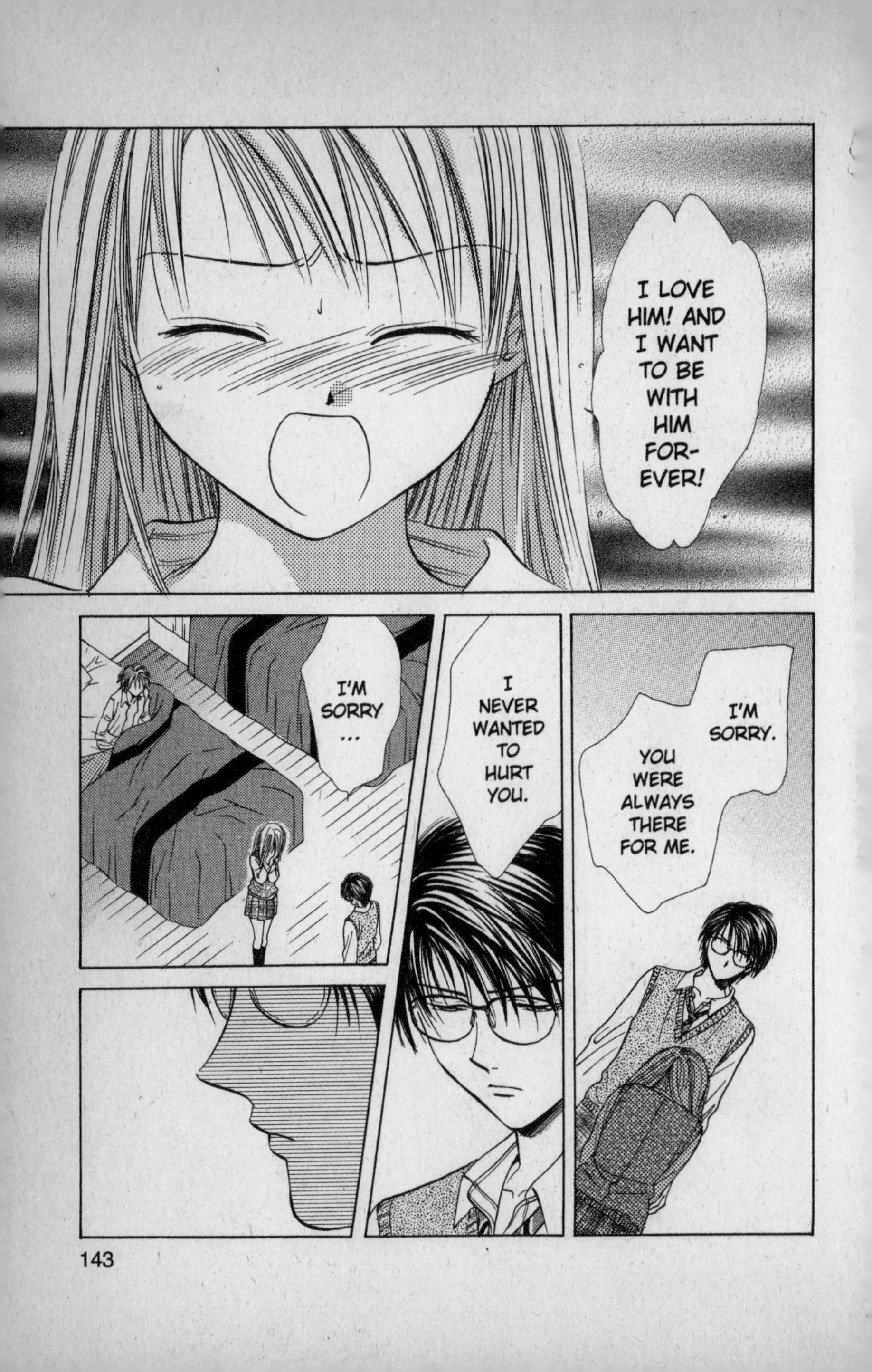
I LOVE HIM! AND I WANT TO BE WITH HIM FOR-EVER!
I'M SORRY.
YOU WERE ALWAYS THERE FOR ME.
I NEVER WANTED TO HURT YOU.
I'M SORRY ...

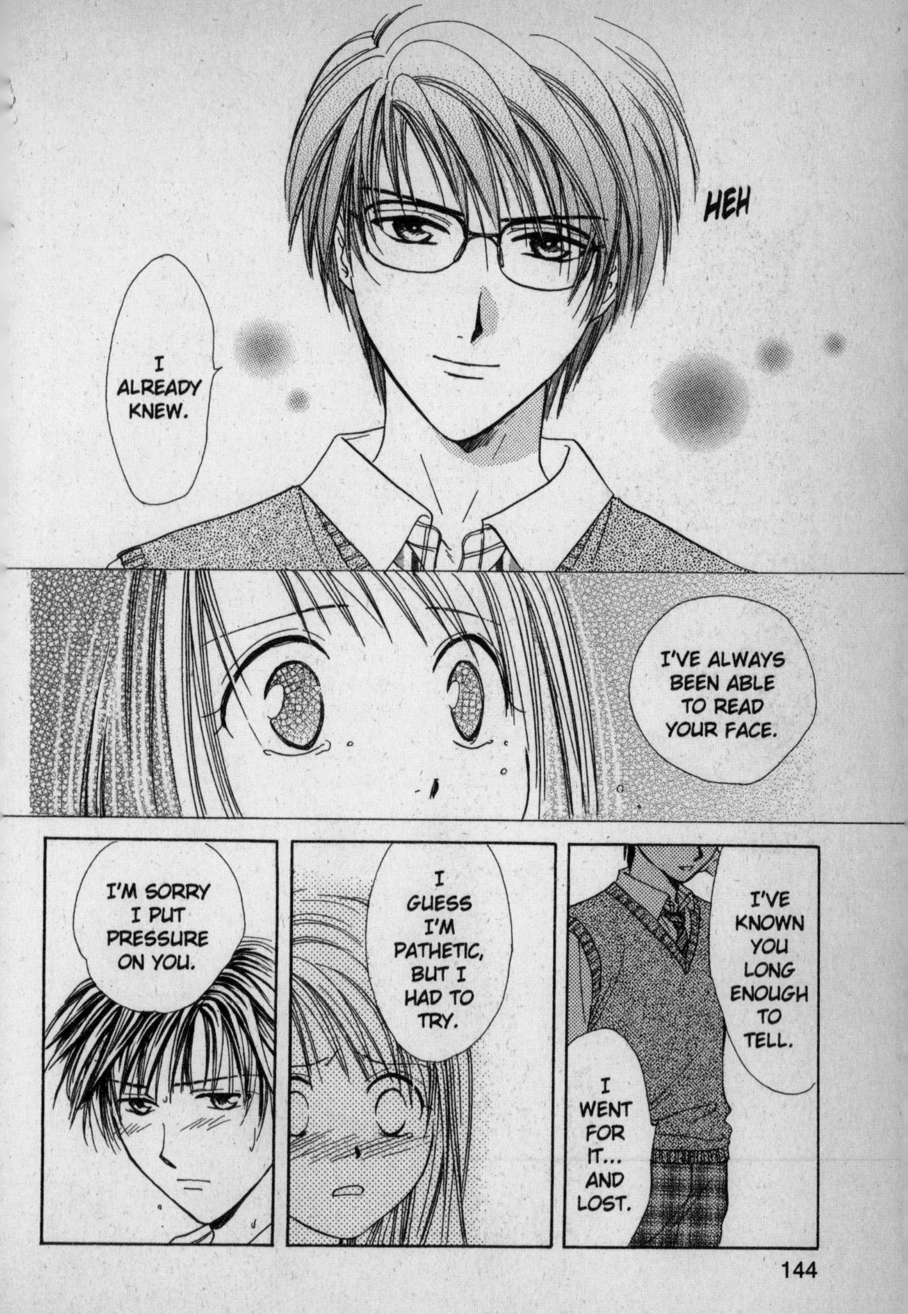
HEH
I ALREADY KNEW.
I'VE ALWAYS BEEN ABLE TO READ YOUR FACE.
I'VE KNOWN YOU LONG ENOUGH TO TELL.
I WENT FOR IT... AND LOST.
I GUESS I'M PATHETIC, BUT I HAD TO TRY.
I'M SORRY I PUT PRESSURE ON YOU.

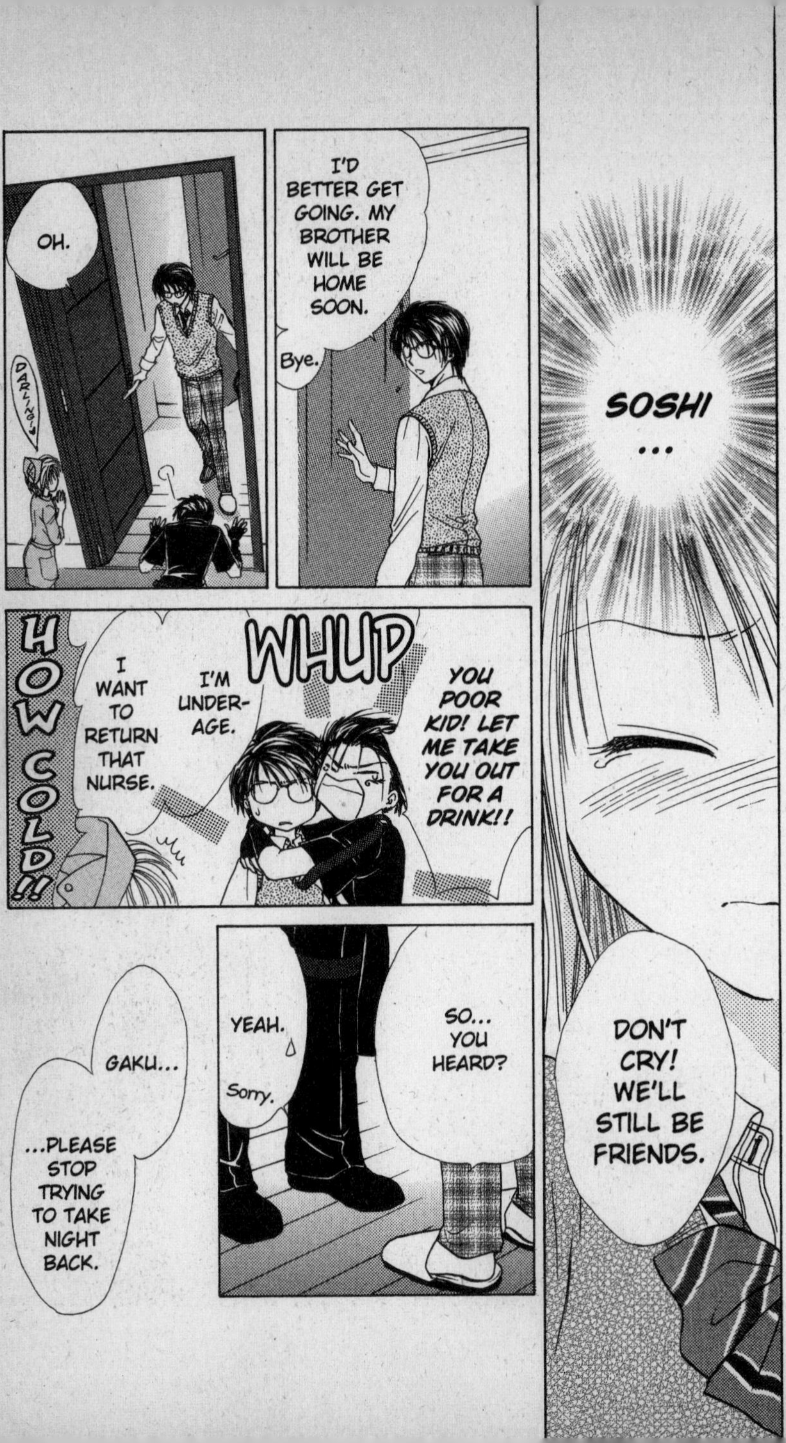
SOSHI ...
DON'T CRY! WE'LL STILL BE FRIENDS.
I'D BETTER GET GOING. MY BROTHER WILL BE HOME SOON.
Bye.
OH.
DARLING!♥
WHUP
YOU POOR KID! LET ME TAKE YOU OUT FOR A DRINK!!
I'M UNDER-AGE.
I WANT TO RETURN THAT NURSE.
HOW COLD!!
SO... YOU HEARD?
YEAH.
Sorry.
GAKU...
...PLEASE STOP TRYING TO TAKE NIGHT BACK.

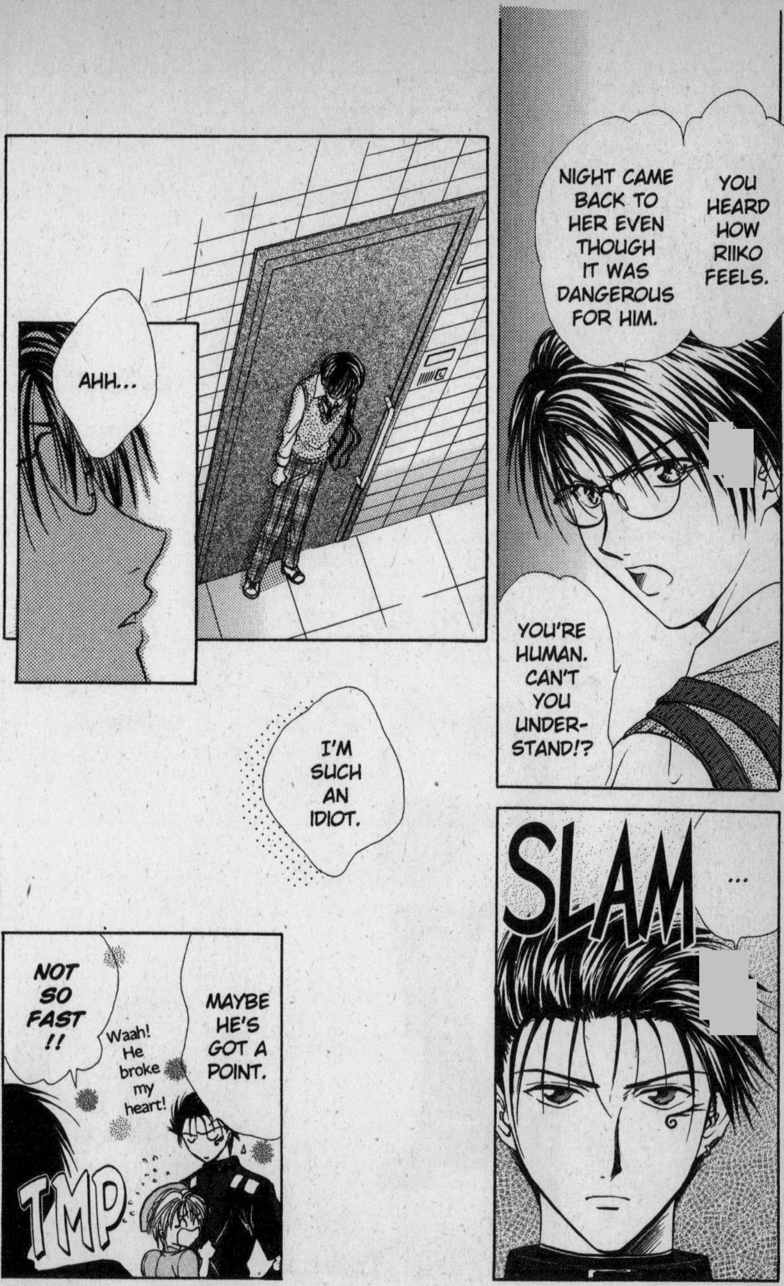
YOU HEARD HOW RIIKO FEELS.
NIGHT CAME BACK TO HER EVEN THOUGH IT WAS DANGEROUS FOR HIM.
YOU'RE HUMAN. CAN'T YOU UNDER-STAND!?
AHH...
I'M SUCH AN IDIOT.
SLAM
...
MAYBE HE'S GOT A POINT.
Waah! He broke my heart!
NOT SO FAST!!
TMP

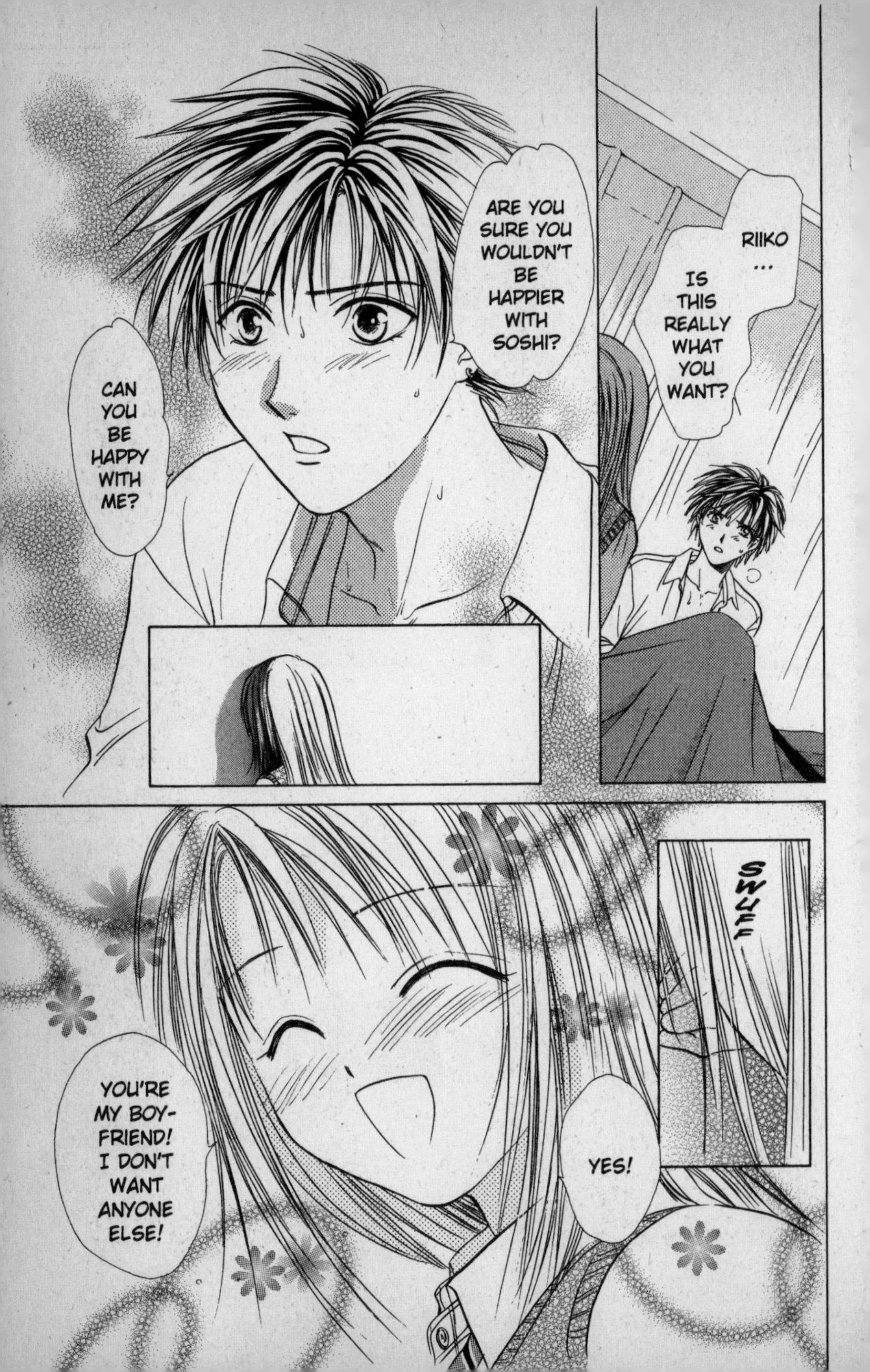
RIIKO ...
IS THIS REALLY WHAT YOU WANT?
ARE YOU SURE YOU WOULDN'T BE HAPPIER WITH SOSHI?
CAN YOU BE HAPPY WITH ME?
SWUFF
YES!
YOU'RE MY BOY-FRIEND! I DON'T WANT ANYONE ELSE!

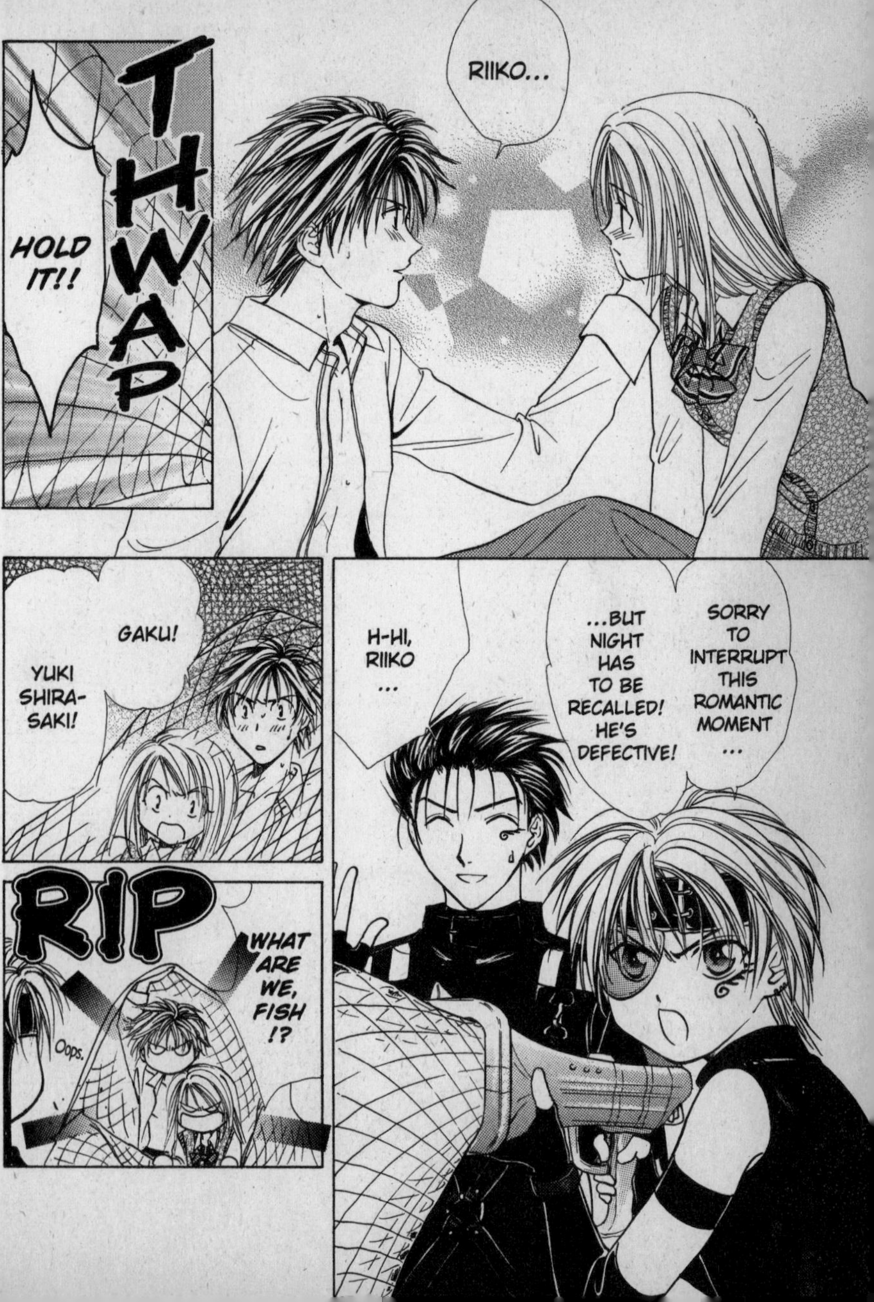
RIIKO...
THWAP
HOLD IT!!
SORRY TO INTERRUPT THIS ROMANTIC MOMENT ...
...BUT NIGHT HAS TO BE RECALLED! HE'S DEFECTIVE!
H-HI, RIIKO ...
GAKU!
YUKI SHIRA-SAKI!
RIP
WHAT ARE WE, FISH !?
Oops.

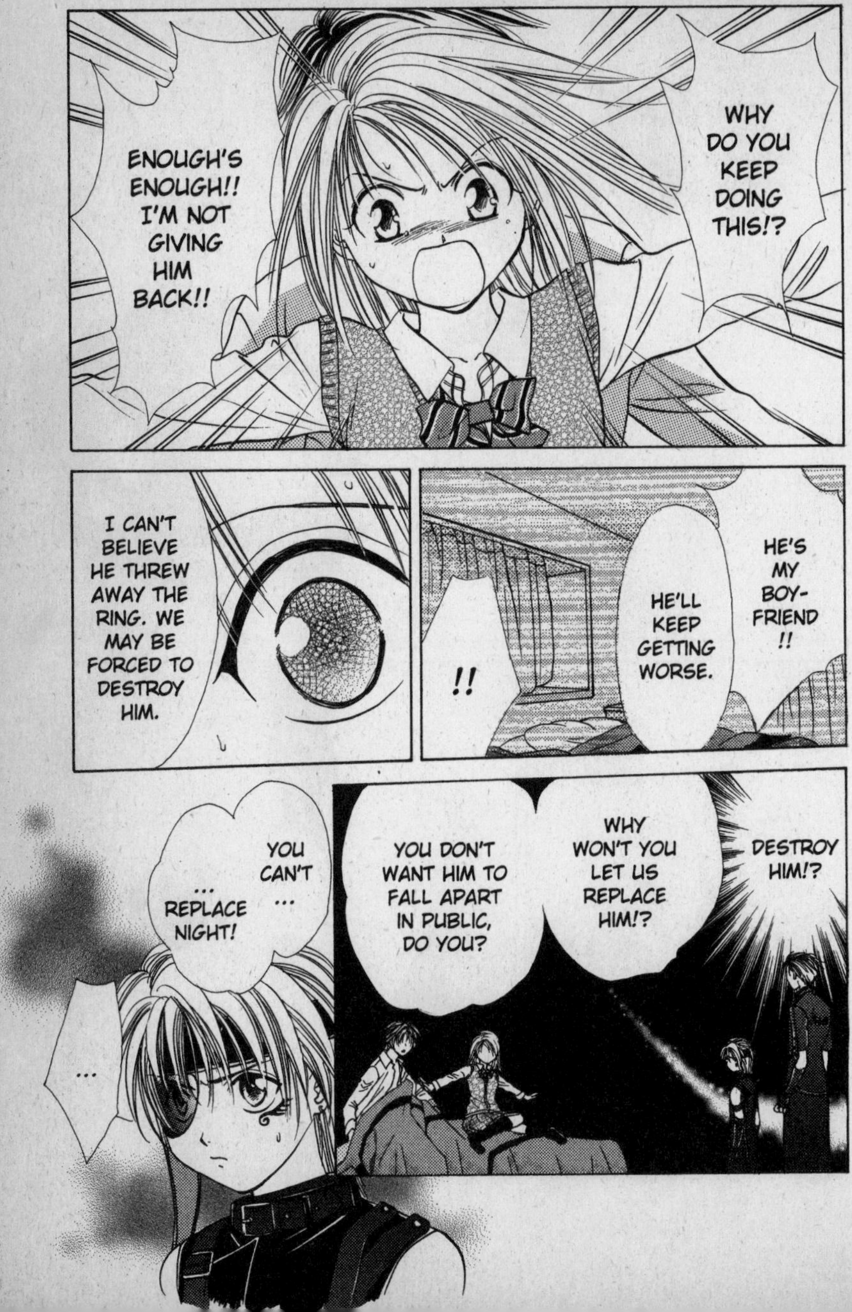
WHY DO YOU KEEP DOING THIS!?
ENOUGH'S ENOUGH!! I'M NOT GIVING HIM BACK!!
HE'S MY BOY-FRIEND !!
HE'LL KEEP GETTING WORSE.
!!
I CAN'T BELIEVE HE THREW AWAY THE RING. WE MAY BE FORCED TO DESTROY HIM.
DESTROY HIM!?
WHY WON'T YOU LET US REPLACE HIM!?
YOU DON'T WANT HIM TO FALL APART IN PUBLIC, DO YOU?
YOU CAN'T ...
... REPLACE NIGHT!
...

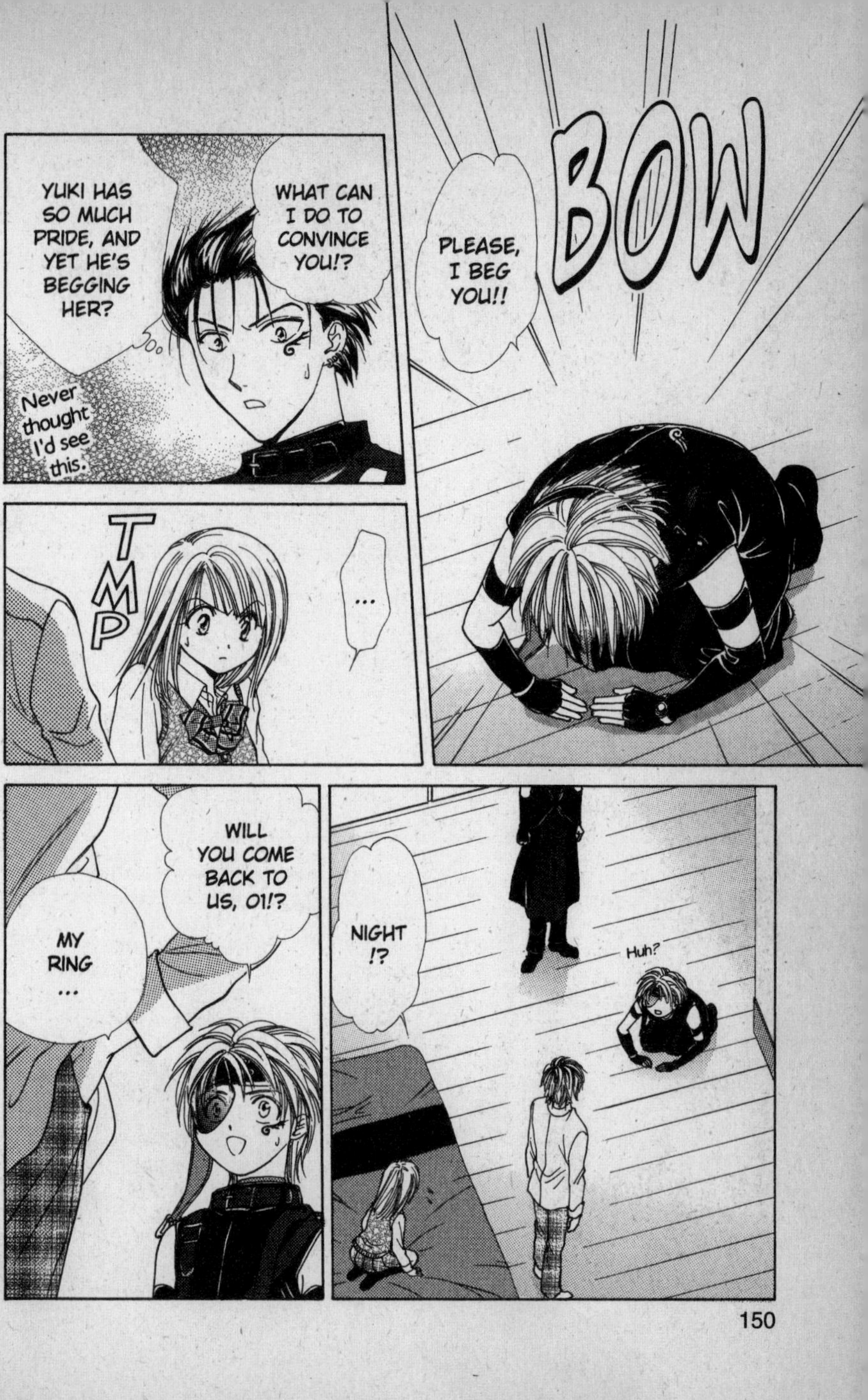
BOW
PLEASE, I BEG YOU!!
WHAT CAN I DO TO CONVINCE YOU!?
YUKI HAS SO MUCH PRIDE, AND YET HE'S BEGGING HER?
Never thought I'd see this.
...
TMP
NIGHT !?
Huh?
WILL YOU COME BACK TO US, 01!?
MY RING ...

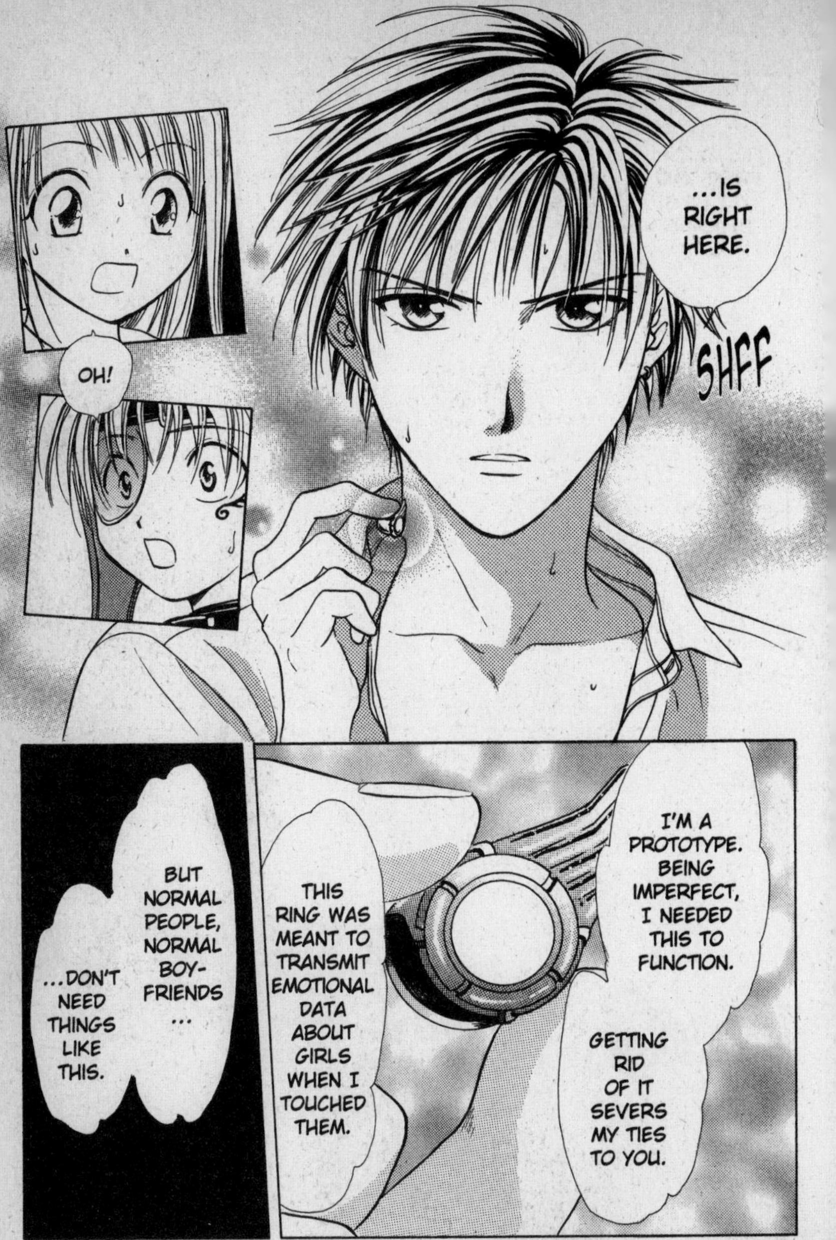
...IS RIGHT HERE.
SHFF
OH!
I'M A PROTOTYPE. BEING IMPERFECT, I NEEDED THIS TO FUNCTION.
GETTING RID OF IT SEVERS MY TIES TO YOU.
THIS RING WAS MEANT TO TRANSMIT EMOTIONAL DATA ABOUT GIRLS WHEN I TOUCHED THEM.
BUT NORMAL PEOPLE, NORMAL BOY-FRIENDS...
...DON'T NEED THINGS LIKE THIS.

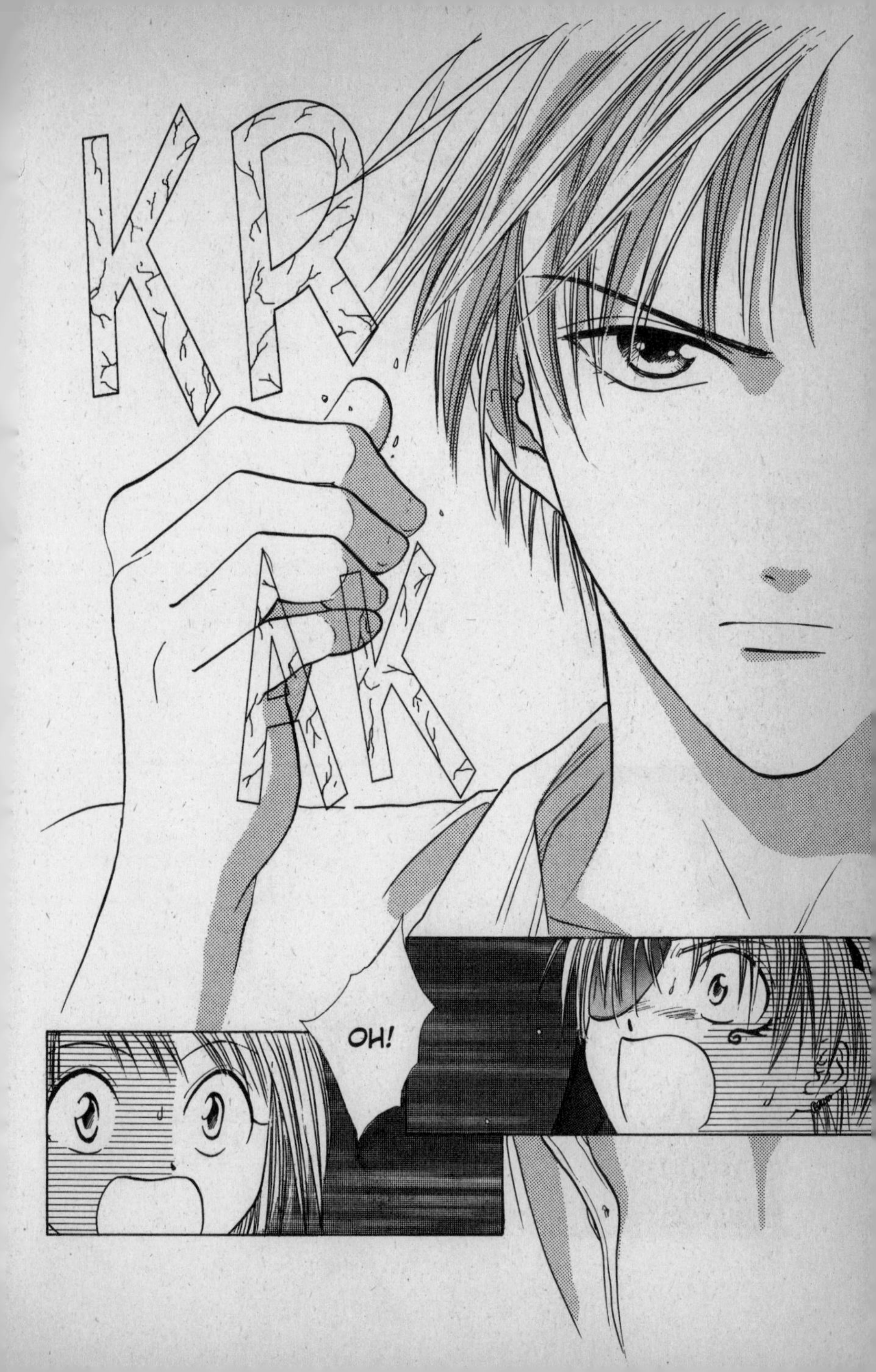
KRAKK
OH!

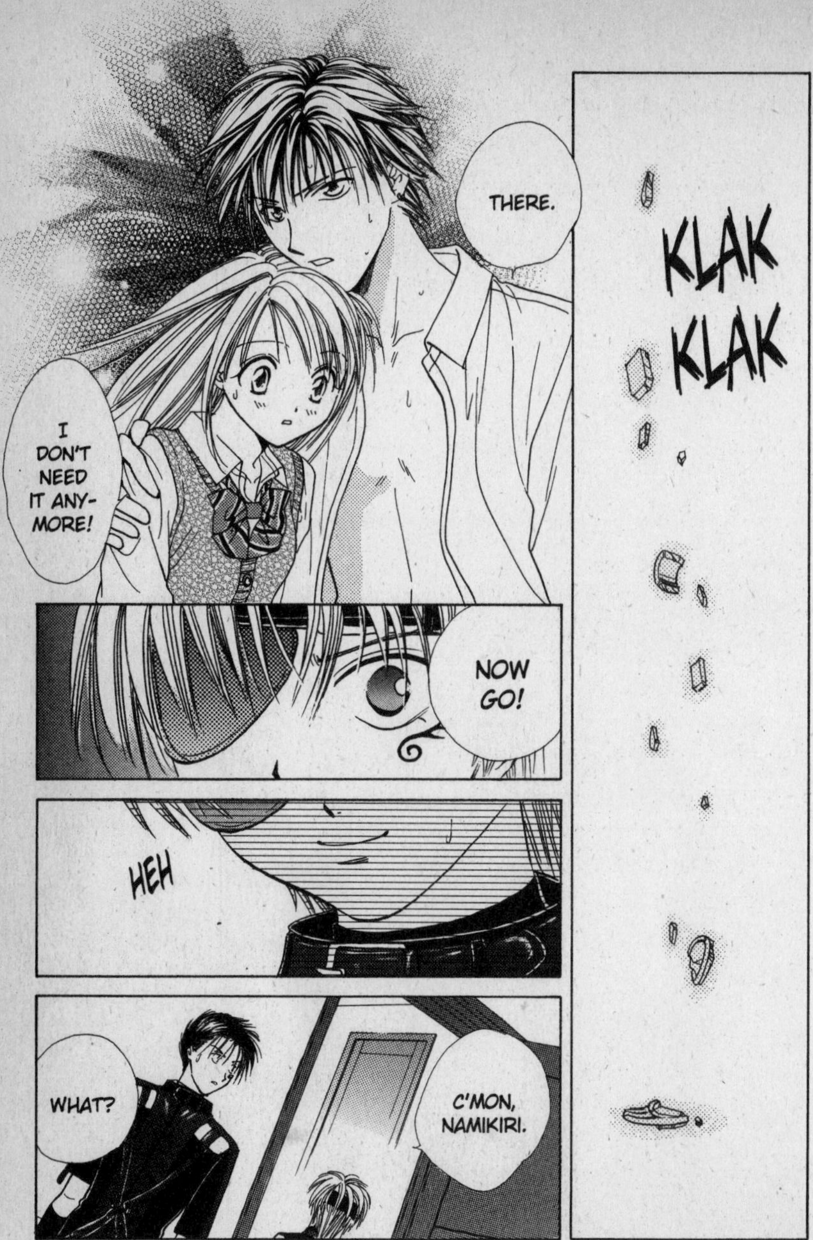
KLAK KLAK
THERE.
I DON'T NEED IT ANY-MORE!
NOW GO!
HEH
C'MON, NAMIKIRI.
WHAT?

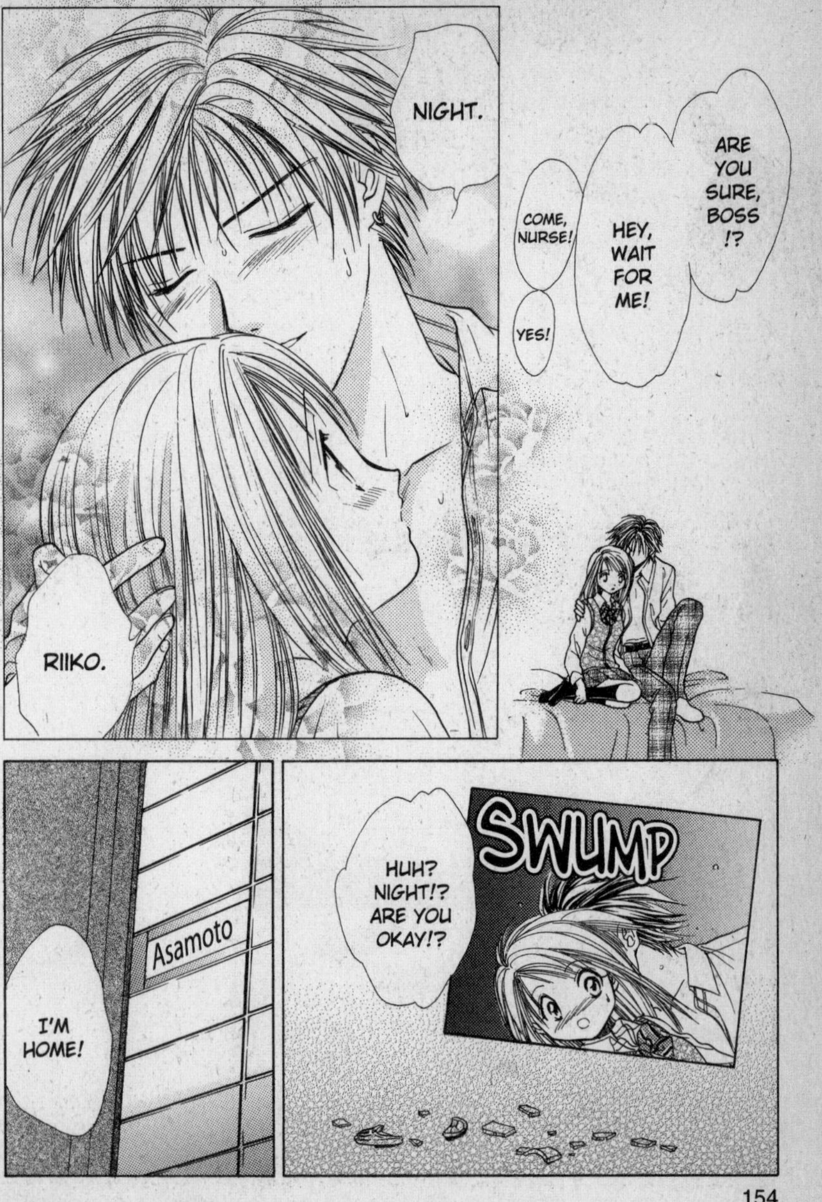
ARE YOU SURE, BOSS!?
HEY, WAIT FOR ME!
COME, NURSE!
YES!
NIGHT.
RIIKO.
SWUMP
HUH? NIGHT!? ARE YOU OKAY!?
Asamoto
I'M HOME!

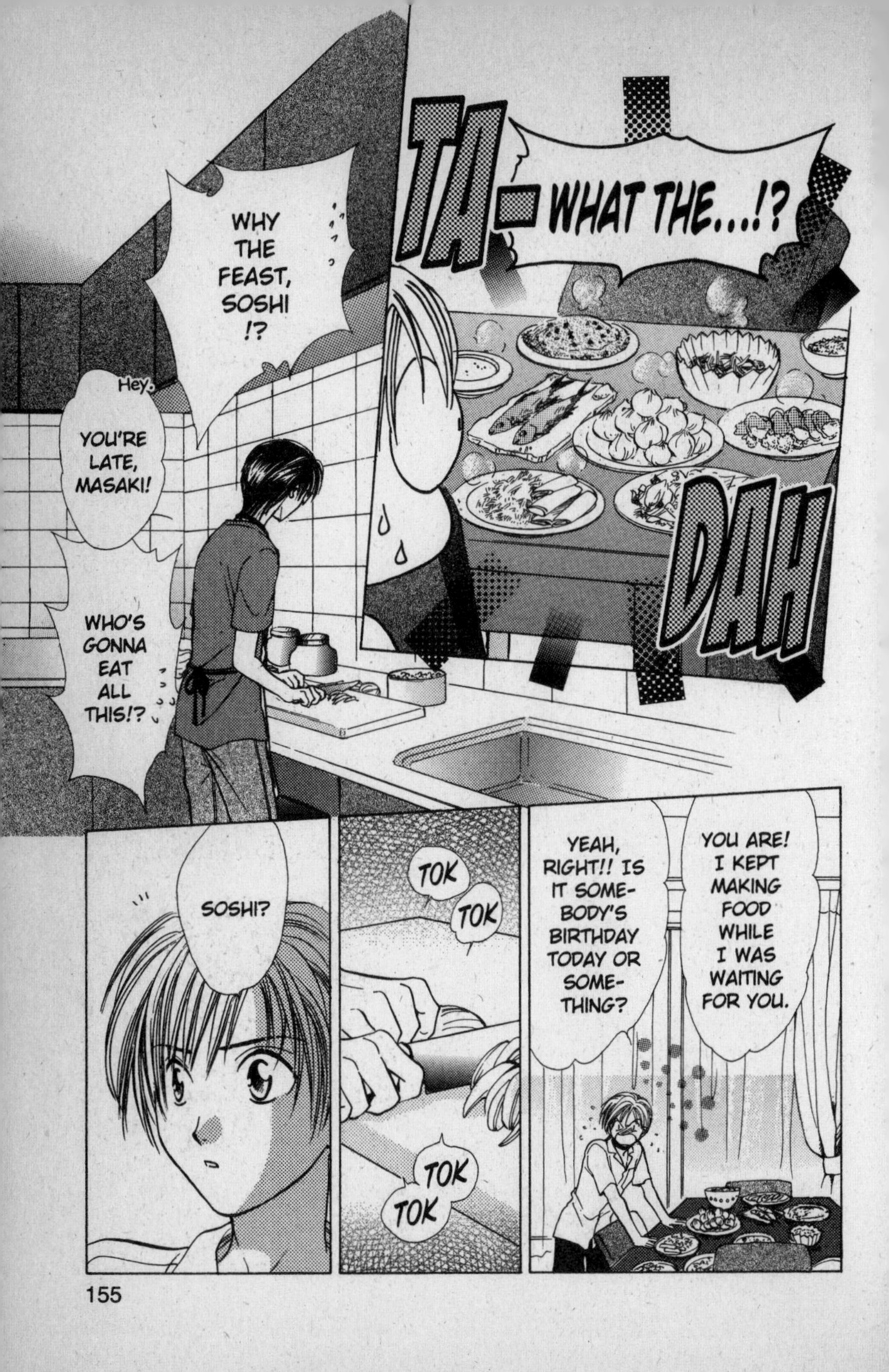
TA-
DAH
WHAT THE...!?
WHY THE FEAST, SOSHI!?
Hey.
YOU'RE LATE, MASAKI!
WHO'S GONNA EAT ALL THIS!?
YOU ARE! I KEPT MAKING FOOD WHILE I WAS WAITING FOR YOU.
YEAH, RIGHT!! IS IT SOME-BODY'S BIRTHDAY TODAY OR SOME-THING?
TOK
TOK
TOK
TOK
SOSHI?

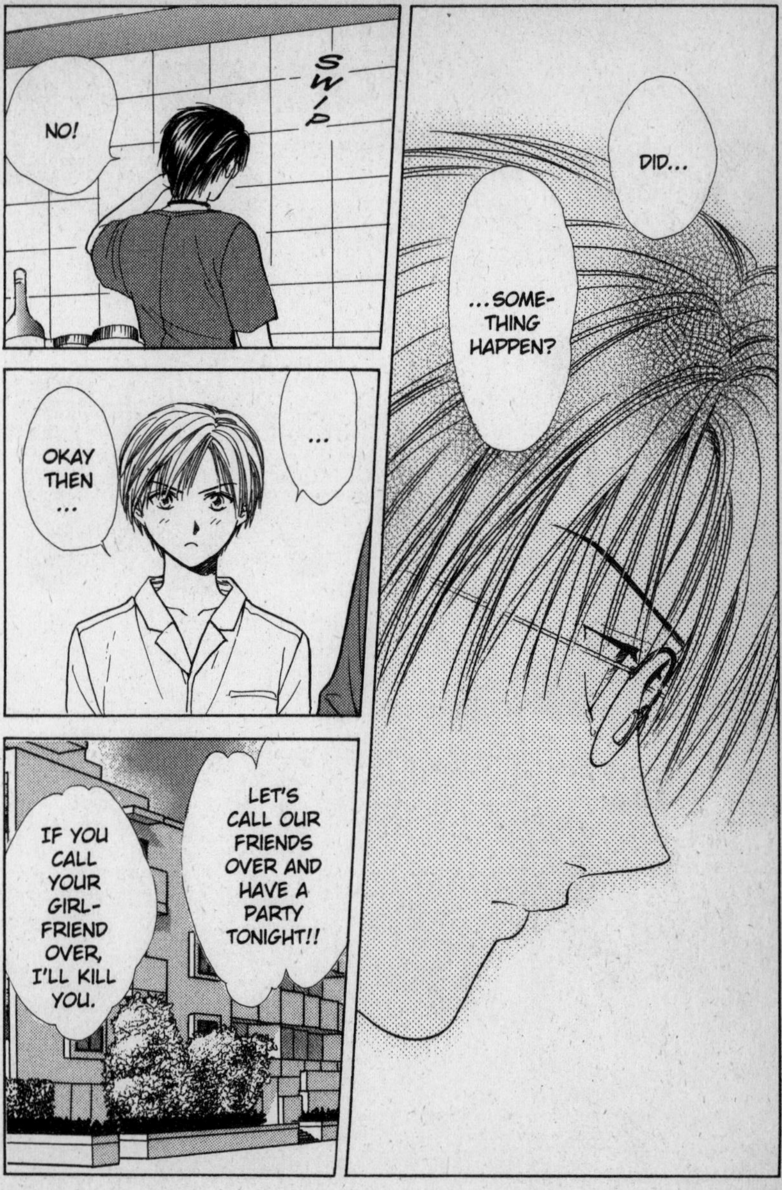
DID...
...SOME-THING HAPPEN?
SWIP
NO!
...
OKAY THEN ...
LET'S CALL OUR FRIENDS OVER AND HAVE A PARTY TONIGHT!!
IF YOU CALL YOUR GIRL-FRIEND OVER, I'LL KILL YOU.

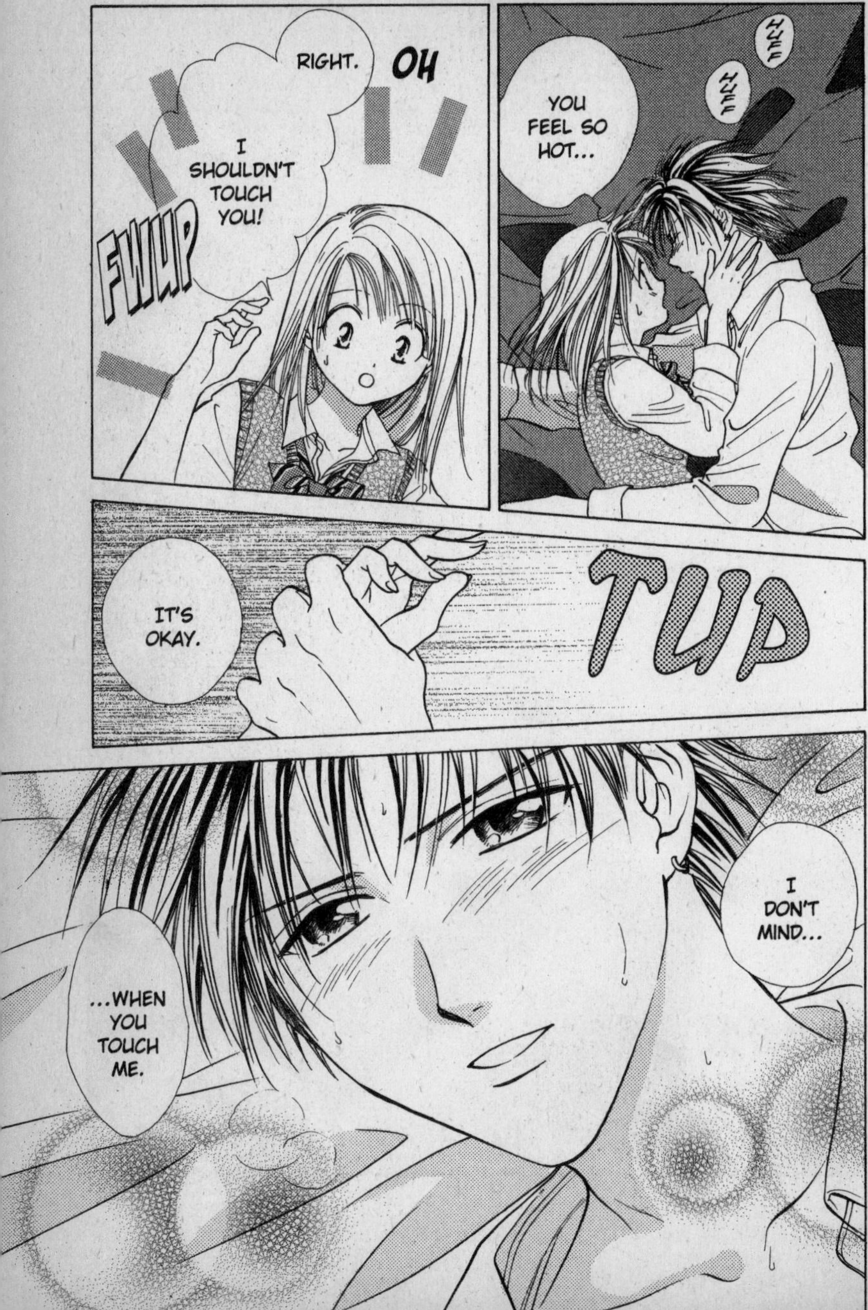
HUFF
HUFF
YOU FEEL SO HOT...
OH
RIGHT.
I SHOULDN'T TOUCH YOU!
FWUP
TUP
IT'S OKAY.
I DON'T MIND...
...WHEN YOU TOUCH ME.

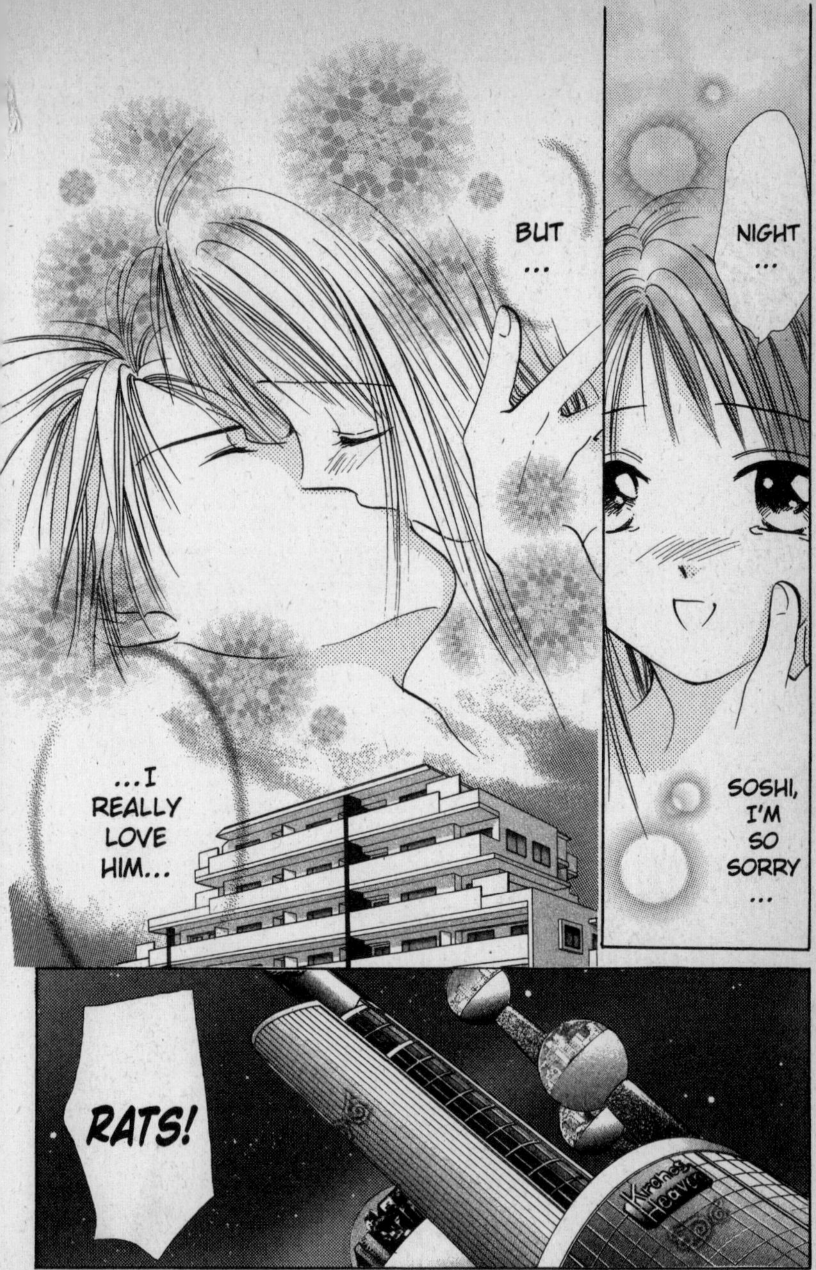
NIGHT...
SOSHI, I'M SO SORRY...
BUT...
...I REALLY LOVE HIM...
RATS!

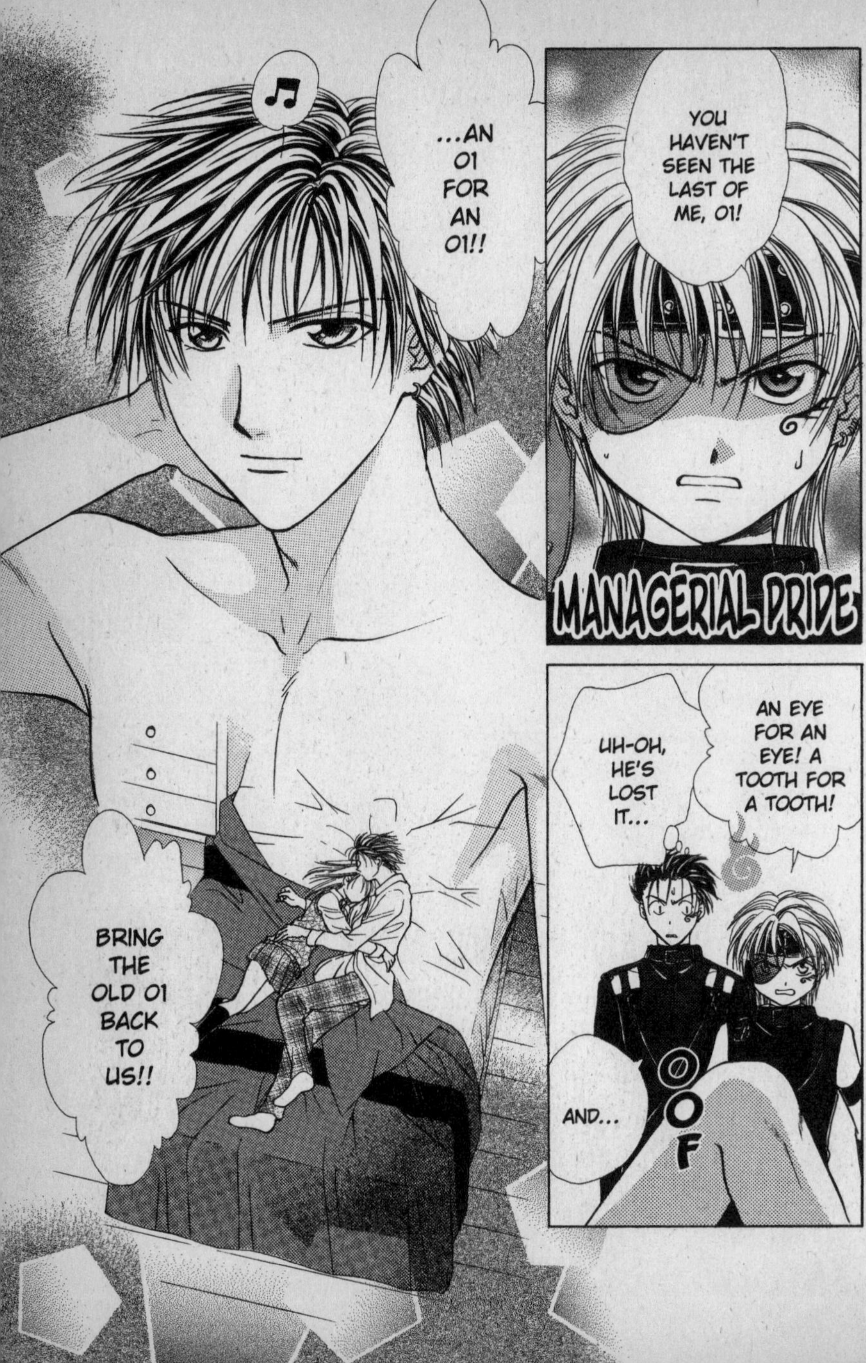
YOU HAVEN'T SEEN THE LAST OF ME, 01!
MANAGERIAL PRIDE
AN EYE FOR AN EYE! A TOOTH FOR A TOOTH!
UH-OH, HE'S LOST IT...
AND...
OOF
...AN 01 FOR AN 01!!
BRING THE OLD 01 BACK TO US!!

Absolute Boyfriend

Act 30: The War Over the Girlfriend

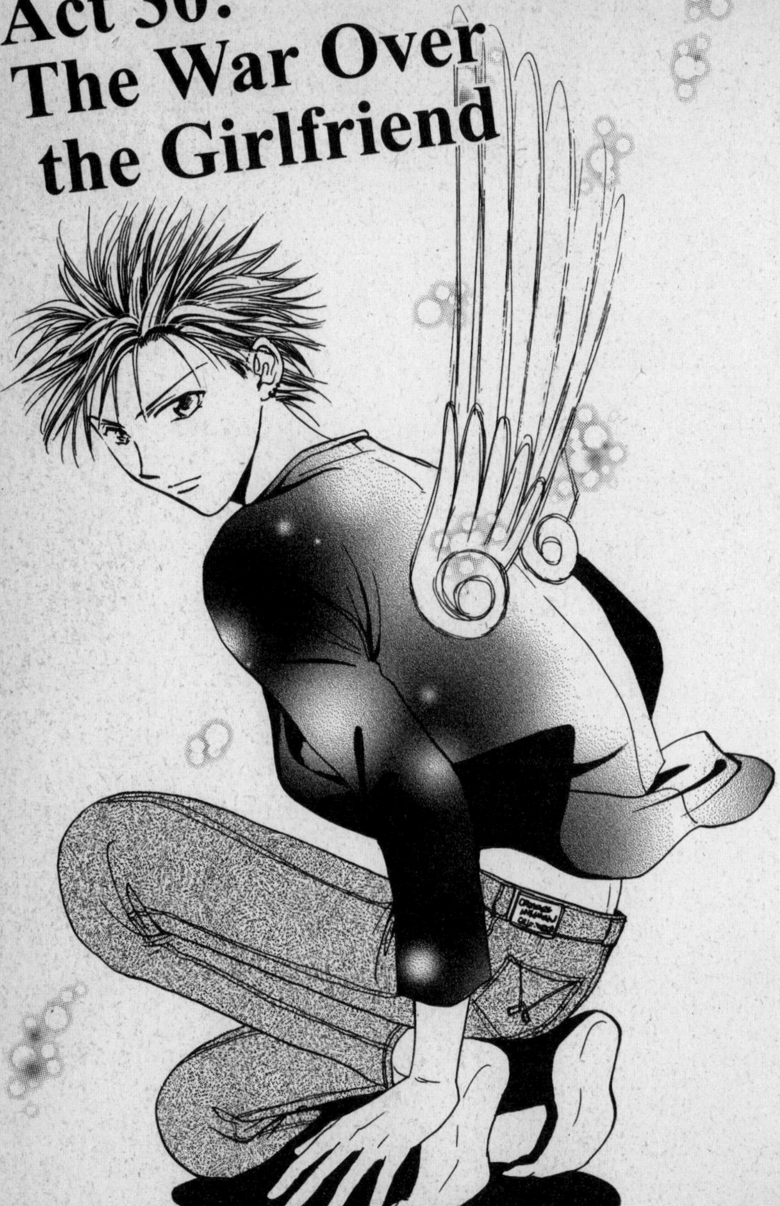

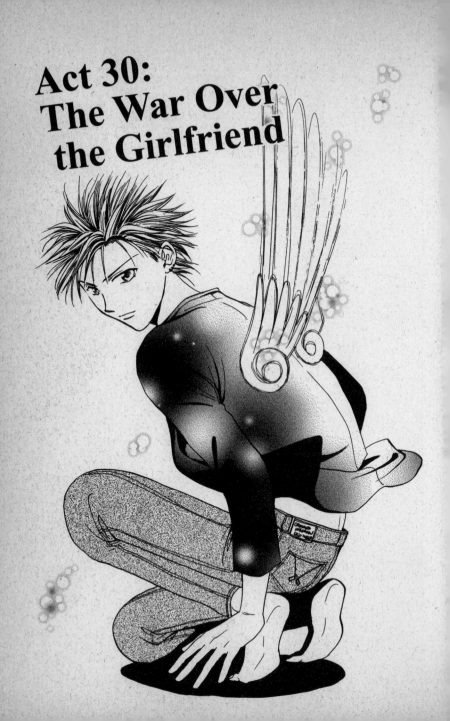

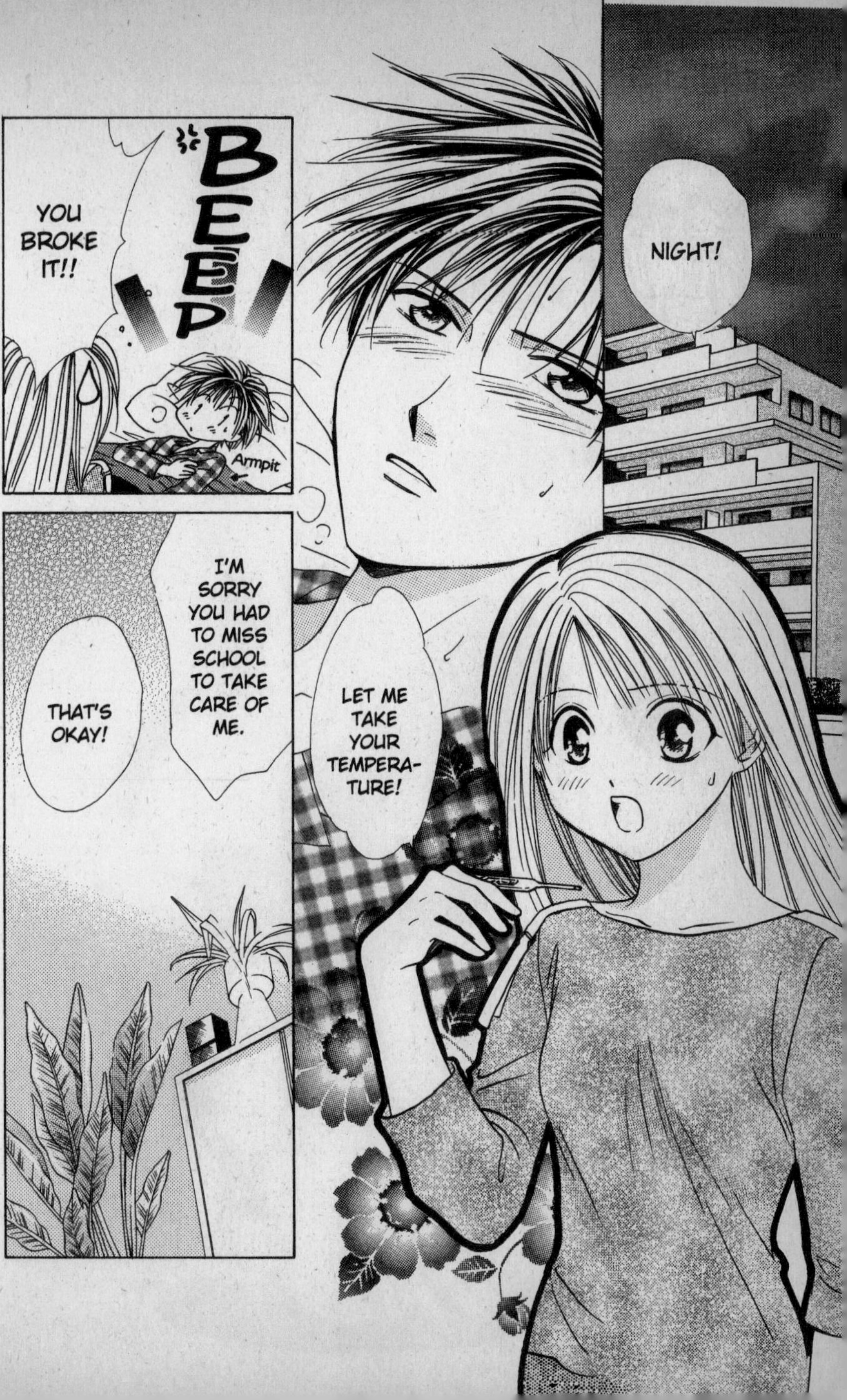
NIGHT!
LET ME TAKE YOUR TEMPERATURE!
BEEP
YOU BROKE IT!!
Armpit
I'M SORRY YOU HAD TO MISS SCHOOL TO TAKE CARE OF ME.
THAT'S OKAY!

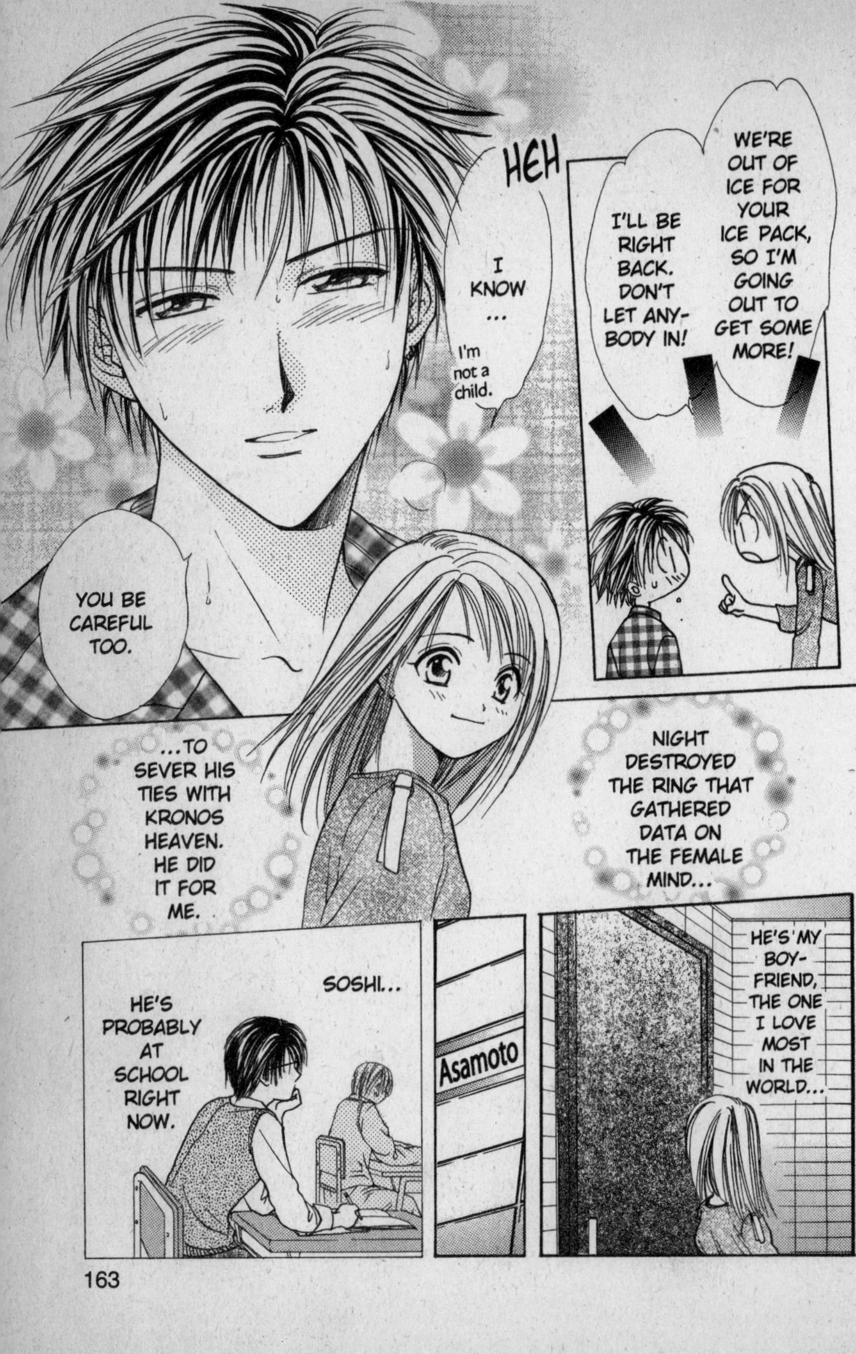
WE'RE OUT OF ICE FOR YOUR ICE PACK, SO I'M GOING OUT TO GET SOME MORE!
I'LL BE RIGHT BACK. DON'T LET ANY-BODY IN!
HEH
I KNOW ...
I'm not a child.
YOU BE CAREFUL TOO.
NIGHT DESTROYED THE RING THAT GATHERED DATA ON THE FEMALE MIND...
...TO SEVER HIS TIES WITH KRONOS HEAVEN. HE DID IT FOR ME.
HE'S MY BOY-FRIEND, THE ONE I LOVE MOST IN THE WORLD...
Asamoto
SOSHI...
HE'S PROBABLY AT SCHOOL RIGHT NOW.

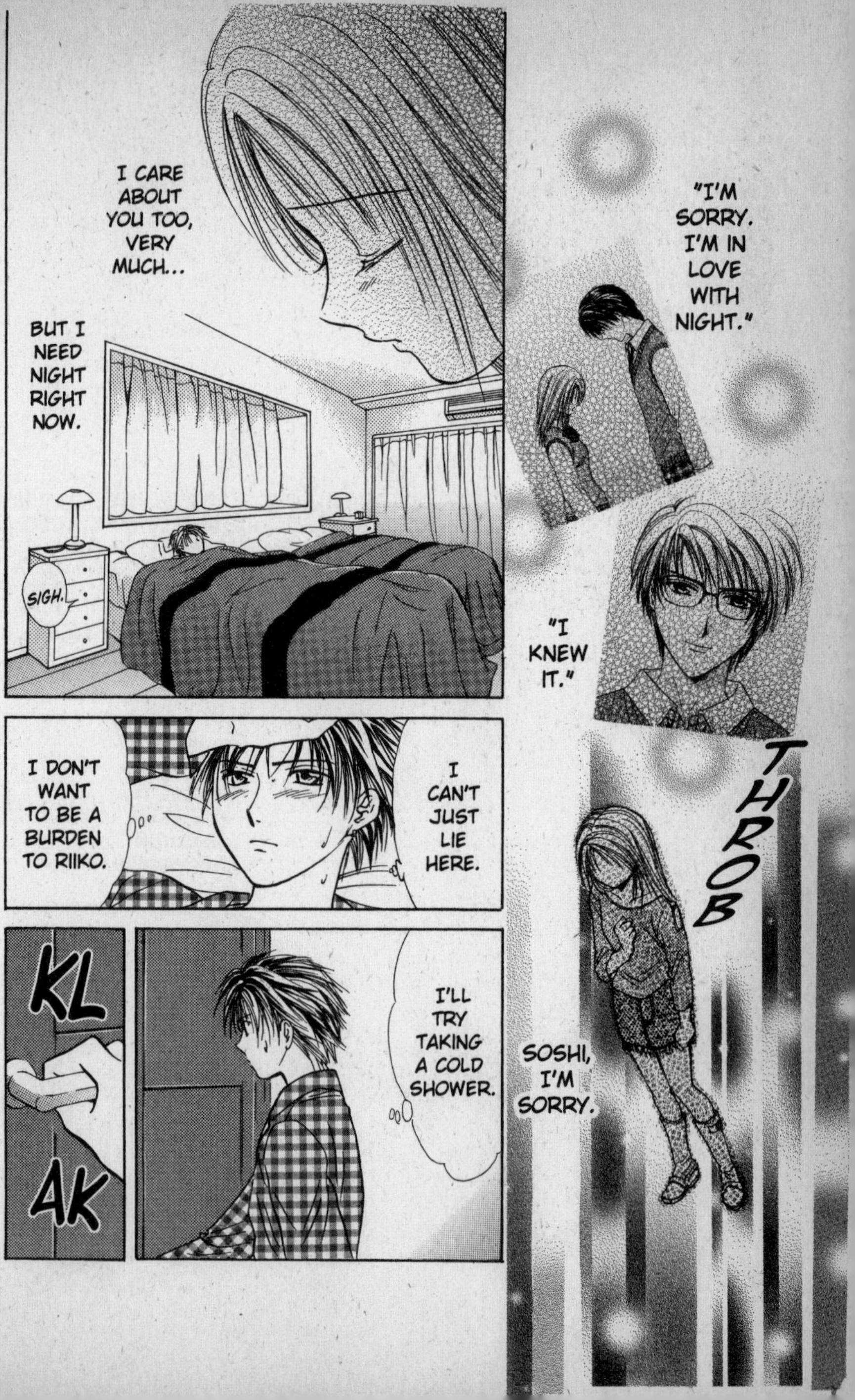
"I'M SORRY. I'M IN LOVE WITH NIGHT."
"I KNEW IT."
THROB
SOSHI, I'M SORRY.
I CARE ABOUT YOU TOO, VERY MUCH...
BUT I NEED NIGHT RIGHT NOW.
SIGH.
I CAN'T JUST LIE HERE.
I DON'T WANT TO BE A BURDEN TO RIIKO.
I'LL TRY TAKING A COLD SHOWER.
KL
AK

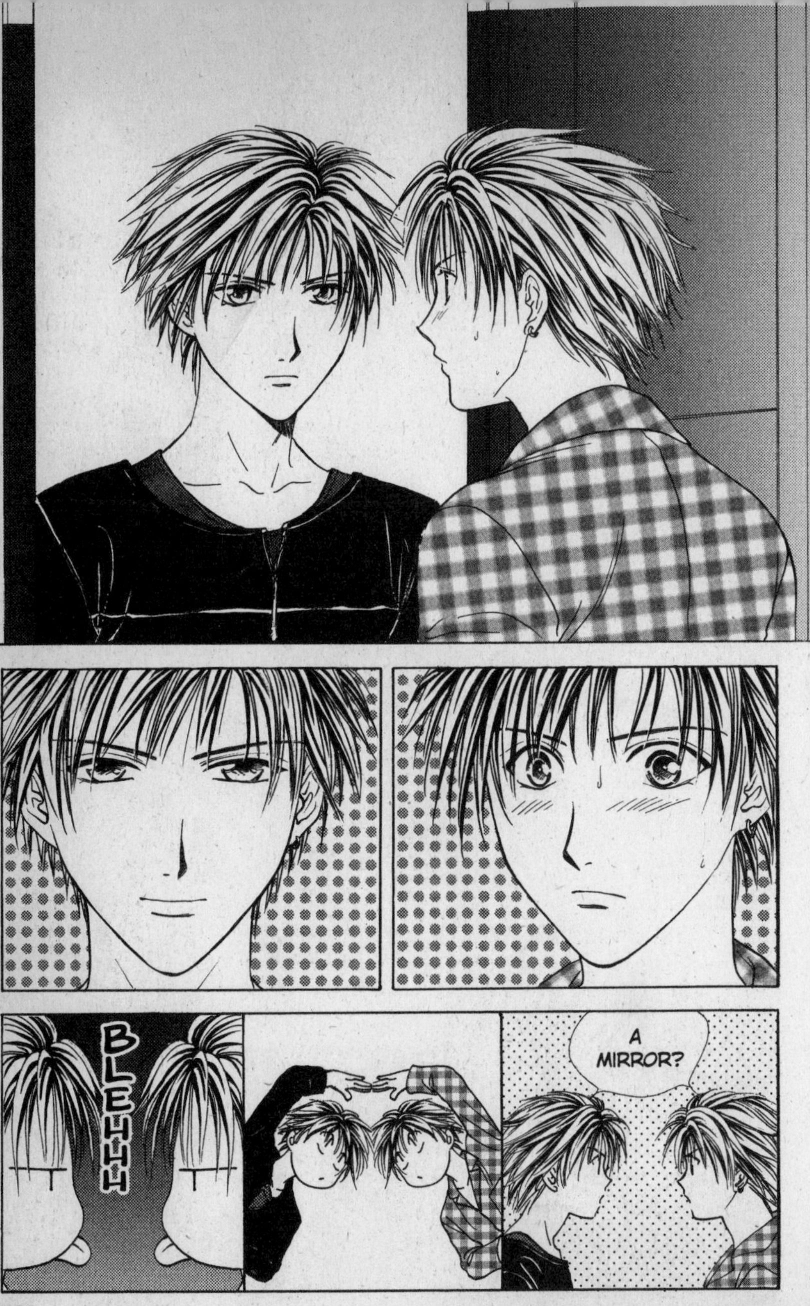
A MIRROR?
BLEHHHH

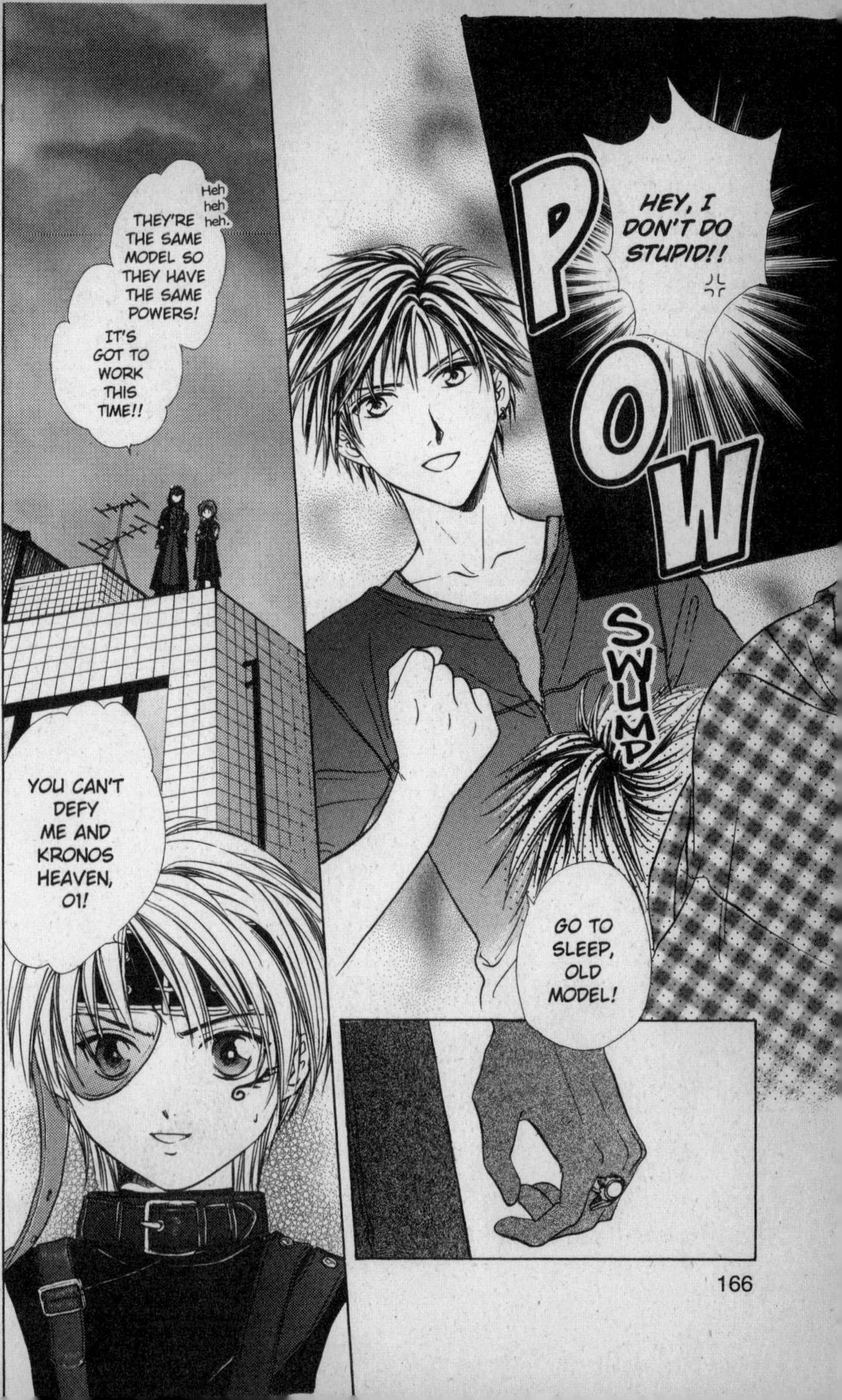
HEY, I DON'T DO STUPID!!
POW
SWUMP
GO TO SLEEP, OLD MODEL!
Heh heh heh.
THEY'RE THE SAME MODEL SO THEY HAVE THE SAME POWERS!
IT'S GOT TO WORK THIS TIME!!
YOU CAN'T DEFY ME AND KRONOS HEAVEN, 01!

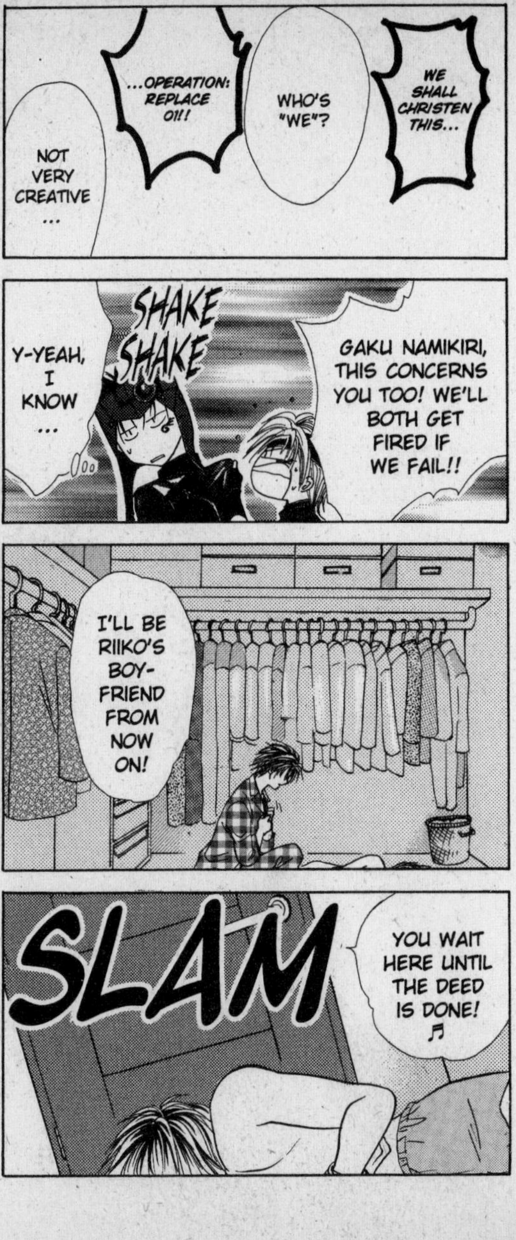
WE SHALL CHRISTEN THIS...
WHO'S "WE"?
...OPERATION: REPLACE OI!!
NOT VERY CREATIVE...
GAKU NAMIKIRI, THIS CONCERNS YOU TOO! WE'LL BOTH GET FIRED IF WE FAIL!!
SHAKE SHAKE
Y-YEAH, I KNOW...
I'LL BE RIIKO'S BOY-FRIEND FROM NOW ON!
YOU WAIT HERE UNTIL THE DEED IS DONE! ♬
SLAM

It's almost time to say goodbye. The next volume will be the last! Hmm, what will happen? ^^; I wonder what kind of fan reactions I'll get... Heh heh heh heh heh... (sinister laugh)
Anyway, I find it hard to read online posts and e-mails from teenagers these days. (All that "j00" and "roxx0rz" stuff.) I don't get why they type this junk.
Oh well. At least they don't write that stuff in handwritten letters. ^^; It's kind of interesting. But these days, I'm more fascinated by the beauty of classical Japanese language. Modern Japanese is so screwed up. My usage is pretty messed up too, though.
Especially when I get tired, words come out of my mouth all wrong. Sometimes I surprise myself. It's like my brain stops working.
Thanks so much for reading! See you in the next volume!

And then...
And then...

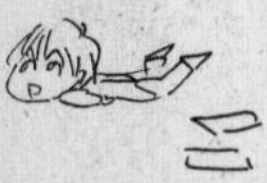

Stop dreaming.

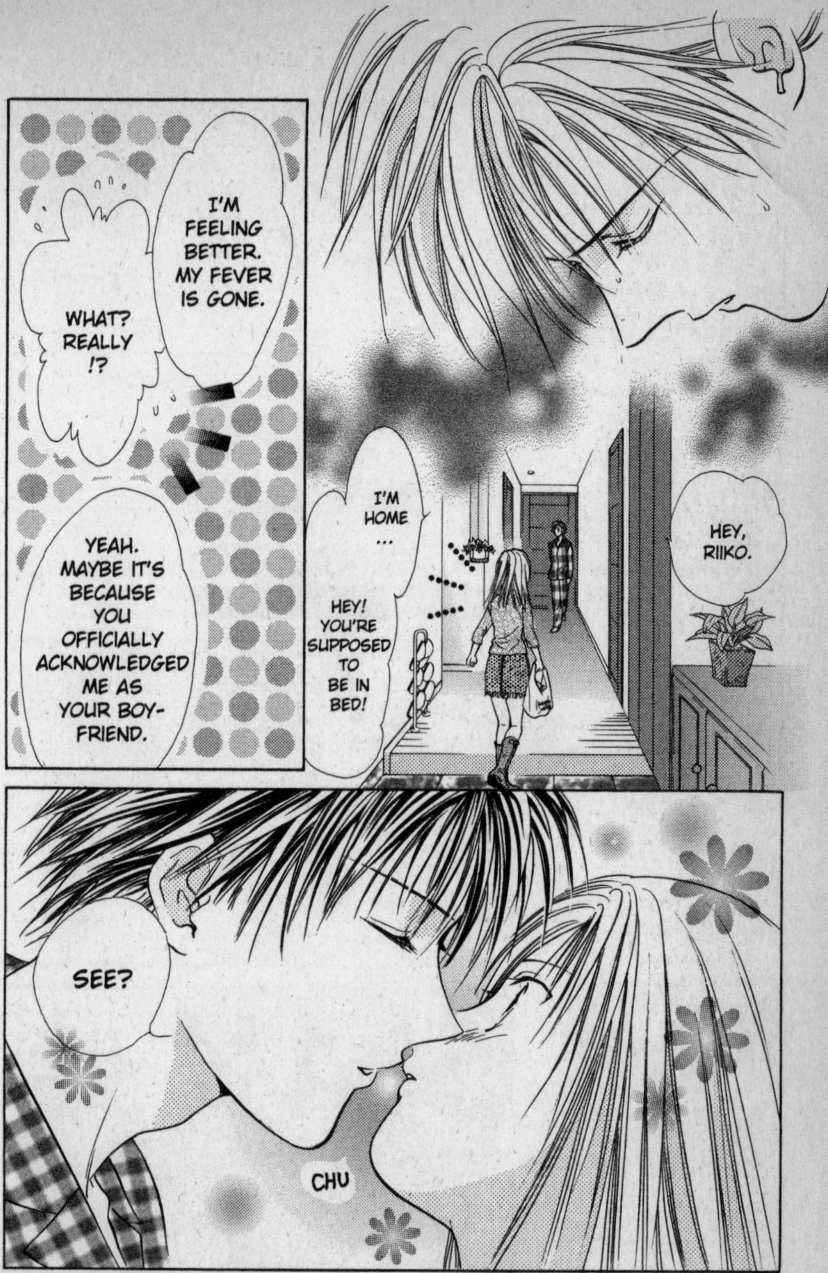
HEY, RIIKO.
I'M HOME ...
HEY! YOU'RE SUPPOSED TO BE IN BED!
I'M FEELING BETTER. MY FEVER IS GONE.
WHAT? REALLY !?
YEAH. MAYBE IT'S BECAUSE YOU OFFICIALLY ACKNOWLEDGED ME AS YOUR BOY-FRIEND.
SEE?
CHU

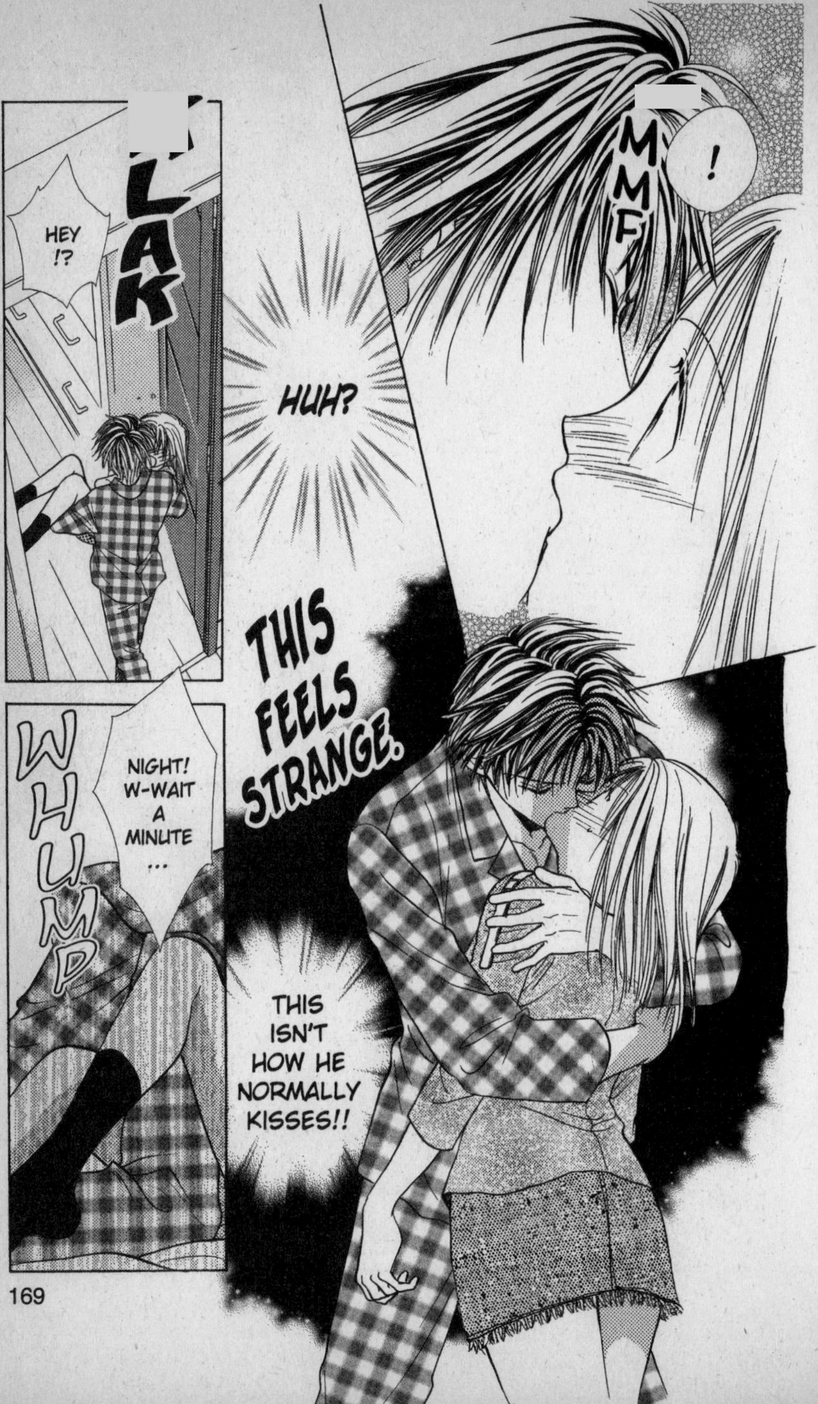
!
MMF
HUH?
THIS FEELS STRANGE.
THIS ISN'T HOW HE NORMALLY KISSES!!
LAK
HEY !?
WHUMP
NIGHT! W-WAIT A MINUTE ...

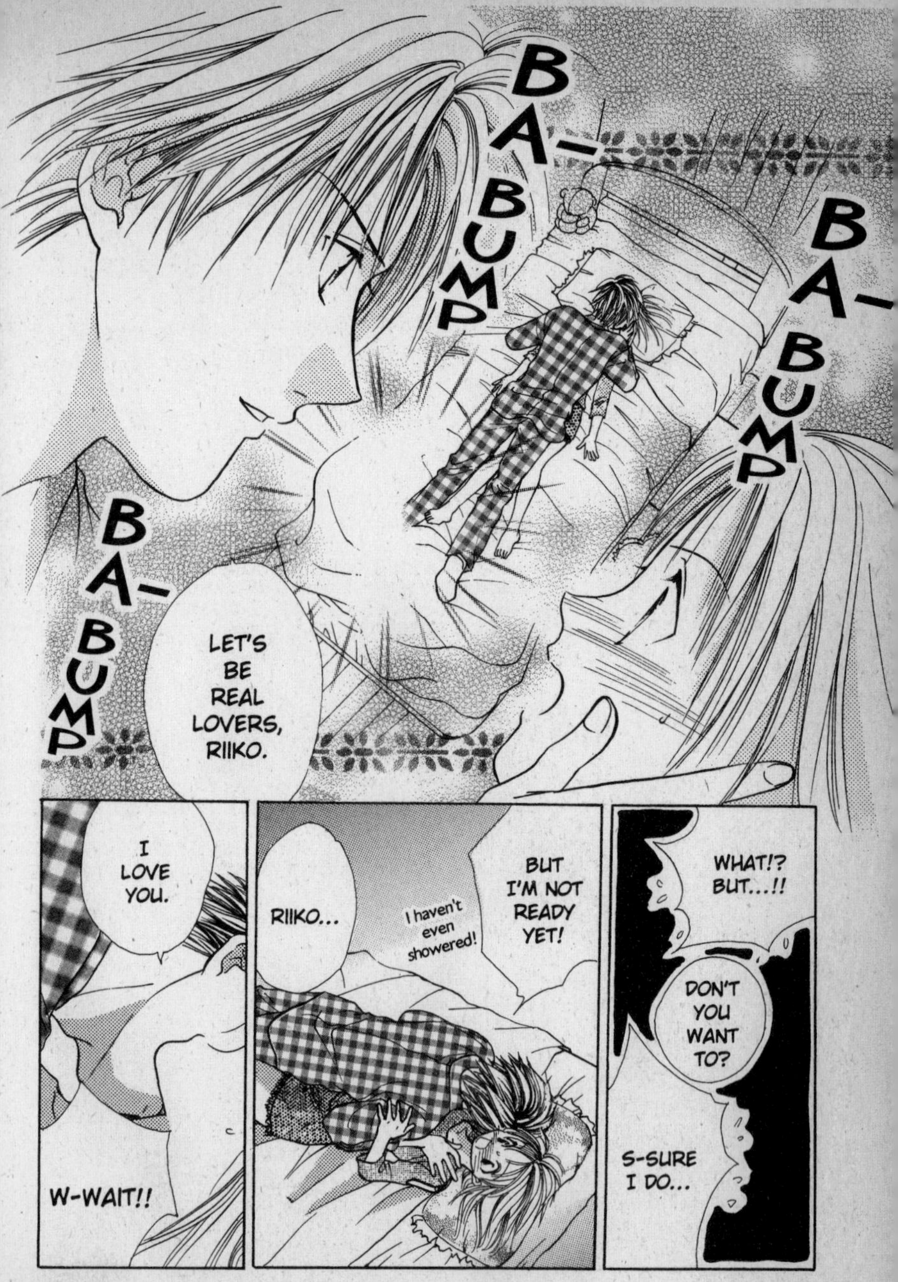
BA-BUMP
BA-BUMP
BA-BUMP
LET'S BE REAL LOVERS, RIIKO.
WHAT!? BUT...!!
DON'T YOU WANT TO?
S-SURE I DO...
BUT I'M NOT READY YET!
I haven't even showered!
RIIKO...
I LOVE YOU.
W-WAIT!!

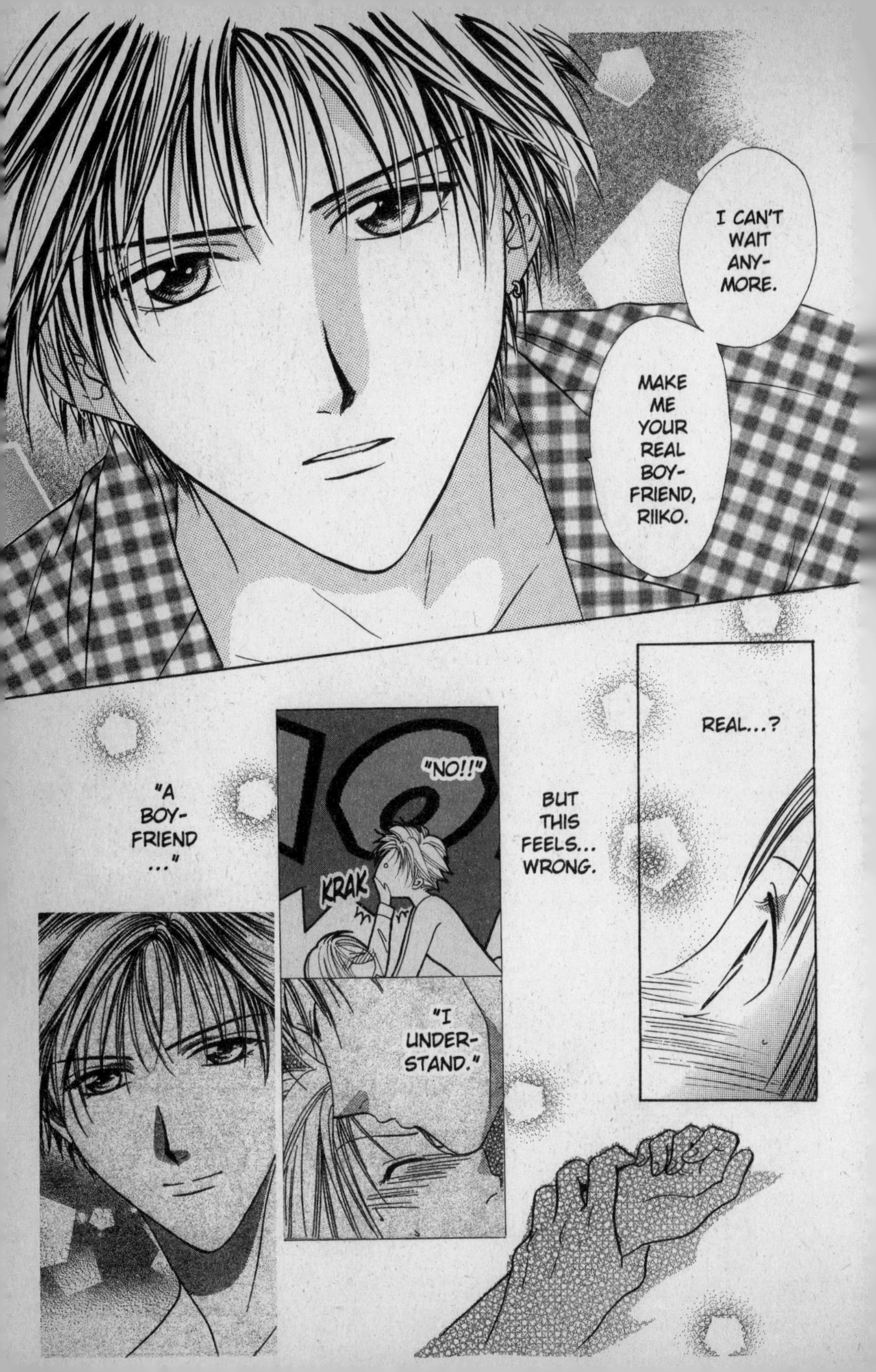
I CAN'T WAIT ANY-MORE.
MAKE ME YOUR REAL BOY-FRIEND, RIIKO.
REAL...?
BUT THIS FEELS... WRONG.
"NO!!"
KRAK
"A BOY-FRIEND..."
"I UNDER-STAND."

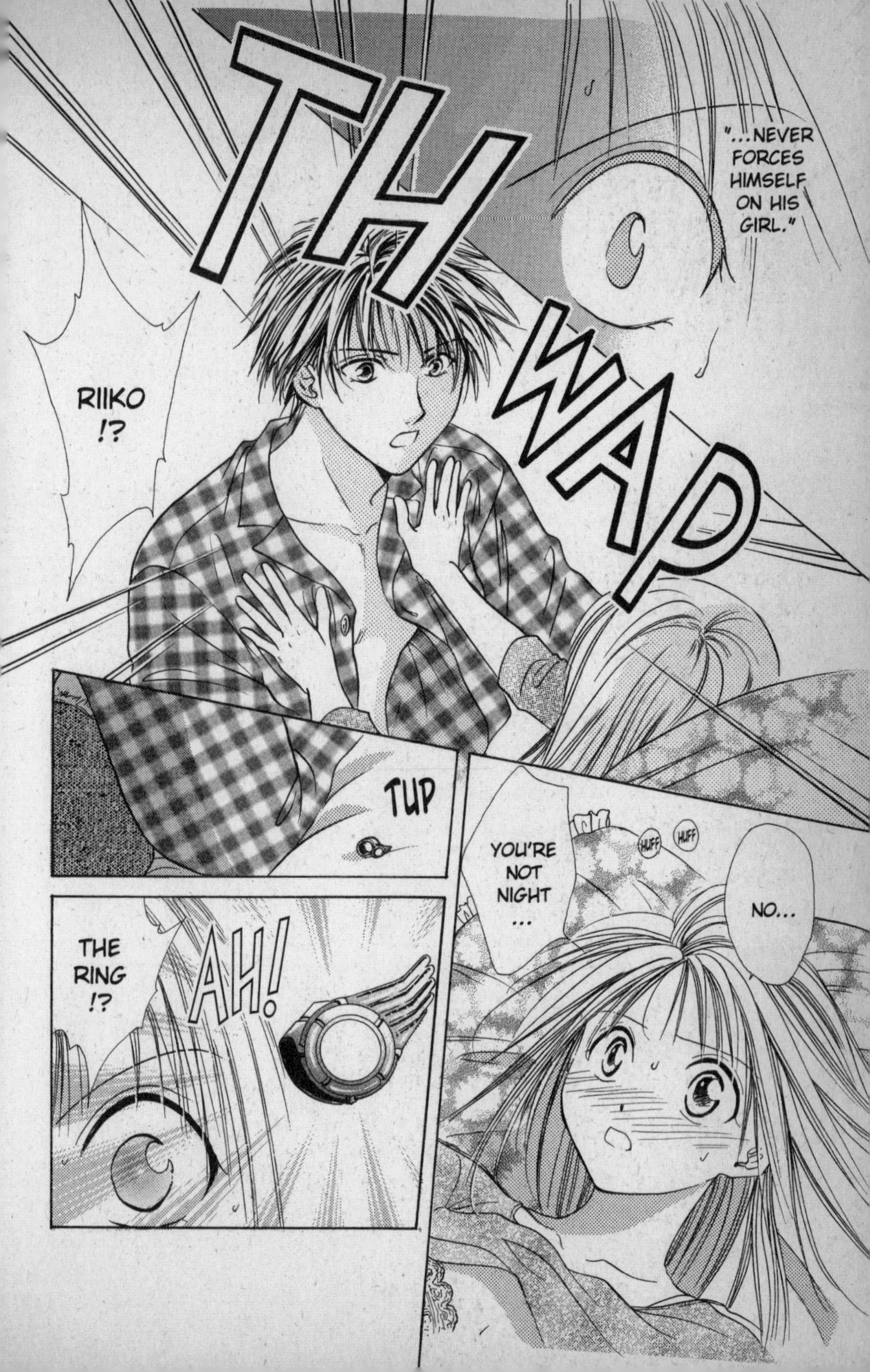
"...NEVER FORCES HIMSELF ON HIS GIRL."
THWAP
RIIKO!?
NO...
HUFF
HUFF
YOU'RE NOT NIGHT...
TUP
AH!
THE RING!?

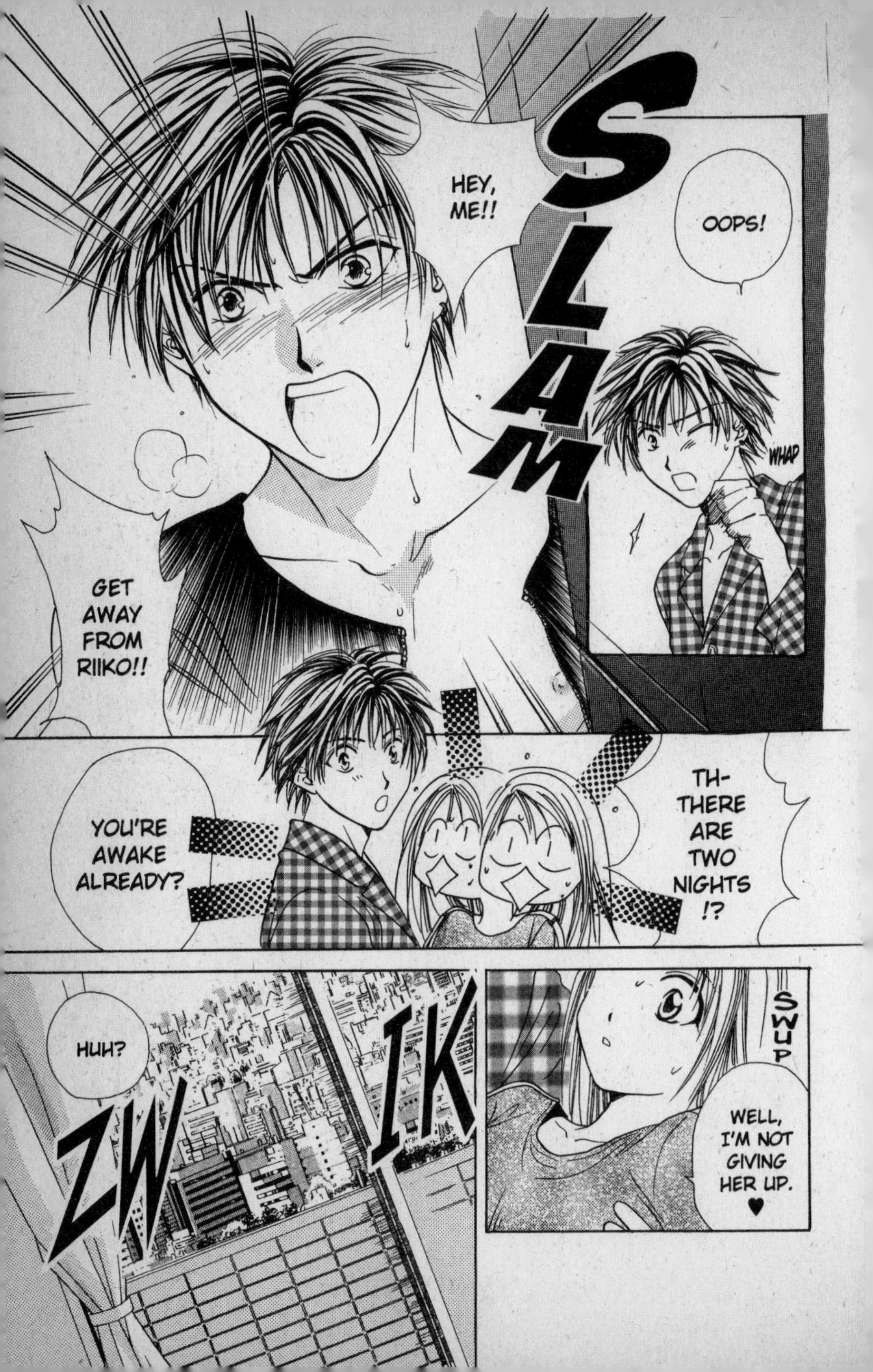
OOPS!
WHAP
SLAM
HEY, ME!!
GET AWAY FROM RIIKO!!
TH-THERE ARE TWO NIGHTS !?
YOU'RE AWAKE ALREADY?
SWUP
WELL, I'M NOT GIVING HER UP. ♥
HUH?
ZWIK

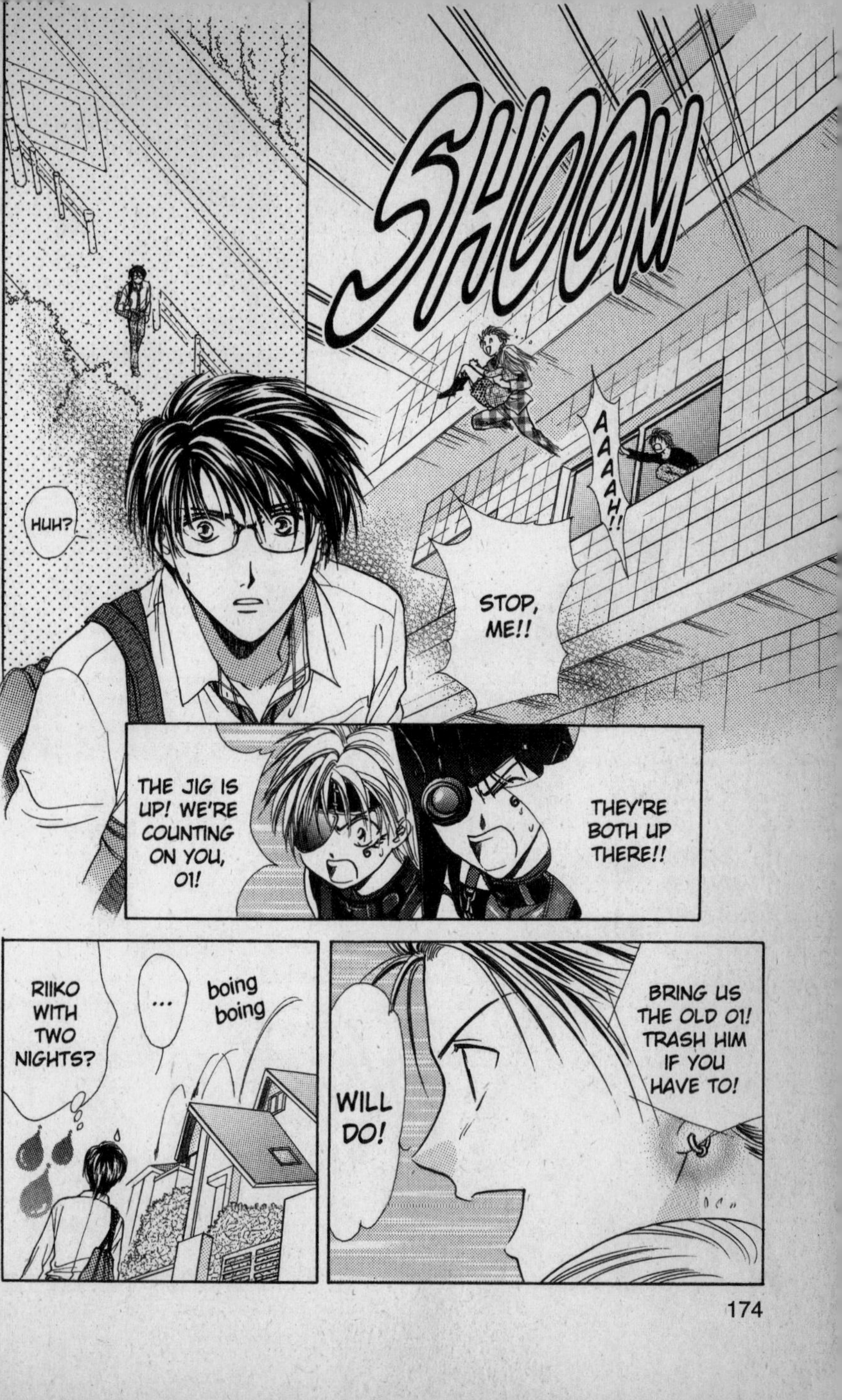
SHOOM
AAAAH!!
STOP, ME!!
HUH?
THEY'RE BOTH UP THERE!!
THE JIG IS UP! WE'RE COUNTING ON YOU, 01!
BRING US THE OLD 01! TRASH HIM IF YOU HAVE TO!
WILL DO!
boing boing
...
RIIKO WITH TWO NIGHTS?

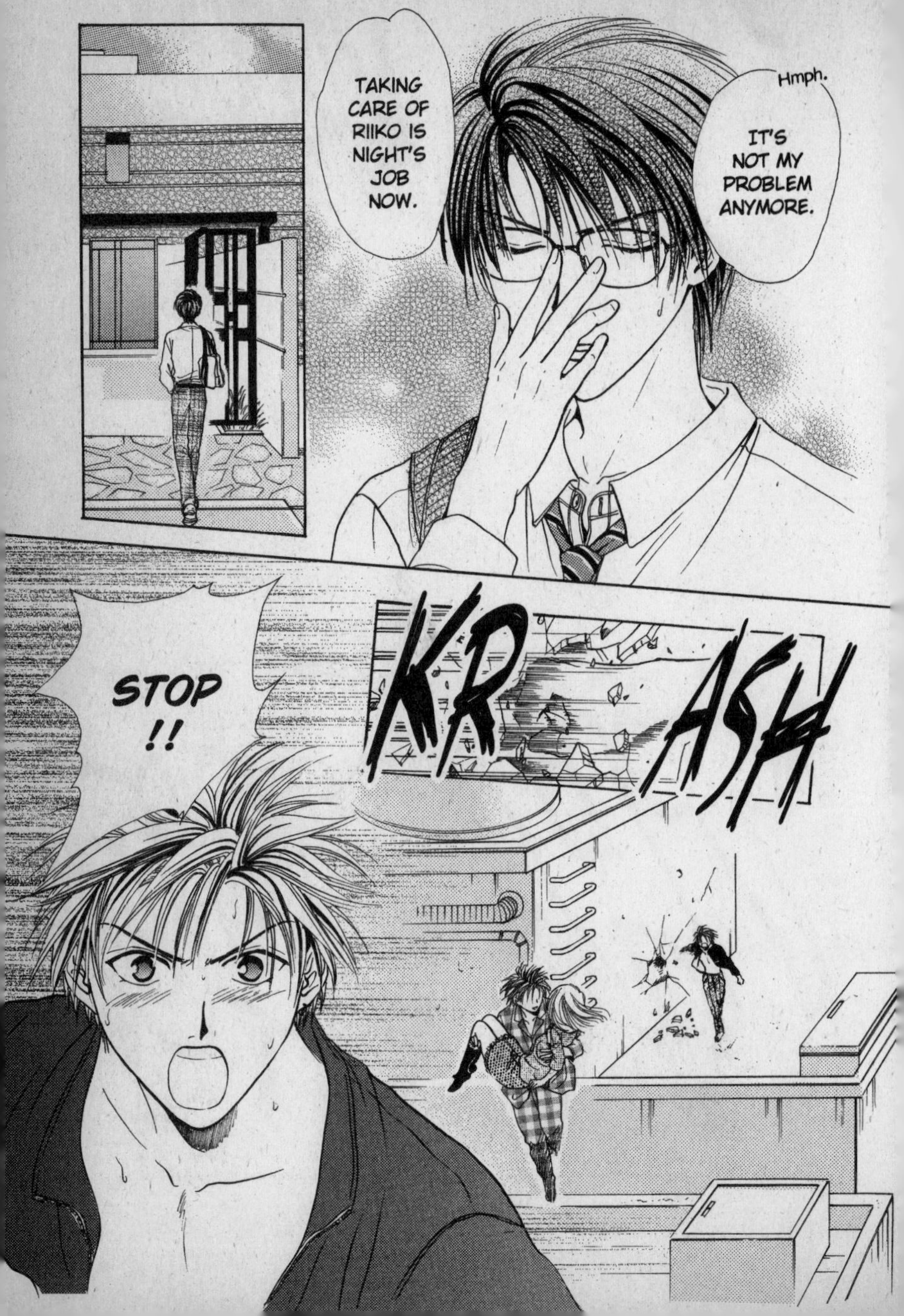
Hmph.
IT'S NOT MY PROBLEM ANYMORE.
TAKING CARE OF RIIKO IS NIGHT'S JOB NOW.
KRASH
STOP !!

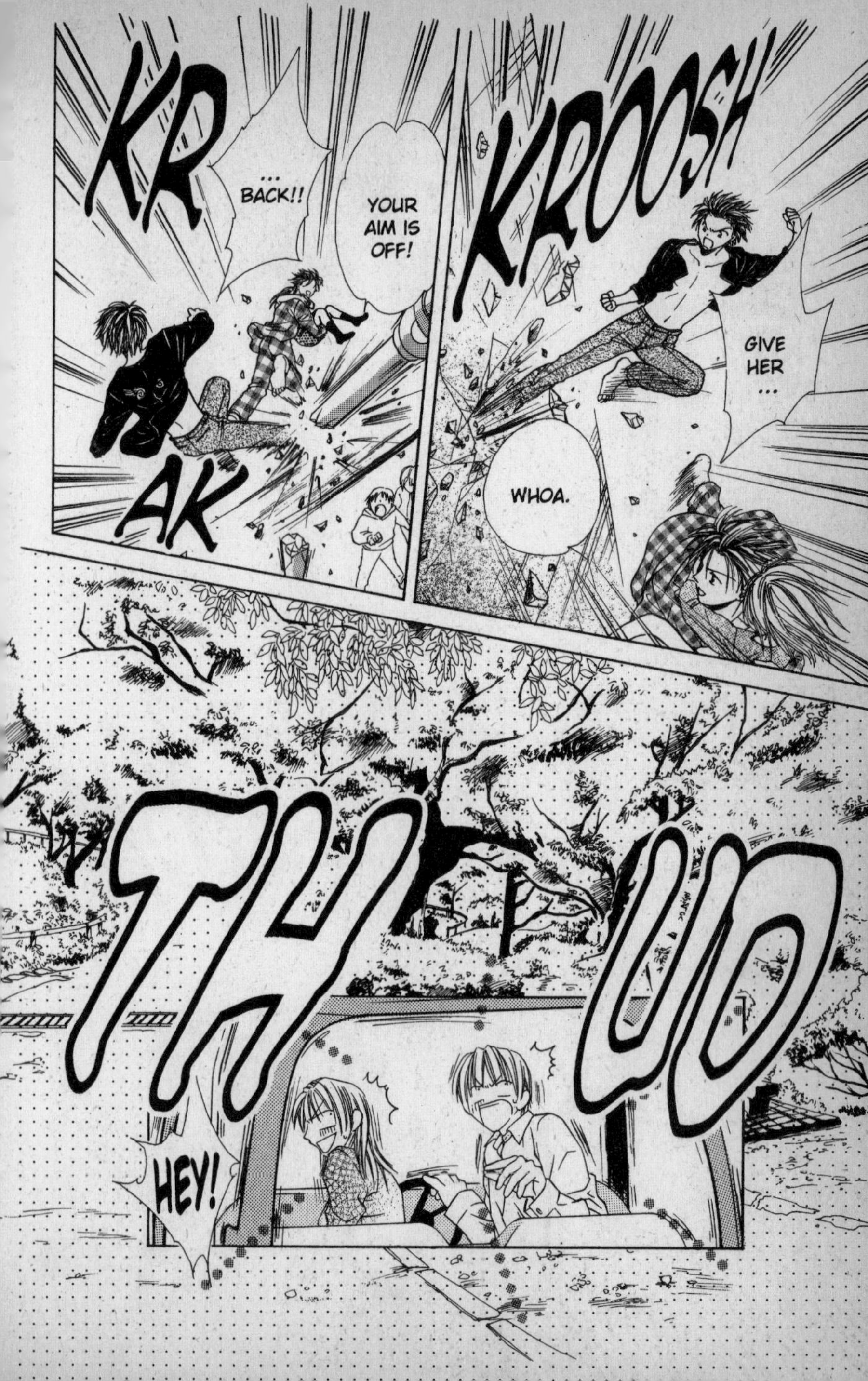
KROOSH
GIVE HER ...
WHOA.
... BACK!!
YOUR AIM IS OFF!
KR
AK
THUD
HEY!

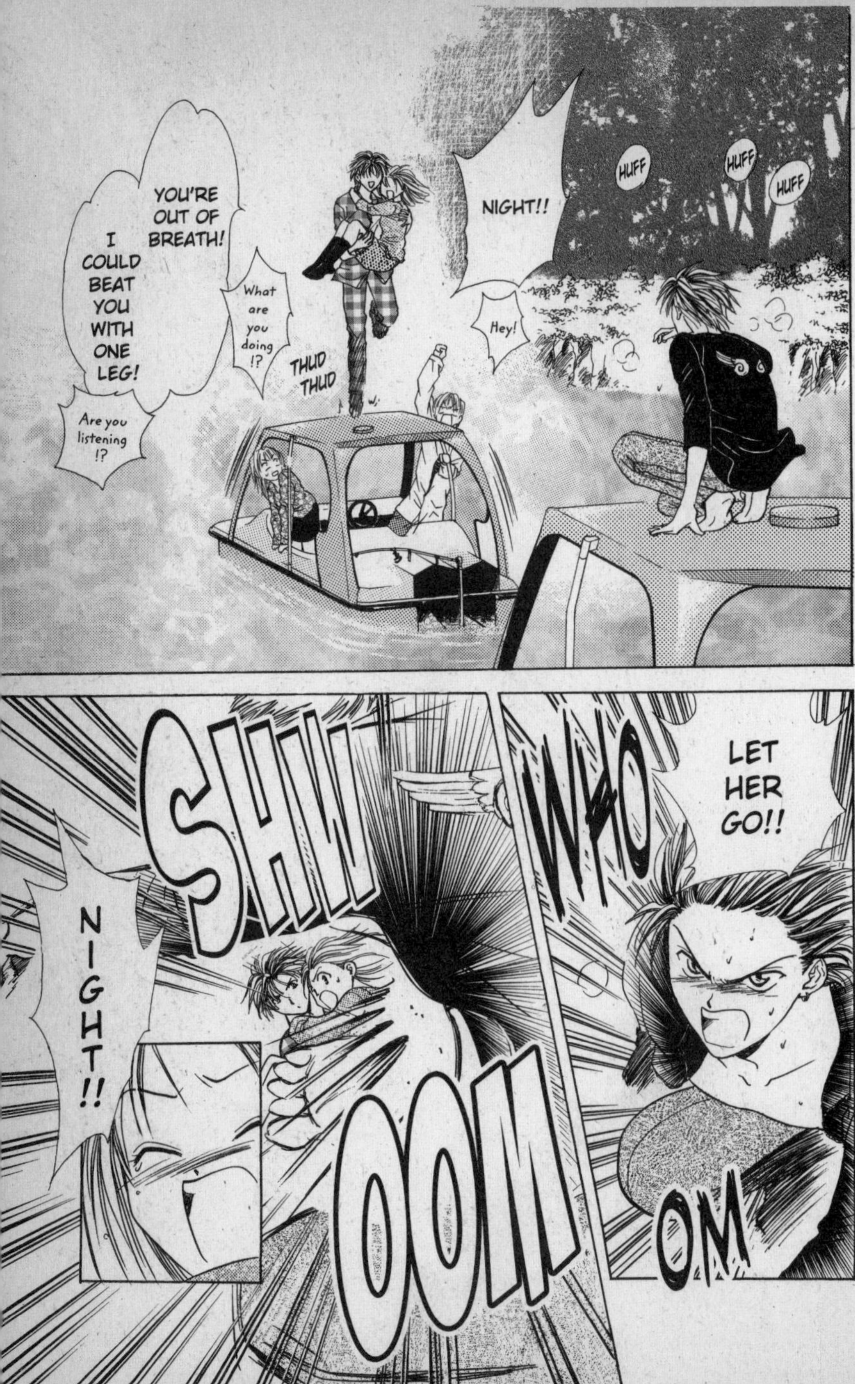
HUFF
HUFF
HUFF
NIGHT!!
Hey!
What are you doing !?
THUD THUD
YOU'RE OUT OF BREATH!
I COULD BEAT YOU WITH ONE LEG!
Are you listening !?
LET HER GO!!
WHO
OM
SHW
OOM
NIGHT!!

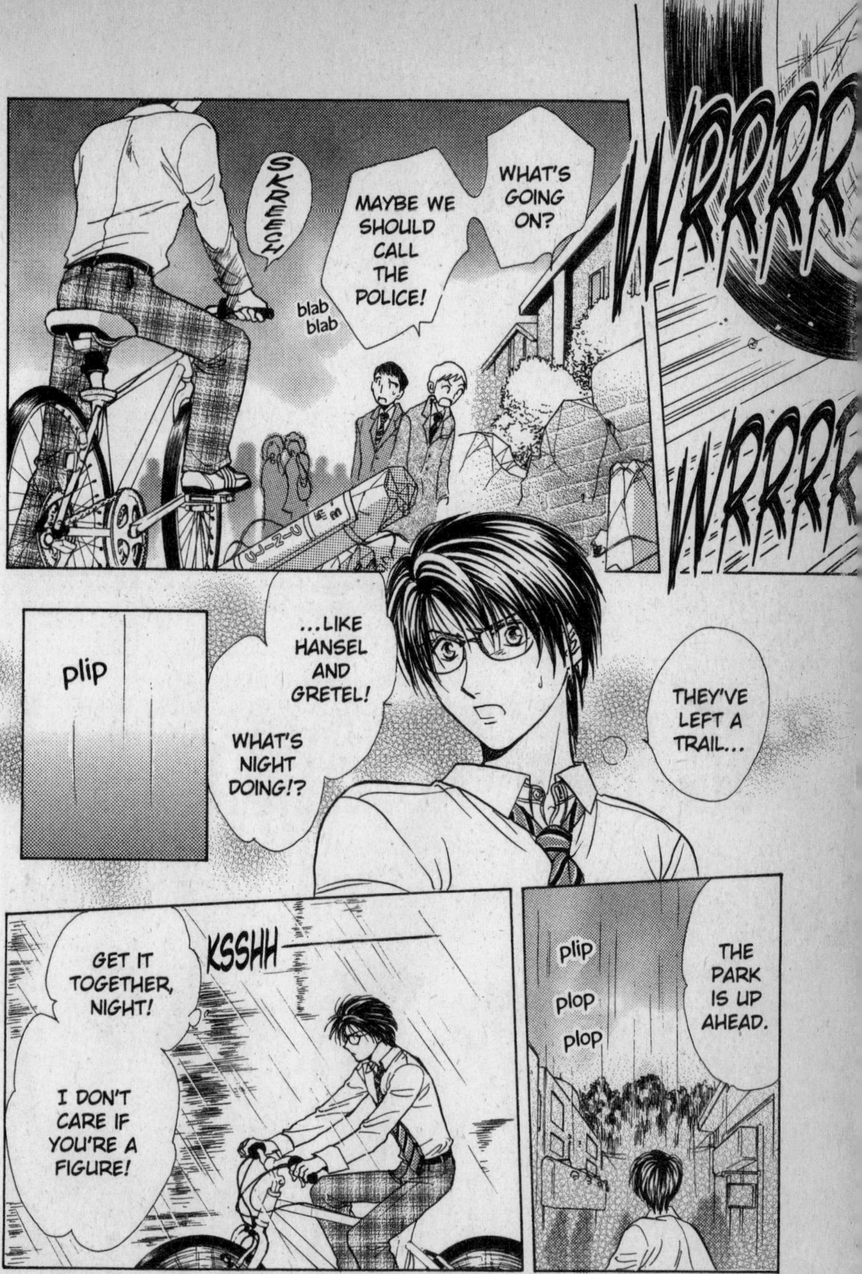
WRRRR
WRRRR
WHAT'S GOING ON?
MAYBE WE SHOULD CALL THE POLICE!
blab blab
SKREECH
THEY'VE LEFT A TRAIL...
...LIKE HANSEL AND GRETEL!
WHAT'S NIGHT DOING!?
plip
THE PARK IS UP AHEAD.
plip
plop
plop
KSSHH
GET IT TOGETHER, NIGHT!
I DON'T CARE IF YOU'RE A FIGURE!

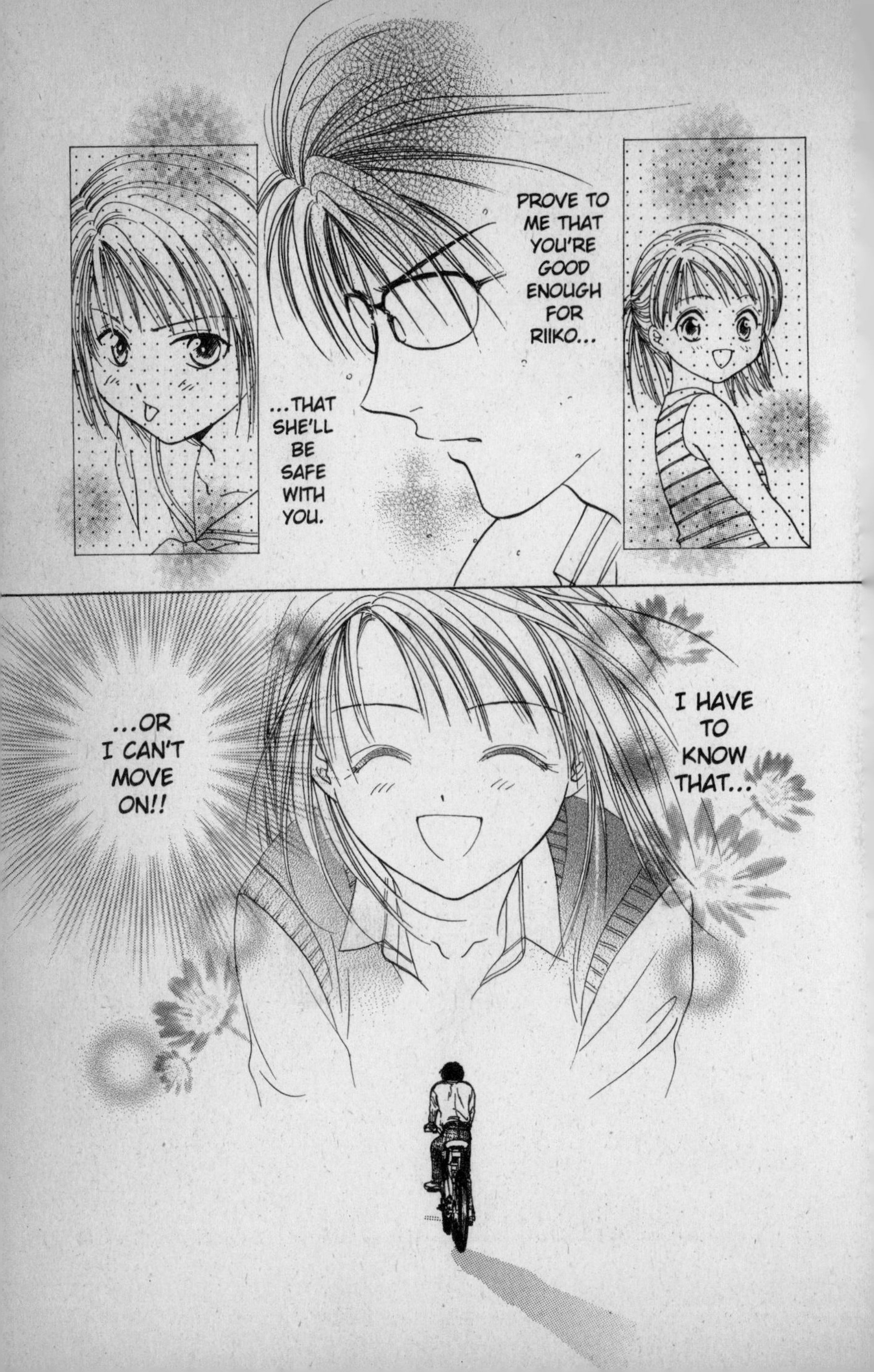
PROVE TO ME THAT YOU'RE GOOD ENOUGH FOR RIIKO...
...THAT SHE'LL BE SAFE WITH YOU.
I HAVE TO KNOW THAT...
...OR I CAN'T MOVE ON!!

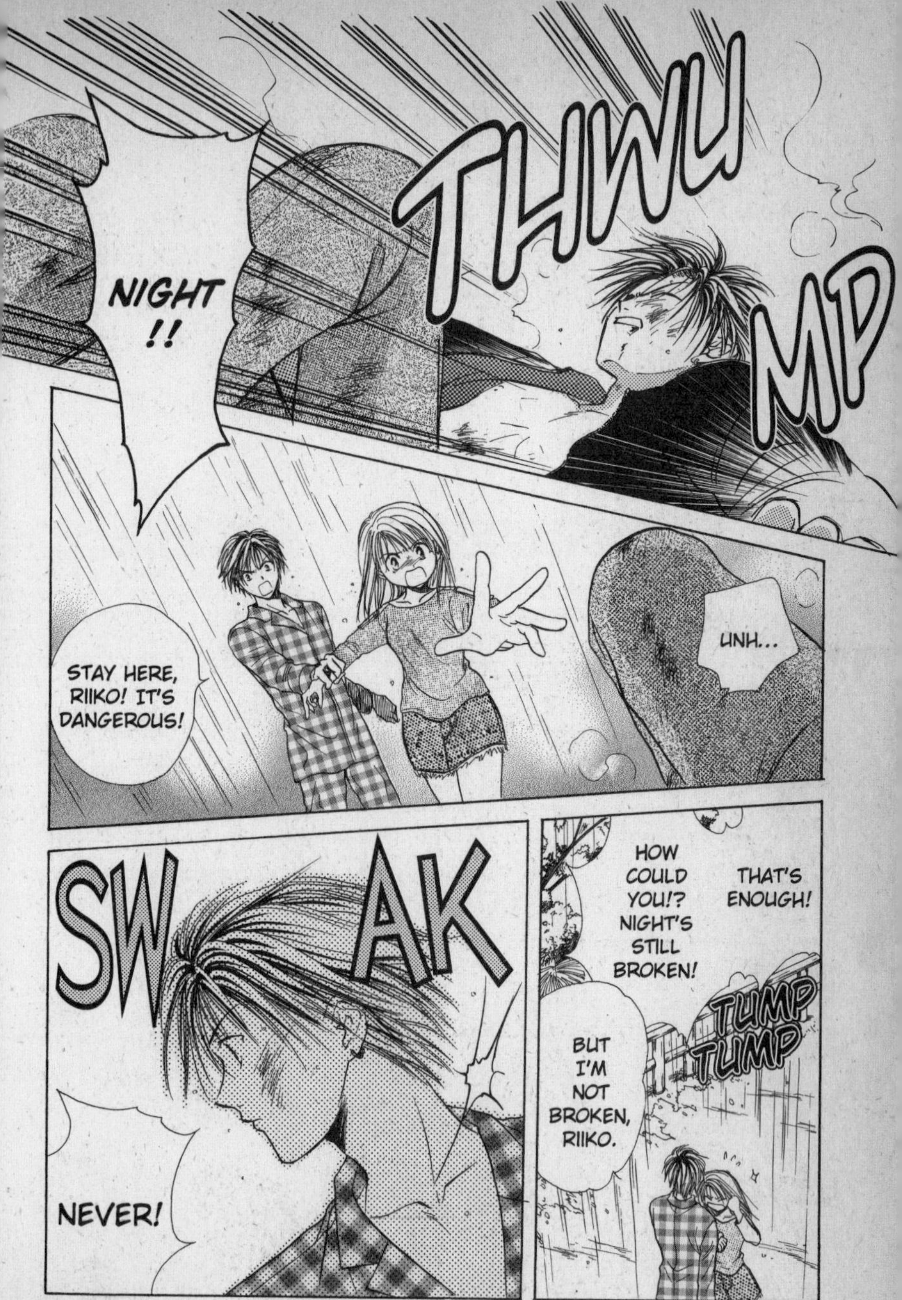
THWUMP
NIGHT !!
UNH...
STAY HERE, RIIKO! IT'S DANGEROUS!
THAT'S ENOUGH!
HOW COULD YOU!? NIGHT'S STILL BROKEN!
TUMP TUMP
BUT I'M NOT BROKEN, RIIKO.
SWAK
NEVER!

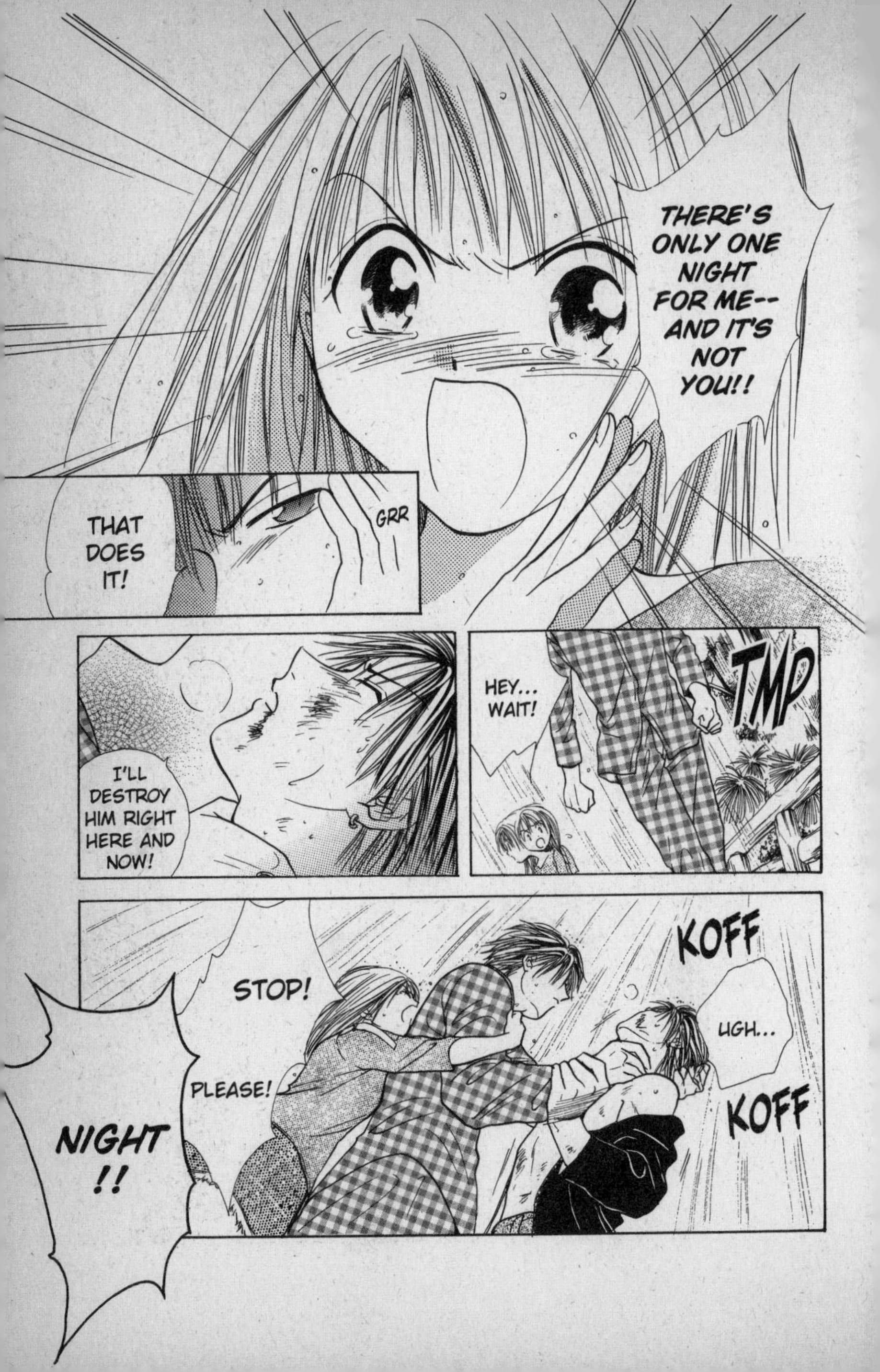
THERE'S ONLY ONE NIGHT FOR ME-- AND IT'S NOT YOU!!
GRR
THAT DOES IT!
TMP
HEY... WAIT!
I'LL DESTROY HIM RIGHT HERE AND NOW!
KOFF
UGH...
STOP!
KOFF
PLEASE!
NIGHT!!

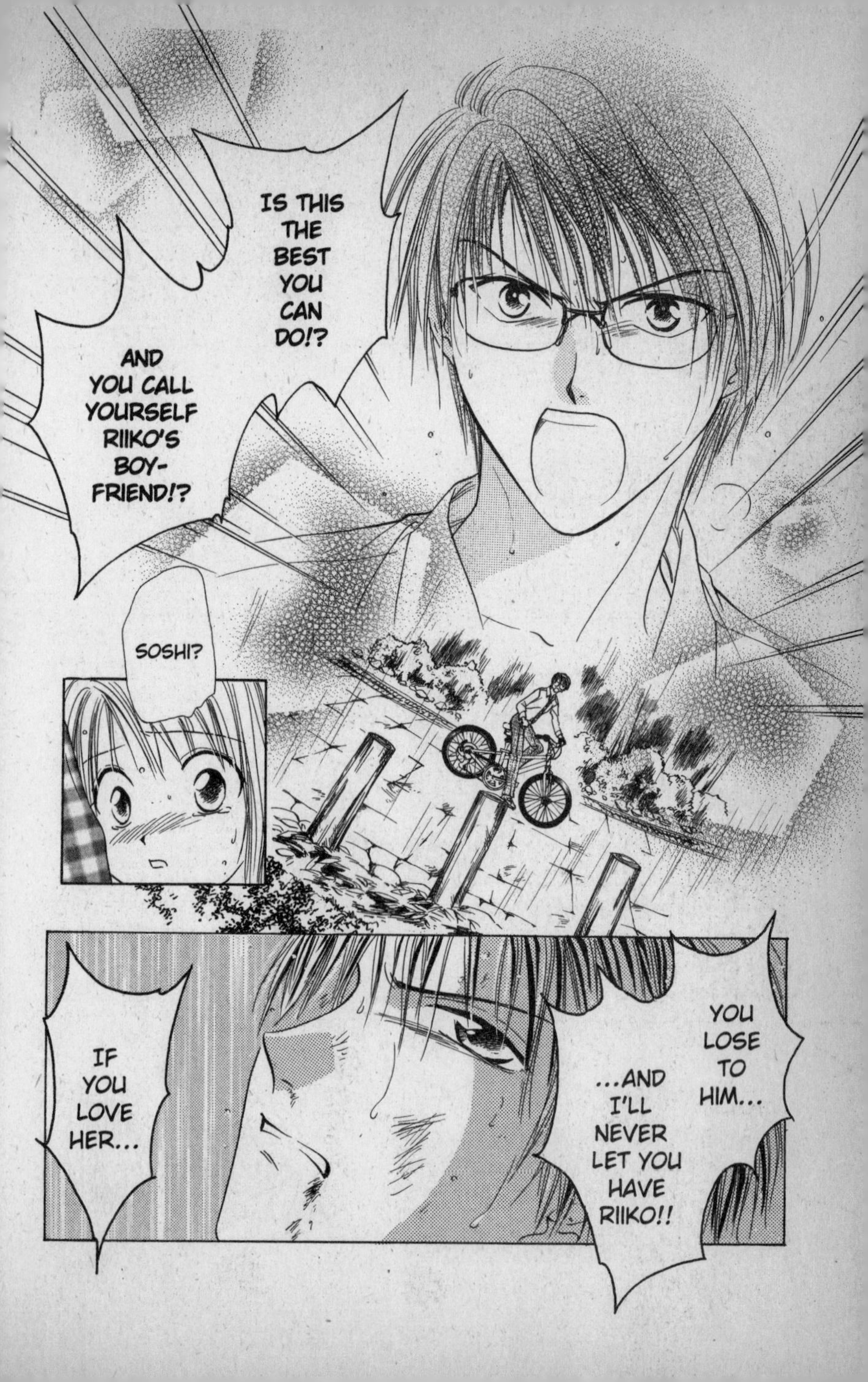
IS THIS THE BEST YOU CAN DO!?
AND YOU CALL YOURSELF RIIKO'S BOY-FRIEND!?
SOSHI?
YOU LOSE TO HIM...
...AND I'LL NEVER LET YOU HAVE RIIKO!!
IF YOU LOVE HER...

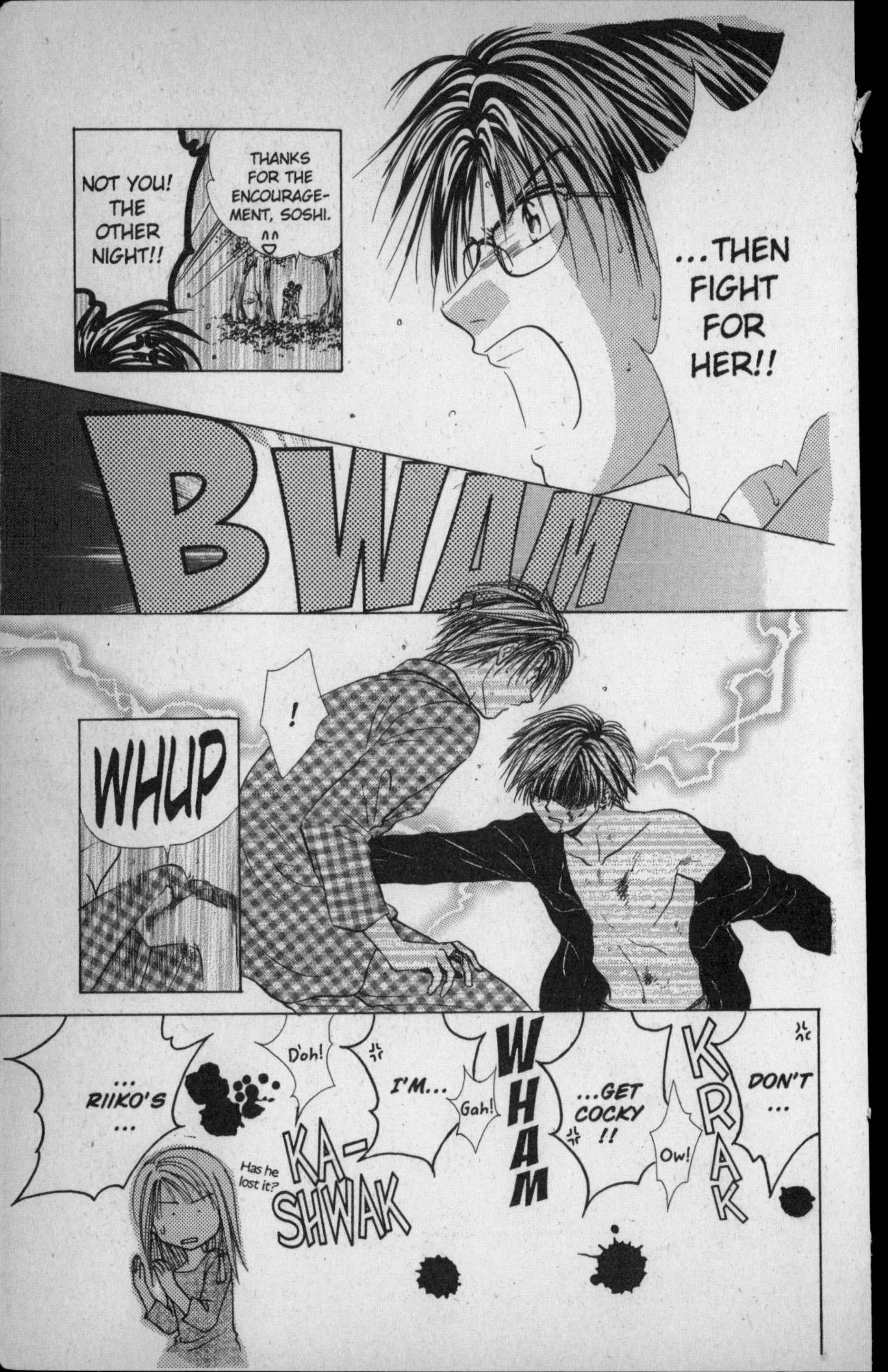
...THEN FIGHT FOR HER!!
THANKS FOR THE ENCOURAGE-MENT, SOSHI.
NOT YOU! THE OTHER NIGHT!!
BWAM
!
WHUP
DON'T ...
KRAK
Ow!
...GET COCKY !!
WHAM
Gah!
I'M...
D'oh!
KA-SHWAK
Has he lost it?
... RIIKO'S ...

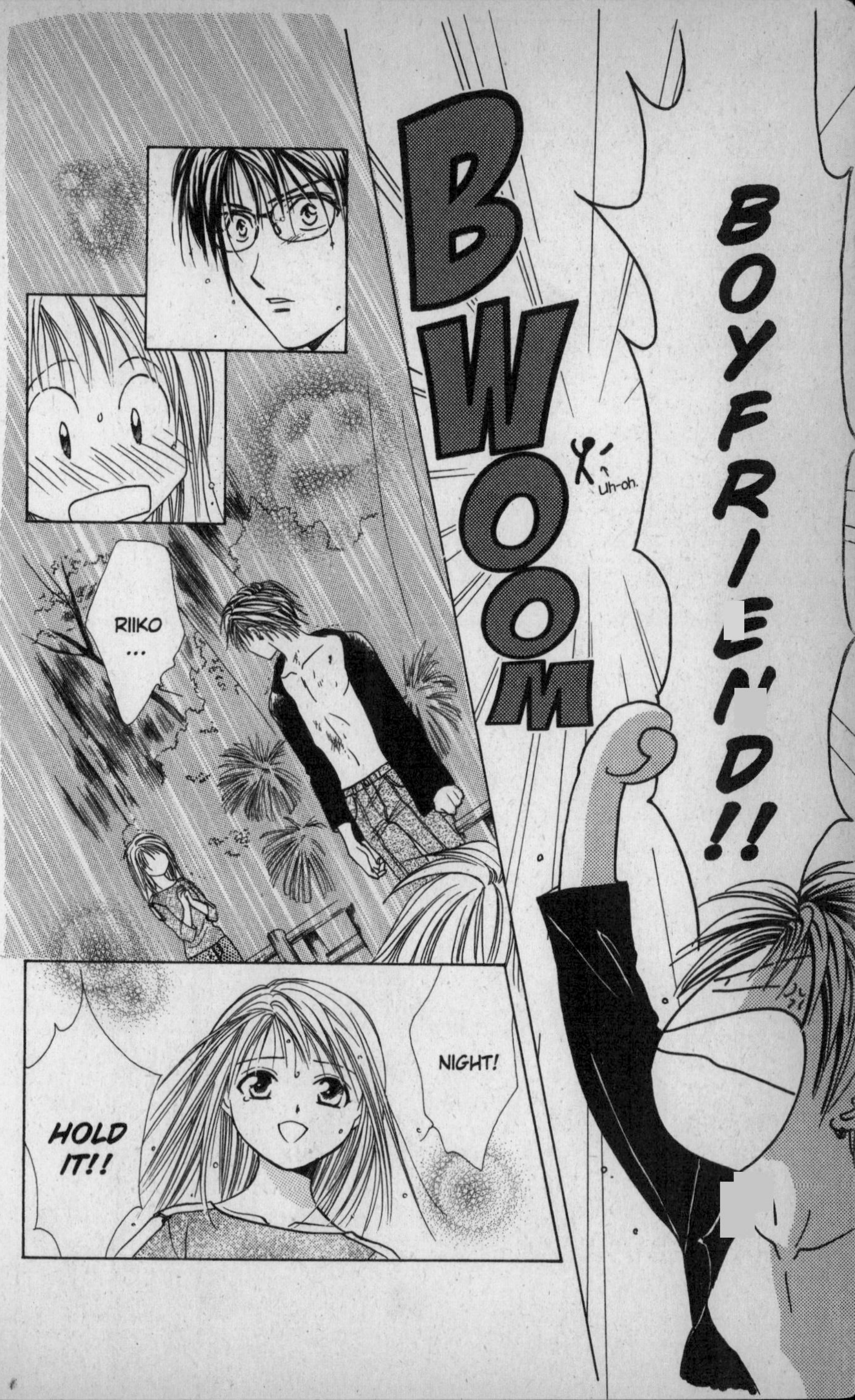
BOYFRIEND!!
BWOOM
uh-oh.
RIIKO ...
NIGHT!
HOLD IT!!

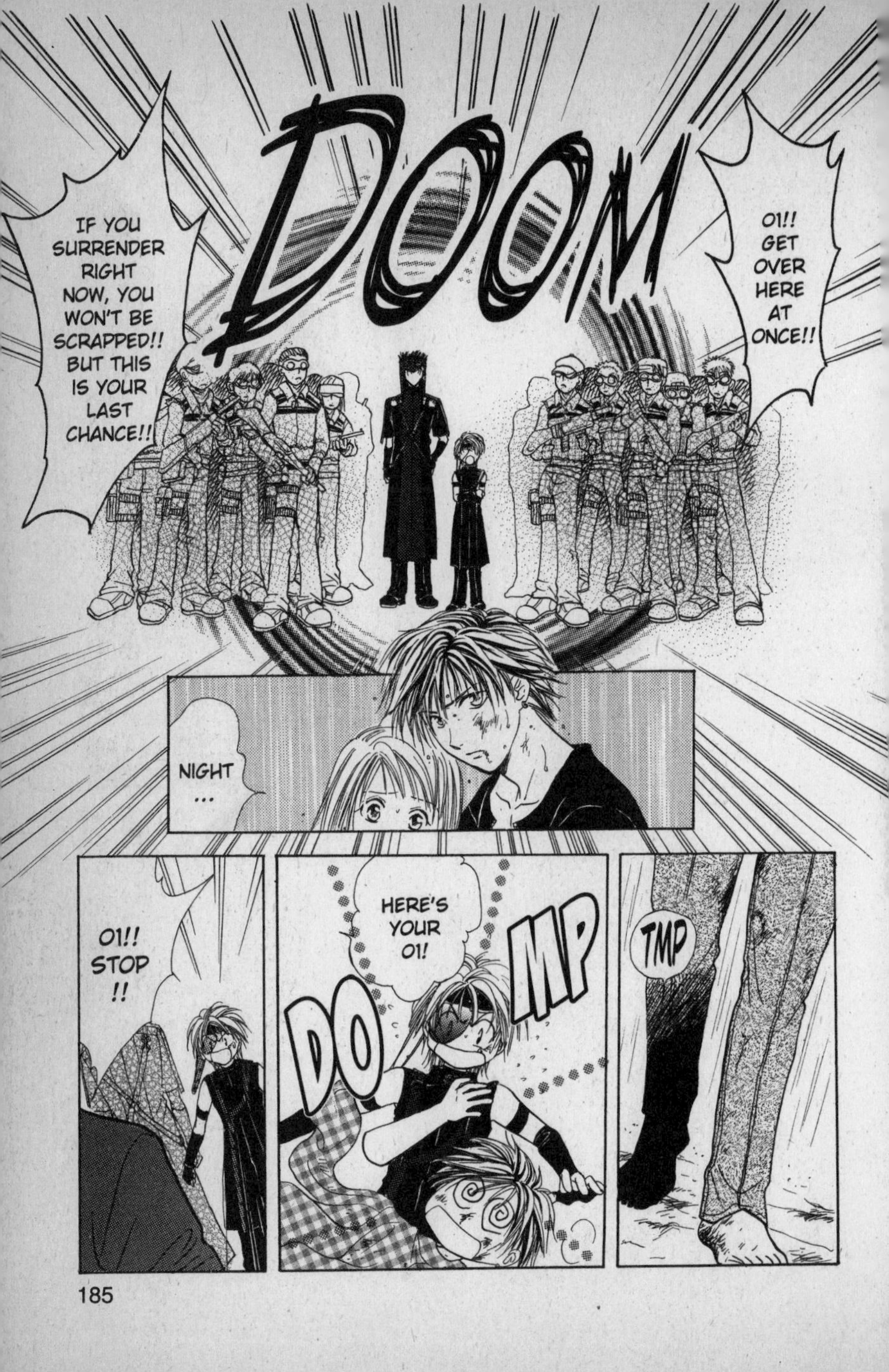
DOOM
01!! GET OVER HERE AT ONCE!!
IF YOU SURRENDER RIGHT NOW, YOU WON'T BE SCRAPPED!! BUT THIS IS YOUR LAST CHANCE!!
NIGHT ...
TMP
HERE'S YOUR 01!
DO
MP
01!! STOP !!

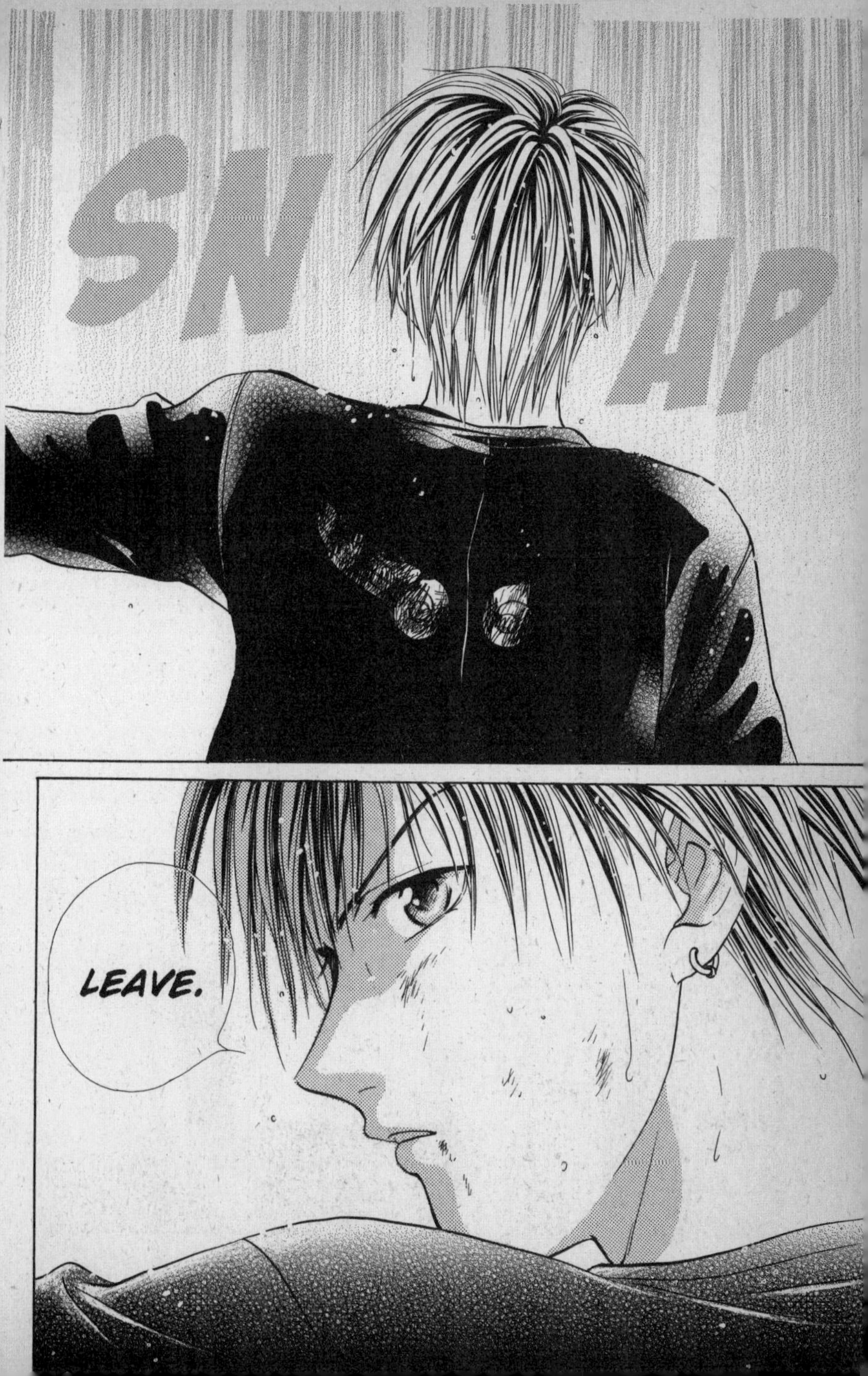
SNAP
LEAVE.

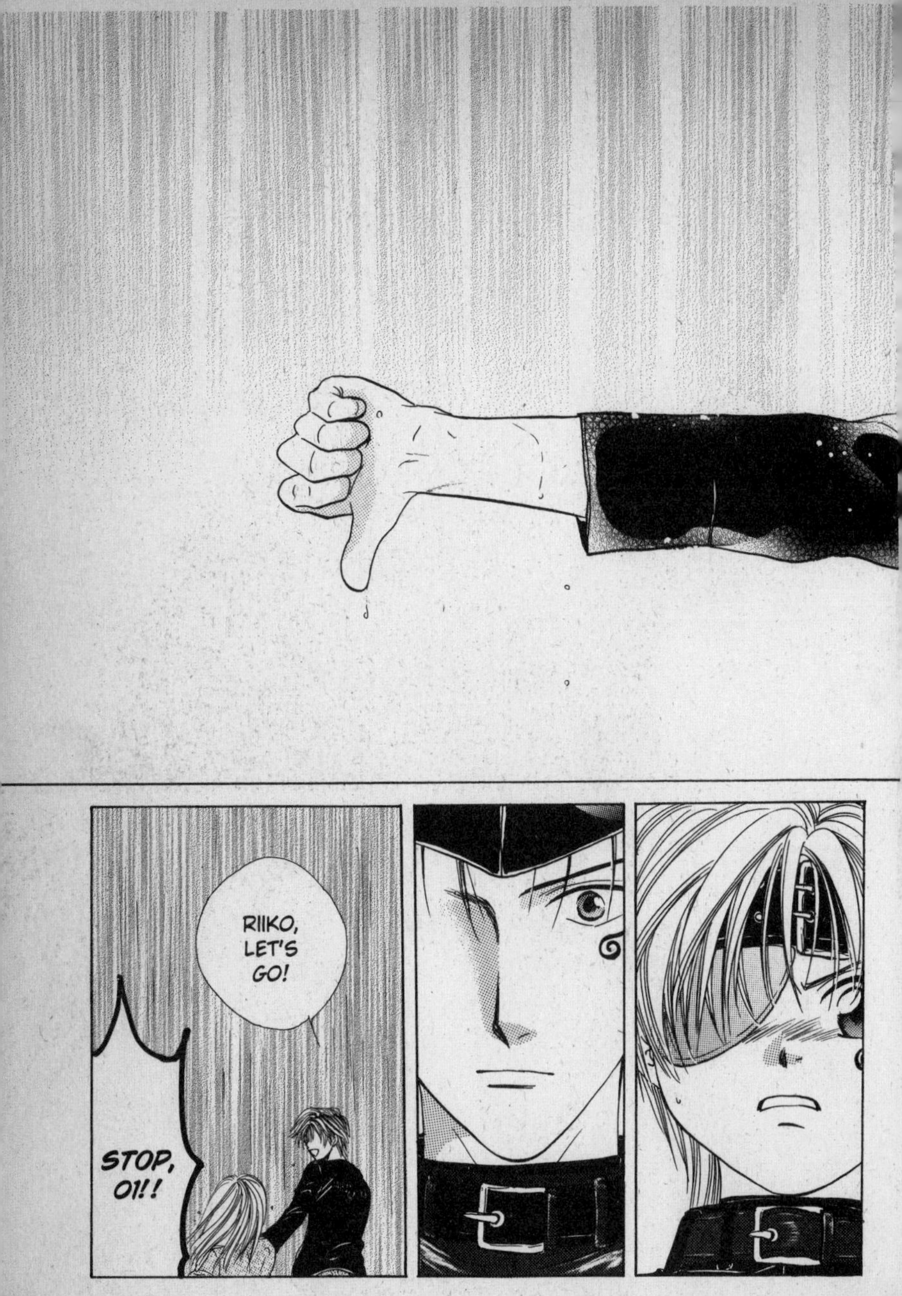
RIIKO, LET'S GO!
STOP, OI!!

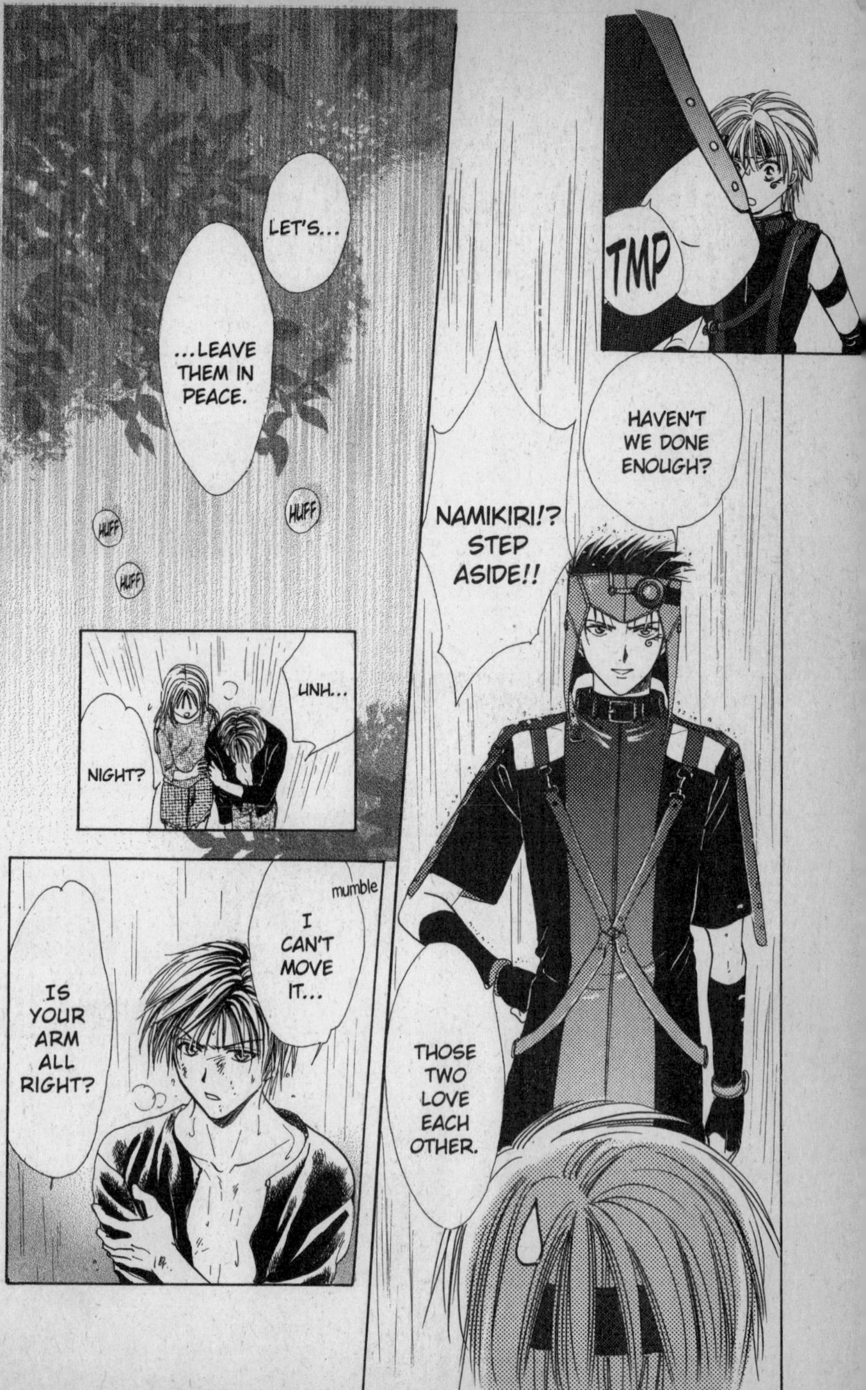
TMP
HAVEN'T WE DONE ENOUGH?
NAMIKIRI!? STEP ASIDE!!
THOSE TWO LOVE EACH OTHER.
LET'S...
...LEAVE THEM IN PEACE.
HUFF
HUFF
HUFF
UNH...
NIGHT?
mumble
I CAN'T MOVE IT...
IS YOUR ARM ALL RIGHT?

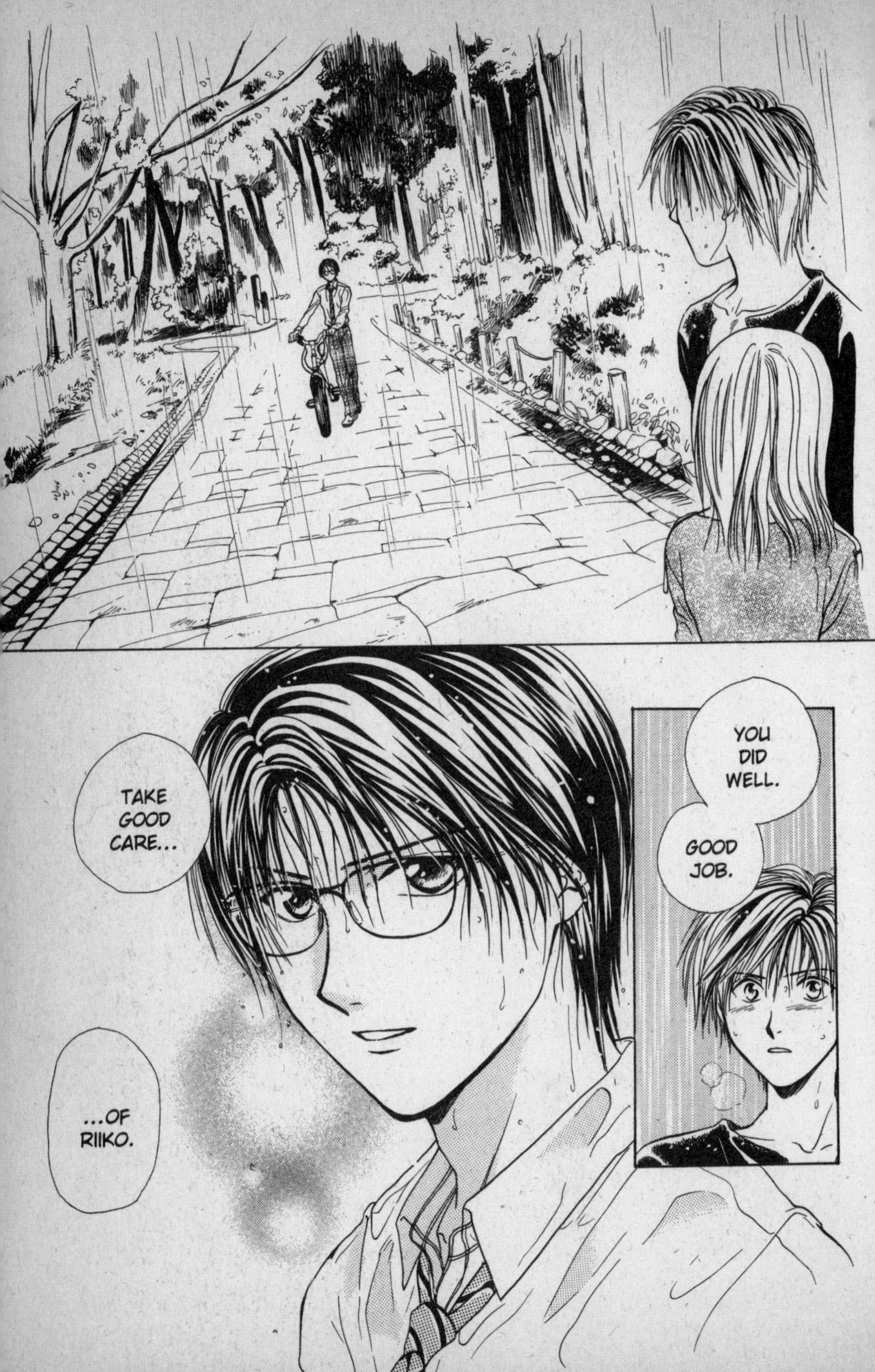
YOU DID WELL.
GOOD JOB.
TAKE GOOD CARE...
...OF RIIKO.

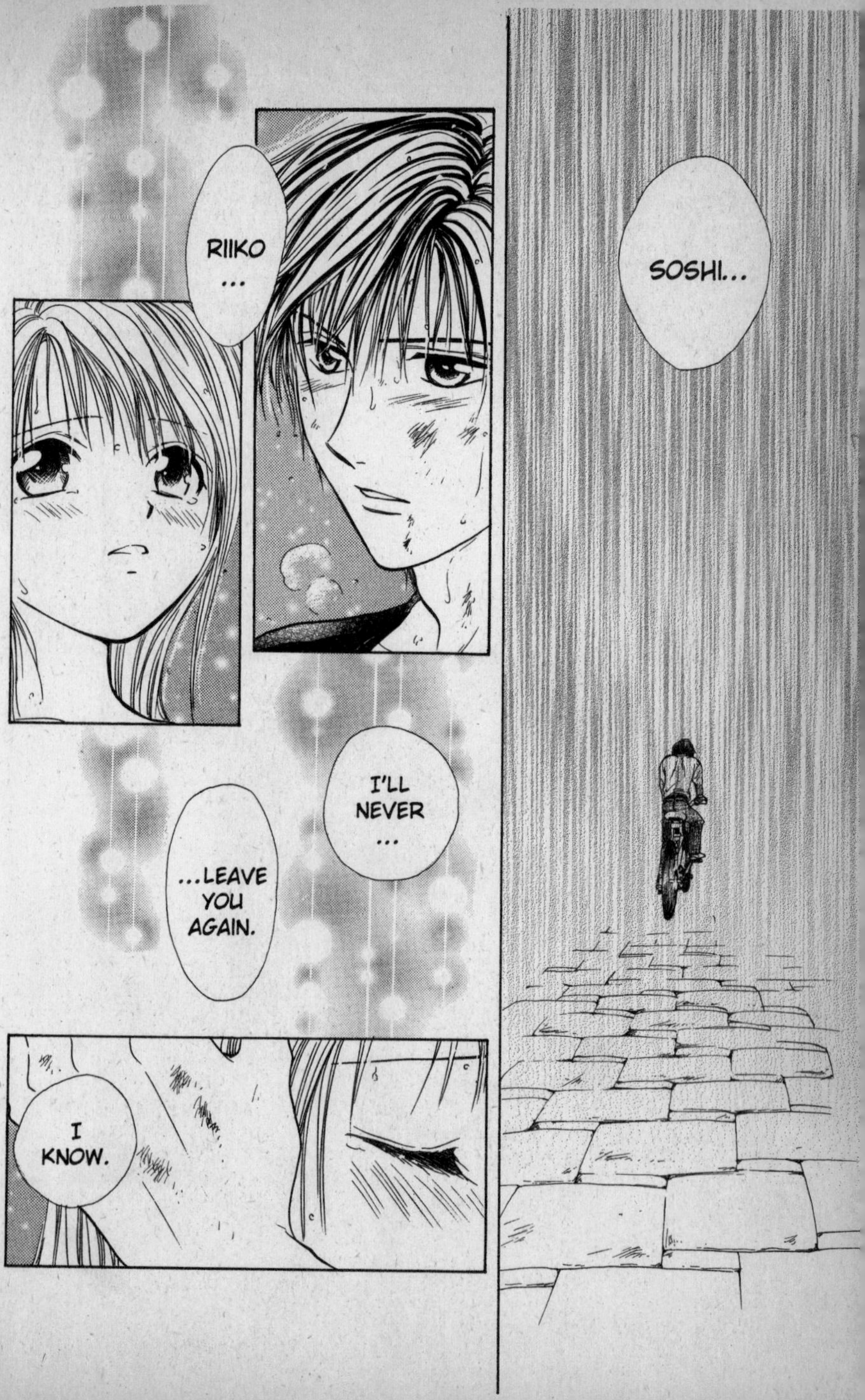
SOSHI...
RIIKO ...
I'LL NEVER ...
...LEAVE YOU AGAIN.
I KNOW.

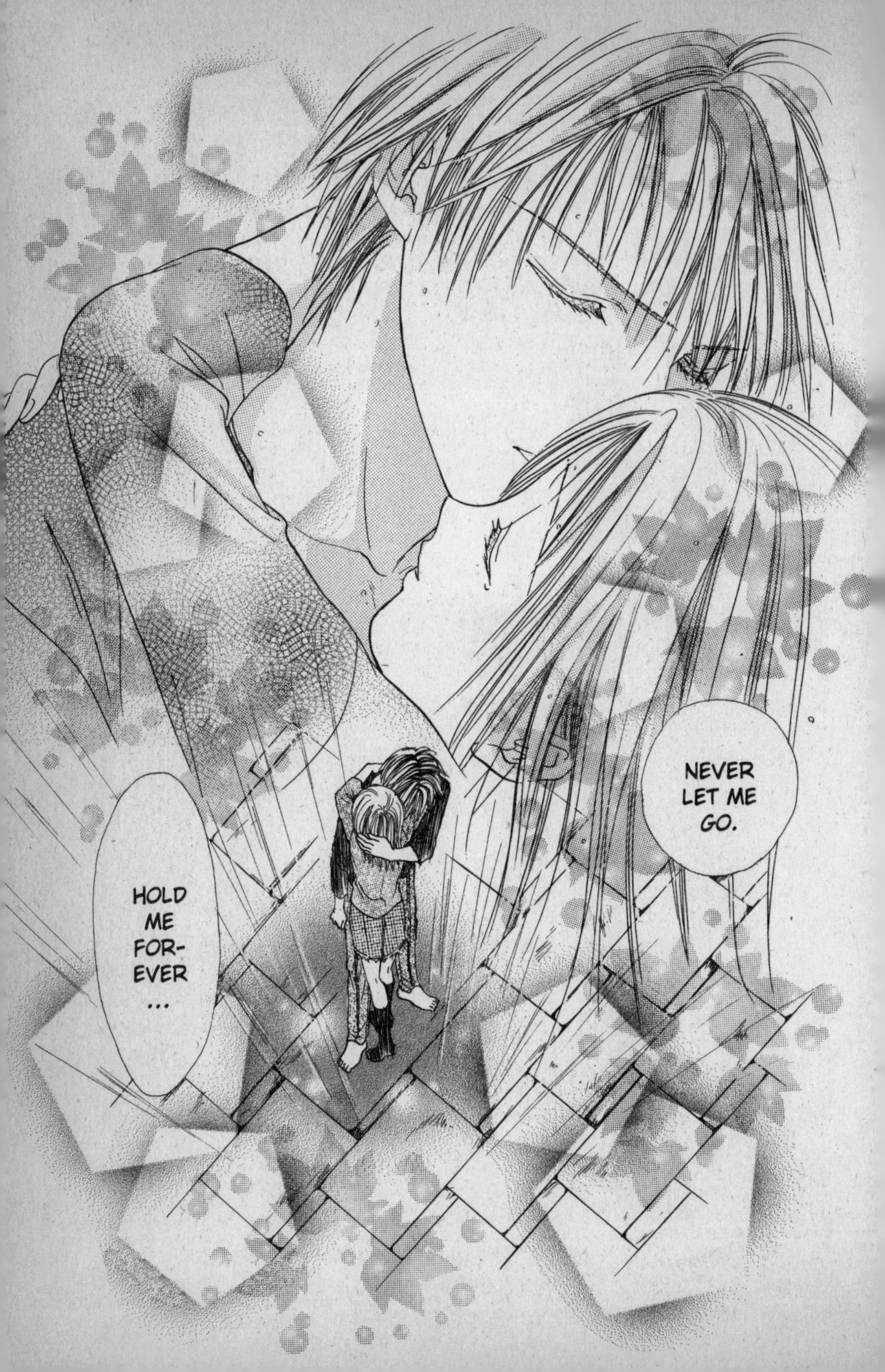
NEVER LET ME GO.
HOLD ME FOR-EVER ...

i try to be a health and wellness fanatic. i forced myself to eat *natto* (fermented soybeans) for the health benefits and now it's one of my favorite foods. i drink soymilk, eat a banana every morning, and drink cocoa regularly because i heard it's good for the stomach. i never forget my daily serving of yogurt. i also went through a wheatgrass juice and turmeric phase. But i always abuse myself with lack of sleep, lack of exercise, and too much stress. They cancel each other out! i guess i can never be a true health nut?

Yuu Watase

Birthday: March 5 (Pisces)

Blood type: B

Born and raised in Osaka.

Hobbies: listening to music, reading. Likes most music besides *enka* (traditional Japanese ballads) and heavy metal. Lately into health and wellness, like massage, mineral waters and wheatgrass juice. But her job is her biggest "hobby"!

Debut title: *Pajama de Ojama* (An intrusion in Pajamas) (*Shojo Comics*, 1989, No. 3)

ABSOLUTE BOYFRIEND
Volume 5
Shojo Beat Edition

Story and Art by
YUU WATASE

© 2003 Yuu WATASE/Shogakukan
All rights reserved.
Original Japanese edition "ZETTAI KARESHI"
published by SHOGAKUKAN Inc.

English Adaptation/Lance Caselman
Translation/Lillian Olsen
Touch-up Art & Lettering/Freeman Wong
Design/Courtney Utt
Editor/Nancy Thistlethwaite

Printed in Canada

Published by VIZ Media, LLC
P.O. Box 77010
San Francisco, CA 94107

10 9 8 7 6 5 4 3
First printing, February 2008
Third printing, August 2011

www.viz.com

www.shojobeat.com

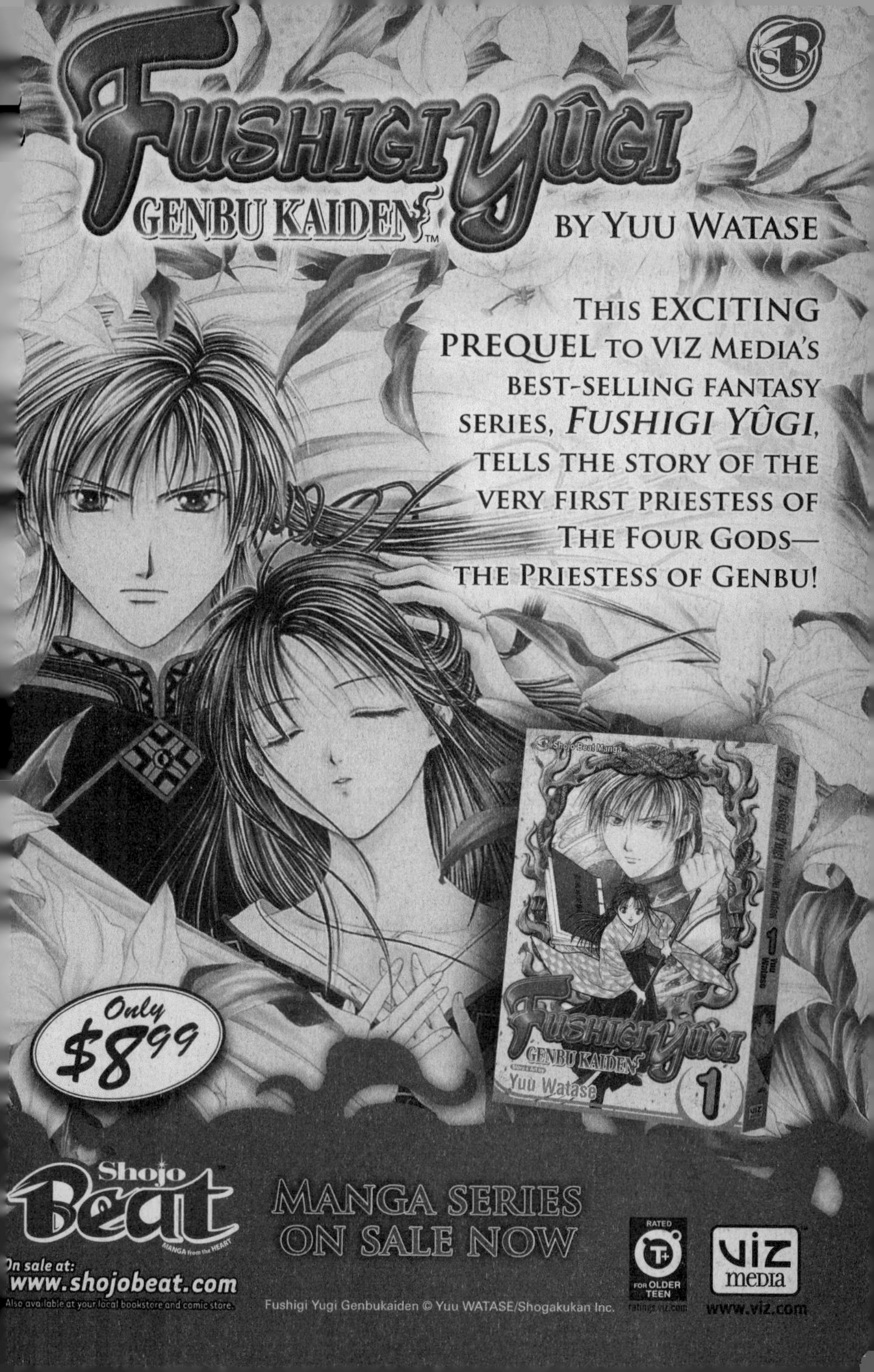
Fushigi Yûgi
Genbu Kaiden™
By Yuu Watase
This EXCITING PREQUEL to VIZ Media's best-selling fantasy series, *Fushigi Yûgi*, tells the story of the very first priestess of The Four Gods—the Priestess of Genbu!
Only $8.99
Shojo Beat Manga
Fushigi Yûgi
Genbu Kaiden
Yuu Watase
1
Shojo Beat
MANGA from the HEART
On sale at:
www.shojobeat.com
Also available at your local bookstore and comic store.
MANGA SERIES ON SALE NOW
Fushigi Yugi Genbukaiden © Yuu WATASE/Shogakukan Inc.
RATED
T+
FOR OLDER TEEN
ratings.viz.com
viz media
www.viz.com

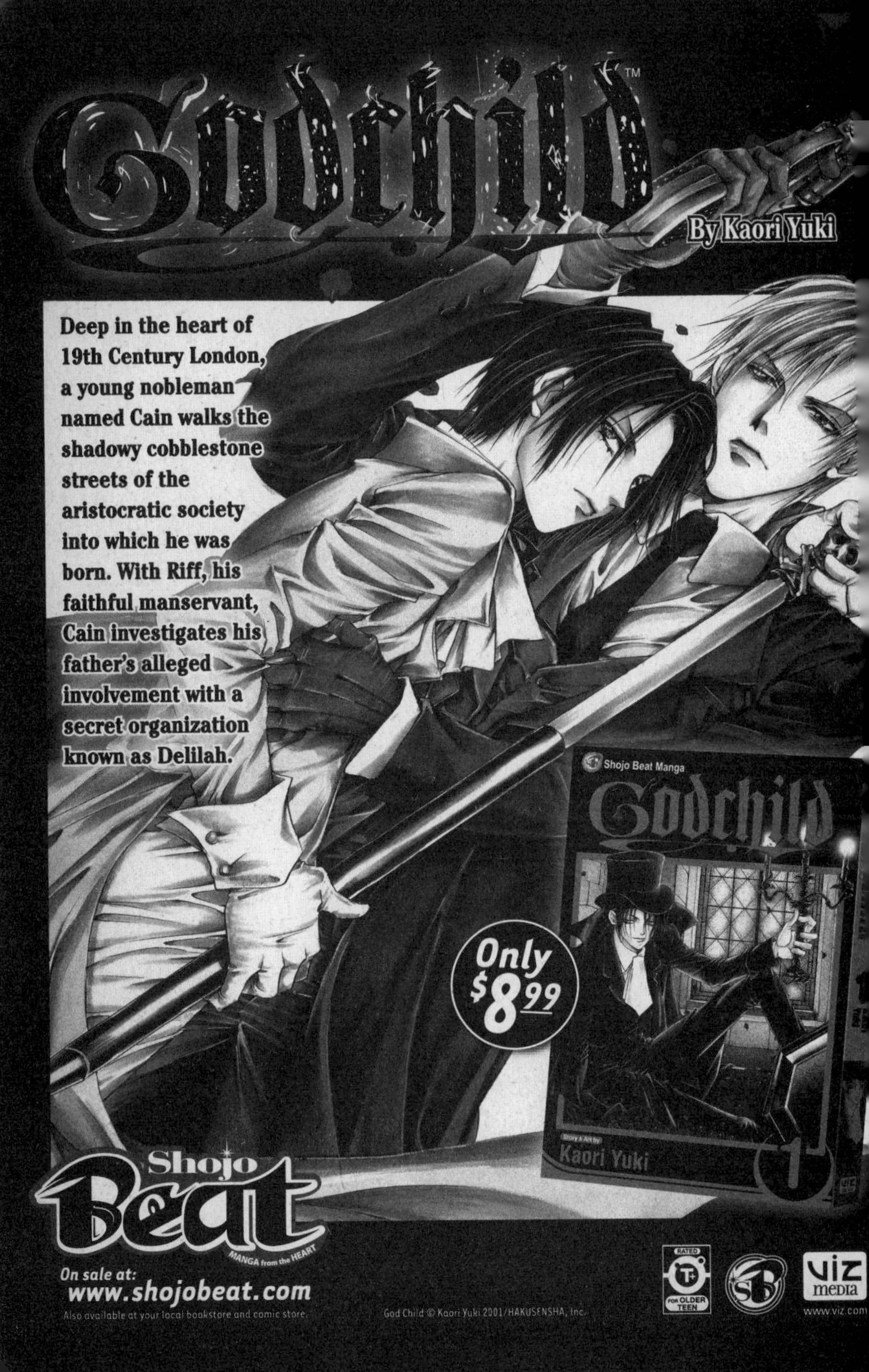
Godchild™
By Kaori Yuki
Deep in the heart of 19th Century London, a young nobleman named Cain walks the shadowy cobblestone streets of the aristocratic society into which he was born. With Riff, his faithful manservant, Cain investigates his father's alleged involvement with a secret organization known as Delilah.
Shojo Beat Manga
Godchild
Story & Art by
Kaori Yuki
1
Only $8.99
Shojo Beat
MANGA from the HEART
On sale at:
www.shojobeat.com
Also available at your local bookstore and comic store.
God Child © Kaori Yuki 2001/HAKUSENSHA, Inc.
RATED T+ FOR OLDER TEEN
viz media
www.viz.com

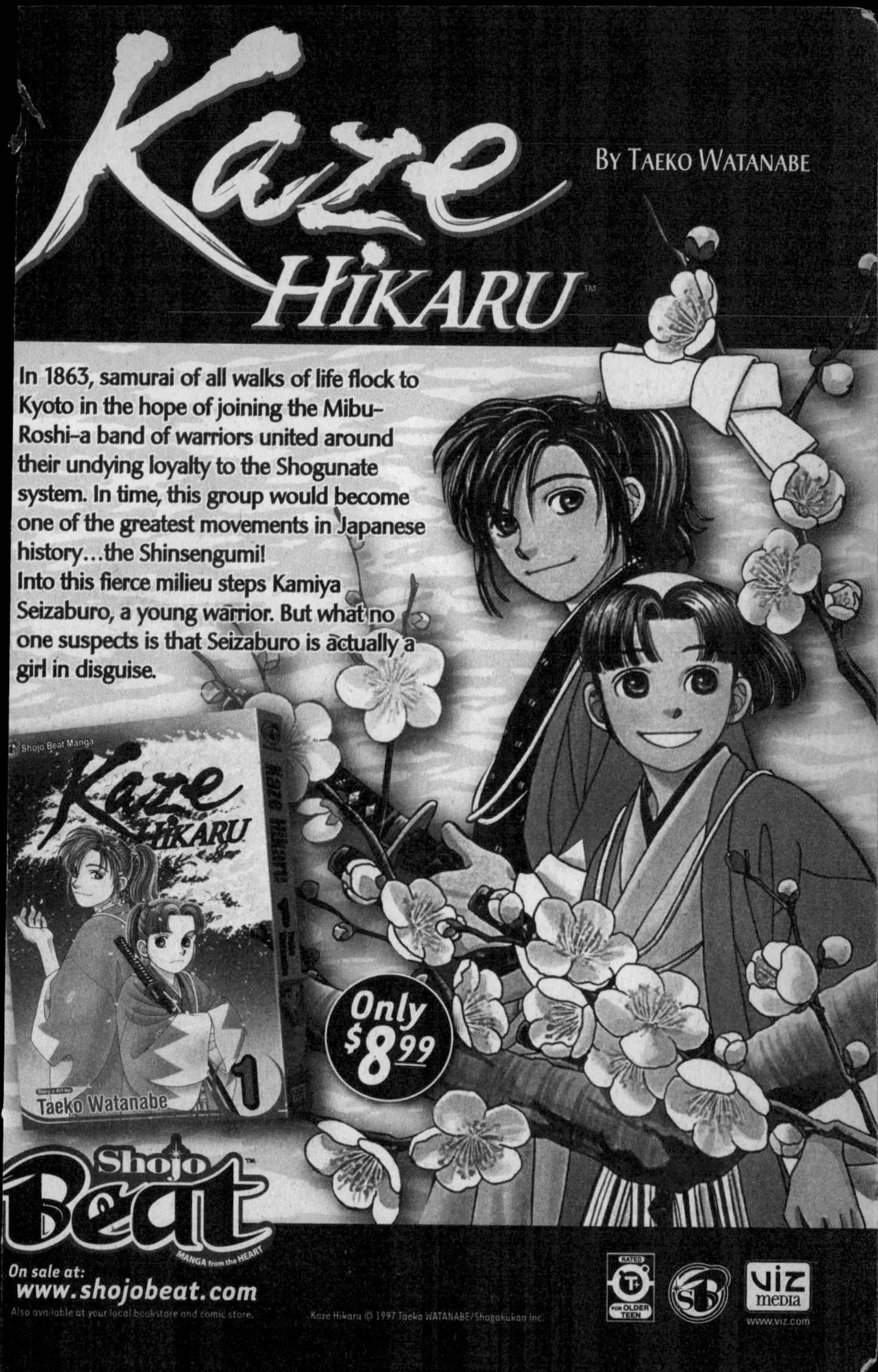

Kaze Hikaru™
By Taeko Watanabe
In 1863, samurai of all walks of life flock to Kyoto in the hope of joining the Mibu-Roshi–a band of warriors united around their undying loyalty to the Shogunate system. In time, this group would become one of the greatest movements in Japanese history…the Shinsengumi!
Into this fierce milieu steps Kamiya Seizaburo, a young warrior. But what no one suspects is that Seizaburo is actually a girl in disguise.
Shojo Beat Manga
Kaze Hikaru
1
Story & Art by
Taeko Watanabe
Only $8.99
Shojo Beat™
MANGA from the HEART
On sale at:
www.shojobeat.com
Also available at your local bookstore and comic store.
Kaze Hikaru © 1997 Taeko WATANABE/Shogakukan Inc.
RATED T+ FOR OLDER TEEN
viz media
www.viz.com

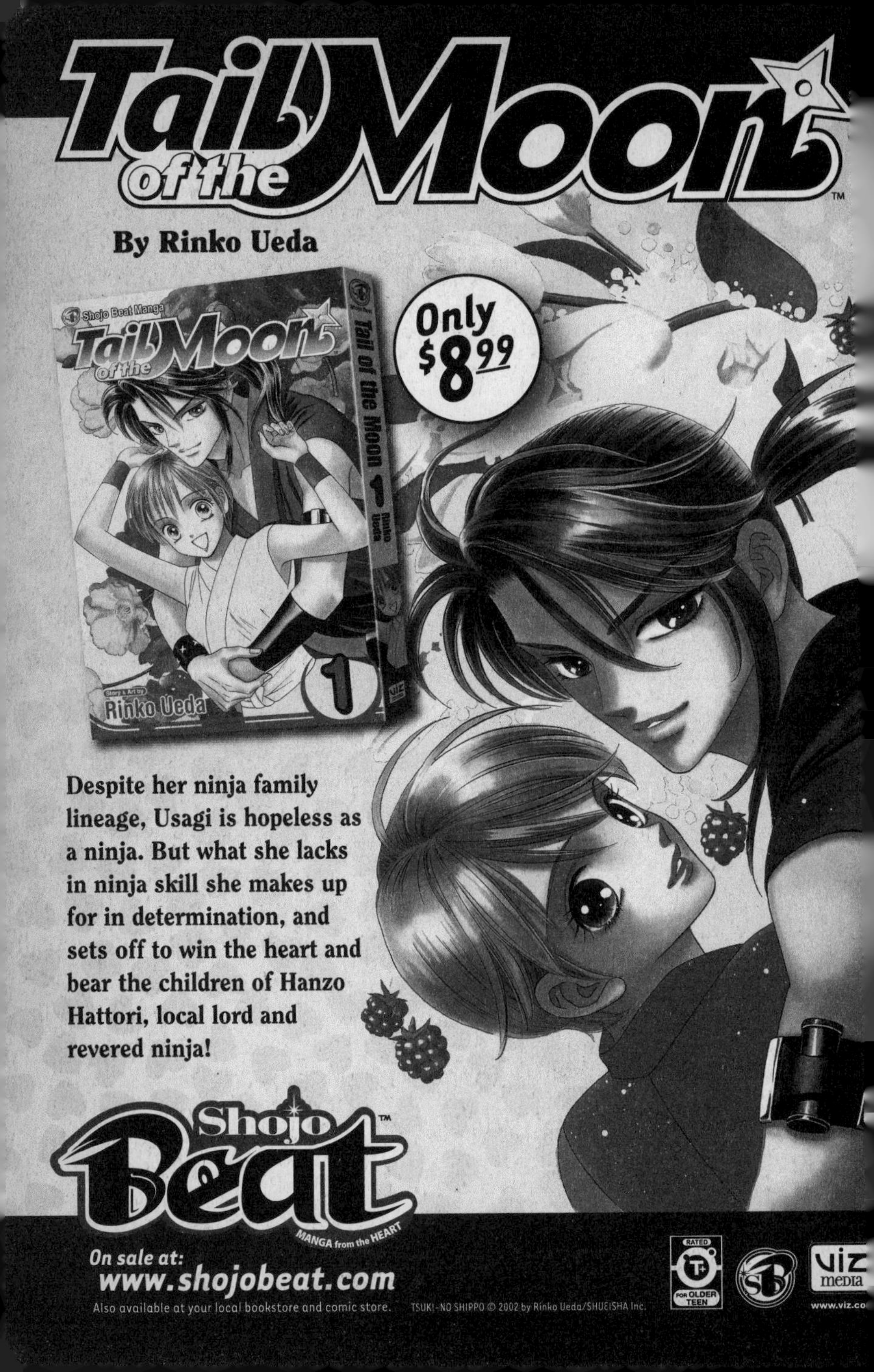
Tail of the Moon™
By Rinko Ueda
Only $8.99
Shojo Beat Manga
Tail of the Moon
1
Story & Art by Rinko Ueda
Despite her ninja family lineage, Usagi is hopeless as a ninja. But what she lacks in ninja skill she makes up for in determination, and sets off to win the heart and bear the children of Hanzo Hattori, local lord and revered ninja!
Shojo Beat™
MANGA from the HEART
On sale at:
www.shojobeat.com
Also available at your local bookstore and comic store.
TSUKI-NO SHIPPO © 2002 by Rinko Ueda/SHUEISHA Inc.
RATED T+ FOR OLDER TEEN
VIZ media
www.viz.com

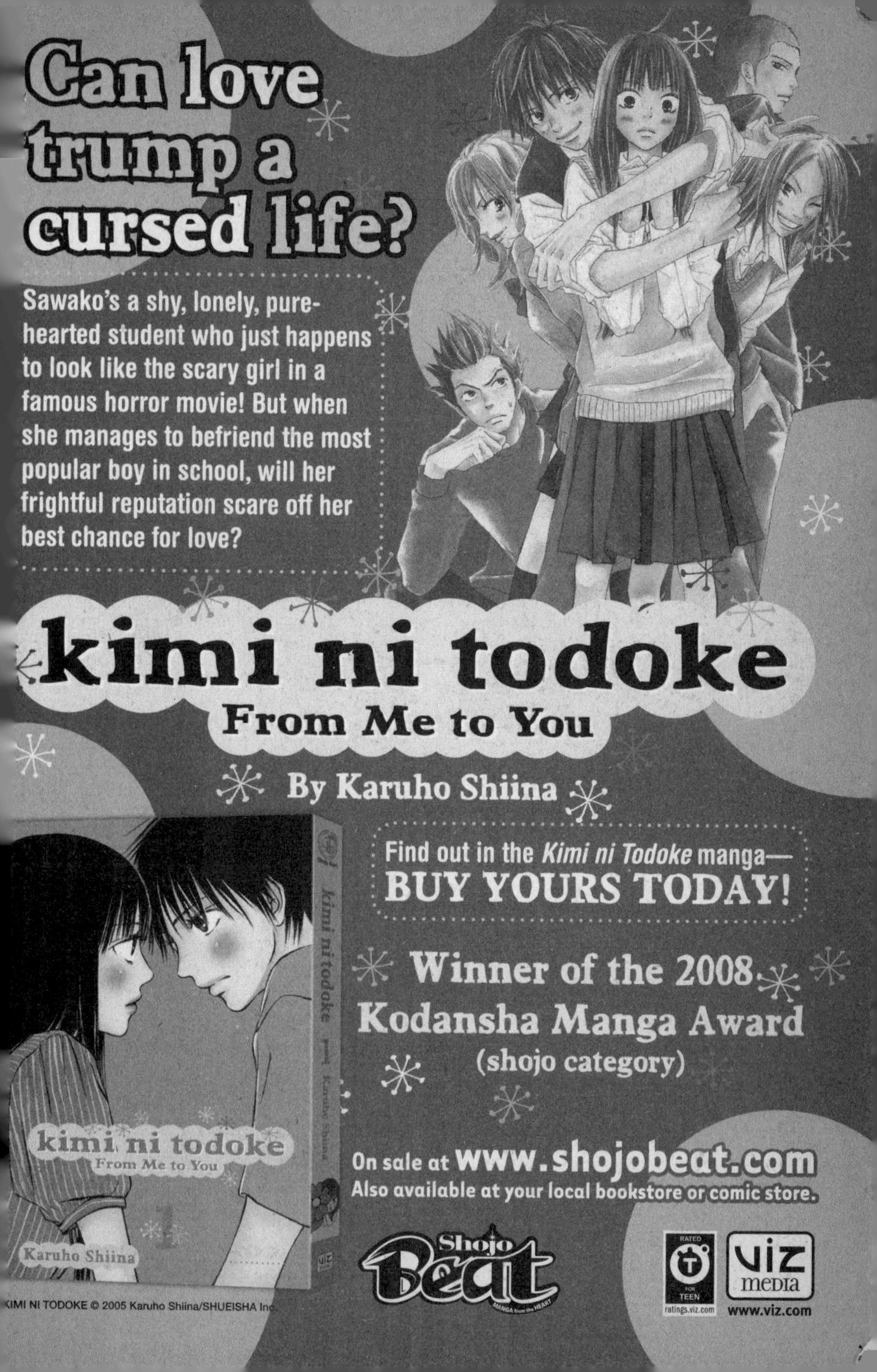
Can love trump a cursed life?
Sawako's a shy, lonely, pure-hearted student who just happens to look like the scary girl in a famous horror movie! But when she manages to befriend the most popular boy in school, will her frightful reputation scare off her best chance for love?
kimi ni todoke
From Me to You
By Karuho Shiina
Find out in the Kimi ni Todoke manga—
BUY YOURS TODAY!
Winner of the 2008 Kodansha Manga Award (shojo category)
kimi ni todoke
From Me to You
Karuho Shiina
On sale at www.shojobeat.com
Also available at your local bookstore or comic store.
Shojo Beat
RATED T FOR TEEN
ratings.viz.com
VIZ media
www.viz.com
KIMI NI TODOKE © 2005 Karuho Shiina/SHUEISHA Inc.

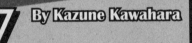

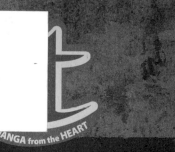

MANGA from the HEART

OTOMEN
**STORY AND ART BY
AYA KANNO**

VAMPIRE KNIGHT
**STORY AND ART BY
MATSURI HINO**

Natsume's BOOK of FRIENDS
**STORY AND ART BY
YUKI MIDORIKAWA**

Want to see more of what you're looking for?

Let your voice be heard!

shojobeat.com/mangasurvey

Help us give you more manga from the heart!

RATED TEEN
rating.viz.com

RATED FOR OLDER TEEN
rating.viz.com

VIZ media
www.viz.com